MODERN LANDSCAPE ARCHITECTURE

MODERN LANDSCAPE ARCHITECTURE:

edited by
Marc Treib

A CRITICAL REVIEW

The MIT Press
Cambridge, Massachusetts
London, England

Designed by Marc Treib.

This book was set in Century Old
Style and Gill Sans by DEKR
Corporation and was printed and
bound in the United States of
America.

Library of Congress Cataloging-in-
Publication Data

Modern landscape architecture :
a critical review
/ edited by Marc Treib.
        p.   cm.
Based on papers presented at a
symposium held in 1989, at the
University of California at Berkeley.
Includes bibliographical
references and index.
  ISBN 0-262-20092-9
1. Landscape architecture—
Congresses.   I. Treib, Marc.
SB469.23.M64   1992
712'.09'04—dc20   92-11571
                CIP

for Dorothée Imbert

Garrett Eckbo, Dan Kiley, and
James Rose (from left to right) at
the symposium, October 1989.
[Ben Blackwell, courtesy
University Art Museum, Berkeley]

I

The story of modern landscape architecture remains to be told. And to begin its telling, the symposium "Modern Architecture [Re]Evaluated" was held in October 1989 at the University of California at Berkeley. The impetus for the symposium was to review and assess the tenets, accomplishments, and limits of modernism in landscape architecture and, as a result, to formulate ideas about possible directions for the discipline. Happily, three of the four founding figures of modern American landscape architecture—Garrett Eckbo, Dan Kiley, and James Rose—were able to attend (James Rose later passed away in the autumn of 1991), and the symposium became a vehicle for a historic reunion of these creative forces for the first time in nearly half a century.

Typically, those who followed—now extending to a third generation—have accepted certain ideas and forms and built upon them, while rejecting other aspects of the founders' work. Ultimately, of course, new ideas are embodied in their own work. Representing this group of landscape architects were Peter Walker, Warren Byrd, Martha Schwartz, and Alexandre Chemetoff.

Despite comments to the contrary, designers do not always maintain a firm perspective on what they are doing. As we all know, the argument for a project is usually elaborated long after the fact, at times depicting the process as far more rational, purposeful, and clear than it ever really was. To balance the inside perspective of the designers, and to extend insight, representatives from the disciplines of landscape history, cultural geography, and art were included in the program: Peirce Lewis, Catherine Howett, John Dixon Hunt, and Robert Irwin. Their views critically examined the cultural and historical matrices within which landscape designers work, and established parallels with the development of modernism in other disciplines.

During the course of the symposium, certain names and clusters of ideas became conspicuous in their absence: Christopher Tunnard, Thomas Church, the French modernist gardens of the 1920s, the experiments with the stylized naturalism developed by Erik Glemme and others for the Stockholm park system, for example. To plug some of these gaps, additional essays were solicited from Thorbjörn Andersson, Gregg Bleam, Dorothée Imbert, Lance Neckar, and Reuben Rainey. At the end of the 1930s and through the 1940s, landscape architects—James Rose, Fletcher Steele, and

Christopher Tunnard foremost among them—published a series of essays that have become central to landscape literature. Because so many of the essays are inaccessible to most readers, a selection of them has also been reprinted here.

It has been said that ideas in architecture follow about 15 years after those in art, while those in landscape architecture are 15 years further behind. A simple reason for this time lag might be based on biophysical forces: plants take time to grow. But this explanation is incomplete. Designing a landscape is informed by technical and design issues as well as cultural values. Unlike buildings, there are few—if any—really ugly trees or shrubs or flowers. Thus, to plant four trees of any sort, in any arrangement, will be perceived by most people as a positive environmental contribution. The primary amenity level is so great that the question of what could be achieved at a higher plateau is rarely posed. It is the quality of the second plateau that distinguishes landscape architecture from mere planting, and it is only there that new ideas are usually developed.

A second factor hampering new ideas in landscape architecture is the nagging persistence of the naturalistic or picturesque tradition. As the urban world grows, the natural world shrinks. Design in a naturalistic form becomes more attractive as an alternative to the order or chaos of the city. Thus, some will resent formal landscapes on the grounds that they don't appear natural. But this categorical dismissal of formality disregards the power of apparent design, and the strength of landscape art to achieve the level and effect of a considered poetry. The art of landscape architecture can be expressed in both naturalistic and formal vocabularies. As the modernists argued, formality or informality is not the real issue.

There is no one answer, no one style, no one approach, no one correct way of creating a viable and, if I may say, beautiful landscape architecture for our century. My own hopes in organizing the symposium and in editing this volume have been simple. I believe that like architecture, landscape design, too, constitutes an art. This is not to imply irresponsible social practice, nor a neglect of the site, climate, or ecology. But as has become increasingly clear in the discipline of architecture, a well-intentioned playground or park, with or without citizen participation, may be no better socially and far less attractive formally when the designer

lacks art, that is, lacks the means to express artistically the analytical findings and social concerns of a given program. One side considers and addresses the parameters; the other side gives them form.

Obviously one volume of collected essays cannot respond to the full range of questions nor substitute for the series of comprehensive studies the subject of modern landscape architecture requires. But it can address specific issues raised by the emergence of modernism in landscape design. Holes in the discourse and critique are bound to remain. Yet perhaps we can assemble certain parts of the puzzle as a means to formulate the story of landscape architecture in the twentieth century, and with new vigor begin to learn from our immediate past.

II

Unlike architecture and painting, modern landscape design made no cataclysmic breach with the past. It retained, for the most part, the materials and many of the conceptual structures of previous eras: the site as the point of departure for the design, for example. Gardens and public spaces in traditional forms continued well into the twentieth century, with few landscape designers attempting to create the world anew.

There were notable exceptions, however. In France, a group of architects (for the most part) attempted to apply the lessons of modern art in general, and cubism in particular, to the garden. Centering on the Art Deco exposition of 1925, and paced by the extravagant work of Gabriel Guevrekian, a small but intensive series of projects issued from solo or collaborative designs. By 1937, however, the call for a social program—rather than an aesthetic fixation—and the provision for activity and recreation brought these experiments to a conclusion. Modernist architects such as Le Corbusier regarded the landscape and plant materials almost as generic greenery, returning as a subject to be viewed or serving as the vegetal buffer between buildings.

In the United States, the classicism of the nineteenth-century revivals held sway among the upper classes enfranchised to build the large estates. During the thirties, however, three landscape architects—Garrett Eckbo, Dan Kiley, and James Rose—consciously tried to integrate modernist architectural ideas into their work and to design a landscape more in accord with present life. Garrett Eckbo produced a tremendous number of gardens in California and elsewhere, gardens that strove toward integrating inside and outside, utilizing new materials, and accommodating developments in American domestic patterns. In time his practice evolved into a series of firms that undertook larger and larger projects, extending from the small plot to the region. James Rose based his practice on the particularities of the site, and a sensitivity toward process that reflected an interest in Eastern thought; for the most part, he kept to projects of limited scale over which he could maintain detailed control. Unfortunately, his illness and passing have made it impossible to secure illustrations of his more recent work. Dan Kiley, on the other hand, has executed a host of projects that range in scale from the small private garden to the vast airport complex, developing an idiom that fuses modern forms with a classic sensibility. His designs reveal an affinity with the clarity of André Le Nôtre, and evidence a refinement of detail in execution that is extremely rare in landscape architecture today. The fourth of the pioneering modernists, the slightly senior Thomas Church, provided the setting for California living in his gardens, which blended aspects of classical order with modern form. The work of these four landscape architects offered a model for, and a yardstick against which, modern American landscape design could be judged.

During the 1960s the concern for form in landscape architecture suffered a major setback. In the anti-aesthetic throes of social turmoil, and the consequent rise of an ecological consciousness, interest in the shaping of landscape design was seriously undermined. The Olmsted picturesque aesthetic continued to hold sway as landscapes emulated the natural. Only recently—within the last ten or so years—have a small number of landscape architects attempted to grapple with the discipline, the art, and the profession as a vital artifact of contemporary culture.

In some ways, they were pushed into it. Beginning in the 1960s, a group of sculptors utilized the landscape as the substance of their art. Their "earthworks" involved the particularities of the site, its shape, its material, and its situation, as the content of the sculpture. In many ways the concept of reordering was basic to their art, although the scope of their purview could be limited. Architects, on the other hand, propelled by the resurgence of the classical style and ideal, reenvisioned the landscape as the continuation of architecture and the binder of building complexes rather than as a green buffer separating buildings. Landscape architects, by exposure and to some degree in defense, began to assert themselves and to formulate a new landscape aesthetic. The group (this is not to imply any formal affiliation) that has emerged has been active in promulgating their ideas in their work and verbally. But efforts to evaluate the formulation of modernism in landscape architecture and trace its developments have been quite limited.

III

For their support of the original symposium, I would like to thank Jacquelynn Baas, Director of the University Art Museum of the University of California at Berkeley, Dean Roger Montgomery of the College of Environmental Design, and Randolph T. Hester, Jr., then Chairman of the Department of Landscape Architecture. The entire staff of the Department of Landscape Architecture was extremely helpful, in particular Paulette Giron, who handled virtually all of the symposium logistics and served far beyond the call of duty. A core of volunteers including Kris Albert, Teva Hesse, and Martha Punderson also provided tremendous service in helping to run the symposium. Diane Harris should be thanked for organizing a representative exhibition of the work of Gertrude Jekyll and Beatrix Farrand drawn from the College of Environmental Design Documents Collection. I must also thank profusely Nina Hubbs, our liaison with the University Art Museum, who helped plan the program and who always found a solution to any problem—with humor. The Beatrix Jones Farrand Fund provided some funding for symposium logistics.

In the editing and assembling of this book, Ken Tadashi Oshima deserves my gratitude for his tireless research assistance; Kevin Gilson for printing most of the negatives for my chapters; Mary McLeod and Reuben Rainey for critically reviewing earlier versions of my essays; and Mark Francis for continued help and encouragement. Over the years I have benefited enormously from my discussion and friendship with Spiro Kostof, whose untimely passing this month deprived architectural history of one of its most brilliant minds.

I am also indebted to the various museums and institutions that have graciously allowed us to reproduce works from their collections. Thanks are also due to *Progressive Architecture* (formerly *Pencil Points*), *Architectural Record,* and *Landscape Architecture* for allowing us to reprint, respectively, four essays by James Rose; the three jointly authored articles by Eckbo, Kiley, and Rose; and an article each by Fletcher Steele and Christopher Tunnard. Every effort has been made to trace the source of each image and to secure permission for its reproduction.

Part of my research on modern landscape architecture in the United States was funded by the Committee on Research, University of California at Berkeley.

The MIT Press has been exemplary in helping to facilitate the editing and production of the volume: to Roger Conover, acquisitions editor, Matthew Abbate for his tireless and complete editing, and Terry Lamoureux for her knowledgeable production assistance, my humble thanks.

It is customary to end one's credits by acknowledging the person who has made the single greatest contribution to the effort. This dubious honor is due Dorothée Imbert, who has shared her time—willingly or still kicking—producing the graphics for the symposium; visiting with me many of the projects included in this book and offering her critical opinions, some of which have been taken and passed off as my own; sharing her vast knowledge of French landscape design during the 1920s; and being the toughest in-house editor that anyone could want—or fear. It is redundant to add that it couldn't have been done without her.

Marc Treib
December 1991

MODERN LANDSCAPE ARCHITECTURE:

A CRITICAL REVIEW

1

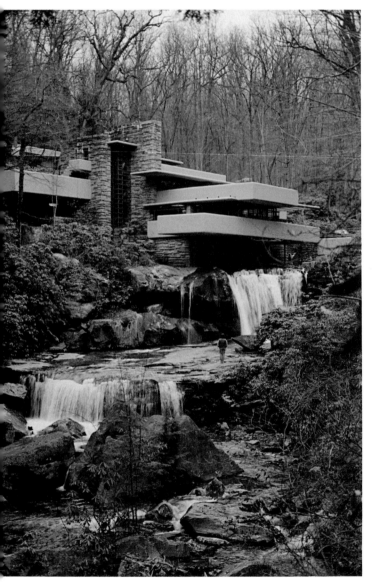

I–1

Peirce Lewis is Professor of Geography at Pennsylvania State University. He teaches and writes about America's ordinary landscapes.

As we look at the world around us, we see an environment that is divided into two very unequal parts. The smaller part is a landscape of designed structures and designed spaces: parks, gardens, formal buildings, and the like. That is the landscape, of course, that attracts the attention of editors and reviewers and critics—the landscape that is liable to end up in portfolios and textbooks—the landscape that teachers of art expect their students to know about (figure 1–1). In the second landscape, a vastly larger one, professional design plays little or no part at all. That second landscape, while not designed by professionals, *is* designed by people who have established stubborn opinions about what a landscape should look like; in short, well-developed landscape tastes. There is, furthermore, a strong communality of landscape taste over large parts of the country, and that is precisely why so much of America looks alike from coast to coast, despite enormous differences in landforms, soil, climate, and location—and that is true of the sacred space of private property, the semipublic landscape along a commercial roadside, and a host of other common objects like water towers and junkyards. The sameness of that ordinary American landscape may annoy us or even bore us; but inevitably, as J. B. Jackson has remarked, that very sameness from coast to coast reminds us that we are a culture.[1]

Popular landscape taste is thus more than just a matter of popular whimsy. Indeed, our tastes in landscape reveal a deeply held and deeply rooted system of shared beliefs[2]—which helps explain why suburbs in North Carolina resemble suburbs in Oregon, and why in both places it is virtually impossible to persuade Americans that they should abolish such things as commercial roadside strips, much as critics and designers may fulminate against them (figure 1–2).

Popular landscape taste is serious business, and that is why professional designers and cultural geographers often find themselves asking the same kinds of questions about it, although for different reasons. Geographers are fascinated with landscape tastes because they are part of a larger value system through which people identify themselves as members of a community. Designers have more immediate reasons to pay attention to public taste. Architects and landscape architects who ignore public taste, or try to defy it, are liable to be dismissed as eccentric or irrelevant; at the simplest level, they will find it hard to get commissions. It is in our common interest, I submit, to try to get our minds around this business of popular landscape taste—not to make judgments about "good taste" or "bad taste" but simply to try to understand it as a fundamental element of culture; to see where it comes from, how it moves through place and across time, how it makes its mark on the landscape—in short, to see how it works.

But taste is not an easy thing to talk about dispassionately. Part of the trouble is semantic—and that is true both at the level of popular conversation and of scholarly discourse. Much of the language used to describe taste is freighted with all manner of pejorative social messages, especially when the word "taste" begins to accumulate modifying adjectives. Phrases like "good taste" and "bad taste," "high-brow taste" and "low-brow taste" are, to put it mildly, loaded invidious expressions, and they tend (quite understandably) to raise hackles, especially when a person or group with "good taste" identifies another person or group as possessing "bad taste." The language smacks of condescension, self-importance, elitism. At the popular level, only arguments over religion or politics are as likely to arouse angry passions as are arguments about taste.

Even academics, supposedly dispassionate, have trouble talking dispassionately about taste. Indeed, a good many social scientists regard taste as a subject that lies wholly outside the realm of proper discourse. Taste, after all, is said to be "subjective" (a statement that is only partly true), and to be accused of subjectivity in some academic circles is roughly the equivalent of being accused of immoral conduct.

The word "popular" causes trouble too. Discussions of popular taste tend to be dismissed along with discussions of "pop" culture, the sort of subject where academics dash off condescending little papers about those quaint people who put Jesus on their dashboards and pink flamingos on their front lawns. I hasten to note that this is not what I mean in this context: by popular I do not mean "pop," and my purpose here is not to discuss pink flamingos.[3]

Even if we manage to wade through this semantic morass, discussions of taste are often put in contexts that make us very uncomfortable. Americans are surrounded by evidence that their tastes are constantly being measured and manipulated in reprehensible ways, for ignoble purposes: advertising agencies do it all the time, as they peddle

1–2

1–1   The designed landscape that art teachers expect their students to know about. Outside Frank Lloyd Wright's Fallingwater. [Marc Treib]

1–2   Such landscapes may annoy or bore us, but their similarity from coast to coast reminds us that we are one culture. U.S. 30, the Lincoln Highway, Breezewood, Pennsylvania, 1985.

everything from underarm deodorants to Scotch whiskey. We despise the techniques, even as we recognize that they work; otherwise the ads would not be run. Our rational nature is revolted by that kind of manipulation; it is as if our most private selves were being invaded and toyed with.

But despite our discomfort in talking about it, taste remains—a stubborn, ineluctable, ubiquitous fact in our personal and collective lives, a fact that demands our serious attention. This essay sets forth three basic canons of American taste, and more particularly of popular American taste as it applies to ordinary human landscape. I call these propositions canons because it seems to me that each of them is basic, axiomatic, and almost immutable. Like religious canons, they give birth to a number of subsidiary ideas. In summary form, they go as follows:

Canon 1: Popular taste is not a trivial matter; it is a fundamental part of all cultures, and a crucial means by which nations and cultures identify themselves and separate themselves from other nations and cultures. It is a fundamental badge of human identity, an essential link in the chain that binds human beings together into communities. One cannot understand a culture without understanding its collectively held ideas about what is or is not beautiful, what constitutes good and bad taste. Landscape taste is an important part of that larger system, simply because landscape is ubiquitous and highly visible.

Canon 2: Landscape taste, like all taste, reveals itself at two quite different levels within any given culture. One level is fundamental; the other is ephemeral. They are not the same, and they should not be confused. Fundamental taste is extremely resistant to change—indeed, almost immutable. It is part of a nation's basic cosmology, and it cuts across lines of time, space, and class. Ephemeral taste, by contrast, is volatile; it changes from time to time, differs from place to place, and identifies important subgroups within the larger culture. Unlike fundamental taste, ephemeral taste is highly susceptible to manipulation.

Canon 3: The cultural landscape is divided into two large spatial categories: areas where standards of taste are routinely invoked, and areas where they are not. In shorthand, we can call these "tasteful" spaces, where designers operate, and "taste-free" spaces where standards of taste are excluded, and which are immune to designers and conscious design. Tasteful space and taste-free space possess quite different properties and operate under different cultural rules.

Canon 1: The Importance of Taste

Canon 1 asserts that taste is not a trivial matter but a fundamental part of all cultures. It is worthwhile reflecting on why this is so.

Consider, first of all, what is meant by taste. In its most elementary form, taste is an expression of aesthetic values. "That's a beautiful woman." "That's an ugly house." "I don't like anchovies on my pizza." It is easy enough to dismiss statements like that as trivial, often because they are couched in language that sounds uninformed, prejudiced, irrational, or even incoherent. How often have we heard expressions like "We-e-e-ll, there's no accounting for taste" or "I know what I like, and that's not it" (figure 1–3)?

But dig below the persiflage and reflect on what such common language really means. All cultures, after all, define themselves by at least three things they hold in common: by their shared material possessions, their shared knowledge of the world, and their shared systems of values and beliefs. Possessions, of course, can come and go, as victims of earthquakes, wars, and bankruptcies will testify. Knowledge, too, can change, and indeed we encourage it: that, after all, is why children are sent to school, and at least one of the reasons that people read books. But shared systems of belief, as any anthropologist will tell us, are often extremely resistant to change.

As in so many other basic matters, Plato summed it up very well: our ultimate values are truth, goodness, and beauty. All societies must deal with all three, but they do it in different ways.

Take the matter of truth, for example. All societies possess a metaphysical system, although they rarely use that term to describe it. Matters of truth or falsity are commonly couched in religious or political terms; it is not by accident that some of the world's most rancorous international disputes spring from religion and politics, and when the two reinforce each other, the results can be murderous. Ireland and the Middle East are egregious examples. Again, it is no accident that people steer away from discussing religion or politics with strangers or casual acquaintances. To enter into a discussion of religion with somebody you don't know is to risk a dispute about the fundamental nature of the universe. To most people, that is perilous ground.

The same goes for the second element in the Platonic triad of values: what is or is not good. I doubt whether any culture exists without at least a rudimentary ethical system. Indeed, there is a certain communality of ethics across the face of the globe, which I suspect stems from our common humanity. Most societies agree, for example, that killing is generally wrong; the law against murder is written into the criminal law and religious codes of most nations. At first blush, it would seem to be an ethical constant. In practice, however, most cultures permit killing under certain circumstances. War is the most common, but the list of exceptions to the law against murder differs considerably from culture to culture. When the Ayatollah Khomeni put

1–3

1–4

1–5

1–3 "I don't know much about architecture, but I know what I don't like." Robert Day in the *New Yorker*, 1966.

1–4 Taste in ordinary things is a means
1–5 by which cultures tangibly express their differences from other cultures. Miners' cemetery, Tonopah, Nevada, 1986. Lawn shrine, Pinconning, Michigan, 1987.

out a contract on Salman Rushdie, on grounds that Rushdie's book *The Satanic Verses* was blasphemous, we in the self-styled civilized world were outraged on what we said were basic ethical grounds. In fact, what we meant was that our list of exceptions to the law against murder did not match the Ayatollah's—which, in anthropological terms, simply revealed that we are members of one culture while the Ayatollah is a member of another— hardly an astonishing insight. Indeed, Americans have their own disputes over what is or is not justifiable killing—and those disputes are among the most bitter, because they reveal *sub*-cultural differences that many would prefer to deny. Americans assume they are all members of the same culture, and therefore share the same value system; they are annoyed and frustrated when they discover they are not. Is abortion murder or isn't it? Is capital punishment murder or isn't it? Neither of these questions will be resolved by rational debate; they illuminate the existence of fundamental cultural cleavages that are not likely to be bridged in any foreseeable future. Most Americans are neither willing nor equipped to confront that stubborn fact.

Which brings us to the third member of the Platonic triad. Just as all cultures and subcultures are united and divided by systems of metaphysics and ethics, they are similarly bound and divided by systems of aesthetics as well—and taste is simply a shorthand to describe parts of that aesthetic belief system. Taste is often expressed in language that sounds trivial—whether or not one likes peanut butter, or button-down shirts, or Georgian architecture. In fact, those matters are not trivial at all when it comes to identifying people as members of a particular culture or subculture (figures 1–4, 5).

Our day-to-day aesthetic likes and dislikes— our tastes—are analogous to our use of language, dialect, and accent: they instantly and publicly identify us as members of any of several cultural groups (nations, cultures, subcultures). What kind of food do you like? How do you like it prepared? What clothing is appropriate for certain occasions? How should you cut your hair? Which do you like best: Brahms, blues, or punk rock? Depending on who is asking, those questions have a right and a wrong answer. If your answer is right, you're in, a member of the group; if it's wrong, you're out, banished to limbo.

Landscape tastes are peculiarly interesting, simply because they publicly advertise our membership in subcultural groups with blinding visibility. What should a proper house look like? What sorts of landscaping should you have around your house? What should a church look like? Individually, our answers to those questions may sound trivial or idiosyncratic; in combination, our tastes identify who we are, and our shared tastes identify the community of which we are a member. Statements of taste are passwords. "Real men don't eat quiche": one's taste in food (and all sorts of other things) are a dead giveaway to one's cultural identity. Gaylord Hauser had it right half a century ago when he re-

1–6

marked: "You are what you eat." Hauser meant it biologically, but the remark is equally true in terms of culture. "By your tastes shall we know you." Indeed, "by your tastes in landscape shall *everybody* know you."

This first canon has several major corollaries. The first seems paradoxical: popular tastes tend to be strongest and most revealing of community membership when applied to essential things, the biological necessities without which humans cannot survive. The list of such things is short. People cannot survive, individually, without clothing, shelter, food, and the periodic excretion of bodily wastes. And people will not survive collectively without sex which allows them to procreate.

Each of these necessary activities is heavily freighted with aesthetic baggage. Thus, members of a particular group say to each other and to outsiders: "We know that we must do all these things in common with other humans. But only we, in our group, have the good taste to do them correctly. You others, lacking our superior knowledge and superior taste, lacking our special discernment, do not. And because you do not possess this special knowledge, you are outsiders—at best pitiable, at worst despicable." Having correct taste is like possessing the password to a secret society that admits few and excludes most. Taste in essential matters is a hallmark of our cultural identity.

Consider shelter, for example. Paint your house a tasteful color, or risk ostracism by your neighbors (figure 1–6). Clothing? If you wear inappropriate clothing, many restaurants will not allow you in the door (figure 1–7). As for food, the examples are endless, but the message is the same: eat and serve tasteful food, or take the consequences. (Try serving roast rat or fricasseed cockroach the next time you have guests for dinner and see what happens.) Excretion of bodily wastes? All humans must do it regularly or they will promptly die; but to urinate or defecate by the public roadside in the United States is to risk arrest. Sex, of course, is the most heavily circumscribed of all biologically necessary behaviors. Sexual proscriptions are often justified on grounds of ethics. In fact, the grounds for sexual prohibitions are less ethical than they are aesthetic. Many kinds of sexual behavior are prohibited not because they are morally wrong, but rather because (like eating worms and rats) the majority think they are aesthetically disgusting.

The implications of this idea are fascinating. Because certain behaviors are biologically essential, we tend to think of the aesthetics as a kind of surface overlay; but in cultural terms it is quite another matter. Humans nearly always apply elaborate aesthetic codes to those biological necessities. The conclusion, I think, is inescapable. Taste is not mere frosting on the cultural cake; it is an inherent part of the cake itself.

There is a second important corollary to the basic canon, and it can be stated simply. If taste is important as a kind of cultural litmus paper, then it follows necessarily that changes in popular taste are signals to changes in the basic culture itself. When a nation changes its tastes in hairstyles, it may not seem very important. But when a nation like the United States, in the course of a decade, changes its tastes in haircuts, in architectural styles, and in sexual behavior—as it did in the 1960s and 1970s— one is led to suspect that American culture is undergoing not just a change in cosmetics but a basic sea change. Exactly what prompted that change one can only speculate: losing a major war, perhaps; forcing a president to resign, perhaps; discovering that the nation could not or would not pay its bills, or keep its cities running, or prevent its children from taking drugs. But during those wrenching times, America's popular tastes underwent drastic change, and one is inclined to suspect that the timing of that change was not accidental.

There is a third corollary about the importance of popular taste. Despite its primary cultural importance, taste is a subject that is almost always off limits to rational discourse. Indeed, taste often seems off limits to any kind of discourse at all. The common saying "There's no accounting for taste" is often uttered in a sententious tone that implies that you'd better not try to account for somebody's taste, because you won't get anywhere. The French take the same line; *chacun à son goût* seems to suggest that everyone's taste is as good as anybody else's—but nobody really believes that, certainly not the French. "Everyone to his own taste" simply means that taste is a matter that lies outside the realm of logic, and that you had better not try to talk about it logically.

There is good reason for this prohibition: it serves as a kind of cultural defense mechanism. Unquestioned tastes, like unquestioned religious or political beliefs, are so important as an earmark of

1–7

1–8

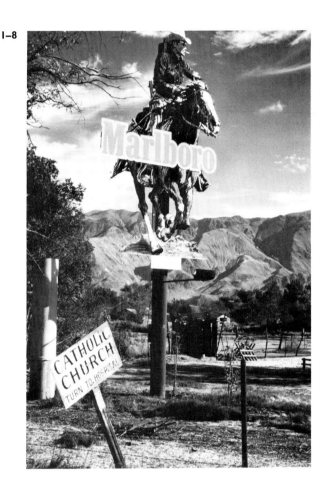

community identity that the discussion of taste (which suggests the possibility of change) threatens the stability and continuity of the community. Or, to put it in slightly different terms, stable communities have stable value systems—and that means stable tastes. To question those tastes is to rock the cultural boat—a dangerous and unsettling act. All societies have a host of built-in mechanisms to punish threats and to protect themselves against danger. So it is risky to question a society's basic value system. It is often risky even to talk about taste.

That does not mean, of course, that popular taste cannot be changed; it happens all the time. It only means that changes are effected by non-rational means: for example, by establishing a connection between smoking Marlboro cigarettes and a healthy masculine appreciation of the great outdoors (figure 1–8). This kind of appeal, of course, drives thoughtful people crazy, because it is so totally irrational, and because its devastating effectiveness is based on forensic dirty tricks. But that is precisely the point. Taste and logic use different languages, and our disapproval will not change that fact.

The moral for environmental designers, I think, is fairly clear. If an architect or landscape architect wants to change the character of a particular environment, he or she would be well advised to pay attention to the popular tastes of those who inhabit that environment. That is likely to be a task requiring more than a little subtlety. Taste, to put it mildly, is not monolithic. And that is the province of the second canon of popular taste.

1–6   In terms of shelter, the color of one's house is immaterial. In terms of group identity, one's chromatic tastes are crucial, as in this Vermont village, 1968.

1–7   Wear tasteful clothes or take the consequences. Atascadero, California, 1988.

1–8   Much successful advertising is based on a totally irrational association between unrelated phenomena: Marlboro sign, Bishop, California, 1986.

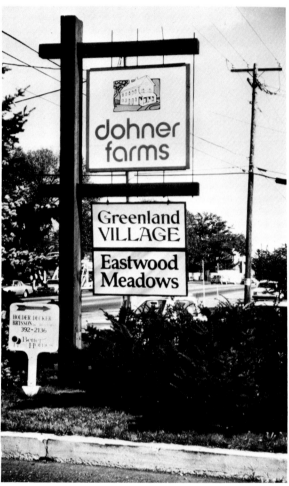

1-9

1-9   Rurality permeates the naming of
        new American places. Real estate
        signs, Lancaster County,
        Pennsylvania, c. 1985.

1-10   The American fondness for an
1-11   English bucolic vision is reflected
        in the common landscape.
        Constable's *Wivenhoe Park, Essex*
        (c. 1825) is reborn in Loudoun
        County, Virginia, 1989.

Canon 2: The Two Layers of Taste

The second canon holds that popular taste occurs at two very different levels in all societies. One level, which can be termed primary taste, is an inherent part of a society's permanent aesthetic value system. The second level, ephemeral taste, is represented by fashions that change from season to season. Ephemeral taste floats on top of primary taste and sometimes even conceals it. Ephemeral taste tends to be conspicuous; it catches our attention like flotsam and jetsam on the surface of a deep river channel. An observer, looking at the river from close by, sees only the surficial debris bobbing and swirling in bewildering patterns. But underneath, the underlying current moves steadily and immutably, paying no attention to the stuff on top.

Primary taste springs from a culture's collective memory and is often deeply rooted in mythic history. If it changes at all, the rate of change is geologic, hardly noticeable in the span of a human lifetime. Because it is virtually permanent, it is taken for granted and is rarely discussed. But it permeates nearly all of adult society. Those who do not share a society's collective primary taste— those who ignore or try to defy it—will be labeled by society in one of several disagreeable ways. They may be labeled as perversely eccentric; avant-garde landscape designers are commonly put into that category. Or they may be labeled as immature: little children, for example, cannot be expected to understand the adult rules of primary taste but are expected to learn them in the process of growing up, sometimes in school or more often just by osmosis. (Teenagers commonly flout primary taste, even when they know what it is, and that is one thing that makes teenagers "difficult.") Or offenders against primary taste may be marginalized. When ethnic and racial minority groups, for example, do not share primary tastes with the mainstream population—by playing music too loudly, for example, or cutting their hair wrong—it is seen as a signal that they are deviant, "not nice." Indeed, when a minority group exhibits "bad taste," as defined by mainstream culture, it is a cause for denunciation and shunning. One of the most visible signs that a minority group is becoming assimilated into the mainstream population is the adoption, by that minority group, of primary tastes in architecture and landscape design.

Americans, like all people, reveal their primary tastes in all kinds of ways, but nowhere more obviously than in the ordinary landscapes they have created and continue to create.[4] Three examples are especially visible:

(1) A fondness for rural as opposed to urban things.

(2) A fondness for a mythic historical past, associated with Europe and more particularly with England.

(3) A deeply held belief in the virtue and sanctity of private property.

Each has far-reaching implications.

A fondness for rural things goes back into the misty recesses of American history. In Richard Hofstadter's fine phrase, "the United States was born in the country and moved to the city."[5] Even though less than five percent of the American population now actually makes its living from farming, the emotional heart of America still lives in the country, or at least in a small rural town, surrounded by the symbols of a purified mythic rural past. The evidence is all around us.

For example, the universal popularity of green lawns, however small, carefully fertilized, watered, and mowed to pasture-like smoothness.

For example, the commonness of gentleman farming as a way for the affluent not merely to evade taxes but to exhibit their bucolic good taste.

For example, the association of rurality with wholesomeness. (Americans are surrounded by "country cooking" but manage to forget the scent of manure.)

For example, the predilection of American real estate developers for rural names, especially when applied to newly created residential subdivisions (figure 1–9).

For example, the universal nostalgic appeal of rural and small town themes in popular advertising.

It is no accident that many of America's most famous and most urbane designs have a countryfied touch to them: buildings like Fallingwater, environments like Central Park—*rus in urbe,* not the other way around. Americans are excellent engineers, maybe the best bridge builders in the world, but they have a poor track record when it comes to designing and building livable cities. That is not because American urban designers are incompetent, I think; it simply reflects the ineluctable fact that Americans prefer the country to the city, as Gallup polls regularly report. A fondness for rural things is a cornerstone of American primary taste.

Another of America's primary landscape tastes is an uncritical fondness for the past. It is seldom the real past, more often a fuzzy romanticized version of some far-off time and some far-off place—commonly European, and more particularly English. America's most popular architectural styles over the last two centuries, while they have changed mercurially in their particulars, are entirely of European or pseudo-European origin. A list of dominant architectural fashions since 1800 makes the point: Georgian, Greek revival, Gothic revival, Italianate revival, neo-Romanesque, Tudor revival, Dutch colonial, Spanish colonial revival, and now postmodern, with its witty historic allusions to any of those revivals, singly or in combination. David Lowenthal has put it nicely in the title of a recent book: *The Past is a Foreign Country.*[6]

British styles are particularly enduring. The permanent fondness for Anglophilic landscapes is reflected in the continuing popularity of Constable's bucolic paintings (figure 1–10) and of expensive exurban landscapes that are earnestly trying to bring Constable back to life in Virginia's green and pleasant land (figure 1–11). It is significant, I think, that

1–10

1–11

the one "historical" style of architecture that has never gone completely out of popular favor in the United States is some variant of Georgian, variously called colonial, Cape Cod, Williamsburg, federal, or whatever. Americans have been building such houses for about two centuries, and they continue to do so with unremitting zeal. While would-be architectural tastemakers wrangle over postmodernism, deconstruction, and a variety of other neologisms, popular builders are erecting neo-Georgian houses.

The reverse side of that coin is what Americans collectively do not like. The International Style reigned supreme in high-style American architectural circles for more than fifty years, but it took hold only in commercial, industrial, or institutional settings. When individual Americans chose styles for their domestic dwellings, their home and hearth, so to speak, they spoke with one voice. Despite periodic attempts on the part of academic architects to persuade Americans to build or buy houses in the International Style, Americans would have no part of it. The reason for popular rejection of internationalism, I think, is fairly obvious. Internationalism consciously rejected historic allusions, and by so doing it flew in the face of Americans' primary taste. Correspondingly, the somewhat tepid embrace of postmodern detailing in recently built suburbs carries the same message; if postmodern gestures are recognizably historical, recognizably European, they are likely to be acceptable. Significantly, most successful real estate developers have refrained from pressing postmodernism much beyond a gesture or two; Michael Graves can get away with it on a few of his big public buildings, but extreme postmodernism (like extreme internationalism) has not worked in the suburbs—nor is it likely to. High-style architects may fulminate over such stubborn public resistance to innovation, but it is not likely to do them much good.

One final element in American primary taste is the persistent affection for clearly defined private property. Again the evidence is almost everywhere. No single element in the ordinary American domestic environment is so wildly successful as the single-family house, detached from all others, surrounded by its own private yard and lawn (figure 1–12). Significantly, in the fastest-growing parts of Florida and the Southwest, where real estate prices are too high for many people to buy a single-family freestanding house, the favored alternative is not an apartment or a condominium but instead an immobile mobile home, set down on a tiny patch of private land. Nobody claims that they amount to much architecturally, but they do one thing superbly well: they satisfy Americans' primary taste for private dominion over private space.[7]

Contrasting sharply with primary taste is ephemeral taste, revealed in the transitory fashions and fads that continually flit across the cultural landscape. A well-developed system of ephemeral taste is an important earmark of the modern Europeanized world. Traditional societies (by which I mean

1–12

1–12   No single element in the ordinary American landscape is so popular as the single-family house, detached from all others, on its own private patch of earth. Crookston, Minnesota, from the air, 1983.

societies where behavior is guided by rules handed down from generation to generation by word of mouth or by tribal custom) take their cues from the past. There is no place in traditional society for a congeries of tastes that shifts from day to day. The Euro-American imperial system, however, changed all that. Today, when we talk about "developing countries," we are talking about places where Europeans and Americans have imported a belief in the virtues of change, of "progress," of ephemera.[8]

Particular ephemeral tastes are almost never shared by the whole society; indeed, differences in ephemeral taste are major hallmarks of subcultural differences. The reason is not hard to find: ephemeral tastes not only change from time to time, they move from place to place and from class to class—indeed, they tend to move through a culture along certain fairly predictable paths. We know that instinctively. Some groups of people adopt new fads readily (the yuppies come to mind); others do so more slowly; some (like the old order Amish of Pennsylvania) not at all. All cultural groups, without exception, are choosy about where their tastes come from: the *New Yorker*, perhaps? Or *Reader's Digest* and *People Magazine*? Or the traditional wisdom of your grandmother? In fact, all people define their position inside a larger culture by the particular ephemeral tastes that they are willing to entertain. How do you cut your hair? What kind of salad dressing do you use? Do you drink alcoholic beverages, and if so what kind? (A little-known but exquisite single-malt—"just a splash, please, and of course no ice"—or a slug of fortified sweet Muscatel, straight out of the upended bottle?)

Theoretically, of course, our ephemeral tastes should be entirely voluntary, but that, of course, is myth. In fact, ephemeral tastes are routinely manipulated, and a huge and immensely profitable advertising industry has grown up, ready and eager to do the manipulating. In fact, Americans often volunteer to have their tastes manipulated. The reason stems from their peculiar geographic mobility. Ever since the settlement of Jamestown, Americans have been in motion, constantly searching for new and better places to live and make a living. Once settled in a new place, the immigrants inevitably sought ways to adjust themselves to a novel and often unfamiliar habitat.

Ministering to the needs of those migrants has long been a profitable enterprise in the United States. Two of the nation's most successful magazines in the last half-century are *Sunset Magazine*, published in Menlo Park, California, and *Southern Living*, of Birmingham, Alabama. Both magazines succeed by doing the same thing: showing newcomers to the fastest-growing parts of the country how to comport themselves—how to fit into the tastes and lifestyles of the West and the South. *Sunset* and *Southern Living* provide the aesthetic ground rules for living in those environments. From 1929 onward, *Sunset* has been teaching displaced Midwesterners about the tastes of middle-class suburban California: how to decorate a house tastefully, how

to plant a garden tastefully, how to prepare food tastefully, and even how to travel tastefully. Starting in the 1960s, *Southern Living* did the same thing for new arrivals in the upper-middle-class South. An editor of *Southern Living* once remarked to me that the magazine's main target is epitomized by the doctor's wife, recently moved from Pittsburgh to Baton Rouge, with a substantial income, a busy husband, and a keen desire to live tastefully—and to be seen to live tastefully according to southern standards. The success of that formula can be gauged by two measures. Several years ago, Time-Life, Inc., bought *Southern Living* for the unprecedented sum of 475 million dollars—this for the privilege of taking their advertising accounts into the homes of several million affluent southerners who wanted to try out new lifestyles but wanted to stay southern at the same time—in short, people who were not exactly sure of their tastes and needed a bit of help. For the other measure of *Southern Living*'s success, one has only to drive the streets of any affluent southern suburb and look around. *Southern Living*'s garden plans are spread all over the place for visitors to see, just as *Sunset*'s gardens can be seen over the length and breadth of suburban California and indeed of the whole suburban West.

There is nothing pernicious, of course, about teaching newcomers how to make their gardens grow; in fact, it seems the hospitable thing to do. But Americans have not been satisfied moving laterally from one geographic location to another. Most also want to move up, to gain a better life for themselves and their children; that, after all, is why they and their ancestors moved to this country (and why they still do, as immigration figures continue to demonstrate). But vertical mobility is not just a question of economics; it is a matter of social class as well. Newcomers to America quickly learned that class in their adopted country meant something quite different from what it meant in the rigidly stratified societies of England, France, Germany, and Italy. Unlike those old class-bound cultures, where a person "knew his place" and was expected to stay there, in America one could move quite readily from one social level to another.

But if people intended to move up to new social levels, they needed guidance. Americans knew instinctively that their tastes—especially their ephemeral tastes—were overt advertisements of the class they belonged to. If a person wanted to move to a new social level, and be accepted at that level, he or she needed guidance in behavior and taste—and furnishing such guidance has been a highly profitable enterprise in America ever since the first printing press was put ashore. Nowadays, aspiring members of the middle class can look to Miss Manners for guidance; our mothers and fathers looked to Gloria Vanderbilt and Emily Post, and our nineteenth-century ancestors sought guidance in the same way. That century, perhaps the most socially mobile time in all of American history, was littered with books and tracts and magazines telling people (especially new immigrants from other cultures) what particular tastes they should adopt if they intended to be accepted as full-fledged members of American society and then to move upward within that society.

Many of those tastes were ephemeral, and that is why people needed guidance. Aesthetic rules were changing all the time, and there was no telling what would come next in the way of acceptable behavior, acceptable dress, acceptable speech, or acceptable design. New immigrants like Hyman Kaplan went to night school to learn how to speak proper tasteful English.[9] Carpenters' handbooks revealed the secrets of building tasteful houses. *Harper's Magazine* was ready to inform its readers how to plant their front yard—if they had the good fortune to have a front yard.[10] And because most of these styles and tastes were ephemeral, aspiring members of the middle class had to keep buying those guides, to make sure that their manners, designs, and language were tastefully *au courant* for their new hoped-for station in society.

Nobody has written more perceptively and engagingly about this subject than Russell Lynes. His best-known essay, "Upperbrow, Middlebrow, and Lowbrow," was first published in 1949.[11] Lynes was interested in the origins of taste, not just high-style taste but popular stuff as well. He was also fascinated by the ways that taste is passed from level to level within society. Judging from the number of times the essay has been updated and reprinted, one guesses that Lynes was not too far off the mark in describing the dynamics of taste in American society.

In Lynes's vocabulary, "upperbrows" are a tiny self-appointed elite who manufacture taste in a precious hothouse world of art makers, art critics, and literati, and who answer to nobody except to other members of their self-admiring class. Most of the world, however, is made of "middlebrows," who aspire to become upperbrows by imitating their art, their clothes, their houses, their landscaping, and their ways of eating, drinking, and speaking. To do that is impossible, however, since one of the earmarks of upperbrowism is imitating nobody. Or, in other words, the moment you try to imitate somebody else's taste, you mark yourself as a would-be social climber—ipso facto a middlebrow. It is Catch 22, of course: once a middlebrow, always a middlebrow. At the bottom of Lynes's aesthetic heap are the "lowbrows," free spirits who

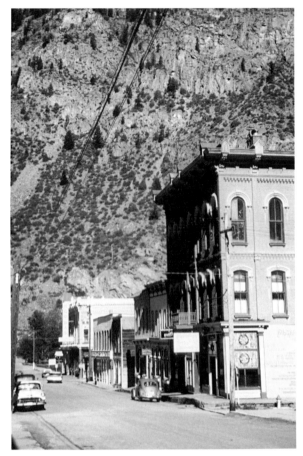

I–I3

I–I3 Taste does, in fact, trickle down. 1870s Italianate architecture dominates the main street in Georgetown, Colorado, 1963. In the foreground is the correct highbrow version. Farther down the block, and built considerably later, the Italianate is diluted to the point that nothing is left but rectangular false fronts.

pay no attention to anyone's taste but their own. Lynes observes that upperbrows despise the middlebrows, because, by their very nature, middlebrows imitate (and inevitably debase) upperbrow tastes and styles. Thus, when an avant-garde upperbrow architectural style is recognized and adopted by middlebrows, the upperbrows—deeply offended—drop it instantly and go on to something else, leaving the hapless middlebrows to imitate styles that are suddenly passé. Meantime, the upperbrows, who regard themselves as free spirits, greatly admire the free-spirited lowbrows, who drink beer from cans, watch mudwrestling on late night TV in their undershirts, scratch their buttocks, and don't care what anybody else thinks. The poor middlebrows are caught in the middle: condemned eternally to worry about other people's opinions of them, and to wait for the next fashion to trickle down to them from above.

Lynes's argument, if taken seriously, has the capacity to send some American intellectuals into a state of near hysteria. After all, Lynes is saying that America is a class-bound society, dominated by a small arrogant elite, and furthermore that armies of Americans seem to like it that way. Even worse, he is suggesting that the majority of middlebrow Americans are like sheep, endlessly driven by herd ambition to become something they can never be, and endlessly manipulated by arrogant puppetmasters who pursue their private goals for selfish purposes.

Trying to deal with Lynes in a contemporary context is not easy; partly the essay was written tongue in cheek, while his most furious critics were dead serious. But it is worth trying to understand why that essay has been in print for about forty years, and why it doubtless will remain in print. There is a good deal of truth in what Lynes says.

There *are* tastemakers in society, and their motives are not necessarily exalted. Ephemeral taste can be and is manipulated. The advertising industry spends its whole time doing that; indeed, there is a whole new field of enterprise devoted to what is called "market segmentation," with demographers hired to identify subcultures by zip code according to age, race, income, ethnicity, housing, and so on, in order to discover the potential tastes for various products that exist within those zip code areas.[12] For example, people in certain zip code areas simply won't buy yogurt, and there is little point for an advertiser to waste money trying to sell it there. Or if a zip code area is known to be inhabited mainly by poor Hispanics and blacks, the market segmenters can advise the salesmen of Gucci shoes to peddle their products elsewhere. Judging by the amount of money that market segmentation commands nowadays, the technique seems to work—which is just another way of saying that most people are not entirely free agents either in terms of income or of taste.

It is also clear, as Lynes argues, that taste is hierarchical: taste does trickle down. The history of American popular architecture, for example, is a long repeating procession of changing styles, introduced or invented by high-style architects and subsequently imitated, simplified, and spread across the land (figure 1–13).[13] Plainly enough, America is not a classless society—although it is equally plain that class in late twentieth-century America does not mean the same thing that it meant to Karl Marx in England of the 1850s.

I–14

Canon 3: The Spaces of Taste

The third and final canon is geographical. There exist in America today two large general categories of space: areas where aesthetic standards are routinely invoked and areas where they are not; "tasteful" space and "taste-free" space.

Tasteful spaces are those where society considers it legitimate and normal to pass judgment about environmental beauty or ugliness. ("That's a beautiful garden. That's an ugly house.") Tasteful space is considered by society at large to be the legitimate province of designers—architects, landscape architects, and amateur gardeners of all kinds, all striving to create beauty, however defined. Taste-free spaces, by contrast, are those where aesthetic value judgments are considered to be out of bounds—where judgments by designers or critics are considered inappropriate or even perverse.

The difference between those two kinds of spaces are obvious to us when we go outdoors (figure 1–14). No designers have gotten near the local junkyard, nor are they likely to. The Highway Beautification Act of 1965 tried to make the owners of junkyards put fences or hedges around their properties so the tastes of passersby would not be offended. Nobody took those fences seriously, nor were they much surprised when the obligatory fences were often built of scrap metal and old hubcaps and consequently looked rather like the space they were supposed to be concealing. The 1965 act failed in this respect for the devastatingly simple reason that junkyards are quintessential taste-free spaces. At the other end of the scale is the American front yard, clearly intended to be tasteful and subject to heavy neighborhood opprobrium if it fails.

Two properties differentiate tasteful from taste-free space and help define them both: how they function and how they are bounded. In terms of function, objects and spaces that serve obvious and serious utilitarian purposes are likely to be taste-free and consequently off limits to designers. For example, few people would dream of designing an irrigation ditch, an airport runway, or an open-pit coal mine to be beautiful: like junkyards, they are designed to perform a useful function, and that is generally regarded as quite enough. The same goes for things like container terminals, oil refineries, and parking lots. Now and then, of course, one of those utilitarian landscapes turns out to be astonishingly beautiful. I think of certain freeway interchanges when seen from the air, or oil refineries at night, or grain elevators that stand above the horizon of the Great Plains like medieval cathedrals. But even when such things turn out to be inadvertently handsome, it is not customary to admit the fact. To say "that's a beautiful steel mill" would be deemed perverse by most people. Steel mills are not designed to be beautiful; they are designed to be useful. In fact, most people have come to accept a certain level of ugliness as an inevitable concomitant of extremely useful things; indeed, extremely

I–14　The boundary between tasteful and taste-free space is often very obvious. Lawns are tasteful; parking lots are not. The boundary here is made of hardened steel. State College, Pennsylvania, c. 1980.

I–15　Walls around recently built western subdivisions are unambiguous boundaries of tasteful space. Suburban Denver, 1978.

utilitarian spaces are often expected to be ugly. If they turn out otherwise, most people simply ignore them.

In terms of boundaries, tasteful spaces tend to be sharply separated from the rest of the world. The private front yard, for example, commonly has unambiguous edges—sidewalks, curbs, hedges, or walls. I am intrigued, as all students of American landscape must be, with the walls that are springing up all over the arid West to enclose newly built residential subdivisions (figure 1–15). Several explanations suggest themselves for the huge popularity of such walls. In newly settled spaces, where people are striving to define their own rules of community, such walls serve a variety of useful purposes. They keep strangers away; they define the boundaries of ownership in an unambiguous way. But one of their main purposes, I think, is to establish the limits of aesthetic responsibility. It is as if the wall builder is saying, "inside this wall is my world, the world of my friends and neighbors who agree with me on all sorts of grounds; the world outside is wilderness—somebody else's responsibility." Those walls help define space and reduce it to manageable proportions in an endless physical and human wasteland that seems to have no landmarks. With those walls, as in so many other ways, people define their place in the world by the tastes they hold up and display to the world at large. It is important that people know where those boundaries are—between them and the world outside.

The ownership of and responsibility for tasteful space is usually unambiguous. Those walls, for example, declare a sharp unarguable boundary between the owner of a space and something else. The same is true for the facade of an owner-occupied house, a corporate headquarters building, a municipal park or square: we know who owns them, and we consequently know who is responsible for their aesthetic properties. That is much less likely to be true of taste-free space. Rental properties, for example, often tend to be taste-free, in part because nobody is really sure who is responsible for them—the owner or the occupant. The same is true of vacant lots, parking lots, and public roadsides.[14] It is not clear who has dominion over those places, and their boundaries are often fuzzy.

A good deal of geographic space, of course, does not fall neatly into either category, and it is in that never-never land between tasteful and taste-free space that some of our most rancorous social and political disputes arise—where there are conflicting aesthetic claims over a particular jurisdiction. Well-tended farmland, for example, is usually held to be beautiful by most Americans, who repeatedly assert that government should help to preserve that beauty, by legislative fiat if necessary (figure 1–16). But most farmland is private property, and, to quote the popular aphorism, "a man's got a right to do what he wants with his own property." To make matters still more complicated, farmland is quintessentially useful and should by all rights be off limits to aesthetic claims. Small won-

1–15

I–16

der that our fiercest disputes over land use tend to focus on subjects like the legal preservation of agricultural land.

And what about those redwood forests? Are they utilitarian timberland and thus taste-free space? Or are they tasteful space, to be set aside on aesthetic grounds? That argument, of course, is not trivial; it reflects the chasm between world views that for more than a century has separated people like John Muir and the National Park Service on the one side from Gifford Pinchot and the National Forest Service on the other—or between the Bureau of Land Management and members of the Sagebrush Rebellion.[15] It is as fundamental as the disputes over abortion or gun control. The argument has not been settled yet, nor will it be soon. It is, to a degree not widely admitted, a matter of popular taste, and consequently off limits to rational discourse. Many people, of course, hotly refuse to admit that, asserting that redwood cutting is an ethical question and simply wrong, or that redwood cutting should be judged on instrumental grounds (banned to prevent soil-erosion, or sanctioned to preserve jobs in the lumber industry). But those arguments, I submit, conceal the root of the matter. The argument about cutting redwoods is in large part a matter of taste—of deeply held aesthetic values. It is, by nature, undebatable, and by nature will continue to be acrimonious. Environmentalists and loggers represent two quite different cultures, each possessing its own peculiar aesthetic standards, indeed its own special language. (The two cultures often use the same words but assign those words quite different meanings.) For that quite primitive reason, they are not likely to reach agreement.

That dispute about cutting redwoods is not an isolated matter. Like so many other disputes that sunder modern American society, it is a matter of taste. And taste goes to the very heart of our culture, of our belief system, of our existence as human beings and members of human communities. Whether we are geographers, designers, or simply citizens of the world, we would be well advised to take matters of taste seriously.

I–16 Tasteful or taste-free landscape? Amish farms, Kishacoquillas Valley, Pennsylvania, c. 1983.

Notes

1 "I happen to be one of those (and I think we're very numerous) who like sameness, who like familiarity. . . . That is one of the characteristics of the American landscape which is an indication that we are a culture. That is why I never cease to be interested and respectful of certain commonplace aspects of the American landscape. . . . [It] is very uniform throughout much of the United States, and that is what I like, that is what I look for: repetition, composition, monotony, uniformity, classicism." From "Figure in a Landscape: A Conversation with J. B. Jackson," a film by the Conservation Foundation in cooperation with the Film Study Center, Harvard University; Claire Marino and Janet Mendelsohn, producers and directors, 1987.

2 David Lowenthal, "The American Scene," *Geographical Review* 58 (1968), 61.

3 Having said that, I cannot resist noting that there is ample room for serious work to be done on those pink flamingos and things like them. No common element in the human landscape ought to be out of bounds to a curious academic merely because it is unfashionable.

4 Landscape tastes are highly specific to particular cultures, which is why the Japanese landscape looks Japanese and the American landscape looks American. For a perceptive Anglo-American view of this matter, see David Lowenthal and Hugh C. Prince, "The English Landscape," *Geographical Review* 54 (July 1964), 309–346.

5 Richard Hofstadter, "The Agrarian Myth and Commercial Realities," in *The Age of Reform* (New York: Vintage Books, 1955), 23.

6 David Lowenthal, *The Past Is a Foreign Country* (Cambridge: Cambridge University Press, 1985).

7 J. B. Jackson has written eloquently and sympathetically about this topic. See especially "The House in the Vernacular Landscape," in Michael P. Conzen (ed.), *The Making of the American Landscape* (Winchester, Mass.: Unwin-Hyman, 1990), 355–369.

8 In the recently colonized Third World, the introduction of ephemeral Euro-American tastes is not a trivial matter. In countries that can barely afford basic nutrition, imported tastes for Scotch whiskey, gigantic sports arenas, and stretch limousines can do serious economic damage.

9 Leo Rosten's Hyman Kaplan stories are not read much any more, but they should be. *The Education of H*Y*M*A*N K*A*P*L*A*N* (for example) is a wonderfully funny and devastatingly perceptive account of how the American WASP establishment inculcated newly arrived immigrants with the English language along with American WASP values—including taste. See also *O K*A*P*L*A*N My K*A*P*L*A*N!* (New York: Harper and Row, 1976).

10 See John Maass, *The Gingerbread Age: A View of Victorian America* (New York: Rinehart, 1957), a lively and well-illustrated account of how, among other things, the nineteenth-century media helped aspiring Americans to arrange their domestic affairs suitably and tastefully. See also Tamara Plakins Thornton, "Cultivating the American Character," *Orion* (1987), 10–19, for an account of how nineteenth-century tastes in domestic horticulture were manipulated in the name of morality.

11 It first appeared in Russell Lynes, *The Tastemakers* (New York: Grosset and Dunlap, 1949).

12 See, for example, Michael J. Weiss, *The Clustering of America* (New York: Harper and Row, 1988). See also Art Weinstein, *Market Segmentation: Using Demographics, Psychographics and Other Segmentation Techniques to Uncover and Exploit New Markets* (Chicago: Probus Publishing Co., 1987). For an insider's guide to how this machinery works, see *The ACORN Market Segmentation System, User's Guide* (Fairfax, Va.: CACI, 1988).

13 Peirce Lewis, "Common Houses, Cultural Spoor," *Landscape* 19, no. 2 (1975), 1–22.

14 Over the last few years, various states have sought to deal with roadside litter by persuading local organizations to "adopt" a section of roadside—to take responsibility for keeping it clear of litter. In return, the state erects a sign giving credit to that organization for its civic virtue. Although the purpose of the program was initially economic—meant to save the state the cost of removing litter—in effect, by shifting responsibility for cleaning up litter, taste-free space has been inadvertently converted into tasteful space. The sign says that the roadside shall be cleaned, and identifies the parties responsible for doing so. The program in many states has been remarkably successful.

15 To savor the ferocity of this dispute, and to appreciate the aesthetic roots of the supposedly ecological argument, read "Hetch-Hetchy," in Roderick Nash, *Wilderness and the American Mind* (New Haven: Yale University Press, 1973). For an excellent account of the Sagebrush Rebellion and its long history (indeed much longer than is commonly appreciated) see William L. Graf, *Wilderness Preservation and the Sagebrush Rebellions* (Savage, Maryland: Rowman & Littlefield, 1990).

2

2–1

Catherine Howett is Professor in the School of Environmental Design at the University of Georgia. Her research and writing interests are centered in nineteenth- and twentieth-century American architecture, landscape architecture, and public art.

The approaching centennial of the World's Columbian Exposition at Chicago offers a useful vantage point from which to review a century of development within the profession of landscape architecture. The fair epitomized this nation's optimistic faith that a civilization greater than any the world had yet seen was about to be realized through revolutionary progress in American industry, science, and the arts. But a curious tension between almost servile reverence for the past achievements of Western European culture and excited anticipation of radical change, catalyzed by the New World's native genius, charged the atmosphere of debate and decision making surrounding plans for the fair. To a remarkable degree that tension persisted in the practice of architecture and landscape architecture throughout the early decades of the new century, as American designers struggled self-consciously to define a style or styles appropriate to their time and their perception that their country and its culture had come of age.

Since responsibility for the fair's master plan was one of the culminating events in the long career of Frederick Law Olmsted, the inspiration that the "White City" gave to the subsequent City Beautiful movement may be seen as a projection into the twentieth century of certain of the urbanistic values for which Olmsted had struggled. On the other hand, the decision of the participating architects to enforce a Beaux-Arts canon in site planning and architecture violated Olmsted's commitment to urban design that provided ample opportunities for the experience of natural scenery. He suffered a great deal of anxiety during the difficult months of superintending the planting of the lagoons, because he feared that the transplanted shrubs and native water plants would not achieve the size and lushness needed to counterpoise the glittering mass of the building complexes; and he fought a losing battle to make the picturesque fifteen-acre Wooded Isle (figure 2–1) the most significant landscape feature of the entire scheme, free of any displays.[1]

As it turned out, however, the intrusion of the Japanese government's pavilion, a reconstruction of the Ho-o-den temple (figure 2–2), seemed not to violate the atmosphere of serene retreat within a shaded grove that Olmsted had wanted the Wooded Isle to convey. The contrast between the architecture of this timber building and that of the buildings surrounding the Court of Honor could not have been more striking, although in both places a distinct aura of imposing architectural presence was manifest. For the young apprentice Frank Lloyd Wright, visiting the Ho-o-den on lunch hour breaks from the office of Adler and Sullivan where he was employed, the mystery to be unraveled was the source of the simple dignity and beauty of this small building sheltered within Olmsted's green island bower. In that place the sensibilities of these two men of genius came together in a passing moment full of portent for the future of American architecture and landscape design.

The example of Olmsted's career had brought the profession of landscape architecture to a position of equality with the other civic arts—architecture, city planning, and public sculpture—by the end of the nineteenth century. Indeed, Charles Eliot Norton proclaimed that "of all American artists," Olmsted stood "first in the production of great works which answer the needs and give expression to the life of our immense and miscellaneous democracy." On the same occasion, Daniel Burnham described Olmsted as one who deserved the nation's gratitude not just for his legacy of public works, but "for what his brain [had] wrought and his pen [had] taught for half a century."[2] Olmsted himself confessed, in a letter to a friend, his belief that he had personally elevated landscape architecture "from the rank of a trade, even of a handicraft, to that of a profession—an Art, an Art of Design," and that the influence of his work would shape future practice.[3] It does seem clear that Olmsted's acknowledged intellectual and artistic leadership generated design energies and directions that sustained the profession through the opening decades of the new century, and not just in the area of urban design and park planning.

For second only to the task of laying out the grounds for the Chicago fair in its importance as a last major work was Olmsted's responsibility for the design of George Vanderbilt's Biltmore estate in western North Carolina, which occupied him between 1889 and his retirement from practice in 1895. In its scale and opulence—formal gardens, forest preserve, and park surrounding a mansion designed by Richard Morris Hunt on the model of the royal chateau of Blois—the project was a cynosure for the era of country house estate building that provided most of the work for landscape architects in the years from the turn of the century until the Great Depression.

2–2

2–1   The Court of Honor, World's Columbian Exposition Chicago, 1893. [from *Photographs of the World's Fair* (Chicago: The Werner Company, 1894)]

2–2   From the Government Lantern, the wooded island with the Ho-o-den Palace to the left, World's Columbian Exposition [from *Photographs of the World's Fair* (Chicago: The Werner Company, 1894)]

This period of Beaux-Arts eclecticism is usually described as a neoclassical revival in reaction against the picturesque eclecticism dominant in England and America during most of the nineteenth century. Vincent Scully has argued, however, that the renewed interest in baroque architecture may be seen as an extension of values long operative within the picturesque tradition. When the world view predicated upon historic traditions of hierarchy and control collapsed under the pressure of new political, social, and scientific realities, the baroque aesthetic that had dominated European art and architecture from the sixteenth to the mid-eighteenth centuries ceased to serve as a viable expression of western society's perception of the world or the significance of human action:

> Since the spatial . . . and sculptural . . . qualities of the old forms per se were now devoid of specific meanings, they could be chosen as seemed appropriate and rearranged as desired. Since this "eclectic" method was purely one of optical titillation, having nothing intrinsic to do with the program or structure of a building, but producing a great variety of effects, it partook of the pictorial freedom of painting and was thus doubly "picturesque." . . . A kind of psuedo-baroque design, drained of emotional focus and of meanings other than theatrical ones . . . became the stock in trade of architectural schools by the end of the century.[4]

From this perspective, the ascendancy of Beaux-Arts academic classicism—the triumph of the imagery of the "White City"—failed to redirect in any essential way the preoccupation of both architects and clients with historical models. The substitution of Roman temples and Renaissance palazzi for buildings meant to evoke, however remotely, the European Middle Ages did not represent the abandonment of compositional concerns that were fundamentally scenographic in nature.

Within the domain of landscape architecture, Reginald Blomfield's defense of formalism against the attacks of William Robinson in England laid the groundwork in this country for endless analyses of the respective advantages of the formal versus the "natural" style. This battle over styles, however, was chiefly phrased in terms of the *look* of geometric order, with its pleasing references to Italian villas, French chateaux, or colonial American gardens, versus the *look* of pastoral scenery, with its equally pleasing references to the landscaped parks surrounding English manor houses (figure 2–3). Ideally, of course, one might bring both styles together in the same place, as Olmsted did for George Vanderbilt at Biltmore, where the formal gardens and terraces open out to spectacular views of forested countryside; or, for that matter, as the styles were frequently combined on rural or suburban properties of much smaller scale, by siting a neoclassical house and formal garden within a landscape plan that accommodated a curving drive and a broad lawn on which trees were informally arranged (figure 2–4).

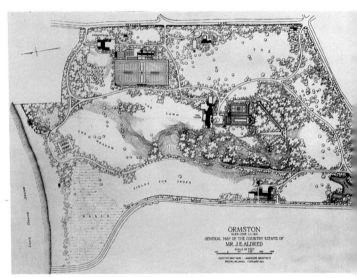

2–3

2–4

Olmsted's intellectual leadership of his own profession, as well as his national reputation as a designer and as an advocate for well-planned cities and suburbs, actually had very little to do with the particular style, derived from English landscape gardening tradition, that became the hallmark of much of his work. This explains, in some measure, the ease with which he undertook the formal gardens at Biltmore and recognized in that project a direction that would account for an important part of his firm's work in future years. His frequent criticism of proposals to introduce formal architectural elements or complexes into public parks was instead related to a lifelong defense of specific values that he believed were essential to the physical and psychological well-being of the inhabitants of the new world that urbanization and industrialization had lately brought into being. These values were partially based in visual experience—the calming and restorative effect of seeing "broad ranges of space"—but embraced as well the notion that the more fully kinesthetic experience of a predominantly natural environment had a profound and wholesome, healing effect upon the human psyche. This theme informed his cause in every strident political battle in which he engaged; it prompted as well such daring conceptual programs as his intention to stir ancestral memories of the earliest encounters of European settlers with coastal Massachusetts through the restoration of a community of salt marsh vegetation in Boston's Fenway.[5]

The more superficial stylistic conventions of the large body of Olmsted's design work were easily perpetuated by his own firm and by legions of disciples and imitators after his death. What did not endure was the philosophical foundation of his practice: the belief that the mission of landscape architecture was to answer the primal need of human beings to interact with environments in which natural elements remained dominant, even if transformed in some measure through art or other human agency. This conviction was not sentimentalized in Olmsted's theory; sanity and health, not emotional attachment to pastoral or picturesque scenery, were at stake when opportunities for this kind of contact with nature were created or denied.

The quasi-religious intensity of this conviction is related, of course, to the formative effect of his reading of such authors as Emerson, Ruskin, and Lowell,[6] all of whom drew upon a romantic tradition responsive to Wordsworth's call for a "wise passiveness" in contemplating the natural world. Barbara Novak has traced the development of a distinct nineteenth-century American expression of this tradition, one that found in landscapes, painted or real, a vehicle for identifying with the indwelling Divine:

> God in nature speaks to God in man. . . . And man can also commune with *man* through nature—a communing which requires for its representation not the solitary figure, but two figures in a landscape, the classic exemplar of which, in American landscape art, is Durand's portrait of Cole and Bryant, *Kindred Spirits* [figure 2–5].

2–5

2–3   Site plan of Ormston, the country
       estate of J. E. Alfred
       Near Glen Cove, Long Island,
       New York, 1922. Olmsted
       Brothers, landscape architects.
       [Frederick Law Olmsted National
       Historical Site/National Park
       Service]

2–4   Residence designed for
       Mr. Livingston Wright
       Atlanta, 1922, Neil Reid, architect.
       [Dennis O'Kain]

2–5   *Kindred Spirits*
       1849. Asher B. Durand.
       Oil on canvas.
       [The New York Public Library,
       Astor, Lenox, and Tilden
       Foundations]

2–6　Garden facade, Avery Coonley
House
Riverside, Illinois, 1908.
Frank Lloyd Wright, architect.
[Frank Lloyd Wright Archives]

2–7　Coonley House plan
From *Ausgeführte Bauten und
Entwürfe von Frank Lloyd Wright*
(Berlin: Verlag Ernst Wasmuth, 1910).
[Frank Lloyd Wright Archives]

2–6

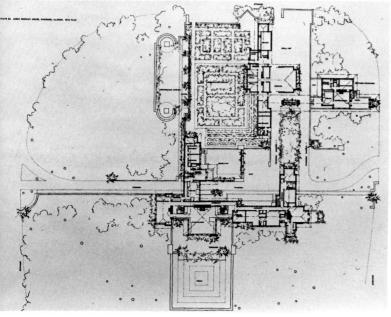

2–7

This picture is evidence not only of singular contemplation after a transcendental model, but of a sharing through communion, of a potential community.[7]

Olmsted's intellectual and emotional commitment to this myth was probably subconscious; he seemed to avoid explicitly religious imagery in describing the experience of nature that his landscape designs made available. But both of the key elements of his understanding of the purposes of the great parks are brought together in Novak's reading of the landscape myth. Olmsted believed that a generous scale of expansive natural scenery, uncompromised by too many traces of human enterprise, was essential to communion with nature, the experience of a euphoric sense of oneness with the whole of creation; and that the *shared* experience of nature was an effective instrument for nurturing a spirit of brotherhood and civic responsibility within a democratic society.

The same values, from Olmsted's point of view, were cultivated within suburban developments that balanced the urban world of work with the pleasures of country living, while fostering "intimate relationship and constant intercourse, and interdependence between families."[8] The Garden City movement represents one of the few developments early in the next century that significantly extended and refined Olmsted's ideas. Walter Creese suggests that Ebenezer Howard, the English originator of the Garden City concept, was inspired by his exposure to Olmsted's work at Riverside during a brief period of employment in Chicago.[9] Landscape architects were not, however, in the vanguard of the Garden City movement in this country.

Frank Lloyd Wright was no less obsessed than Olmsted with the central importance of engagement with the natural world for modern men and women desiring to lead happy, healthy, and productive lives. Nor was he any less convinced that cities, suburbs, and homes needed to be designed in ways that affirmed the highest aspirations of American democracy, by making it possible for every person to discover the beauty and truth that great art and architecture make accessible to human understanding. The most important lesson passed on to Wright by his *lieber Meister* Louis Sullivan was that since disharmony with nature was at the root of most of the ills of the modern world, the architect is called to serve as nature's instrument of reconciliation.[10] Wright's challenge was to conceive an American building that was itself a part of nature, not separate from it—a "noble organic expression of nature." Such an architecture would have to sever at last the "umbilical cord to the Colonial or the French chateau, the English manor house or the grandomania of [the] Beaux-Arts"; it must substitute for the catalogue of styles an architecture that sought to express through its forms the authentic experience of generations of Americans who had come to know the land intimately. We had to know better, Wright said, "the here and now of *our own life* in its Time and Place."[11]

The landscape of the midwestern prairie provided Wright with the first grounding of his metaphors of place in actual form and materials. On the outside, the house "began to associate with the ground and become natural to its prairie site" through "extension and emphasis of the planes parallel to the ground," especially roof lines and windows. Wide windows and glazed doors opened onto terraces, courts, and gardens, making both light and landscape more present within the house and achieving that interpenetration of house and garden that Wright so admired in Japanese architecture (figure 2–6). In the interior, a new openness prevailed—in his terms, "wholly plastic, instead of structural . . . the ceilings and floors and enclosing screens to flow into each other as one large enclosure of space"—analogous, we may infer, to the spatial expansiveness on the horizontal plane of the prairie vista (figure 2–7). The houses were to convey "a sense of shelter" and rigorous simplicity, as if to show their descent from the primitive cabins of the pioneers who settled the prairie wilderness. The fussy and dysfunctional "mantels" of popular fashion were replaced by "the *integral* fireplace," with a great chimney rising on the outside; "it refreshed me to see the fire burning deep in the masonry of the house itself," Wright said of this revitalized feature.[12]

Wright's organicism, then, denies the possibility of an architecture whose formal language or material details can be conceived separately from the site with which it forms a single, cohesive environment. The forms of a building must respond to a functional program, but the expressive quality of those forms is also, in a sense, functional, and derives from the architect's conceptual and intuitive responses to the topology of site and region. "Oh yes," he wrote in 1931, in criticizing the practice of some who called themselves modern architects, "a house is a machine in which to live, but by the same token a heart is a suction pump. Sentient man begins where that concept of the heart ends."[13] Wright's understanding of the motive force of *place*—what is historically described as the *genius loci*—deepened over the course of his long career, becoming less literal, more complex and ambiguous.

In the early years, he sought to discover the essential character of the regional landscape in order to generate an appropriate architectural style. The Prairie houses represent just such an effort to embody the physical and mythic character of the region in an objective architectural medium. Passages in Wright's autobiography describe his similar effort to think freshly about the nature of the California landscape, during the period after his return from Japan when he was gestating ideas for the Millard house, La Miniatura. He begins with a poetic evocation of the "real" California landscape:

Near [the site] that arid, sunlit strand is still unspoiled. . . . Curious tan-gold foothills rise

from the tattooed sand-stretches to join slopes spotted as the leopard-skin, with grease-bush.

This foreground spreads to distances so vast—human scale is utterly lost as all features recede, turn blue, recede and become bluer still to merge their blue mountain shapes, snow capped, with the azure of the skies. . . . Water comes, but comes as a deluge once a year to surprise the roofs, sweep the sands into ripples and roll the boulders along in the gashes combed by sudden streams in the sands of the desert— then—all dry as before.[14]

Wright then describes the "Yankeefied" houses and yards built by the droves of midwesterners who had migrated to California, seeking the mild climate but unprepared to surrender to the real nature of the place in which they now lived. When their houses imitated the styles familiar to them from "back home," they appeared to him "hard," all of them wearing the "same fixed face" and still projecting "bristling defenses" against severe weather for which there was absolutely no need. The newcomers used exotic rather than indigenous vegetation in "neat, curious little 'collection[s]'—all nicely set out together on the clipped lawns of little town-lots." In a second phase, Wright noted, "decorative picturizing architects" introduced Californians to Spanish style. Copying Spanish mission buildings, copying as well their furniture and their cool patios and vivid gardens, the Californians "have yet nothing to say for themselves in all this except acquired taste for the Spanish antique."[15]

La Miniatura, by contrast, was to be a building that started fresh, searching for all that was missing in the sterile, sentimental copies of historic styles. "And what was missing?" Wright asked. "Nothing more or less than a distinctly genuine expression of California in terms of modern industry and modern life." La Miniatura would therefore grow "as a cactus grows," from a vision of "a new Architecture for a new Life—the life of romantic, beautiful California." Wright rejected the "treeless lot originally purchased by Mrs. Millard" in favor of a wooded eucalyptus ravine costing half as much, then set the house at the rear of the property in order to use the ravine in front as a "sunken garden" to which balconies and terraces would lead down (figure 2–8). In order to give Alice Millard the fireproof house she wanted as protection for works of art, he would "take that despised outcast of the building industry—the concrete block" and weave it, "make it live as a thing of beauty—textured like the trees. . . . The building would be made of the 'blocks' as a kind of tree standing at home among other trees in its own native land."[16]

Wright liked to use the metaphor of the building as tree to explain what he meant by organic architecture—an organic integration of building and site, of indoors and outdoors. The idea of an appropriate *regional* style is gradually absorbed into a theory that focuses more specifically on the unique character of an individual site, as the following pas-

sage from *The Natural House,* first published in 1954, suggests:

> We have no longer an outside and an inside as two separate things. Now the outside may come inside, and the inside may and does go outside. They are *of* each other. . . .
>
> It is in the nature of any organic building to grow from its site, come out of the ground into the light—the ground itself held always as a component basic part of the building itself. . . . A building dignified as a tree in the midst of nature. . . . But instead of "organic" we might say "natural" building. Or we might say integral building.[17]

One might dismiss Wright's search for metaphors to describe his "new architecture" as little more than rhetorical posturing, given his rather grandiloquent prose style, and given as well the number of projects that emerged from his office over the years in which no particular care seems to have been taken to acknowledge special features of the site in siting or design of the building and its landscape. But such a dismissal would fail to appreciate the profound significance to his work of certain key iconic images, of which one of the most important is the visual metaphor of the building as a living tree growing out of the ground on which it stands. Like the tree, the building should be penetrated by ceaselessly shifting light and shadow, sheltering at its center and yet broadly spreading—downward into the layered soil, outward toward the enveloping sky—literally breathing to the pulse of dynamic systems tied to the earth and the air.

The architecture of Fallingwater, designed for the Kaufmann family at Bear Run, Pennsylvania (figure 2–9), can only be understood in terms of such an organic metaphor—not in the sense that the forms of the house are abstractions of the idea of "treeness," in the way that regional metaphors might be translated into a formal and textural vocabulary constituting a regional style, but in the sense that the body of the house has become an extension of the body of the earth in that place—water, rock, soil, slope, and vegetation. In his design of Fallingwater, Wright pressed the organic metaphor with so much daring that what Kenneth Frampton has described as the "fundamentalist assimilation of the building . . . to the processes of nature" moves beyond the cycle of generative process to curve imperceptibly—over the course of years in which water seeps and erodes, roots spread, pressures build, and materials decay—toward a heroic engagement with the entropic forces of nature as well. Frampton sees in Fallingwater's embrace of darkness a hint of the ancient cave:

> Its fusion with the landscape is total, for, despite the extensive use of horizontal glazing, nature permeates the structure at every turn. Its interior evokes the atmosphere of a furnished cave rather than that of a house in the traditional sense. That the rough stone walls and flagged floors intend some primitive homage to the site is borne out by the living room stairs which, de-

2–9

2–8   La Miniatura, residence designed for Mrs. George Madison Millard Pasadena, California, 1923. Frank Lloyd Wright, architect. [Frank Lloyd Wright Archives]

2–9   Fallingwater, residence designed for Edgar Kaufmann, Sr. Near Bear Run, Pennsylvania, 1936. Frank Lloyd Wright, architect. [Marc Treib]

scending through the floor to the waterfall below, have no function other than to bring man into more intimate communion with the surface of the stream.[18]

Frampton's terms "function" and "communion with nature" relate very closely to an evolution that allows us to see Wright's vision in the twentieth century as intimately connected to that of Olmsted in the nineteenth. Both affirmed the necessity for Americans to live in a way that allowed close contact with nature in spite of accelerating urbanization. Olmsted had remained hopeful that cities could be planned to make this possible by including parks at every scale—from that of the great "central" park to green recreational corridors and neighborhood parks—and through development of suburban communities in which natural scenery was amply preserved. Wright, on the other hand, hailed the birth of the automotive age as a liberation by which Americans could retain the antiurban bias that went back at least as far as Jefferson's fear of great cities as "pestilential to the morals, the health, and the liberties of man."[19] In his model of Broadacre City, and in his 1932 book *The Disappearing City* that outlined the planning principles on which Broadacre was based, Wright advanced the view that the decentralization made feasible by the automobile would ultimately produce a new urban form in which the city was simply absorbed into the larger countryside all across America. In the meantime, Wright urged his clients to flee the cities built on the old pattern of concentrated population and services:

My suggestion would be to go just as far as you can go—and go soon and go fast. . . .

We have all the means to live free and independent, far apart—as we choose—still retaining all the social relationships and advantages we ever had. . . . You would enjoy all that you used to enjoy when you were ten to a block, and think of the immense advantages for your children and for yourself: freedom to *use* the ground, relationship with all kinds of living growth.[20]

Wright's vision of a free and independent life lived in one's own domain, in daily and intimate relationship with the natural world and yet without any sacrifice of the benefits provided by modern industrial technology, is a distinctively American utopian vision. It is rooted, as has already been suggested, in the national experience of encounter with the wilderness and in an enduring romantic tradition that celebrated the natural world as the arena in which self-realization and communal consciousness are both achieved, a tradition linking Emerson, Thoreau, and Walt Whitman as it did Olmsted and Wright.

The vision of a new urban future that Antonio Sant'Elia and the Italian futurists proposed early in the twentieth century could not have been more different. They accepted an environment in which large mobile populations would inhabit a landscape radically transformed by industrialization:

We must invent and rebuild *ex novo* our modern city like an immense and tumultuous shipyard, active, mobile, and everywhere dynamic, and the modern building like a giant machine. . . . The house of cement, iron, and glass, without carved or painted ornament, rich only in the inherent beauty of its lines and modeling, extraordinarily brutish in its mechanical simplicity, as big as need dictates, and not merely as zoning rules permit, must rise from the brink of a tumultuous abyss; the street which, itself, will no longer lie like a doormat at the level of the thresholds but plunge storeys deep into the earth, gathering up the traffic of the metropolis connected for necessary transfers to metal catwalks and high-speed conveyor belts.[21]

While this radical manifesto of 1914 hardly represents the entire modernist movement, the vision postulated here at least serves to underscore the essential foundation of European modernism in an acceptance of both urbanism and the iconography of machine technology.

Wright, of course, had been an important influence on the beginnings of the modern movement in Europe, particularly after the publication of the Wasmuth portfolios in 1910–1911. Like the leaders of the European avant-garde, he rejected historicism and the Beaux-Arts academic definition of architecture as a manipulation of formal and ornamental conventions derived from classical precedent. But Wright had also invented a brilliant alternative model in his designs of the Prairie house years. These houses offered the Europeans instruction in the way that the old relationships of floor, ceiling, wall, column, and roof could be radically reconstructed, becoming newly responsive to a program that demanded experience of the building as a fluid, dynamic space accommodating interlocking functions. The younger European architects, including such seminal figures as Walter Gropius, Le Corbusier, and Mies van der Rohe, were primarily interested in Wright's synthesis of spatial plasticity—the open plan—and a simplified, abstract formal vocabulary. As Neil Levine has observed:

[Their own] steel, concrete, and glass structures of the 1920s . . . showed the way in which Wright's fragmentation and decomposition of traditional form could be used to create an abstract architecture of lines and planes in space. But once Wright's Prairie style was defined and accepted as the catalytic agent in this development toward abstraction, Wright himself was relegated to the role of a forerunner. . . . The later work was never really accepted as part of the canon of modern architecture.[22]

Part of the failure of Wright's later work, from the point of view of these European modernists, was its departure from the kind of typology that the notion of a Prairie "style" seemed to suggest, in favor of much more idiosyncratic and site-specific responses to each major commission. Only Wright's Usonian program possibly contained the seeds of that standardization of materials and planning formula—compatible with a machine aesthetic—that might have met the rigorous demands of European rationalism, particularly as it found expression in Bauhaus philosophy or in the structure of Le Corbusier's Maison Dom-Ino of 1915. Wright's romantic investment in individuality and in consideration of the site as a microcosm of human engagement with the world of nature were totally foreign to the European aesthetic, which aimed instead, in Vincent Scully's words, "to express a separateness between men and nature."[23] Landscape architecture, it should be noted, was not among the industries, arts, and crafts included in the interdisciplinary curriculum and workshops of the Bauhaus.

Le Corbusier's articulation of the theory of the house as a "machine for living" was not meant to deprive architecture of emotional content even beyond the satisfaction of seeing functional requirements intelligently and even elegantly answered. But it was to be through the play of abstract forms—shapes "clearly revealed in light," related in ways that have no necessary "reference to what is practical or descriptive"[24]—that the architect "realizes an order which is a pure creation of his spirit," communicates his ideas, and arouses our "plastic" emotions.[25] Frampton points out that this "drive to resolve the conflict between the Engineer's Aesthetic and Architecture, to inform utility with the hierarchy of myth," inevitably brought Le Corbusier "into conflict with the functionalist-socialist designers of the 1920s."[26] And yet the mythic reach of his architecture is not *into* the nature that surrounds his buildings but precisely in confrontation with it; the delight occasioned by the "spiralling qualities of asymmetry, rotation, and peripheral dispersal"[27] worked out within the severe cubic volume of the Villa Savoye, for example (figure 3–11), is set against the static and idealized landscape above which the rooms of the house, elevated on *pilotis*, seem to float in space. Le Corbusier himself affirms this dreamlike separation of the house from the rural landscape in which it is placed, declaring that the inhabitants "survey their whole domain from the height of the *jardin suspendu* or from the four aspects of their *fenêtres en longueur*. Their domestic life is inserted into a Virgilian dream."[28] The feature of roof gardens, included among the "five points toward a new architecture" of Le Corbusier and Pierre Jeanneret, are defended, curiously, as a replacement for the planar surface of land removed from the landscape by construction of the building,[29] suggesting the degree to which the landscape is conceived to remain unmodified, intact, and separate from the architectural event that takes place within it.

This Cartesian distancing of the occupants of the house from a surrounding landscape that is experienced primarily as panorama was even more explicitly defined and justified by Mies van der Rohe—although not at the beginning of his career, when he was most strongly under the influence of his admiration for Wright. Colin Rowe speaks of the way in which, in contrast to Le Corbusier, in Mies's early work the "vertical planes trail out suggestively, 'peripherically,' into the landscape," and Wolf Tegethoff has attempted a reinterpretation that argues for "manifold interrelationships" between the structure of the Barcelona Pavilion and its landscape context.[30] Tegethoff takes issue with the critical consensus that the early designs of Mies were typical of modern architecture generally in responding to their surroundings "only negatively, only by rejecting them."[31] At the same time, Tegethoff and others have observed a gradual change in the way that Miesian buildings connect with the landscape, related to the architect's growing interest, by the 1940s when he was working in America, in a more autonomous block form. This classicizing tendency has been described by Vincent Scully as a movement in Mies's later work away from asymmetry and forms that move freely in space toward a greater concentration on the building as an idealized, humanistically ordered composition.[32]

Mies reconciled this formal change in his architecture with his earlier interest in the integration of building and landscape by arriving at the position that true unity between architecture and nature exists as an ideal but not as a real possibility; hence the desired unity could only be achieved at a "spiritual" and philosophical level:

> Nature should also have a life of its own. We should avoid disturbing it with the excessive color of our houses and our interior furnishings. Indeed, we should strive to bring Nature, houses, and people together into a higher unity. When one looks at Nature through the glass walls of the Farnsworth House [figure 2–10] it takes on a deeper significance than when one stands outside. More of Nature is thus expressed—it becomes part of a greater whole.[33]

The effect of this commitment to a more abstract and philosophical relationship with nature was deliberately to aestheticize the experience of the surrounding landscape that the later buildings provide. Tegethoff cites the philosopher Nicolai Hartmann to support Mies's position that an essential feature of the aesthetic response to nature is separation, "distance from the object." In this view, to feel oneself "taken up, accepted, surrounded, and . . . one with Nature" by entering or engaging the landscape militates against the possibility of "aesthetic pleasure," which demands that one "confront" the landscape as a spectator. "The essential factor," Hartmann wrote, "is the pictorial character, the limitation, the selectivity [of the scenery]."[34]

Tegethoff uses both the plans for the unbuilt Resor House in Wilson, Wyoming, and the Farnsworth House in Plano, Illinois, as examples of the late style in which Mies used the glass walls to frame carefully controlled views of nature that were meant to be perceived as remote and idealized. Tegethoff writes of the Resor House:

> Looking through the glass wall one is struck . . . by an impression of visual distance, of detachment. The landscape here appears to the viewer no longer as a spatial frame of reference, but takes on a distinctly pictorial, almost stagelike

2–10

2–10 Farnsworth House
Plano, Illinois, 1951 (designed
earlier). Mies van der Rohe,
architect.
[Marc Treib]

character that Mies attempted to make even more apparent by means of the strictly frontal reproduction in parallel planes of the panorama presented. . . . The landscape projected in the opening . . . loses much of its three-dimensionality, . . . essential characteristics of the work of art [i.e., painting] having been imposed upon it.[35] Le Corbusier, Mies, and others among the European modernists would have been profoundly offended by the comparison of this emphasis on pictorial view making, on composing framed vistas from the building outward into the landscape, with the Beaux-Arts tradition that Scully described as the "last, persistently catatonic phase"[36] of picturesque eclecticism. And yet in its emphasis on an abstract, two-dimensional, distanced and compositionally determined *use* of the natural landscape, there are close similarities between this European approach to the "problem" of "tying the space to the landscape" (Mies's phrase)[37] and the scenographic preoccupations that Scully traced.

Scully speaks, in fact, of a "Puritan fleshlessness" and "utter separation from the *place*" (italics added) that became characteristic of American architecture once it had been absorbed within the International Style. Moreover he sees an important connection between this development and the fact, already noted, that except for Mies and Richard Neutra, most of the Europeans who came to America to teach and to practice (especially those in the circle around Walter Gropius) denied the relevance of Wright's work to the ongoing dialogue within the modern movement. "Most serious of all," according to Scully, "they passed this attitude on to most of the excellent students who now flocked to them," a rejection that had a great deal to do with Wright's dwindling influence in the postwar years.[38]

In a way, the Europeans and those American architects who embraced the modernist aesthetic were right about Wright's not being a "modern man" within their terms, so strong in him was the insistence on the experience of nature and of site as the wellspring of creative form-giving. It is possible to show, however, although not within the limits of this essay, that the same values—generated by a widely shared mythic conception of the American nation and of nature—that shaped both Olmsted's and Wright's sensibilities as children of the nineteenth century, endure in our own day and still find expression in literature, the visual arts, cinema, music—and architecture. A more interesting question has to do with American landscape architecture in the twentieth century, and the degree to which mainstream practice within that profession has manifested continuity with this artistic ethos, simply ignored it, or run counter to it, as the European modernist aesthetic seems clearly to have done.

Unfortunately there was little philosophical or critical discourse within the profession in the early twentieth century at a level comparable to the writings of Olmsted and such contemporaries of his as Horace W. S. Cleveland, author of *Landscape Architecture as Applied to the Wants of the West* of

1873. No such discourse seemed necessary, apparently, during the first three decades of this century, when energies of the City Beautiful movement continued to inform landscape architecture in the public domain, and when what Norman Newton has called the "Country Place Era" of residential estate design shaped popular perceptions of the nature of the work that landscape architects performed.

One of the few practitioners who stood against the tide of Beaux-Arts eclecticism in landscape design was the midwesterner Jens Jensen, a Danish immigrant to Chicago who occasionally worked on projects with Wright and was the most important figure in the regional movement to which Wilhelm Miller gave the name "Prairie School of Landscape Gardening."[39] Jensen tapped—and incorporated into such landmark projects as his design of a "Prairie River" in Chicago's Columbus Park (figure 2–11)—a cluster of landscape images of the original prairie of Illinois and Wisconsin analogous to those Wright associated with the forms of his Prairie houses. A consummate plantsman, Jensen had a growing appreciation for the way that indigenous communities of trees and shrubs imposed a unique character on the native landscape, one that reflected the complex contingencies of biotic and other factors at play in a specific place. He strove diligently to cultivate in his clients and in the general public (during the years that he worked for the Chicago parks department) a taste for another kind of beauty than the bland, predictable refinement of traditional ornamental gardening based on reproductions of historical styles. He was outspoken in his criticism of the formal styles that were the stock in trade of "eastern landscape architects," arguing instead for increased use of native vegetation in groupings that replicated the look of natural communities. Such espousal of what the profession viewed as "wild nature," Newton says, earned Jensen a reputation as an "eccentric maverick best allowed to go his own way undisturbed—and unmentioned." He had resigned from the professional association, the American Society of Landscape Architects, after a brief membership.[40]

Although he built a substantial regional practice in the Midwest, Jensen's isolation within the profession of landscape architecture is another indication of the degree to which that profession operated as a firmly entrenched and conservative academy—a Beaux-Arts academy—long after Wright's modernism and European modernism had together shaken the foundations of the White City. Jensen offered another paradigm—the landscape that recreates or dramatizes the authentic character of the region—but even Newton, writing in 1971, criticized the claims made by Jensen and his followers that the "Prairie Style" was "a somehow 'different' way of working," and deplored the use of a descriptive label that seemed to suggest "purely regional applicability—a fate that no sound program of planting design deserves."[41] Wright, who also studied the prairie in order to create an appropriate architecture for his midwestern buildings, who

2–11

studied California in order to discover building forms appropriate to its unique landscape, who studied the Arizona desert in order to make a place that could belong nowhere else in precisely the way that it belongs where it is, would have held with Jensen in this debate, and not with Newton.

There were, of course, creative people within the profession who finally posed to themselves the inevitable questions: if the perpetuation of historical styles, formal or informal in myriad combinations, does not exhaust all possibilities for the designed landscape, what are the alternatives? Can the modern movement, which has revolutionized the look and indeed the very nature of painting, sculpture, and architecture, have an application to landscape architecture? How may rational principles of function, simplicity, and the abstract geometry of transparent structural and spatial relationships be applied to the design of landscapes?

The first response to those questions, among European artists and architects, is best illustrated by the Garden of Water and Light designed for the 1925 Exposition des Arts Décoratifs in Paris by the Armenian architect Gabriel Guevrekian (figure 3–2) and by his later, similar garden at the villa of the vicomte de Noailles on the Côte d'Azur (figure 3–3). Guevrekian's intention in both of these designs was to create a garden that could be experienced as an autonomous art object, one in which the visual impact of formal relationships among the geometric planting beds arranged within the triangle formed by the walls was dominant. Added to this, however, are elements of optical illusion and of movement, including the addition, in the Noailles villa garden, of a Jacques Lipchitz sculpture of a man and woman embracing, which actually moved with "provocative motorized contortions."[42]

While the symmetrical and axial composition of these garden plans represents an abrogation of the "free" planning principles advocated by the early modernists, their ahistoricism and inclusion of mechanical features and materials associated with modern technology link them to the modernist canon. But they are also rigorously self-referential and objectified; the materials of the landscape—water, plants, and such architectural elements as the walls and raised beds—are treated as the material for art-making in the way that the inert materials of any art or craft are transformed into an art object. The design places more emphasis on dazzling visual effects of color, light, and perspective than on the kinesthetic experience of plastic and fluid, volumetric space that was an obsessive concern of the early modernist architects.

It is important to understand this aspect of Guevrekian's gardens, since it may serve as a model for the modernist landscape that is able to provide insight into a considerable body of work by artists and landscape architects as distinguished as Isamu Noguchi and Roberto Burle Marx. The biomorphic forms of Noguchi's UNESCO gardens of the early 1950s (figure 2–12), or of the "signature" works of Burle Marx, represent similar derivations

2–11　Babson House
　　　Riverside, Illinois. Louis Sullivan, architect; landscape design by Jens Jensen.
　　　[reproduced in Leonard K. Eaton, *Landscape Artist in America: The Life and Work of Jens Jensen* (Chicago: University of Chicago Press, 1964)]

2–12　UNESCO gardens
　　　Paris, 1956–1958. Isamu Noguchi.
　　　[Marc Treib]

2–12

2–13

from modernist experiment, although these examples are linked with 1930s exploration of surreal forms and irrational experience in painting, such as those of Joan Miró (figure 2–13) and André Masson, rather than with the rational, hard-edged geometries of De Stijl or cubism. But like Guevrekian, these designers created a "modern" landscape by giving primacy to compositional and pictorial values, in a manner not very different from the seventeenth-century French formalist imperative *forcer la nature*.

This approach to the design of the modern landscape is antithetical to the view of Le Corbusier and Mies in its refusal to allow the landscape to function merely as a foil to the man-made construct that is the building—even as *their* view is in its turn antithetical to Wright's vision of spatial and symbolic integration with natural forces that impress their own dynamic processes upon built forms.

Fletcher Steele and Thomas Church—and in the next generation Garrett Eckbo, Dan Kiley, and James Rose, who were classmates in the landscape architecture program at Harvard's Graduate School of Design when Gropius arrived in the thirties—undoubtedly felt besieged by these conflicting interpretations of modernism as it applied to the design of landscapes. The burden of finding a direction to pursue could be made still more difficult if one accepted the obligation to investigate design, including landscape design, as an instrument of democratic social reform—a Bauhaus ideal that took on added immediacy in New Deal America. Christopher Tunnard, the English landscape architect and author who became the principal spokesman during his tenure at Harvard for the necessity of conceiving a modern landscape commensurate in its conceptual and aesthetic authority to the best of modern architecture, argued that "the right style for the twentieth century is no style at all, but a new conception of planning the human environment."[43] Yet many of Tunnard's own designs, such as his 1949 garden at Newport, Rhode Island, seem to represent the same awkward blending of traditional formal elements and biomorphic forms that he criticized as inappropriate to a twentieth-century design canon that sought to be genuinely responsive to the new realities of modern life.

Fletcher Steele and Thomas Church were both exposed to European modernism through travel in Europe and were stimulated by what they saw. The exhibition "Contemporary Landscape Architecture and Its Sources" that opened in the spring of 1937 at the San Francisco Museum of Art awarded first prize to a Church design for a "City House and Garden on a 25-Foot Lot" (figure 2–14), and featured a photograph of Fletcher Steele's model for a proposed stairway and fountain for the Ellwanger estate in Rochester, New York, on the cover of the exhibition catalogue. Both men absorbed certain values from European modernism, particularly its liberation from the tyranny of academic styles reproduced with almost archaeological fidelity. Michael Laurie has said of Thomas Church's designs that "the central axis was abandoned in favor of multiplicity of viewpoints, simple planes and flowing lines. Texture and color, space and form were manipulated in a manner reminiscent of the Cubist painters."[44]

The success of Church's work, however, would seem to have been only secondarily related to the formal, visual, and spatial qualities that Laurie describes, since such factors fail to take into consideration how closely his projects were identified with California and the emergence of a loosely defined California school of modernists that included Garrett Eckbo and Lawrence Halprin among its principal practitioners. It is impossible to isolate the best work of this group from its identification with a regional lifestyle and an existing regional landscape. Something survived in the California school, even as popularized in the typical *Sunset Magazine* garden layouts, that had its source in both a sensitive response to place, to the *genius loci* that Wright tried to discover for himself, and in what Wright perceived to be the "new life" that might be lived by men and women within that fragile but inviting landscape.

"Inviting" because the new pattern and rhythm of American life that emerged in California was an expression of the gentle climate and the very look and feel of the place—suggesting as it did the richly layered sensuous atmosphere of the ancient paradise garden of Persian and Islamic tradition. This imagery came naturally to Californians by way of their inheritance from Moorish Spain, making it possible finally to conceive of the house as a pavilion within a garden rather than as first and foremost a shelter from the surrounding environment. Their culture was infused as well by the example of Japanese building tradition, with its sympathetic vision of a seamless integration between house and garden.

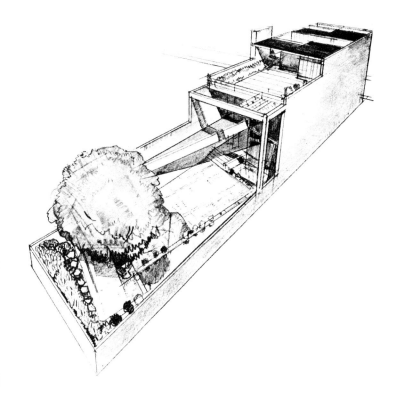

2–14

This is the same vision that the inlander Wright had seen prophetically in the closing years of the nineteenth century, as he touched with his hands, as he surely must have, the transformative frame of the Ho-o-den, which seemed, within the shadow of the White City and at the very heart of the most expansive and dynamic city of the western world, still to belong to Olmsted's Wooded Isle. Architecture and landscape, within this vision, should facilitate and intensify human engagement with the natural world, working against the illusion that contemporary technology has liberated us from our primal psychic and physical dependence upon nature—or at least the need for continual, meaningful, and restorative personal and communal awareness of that deep dependence.

Christopher Tunnard was probably correct in his assessment that the critical questions for architecture and landscape architecture in the twentieth century should have little to do with matters of "style." As a new century approaches, we need to continue the search for an appropriate vision—grounded in philosophical, aesthetic, psychological, and ecological values—to guide the design of contemporary environments that allow us all to live more fulfilling lives, knowing ourselves and the places we inhabit more profoundly, more intimately and joyfully. The challenge to rethink the past and to explore alternative futures is our most important legacy from the modern movement; we may discover through that process, however, that we are building on an American tradition of ideas and images with continuing relevance in our own time.

Notes

1 Report of Frederick Law Olmsted to his partners, April 1892, cited in Laura Woods Roper, *FLO: A Biography of Frederick Law Olmsted* (Baltimore: Johns Hopkins University Press, 1973), 437.

2 Ibid., 447.

3 Letter to Mrs. William Dwight Whitney, 16 December 1890, cited in ibid., 420.

4 Vincent Scully, Jr., *Modern Architecture* (New York: George Braziller, 1982), 15–16.

5 Walter L. Creese, *The Crowning of the American Landscape: Eight Great Spaces and Their Buildings* (Princeton, N.J.: Princeton University Press, 1985), 171–177.

6 Roper, *FLO*, 420.

7 Barbara Novak, *Nature and Culture: American Landscape and Painting, 1825–1875* (New York: Oxford University Press, 1980), 15.

8 Olmsted, Vaux & Company, "Preliminary Report upon the Proposed Suburban Village at Riverside, near Chicago," reprinted in *Civilizing American Cities: A Selection of Frederick Law Olmsted's Writings on City Landscapes*, ed. S. B. Sutton (Cambridge, Mass.: MIT Press, 1979), 303.

9 Creese, *The Crowning of the American Landscape*, 228.

10 Donald Hoffman, "Meeting Nature Face to Face," in *The Nature of Frank Lloyd Wright*, ed. Carol R. Bolon, Robert S. Nelson, and Linda Seidel (Chicago: University of Chicago Press, 1988), 88–89.

11 Frank Lloyd Wright, "A Testament," reprinted in *Frank Lloyd Wright: Writings and Buildings*, selected by Edgar Kaufmann and Ben Raeburn (New York: New American Library, 1974), 28–33.

12 Wright, "Modern Architecture," in Kaufmann and Raeburn, *Frank Lloyd Wright*, 38–55.

13 Wright, "Young Architecture," excerpted in *Programs and Manifestoes on 20th-Century Architecture*, ed. Ulrich Conrads (Cambridge, Mass.: MIT Press, 1970), 124.

14 From Wright, *An Autobiography*, in Kaufmann and Raeburn, *Frank Lloyd Wright*, 211.

15 Ibid., 213–214.

16 Ibid., 214–219.

17 Frank Lloyd Wright, *The Natural House* (New York: Bramhall House, 1959), 50–51.

18 Kenneth Frampton, *Modern Architecture: A Critical History* (New York: Oxford University Press, 1980), 188, 189.

19 Thomas Jefferson to Benjamin Rush, 23 September 1800, in *The Works of Thomas Jefferson*, ed. Paul L. Ford (New York: G. P. Putnam's Sons, 1904–1905), 9:147.

20 Wright, *The Natural House*, 140–141.

21 Antonio Sant'Elia, *Messagio*, cited in Frampton, *Modern Architecture*, 87–88.

22 Neil Levine, "Frank Lloyd Wright's Own Houses and His Changing Concept of Representation," in Bolon, Nelson, and Seidel, *The Nature of Frank Lloyd Wright*, 21.

23 Scully, *Modern Architecture*, 25.

24 Le Corbusier, *Vers une architecture*, cited in Frampton, *Modern Architecture*, 149.

25 Le Corbusier, "Towards a New Architecture: Guiding Principles," in Conrads, *Programs and Manifestoes*, 59.

26 Frampton, *Modern Architecture*, 160.

27 Ibid., 158.

28 Le Corbusier, *Précisions sur un état présent de l'architecture et de l'urbanisme*, cited in ibid., 158.

29 Le Corbusier and Pierre Jeanneret, "Five Points Towards a New Architecture," in Conrads, *Programs and Manifestoes*, 99–100.

30 Colin Rowe, "Neo-'Classicism' and Modern Architecture II," in *The Mathematics of the Ideal Villa and Other Essays* (Cambridge, Mass.: MIT Press, 1976), 144; Wolf Tegethoff, *Mies van der Rohe: The Villas and Country Houses* (New York: The Museum of Modern Art, 1985), 87–89.

31 Wolfgang Pehnt, "Architektur," cited in Tegethoff, *Mies van der Rohe*, 86.

32 Scully, *Modern Architecture*, 33–34.

33 Mies van der Rohe, in an interview with Christian Norberg-Schulz, cited in Tegethoff, *Mies van der Rohe*, 130.

34 Nicolai Hartmann, *Aesthetik*, 2d ed., cited in Tegethoff, *Mies van der Rohe*, 129.

35 Tegethoff, *Mies van der Rohe*, 128.

36 Scully, *Modern Architecture*, 16.

37 Mies van der Rohe, cited in Tegethoff, *Mies van der Rohe*, 128.

38 Scully, *Modern Architecture*, 30, 36.

39 Christopher Tunnard, "Modern Gardens for Modern Houses: Reflections on Current Trends in Landscape Design," *Landscape Architecture* 32 (January 1942), 60. (Reprinted in this volume.)

40 Norman T. Newton, *Design on the Land: The Development of Landscape Architecture* (Cambridge, Mass.: Belknap Press of Harvard University Press, 1971), 435.

41 Ibid., 434.

42 Michel Racine, Ernest J.-P. Boursier-Mougenot, and Françoise Binet, *The Gardens of Provence and the French Riviera*, trans. Alice Parte and Helen Agarathe (Cambridge, Mass.: MIT Press, 1987), 199–201.

43 Tunnard, "Modern Gardens for Modern Houses," 60.

44 Michael Laurie, *An Introduction to Landscape Architecture* (New York: Elsevier, 1976), 46.

3

3–1

Marc Treib is Professor of Architecture at
the University of California at Berkeley,
a practicing designer, and a frequent
contributor to architecture and design
journals. He is the coauthor of *A Guide to
the Gardens of Kyoto* (1980) and author of
Sanctuaries of Spanish New Mexico (1993).

I

The production of a modernist sensibility in American landscape architecture depended to a great degree on a belief that like the other arts, it should develop in accord with the social and technological conditions of contemporary life. Its formulation grew from a disenchantment with the prevalent neoclassical attitude toward designed landscape and the need to address directly the design of the smaller lots of American suburbia. Roots for a vocabulary were found in impulses from other artistic fields. Unlike painting, sculpture, and music, which could enjoy a creation in relative autonomy, however, landscape architecture had to consider two factors characteristic of design professions. The first involves the human presence and, with it, use. The second, planning with living vegetation, requires an understanding of horticulture and ecology. These factors circumscribed and directed the emergence of the modernist sensibility in landscape architecture and distinguished its efforts from those in the other fine arts and design discipline.

Modern landscape architecture evolved only rather slowly, lagging behind developments in other disciplines. Its principal manifesto was Christopher Tunnard's 1938 *Gardens in the Modern Landscape,* first published the previous year as a series of articles in the *Architectural Review* and thoroughly revamped in 1948. Like Sigfried Giedion's coeval *Space, Time and Architecture,*[1] Tunnard's work combined history, criticism, and polemic to establish the historical context in which landscape design has existed and the forces that direct it today. The old values and the old forms, Tunnard asserted, could no longer satisfy contemporary artistic and planning needs. In their place he offered three possible approaches for designing the new landscape: the functional, the artistic, and the empathetic, which takes its inspiration from the Japanese tradition. Each of these would appear, at least to some degree, in the work of the period's most prominent designers.[2]

Unlike the cubist achievements of Georges Braque and Pablo Picasso during the first decades of the century, landscape design produced no epic breakthrough. Nor was there any single figure or any one project that could be identified as the first true manifestation of a modern landscape. With a shrug of his shoulders, landscape architect and critic Fletcher Steele in 1930 offered that "What a modernistic garden may be is everybody's guess. The reason is that it does not yet exist as a type.

We gardeners have always been behind other artists in adopting new ideas."[3] Instead of a coherent doctrine, one finds rambling and imprecise printed discourse, a motley group of individuals, many of whom were not landscape architects by training, and a trail of projects that could be classified as modern only to varying degrees. Contemporary landscape developments in Europe often differed in their attitude to both people and formal idiom, although certain characteristics subsequently were shared by both American and overseas designers.[4] A very broadly sketched overview of the development of modern landscape architecture in the United States is the subject of this essay, including work and figures from abroad only in light of their impact on American landscape design or for their potent realization of shared ideas.

II

At the turn of the century, American landscape architecture was engrossed by the lessons of Beaux-Arts orthodoxy and the naturalistic yearnings of Frederick Law Olmsted; the first was applied to more formal designs, whether civic or patrician, and the second to parks and other public complexes like academic campuses. Rarely were the two modes completely segregated, however. More commonly, formal elements crept into the most naturalistic of parks, while the most rigid classical axis was tempered by the vagaries of a planted edge.

Like their colleagues in the United States and other parts of Europe, French landscape designers were caught in the dual polarities between formality and naturalism, the former represented by the restoration of the great estate gardens, the latter in the public parks of Paris and other major cities. To some degree contemporary garden designers took issue with both traditions, although with the gloss of the contemporary art movements they also borrowed the more formal characteristics of the *style régulier*[5] in developing a modernist landscape.

The Exposition Internationale des Arts Décoratifs et Industriels Modernes of 1925—or the Art Deco exposition as it came to be called—served as a pivotal instant in the development of gardens in France, and perhaps in a larger sphere around the world. Although most of the landscape works at the fair were executed on a relatively small scale, their designers attempted to bring recent impulses in the fine and applied arts outdoors.

3–2

3–I   Vaux-le-Vicomte
       France, c. 1660. André Le Nôtre.
       [Marc Treib]

3–2   The Garden of Water and Light
       Paris, 1925. Gabriel Guevrekian.
       [from Joseph Marrast, *1925
       Jardins*]

3–3

3–3   Garden for the Villa Noailles
Hyères, France, 1927
(reconstructed 1990).
[Marc Treib]

In some ways, these works were visual extravagances, sculptures or bas-reliefs executed in living and inert materials. In other ways, however, these small gardens suggested that the new century and the aftermath of the Great War warranted a substantial overhaul of garden-making ideas and attitudes.

While several landscape works at the exposition might strike only a curious note today—for example, the concrete trees of Robert Mallet-Stevens and Jan and Joël Martel, and the aviaries in Albert Laprade's Garden of Birds—the most influential design was Gabriel Guevrekian's Garden of Water and Light. Tucked into a triangular site on the main esplanade, the garden utilized the triangle as its principal motif. The geometric figure appeared not only in the overall plan and the shape of the principal pool, but also in the glass tiles of the surrounding walls and the shapes of the angled panels of lawn. A sphere of faceted glass revolved by day and night, catching and throwing the light cast upon its mirrored surfaces. In its radical appearance and rigorous execution, the Garden of Water and Light suggested true formal development rather than the mere exploitation of a geometric motif.

The notoriety achieved by the Garden of Water and Light—which was both positive and negative—led the vicomte Charles de Noailles to commission Guevrekian to design a second triangular garden, this one for his villa at Hyères in southern France. The villa's architect was Robert Mallet-Stevens. Built of concrete, prismatic in form, and overtly in the modernist idiom, the villa's basic architectural idea was alien to its locale. The garden that Guevrekian realized there became an icon of modern landscape design, pairing a fashionable pattern of cubist inspiration with a suitably formal equilibrium. More importantly, however, the design showcased inert rather than living materials, upsetting the traditional balance that had almost always favored vegetation.

In resolving the difficulties of a small site on the villa's eastern flank, Guevrekian created a triangular space that rose in shallow steps toward an apex culminating in a rotating statue by Jacques Lipchitz called *Joie de Vivre.* The ascending ground plane was lined with alternating panels of ceramic tile and tulips, partially bracketed on both sides by tilted zigzag planes planted in small blue flowers. As a totality, the composition exploited the constraints of its site and cleverly integrated mineral and living materials within an unrelenting geometric field.

Like so many works of applied art that followed in the aftermath of the Art Deco exposition, the Noailles garden derived its forms from elements of cubist—or better stated, cubistic—inspiration. The basic symmetry and emphasis on patterning the ground plane that characterized Guevrekian's design prevailed in the gardens of the time. Little utilized were the new lessons in space/time and integrated form that cubism had proposed. As Dorothée Imbert has recently shown, these gardens were less paintings, less sculptures, less ar-

chitectural space than bas-reliefs—compositions that barely got off the ground and into the third dimension.[6]

These limitations hardly escaped the notice of Fletcher Steele, who toured frequently and widely and was an important link between the nascent efforts in modern landscape architecture in Europe and those in the United States. Steele traveled in France during the twenties and probably visited both the exposition gardens and others in the new mode. While he was obviously impressed with the direction their designers had taken, Steele was cautious in lavishing praise upon their work. In a 1937 catalogue essay for *Contemporary Landscape Architecture and Its Sources,* Steele expressed his admiration for the ability of these designers to shatter the classical axis, to invigorate the sense of space in their gardens, and to accommodate both the formal and informal modes "hitherto incompatible."[7] He regarded their reliance on architectonic rather than vegetal elements as a shortcoming pervading both their concepts and realized efforts, however. Architects, in Steele's view, rarely understood the full capabilities of the garden, a liability found *in extremis* in the garden designs of the architects Le Corbusier, Pierre Jeanneret, Mallet-Stevens, and Andre Lurçat: "Their work shows an utter lack of interest or understanding of plant life and the myriad ways it might reenforce their ideas and lend them a charm now usually lacking."[8]

Steele's own work was principally for the elite, and like so many designers of his era working for monied clients, he turned to the Italianate and Beaux-Arts models for sources, adding a handling of site and vista that drew principally upon the English tradition. A true eclectic, when the time arrived Steele tried to integrate elements of the new gardens he had seen into his comfortable style, and in these attempts he served as a transitional figure between traditional and modern landscape design. Most notable among Steele's projects is the several decades–long work at Naumkeag in western Massachusetts.

Both the house and the structure of the garden at Naumkeag had been determined by prior designers; Steele accepted these constraints and over the years fitted various gardens to the original armature of allees and roads. The Blue Steps were constructed in 1938 and remain among his most memorable and photogenic works. Curious in form, intriguing in its play of wispy handrails against solid masonry bases, with water spilling through the flights of steps, the architecture of the stairs was designed to contrast with the white birches planted with a studied eye for disorder. The steps provoke interest and appreciation both as sculpture and as landscape. Less successful were Steele's stabs at using the evolving modern forms of the day. His serpentine rose beds at Naumkeag draw or add little from the panel of turf into which they are cut; the fashionable curve used for the Ellwanger residence stair of 1935 appears to be more of a modified fleur-de-lis than a truly modernist shape.

3–4

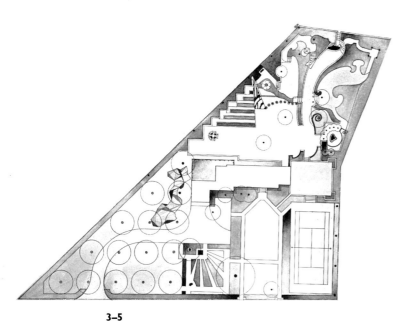

3–5

3–4   The rose garden, Naumkeag
       Stockbridge, Massachusetts,
       1930s. Fletcher Steele.
       [Marc Treib]

3–5   Plan, Smithwick garden
       Gloucester, Massachusetts,
       c. 1929 (unrealized).
       Fletcher Steele.
       [SUNY ESF Archives]

3–6   The Blue Steps, Naumkeag
       Stockbridge, Massachusetts,
       1938. Fletcher Steele.
       [Marc Treib]

If in his own garden designs Fletcher Steele moved only inconclusively into the modern idiom, his writings had a very profound effect on those who formulated and realized the first modern American landscape architecture. In particular, his articles and manner influenced a trio of students completing their studies at Harvard University at the end of the 1930s: James Rose, Dan Kiley, and Garrett Eckbo.[9]

Walter Gropius, who had fled Germany earlier in the decade, headed Harvard's architecture department, introducing modern international currents into what had been a traditional curriculum. If landscape architecture at Harvard was still too locked into the historical tradition manifested in Beaux-Arts doctrine, several young landscape architects would look to other disciplines, foremost among them architecture. Gropius became an important figure in the education of Rose and Eckbo, and the coterie of architects around him offered a potential model for modernist leanings in landscape design.

Modernist Space: Modernist Architecture

In any design profession, there are two basic sources for new ideas: those that develop from the particularities and history of the profession, and those that are adapted from other fields and disciplines and from the social milieu. The free plan and interpenetrating spaces of modern architecture provided a valuable model for rethinking landscape architecture in the United States. Rose, Kiley, and Eckbo coauthored a series of articles in 1938–1941 in *Architectural Record* outlining ideas for the rural and urban landscapes. In subsequent years, Rose remained their principal voice. His exhortation to look at the conditions of the modern world found a public forum in a series of articles published in *Pencil Points,* the predecessor of today's *Progressive Architecture.*

In "Freedom in the Garden," his first important solo publication, Rose positioned landscape design between architecture and sculpture: "In reality, it [landscape design] is outdoor sculpture, not to be looked at as an object, but designed to surround us in a pleasant sense of space relations."[10] Although the dominance of the horizontal dimension in the landscape makes spatial design more challenging, Rose asserts that "ground forms evolve from the division of space" and not vice versa. Space, rather than style, is the true province of landscape architecture. In the article, Rose juxtaposed his own garden project with a painting by Theo van Doesburg and the plan of Mies van der Rohe's 1924 project for a brick country villa to illustrate this sense of continuous space—space without the restrictive coercion of the singular axis.

One could characterize the tectonics of modern architecture as utilizing contemporary materials and engineering strategies, developing an expression from the means of production and a prevalent involvement with volume and space—particularly

3–6

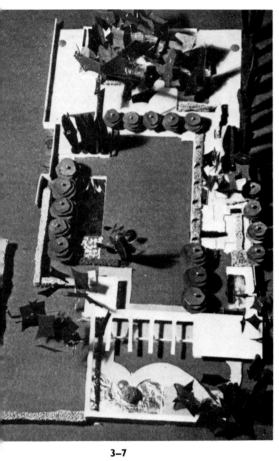

3-7

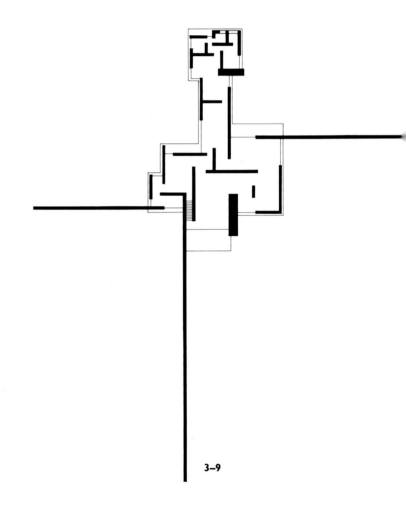

3-9

3–8

spaces that conjoin. Le Corbusier's formulation of a new architecture capitalized on the free plan resulting from the separation of structure and enclosure. By raising the building on columns and creating a garden terrace on its roof, the ground displaced by construction could be reclaimed. His Villa Savoye (1929) at Poissy strove toward integrating spaces horizontally and vertically; the villa as an entity remained detached from its meadow—left conceptually untouched—a "machine in the garden," to use Leo Marx's phrase.[11]

On the other hand, it was Mies van der Rohe's German Pavilion for the 1929 Barcelona Exhibition that became the true archetype of modernist spatial composition. The building was intended to serve only ceremonial purposes; free of functional necessity, its architect created a work in which wall and ceiling planes modulated space treated as a continuum. To distinguish inside from outside becomes arduous; except for the perimeter walls, all planes overlap in space, and no rigid intersections delineate distinct cells within the building's envelope.[12]

Rose's paragons were intended to illustrate the dissolution of discrete spaces such as the outdoor rooms of the classical tradition. Yet in much of Dan Kiley's mature design, aspects of the classical landscape reappear. Kiley is not unkindly regarded as the landscape architect whose work most closely parallels Mies van der Rohe, and as a designer who transformed the formal vocabulary of Le Nôtre by a truly modernist spatial sensibility.[13]

The Miller garden (1955) and the North Carolina National Bank terrace/garden (1988) bookend Kiley's long and prolific career based on the concern for space and its modulation, using both construction and planting. The plan of the Miller garden is disarmingly and splendidly simple, with rectangularly configured spaces defined by hedges, allees, and walls. A subtle play of spaces, ground contour, and elements suggests a multitude of readings in spite of the simplicity of the idiom. The house, designed by Eero Saarinen, is dominated by its living room; all its other spaces pinwheel outward from this center. The garden's design derives from the architectonic order of the house, reverberating in the spaces that radiate from the living room toward the river or road. The garden plan, one feels, is a consequence of architecture engaging its site; or conversely, the house exists as an environmentally conditioned part of the greater garden. As at Barcelona Pavilion, the line between interior and exterior has been subdued by a broad overhanging roof. In effect, building and garden have been rendered spatially coincident; only the shift in vocabulary from living vegetation to inert building materials distinguishes the two realms.

Thirty-three years later, in Tampa, Florida, Kiley demonstrated again that the order of the building is the starting point of landscape architecture, and his heightened ability to interplay more than one system of ordering. If the Miller garden represents a chorus of elements in harmony, the

3–7   Model, garden project
1938. James C. Rose. Published as an illustration for "Freedom in the Garden."

3–8   *Rhythm of a Russian Dance*
1918. Theo van Doesburg. Used by James C. Rose as an illustration for "Freedom in the Garden," 1938.
[Museum of Modern Art, New York, acquired through the Lillie P. Bliss Bequest]

3–9   Perspective and plan, project for a brick country house
1924. Ludwig Mies van der Rohe. The plan was used by James C. Rose as an illustration for "Freedom in the Garden," 1938.
[Mies van der Rohe Archive, Museum of Modern Art, New York]

3–10

3–11

North Carolina National Bank terrace is a complex interweaving of subtle dissonances. The terrace patterning extends from architect Harry Wolf's use of the Fibonacci series of numbers in planning the round office tower and adjacent cubic banking hall. Kiley used this proportional series to modulate the balance between the areas of stone and zoysia grass, the two principal materials of which the terrace is made. While Islam provided the probable inspiration for the watercourses that emanate from the glass roof of the parking garage corridor, the overall style of the terrace is less easily characterized. A grid of washingtonia palms provides the principal structure, with curving plantings of crape myrtles serving as a foil underneath, changing with the seasons and contributing sheets of color when in bloom. This elaboration of orders could actually characterize a postmodern landscape. But it could also be termed a masterful handling of the modernist idiom in which the various voices are structured by the bass line of palms, further enriched by the relationship of plantings to paving and patterning to space. The garden terrace must be seen in section as well as in plan; that is, as a complex spatial entity in which the rambling character of one variety contrasts with the regular planting of a second, and high frond clusters play against low leafy canopies. This one project encapsulates the lessons of several garden traditions; the product, however, is spatial, uniquely modern, and uniquely Kiley's.

Unlike modernist architecture in Europe, with its specific target of improved housing conditions, little in the early writings suggests public betterment through landscape design. The need for a new approach stemmed rather from the notion of *Zeitgeist,* implicit or explicit. Modern architecture in the United States had also been treated to a great degree as a matter of a style appropriate to the century. Public purpose was induced to follow thereafter. "The International Style: Architecture since 1922," the 1932 landmark exhibition at the Museum of Modern Art, established the canons by which buildings would be judged modern or retrograde. The exhibition's curators, Henry-Russell Hitchcock and Philip Johnson, produced a checklist of criteria by which buildings could be judged. Three basic principles applied: first, "a new conception of architecture as volume rather than mass"; second, "regularity rather than axial symmetry serves as the chief means of ordering the design"; and third, the proscription of applied ornament.[14] It appears obvious that James Rose, writing some six years later, borrowed at least two of the characteristics of modern landscape design from architectural: the concern for space and the vituperative rejection of symmetry and the classical axis. The third point, proscribing ornament, was moot. Gardens employ plants, and plants have an inherently decorative quality. Rose never talks against ornament as such, except to note that its role should always be subservient to creating space. With urging from architectural thought, space became the central element of modern landscape thinking.

3–10 German Pavilion, Barcelona
Exposition
1929 (reconstructed). Ludwig
Mies van der Rohe.
[Marc Treib]

3–11 Villa Savoye
Poissy-sur-Seine, France, 1929.
Le Corbusier.
[Marc Treib]

3–12

3–13

3–12 View from the terrace toward the river, Miller garden
Columbus, Indiana, 1955.
Dan Kiley.
[Marc Treib]

3–13 Plan, Miller garden
Columbus, Indiana, 1955. Dan
Kiley.
[Hongcheol Choe, courtesy
Jory Johnson]

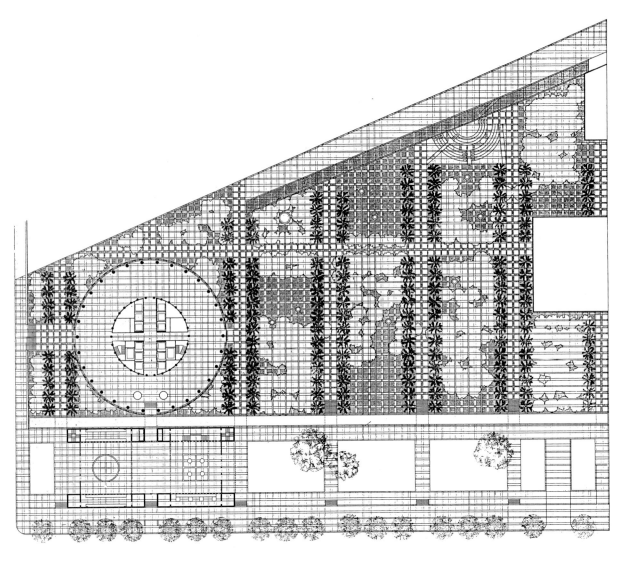

3–14

3–14 Plan, garden/terrace, North
Carolina National Bank
Tampa, Florida, 1988. Harry Wolf,
architect; Dan Kiley, landscape
architect.

3–15 Garden/terrace, North Carolina
National Bank
Tampa, Florida, 1988. Harry Wolf,
architect; Dan Kiley, landscape
architect.
[Marc Treib]

3–15

Sources in the Fine Arts

Emerging modern landscape architects sought a formal vocabulary by which to embody concerns expressed in contemporary architecture, among them a consideration of human activities, twentieth-century technologies, and an augmented understanding of ecology and the greater landscape. They reasoned that one must eschew as inappropriate the formal, symmetrical plan, the axis, and other remnants of the neoclassical landscape, for these expressed the life and culture of prior eras.

Of the twentieth-century art movements, cubism provided the most fecund source for both shapes and structure in landscape architecture. Cubist space offered the images of multiple foci taken from a single vantage point, radically conflated space and time, and replicating the effect of four dimensions in two. But the *spatial* ideas implicit in cubist composition were only of marginal interest to landscape architects. Little of painting's overlapping of views, proportional systems, chroma, or synthetic recomposition was applied to the new landscape. More attractive was a vocabulary of shapes *adapted* from cubism: the zigzag and the piano curve, for example, executed in flowers, paving, or even terrace walls instead of pigment.

Of course, architects had also drawn clues directly from cubist painting, almost from its inception, Le Corbusier and Alvar Aalto foremost among them. And while neither a true cubist architecture nor a true cubist garden ever really existed, several noted designers did employ shapes and features in their work that reflected the influence of cubism and purism. The roof garden of the Villa Savoye, for example, with its curving wall, framed views, and spots of greenery at least loosely suggests a purist painting extruded into the third dimension. Aalto's Villa Mairea in Noormarkku, Finland (1938), on the other hand, applied to architectural design the principle of the cubist collage by disturbing the purity of the white wall surfaces with overlays of saplings and sheathing. Throughout the villa—in the entrance canopy, the contour of the studio, and the free-form pool—the shapes of the new painting are set against an orthogonal layout of columns and walls.[15]

If the cubist view addressed the material and visual complexities of what Martin Heidegger would call our "being in the world,"[16] surrealism, in turn, concerned the depths or heights of the human mind. Surrealist thinking and its products evolved in the 1920s and 1930s, but even from its origins the movement was rent by two opposing concepts. The first fostered automism—the free workings of the human unconscious—as a means of bypassing rational process and the restrictive limitations that inculcation imposes upon the individual. To map the unconscious in the surrealist arts, there must be no impediments to misdirect the intermediate graphic vehicle. Unlike the linear mode of written language, recorded as a "stream of consciousness," painting makes its own demands upon the artist, among

3–16

3–17

3–16   North Christian Church
Columbus, Indiana, 1959.
Eero Saarinen, architect;
Dan Kiley, landscape architect.
[Marc Treib]

3–17   The Oakland Museum
Oakland, California, 1969. Roche,
Dinkeloo and Associates,
architects; Dan Kiley, landscape
architect.
[Joe Samberg, courtesy the
Oakland Museum]

3–18

3–19

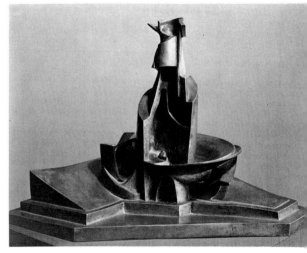

3–20

3–21

3–18   United States Air Force Academy
Colorado Springs, Colorado, 1956–
1968. Skidmore, Owings and
Merrill, architects; Dan Kiley,
landscape architect.
[Stewarts Photographers,
courtesy Dan Kiley]

3–19   *The Painter's Window*
1925. Juan Gris.
[The Baltimore Museum of Art,
Bequest of Saidie A. May]

3–20   *Development of a Bottle in Space*
1912. Umberto Boccioni.
Silvered bronze.
[Museum of Modern Art, New
York]

3–21   South Facade, Villa Mairea
Noormarkku, Finland, 1938.
Alvar Aalto.
[Welin, courtesy the Museum of
Finnish Architecture]

them the need to confront simultaneity, factuality, and facture.[17] The alternate conception, best represented in the work of Salvador Dalí, looked to a realistic painting manner as the means to objectively portray the complexities of the mind and the dream.[18] In many ways the strength of Dalí's paintings derives from their vivid, almost academic techniques, which we have been taught to regard as representative of a reality that accepts the laws of perspective. The seeming reality of the representation conflicts powerfully with the surreality of the matter rendered on the canvas. The internecine dispute among the surrealists was of little consequence to designers, however. More important to them were the biomorphic shapes that came from surrealism, forms that could be applied to design—and landscape architecture—without ideological baggage.

Two artists, Hans (or Jean) Arp and Joan Miró, suggested a cautious middle ground between the two surrealist camps, while providing the foundations for a bridge between the plastic arts and landscape architecture. Arp was a multivalent talent, whose works spanned across surrealism, Dada, and nonobjective art and poetry. His signature paintings and reliefs avoided virtually all chiaroscuro and three-dimensional rendering, offering shapes and forms easily appropriated by designers and landscape architects. In the years following the war, the kidney, the boomerang, and the amoeba—as well as interpretations of surrealism by Yves Tanguy and Arshile Gorky—frequently appeared also in the design of textiles, furniture, curtains, and even the new material, plastic laminate. Conceptually the amoeba seemed to have a particular appropriateness for landscape because as a formal motif it looked "natural," far more natural than the axis or the topiary bush of traditional gardens.

The shapes in Miró's paintings and Arp's prints and sculpture evoked the natural contours of land form or the shapes of lakes or even spindly trees against shifting masses of vegetation. Isamu Noguchi, on the other hand, actually proposed sculpture and stage sets for Martha Graham that were in effect landscapes.[19] His *Monument to the Plow* (1933), for example, presages the earthworks of the 1960s, applying sculptural concerns and a narrative to the prairies. *Contoured Playground, New York* (1941), *Sculpture to Be Seen from Mars* (1947), and other playground projects from the 1950s and 1960s continue his blending of landscape and sculpture. These projects were left unrealized, and only in 1958 was Noguchi able to execute his first major landscape design. His UNESCO garden in Paris, which complemented Marcel Breuer's 1958 concrete megalith, sculptured a groundscape of earth, stone, and water as a transition and escape from the hard terraces surrounding the building.

Today, the trees completing the design have matured and the garden is overgrown almost to the point of indistinction, although the abstract forms of the undulating ground plane below the tree canopy

3–22

3–22 *Painting*
1933. Joan Miró.
[Museum of Modern Art,
New York, Loula D. Lasker
Bequest]

3–23 *Chartres*
1950–1965. Jean Arp.
Painted wood relief.
[courtesy Sidney Janis Gallery,
New York]

3–24 *Objets Celestes*
1961. Jean Arp.
Painted wood relief.
[courtesy Sidney Janis Gallery,
New York]

still reveal the artist's conception of the garden as sculpture. As in his later *California Scenario* of 1984, one can distinguish the work of the artist from that of the designer by its emphasis on form rather than utility and amenity. But in spite of these pragmatic limitations, Noguchi remains an important figure in formulating a vocabulary and an approach to shaping postwar landscape architecture.

As a source of forms appropriated for landscape design, modern art was equally important for telling the viewer what it was not—it was *not* the picturesque and it was *not* the classical—as for what it was: thoroughly modern (in spite of Tunnard's proclamation that "the right style for the twentieth century is no style at all").[20] But why use biomorphic shapes in a garden? I have found no polemics in the professional literature exhorting designers to use the new vocabulary. Contemporary publications tended to describe landscape design factually, without sentiment, with little theoretical embellishment in the rational spirit of the age. Late in life, Jens Jensen, the dean of the prairie landscape, had in fact argued for the curving line, but his call was based on distinguishing the natural from the constructed rather than on any relation to contemporary art. "Curves represent the unchained mind full of mystery and beauty," Jensen claimed in a selection of his memoirs, *Siftings.* "Straight lines belong to militant thought. No mind can be free in a concept of limitations. Straight lines spell autocracy, of which most European gardens are an expression, and their course points to intellectual decay, which soon develops a prison from which the mind can never escape. The free thought that produces the free curve can never be strangled." Worse still, perhaps: "Straight lines are copied from the architect and do not belong to the landscape. They have nothing to do with nature, of which landscaping is a part and out of which the art has grown. Landscape must follow the lines of the free-growing tree with its thousands of curves."[21] But Jensen's vehement argument is rare in the literature, and its words belong to the last century rather than to the new world of technology and modern art. The first cluster of modern landscape architects, in contrast, grappled with the inherent dichotomy of architectural and landscape architectural forms, forging a new design vocabulary in the resolution of the enigma.

Regardless of its conceptual origins, the curvilinear suggested a more suitable relation of built or planted forms to topography and existing vegetation than did the straight line. While applicable at the scale of larger site plans, this would be a less convincing argument for small suburban tracts, where relief bore little importance. But naturalness never really seemed to be the issue. The Brazilian landscape architect and artist Roberto Burle Marx, for example, has relied to a great extent on a free form whose shape rarely coincides with natural terrain. Part of the impetus for these forms may have resulted from Burle Marx's association with architects such as Oscar Niemeyer, Affonso Reidy, and

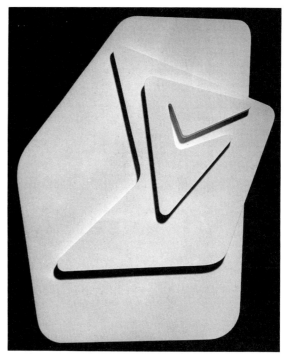

3–23

3–24

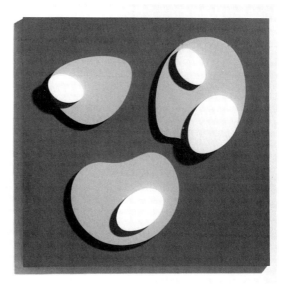

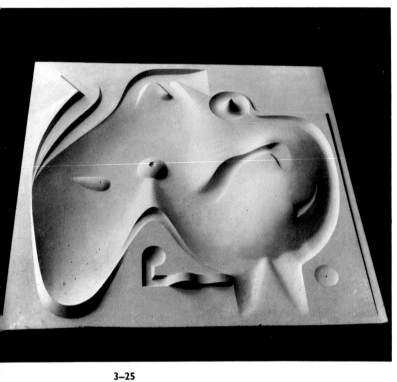

3–25

3–26

3–27

3–25 *Contoured Playground*
New York, 1941. Plaster.
Isamu Noguchi.
[Rudolph Burckhardt, courtesy
Isamu Noguchi Foundation, Inc.]

3–26 Garden, UNESCO Building
Paris, France, 1958.
Isamu Noguchi.
[Marc Treib]

3–27 Kaiser Center roof garden
Oakland, California, 1960.
Osmundson and Staley.
[Bill Wasson, courtesy
Kaiser Center]

Lucio Costa—in turn influenced by Le Corbusier—who included the meandering curve as well as the grid in their architecture. Burle Marx was trained as an artist and hence uses the free shape in a more painterly manner, however. More often than not, he appears to *blanket* the contours in forms deriving from his own flat artworks rather than from the lay of the land. Rarely is there any perceivable attempt to, say, derive a shape from the profile of the topography. Burle Marx has been termed a "painter in plants," resorting to his vast horticultural knowledge to attain precise effects of color and light. Howard Adams has suggested that Burle Marx effects a "bifurcation" of the viewer's perceptions between the plant specimen close at hand and the distant vista.[22] If so, Burle Marx has created the sense of space and depth without relying upon the enframing foreground element or other vehicles used to construct traditional perspective.

In the postwar years, the free form, raised vertically into the softly curving mound, became a principal contributor to landscape projects large and small. Designs such as Osmundson and Staley's roof garden for the Kaiser Center parking garage in Oakland (1960) suggest how even the rational spacing of structural columns, which determined the placement of the trees, can be subverted by a biomorphic design that disguises their locations. A major and skillful design, the Kaiser roof garden also reveals the widespread acceptance of the biomorphic curve by landscape architects and non-professional designers alike. The kidney-shaped pool, after all, became a symbol of life in suburban California.

The free form, the amoeba, and the kidney shape—with more architectonic motifs such as the zigzag—provided a major aesthetic stimulus and charged vocabulary for making the modernist landscape. The new shapes most commonly appeared in plan, in planting beds and clusters of shrubs and bushes, basically continuing the tradition of the parterre. In the collaborative project of Roberto Burle Marx and Oscar Niemeyer for the Tremaine House (1948) in Santa Barbara, on the other hand, the impact is not felt in plan alone; shape and space flow together effortlessly, integrating yet revealing the character and contribution of architecture and landscape.

Unlike the adoption of modern architectural space, biomorphism did little to change the *nature* of the garden; more often than not, it provided only a reinvigorated guise for traditionalist garden ideas. In *Landscape for Living*, Garrett Eckbo wrote that landscape architecture has three concerns: surfacing, enclosure, and enrichment.[23] While there is little doubt that biomorphism recreated an enriched surface, it never quite delivered a new spatial structure. Joan Miró had established that, no matter how grandly conceived, perspective ultimately depicts finite space.[24] By destroying the clues upon which we normally rely for depth perception, the undulating world of biomorphism—like Miró's paintings—suggested infinite space. And while the

shaped meander never actually led to this new world of space within the garden, it did, at least, present us with its promise.

Axioms for a Modern Landscape

In early projects and writings by Eckbo and others one sees an emerging paradigm for modern landscape architecture, as if an imperfect, ill-formed, and implicit manifesto.[25] The axioms of the new landscape design could be summarized as follows:

1. *A denial of historical styles. Instead, landscape expression derives from a rational approach to the conditions created by industrial society, the site, and the program.* Today's landscape architect must reject outright the heritages of the neoclassical and naturalistic landscapes, which are appropriate to neither the current social nor the current aesthetic situation.

2. *A concern for space rather than pattern, deriving a model from contemporary architecture.* "Design should be three-dimensional," Eckbo wrote; "people live in volumes, not planes."[26] This is one of the true foundation stones of modern landscape design, although in their vehement arguments against the Beaux-Arts tradition, the young designers at times overlooked the spatial lessons learned from history. The meanders and clumps of the English landscape garden and the axes and bosks of the French formal garden were equally spatial. Though perhaps outmoded as viable schools of landscape thought, neither tradition relied on pattern alone.

Underlying the modern approach, however, was really an interest in discovering a new *form* of space that superseded those of previous centuries. In an early study, Eckbo proposed 18 schemes for small gardens in tight urban conditions.[27] The designs alternated rigidly geometric arrangements, those relying on curvilinear forms, those that tread lightly on the slope, and those that completely reformed it for increased spatial power. Taken as a whole, these studies sketched out what would become the elements of Eckbo's landscape architecture over a half century.

In general, modern America landscape architecture appeared first in the private garden and thereafter in the corporate campus. In Europe, on the other hand, a more reasoned balance was struck among the public park and housing estate, the private garden, and the tainted landscape of industry. In England, Geoffrey Jellicoe's comprehensive site plan for reclaiming the land around Hope Cement Works (1943), and his aesthetic use of waste soil from motorway construction at Guiness Hills (1959), attempted to reconcile principles of formal composition with contemporary environmental problems.[28]

Eckbo's work provides some of the few notable efforts to address social issues through public landscape design. From virtually the beginning of his career during the closing years of the Depression, Eckbo was involved in larger-scale site plan-

3–28

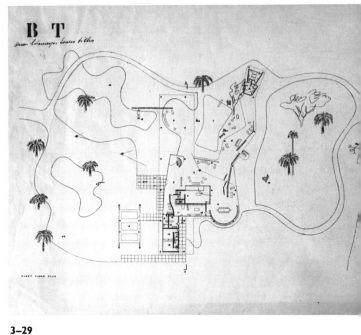

3–29

3–30

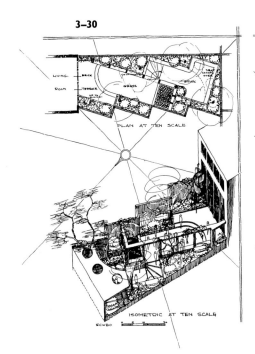

3–31

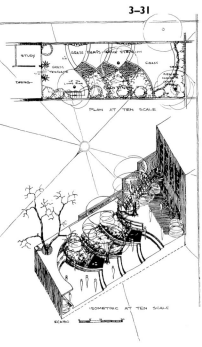

3–28 Garden plan, Burton Tremaine
residence
1948 (project). Roberto Burle
Marx, landscape architect.
[Museum of Modern Art, New
York, gift of Mr. and Mrs.
Burton Tremaine]

3–29 Garden plan, Burton Tremaine
residence
1948 (project). Oscar Niemeyer,
architect; Roberto Burle Marx,
landscape architect.
[Museum of Modern Art, New
York, gift of Mr. and Mrs.
Burton Tremaine]

3–30 Plans and axonometrics, urban
3–31 gardens
1937. Garrett Eckbo.
Used to illustrate "Small Gardens
in the City."

ning to benefit the less fortunate strata of society, an interest he attributes, in part, to the social ideas promulgated by Gropius at Harvard.[29] From 1939 to 1942 Eckbo worked for the Farm Security Administration, for whom he planned a number of settlements for farm workers in impropitious settings such as desiccated lands in rural Arizona and California.[30] In these projects, Eckbo applied the modern model to spaces for specifically assigned purposes, from screening laundry areas to creating private zones for individual families. The axonometric drawings and perspectives from this period resonate with ideas as fresh as those of the 1925 Paris exposition gardens, and reflect the same thoroughness as his didactic studies for small gardens. Each FSA design depicts simple schemes ordered in sophisticated ways, exploiting the properties of vegetation to modulate spaces vertically as well as horizontally. The work for the FSA allowed Eckbo to develop an approach toward the expansive as well as the restrictive nature of sites. Site planning is the name of the enterprise of "the total space organization for a specific construction project on a specific site," Eckbo wrote in a 1942 article in *Architectural Forum.* Comprehensive study establishes the "desirable relationships between buildings, utilities, roads and walks, recreation facilities, planting and open space." The scale of the project is not the issue; each project, whether large or small, requires cohesive site planning, which is "the arrangement of environments for PEOPLE."[31] Given this concern for people, both as individuals and collectively grouped in neighborhoods and society, it is no surprise that firms founded by Eckbo often grew into the corporate offices so characteristic of today's landscape practice, offices whose projects are as much site and regional planning as they are landscape design.

3. *Landscapes are for people.* Although addressed to a variety of purposes, landscape design ultimately concerns making outdoor places for human use (a fact that seemed to escape the attention of the younger generation during the early years of modernism). The question, of course, was what social and economic groups modern landscapes were to be made for, and in discussions of these issues writers such as Eckbo reveal their democratic beliefs. As he wrote in 1937: "People, not plants, are the important things in the gardens. Every garden is a stage, every occupant a player."[32]

4. *The destruction of the axis.* The modern landscape, perhaps influenced by cubist space, is multifaceted and omnidirectional. With the axis removed, the restricted view of linear perspective expands. Here is the clearest connection between landscape architecture and modern architecture and painting. Cubism represented a world in which reality is constructed through simultaneous views—as we think rather than as we see. Rose proposed: "If you wish to consider any line of sight an axis, then you have an infinite number of axes in a garden or anywhere else, and so it should be. By selecting one or two axes and developing a picture from a

given station point, we are losing an infinity of opportunities." Hitchcock and Johnson had argued that "axial symmetry has generally been used to achieve the ordering of irregularity, . . . dominating and relating the confusion of independent features and elaborate detail. Modern standardization gives automatically a high degree of consistency in the parts."[33] Therefore, no need remains for symmetrical organization. As Eckbo proposed: "Let there be rhythm, let there be movement; let there be life and action and gayety. Let there be nothing static, balanced, carefully set."[34]

The argument for standardization, of course, had little application to landscape architecture, since plants rarely grew exactly as predicted without rigorous training. Garden structures, on the other hand, could be rationalized, and in 1948 Rose did, in fact, propose a "modular garden."[35] Where at all applicable, new materials were used in the garden. If the best-known experiment remains Eckbo's use of aluminum in his own garden of the late 1950s, materials such as textured concrete blocks, metal screens, and plastics frequently appeared throughout the southern Californian projects.

5. *Plants are used for their individual qualities as botanical entities and sculpture.* This represents a "scientific" and "economical" use of plants within the garden. Early modernist discourse on the selection and use of plants was plagued by a pervasive ambiguity, as if the writers—most often the designers themselves—were stymied by the basically intransigent characteristics of the natural world. While the argument of formal versus informal continued—to the degree that *not* joining the argument was in itself a symbol of modernity—plant selection remained predicated on the parameters of climate and environment.[36] As late as 1948, for example, Brenda Colvin could write that "architecture is dealing with completely new materials as well as new needs, whereas the natural materials of landscape (land and vegetation) and the *basic* human needs which landscape fulfils are ageless. In garden design and in the wilder landscape, any conscious effort to create a 'new style' will be sterile."[37]

Although he wrote a decade before the first edition of Colvin's book, James Rose seemed to confront her pronouncement in his manifesto "New Freedom in the Garden": "We are told that industrial design and 'so-called' modern architecture came about through the discovery of new materials and methods of construction, but that landscape design cannot change because materials and methods have not changed. We have found our final resting place. Our grave is on axis in a Beaux-Arts cemetery. A monument terminates the vista, and if you approach with reverence, you can see the bromitaph authority has placed there: 'A tree is a tree, and always will be a tree; therefore we can have no modern landscape design.'"[38] Rose's declamation was less the product of aesthetic paranoia than a stance against the prevalent modes. The rooted intransigence of the profession is indicated by British landscape architect George Dillistone's contribution

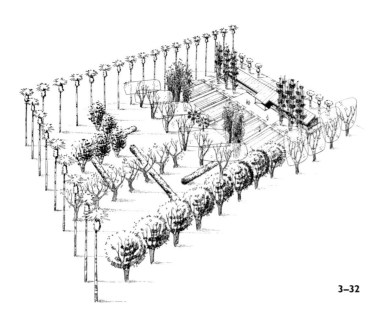

3–32

3–33

3–32 Perspective study, small park, Mineral King Co-op Ranch San Joaquin Valley, California, 1940. Farm Security Administration; Garrett Eckbo.

3–33 Perspective study, camp park space Near Harlingen, Texas, 1940. Farm Security Administration; Garrett Eckbo.

to the 1939 compendium *Gardens and Gardening.* "To talk of a new 'style' in gardens is merely absurd. Even in architecture, a change in style is merely a rearrangement of old forms in different sequence, possibly involving omissions, never additions, to those of the past. In gardening, every known form, colour and contour has been used repeatedly throughout the ages. Garden design is therefore a matter of selecting forms, colours and contours applicable to the site, and not of conformity with the pattern of an elevation or the proportionate composition of the building it surrounds."[39] With such attitudes so deeply rooted, a vigorous polemic for modernism was justified.

Modernist writers reacted against two particular aspects of plant selection and use. The first was the specimen used for its horticultural rather than formal interest; Tunnard argued, instead, for a "structural" use of vegetation, a term obviously borrowed from architecture and seemingly an oxymoron. Planting in "mass" was the second use of plantings against which modernists reacted, a characteristic of formal garden design usually lumped under the notion "Beaux-Arts" but applicable as well to the English landscape garden. To isolate the bush or tree, Rose believed, is to treat it rationally: "It is only by the isolation of specimens that plants can be controlled scientifically, developed to the ultimate of their potential characteristics, and used with elastic tensility."[40] Tunnard is more succinct in his views: "In other cases plants need freedom, sometimes complete isolation, to take their place in the scheme. Selection, not massing for picturesque effect, is the requirement of the modern garden."[41] Seen in retrospect, the multitude of vistas and paths suggested by applying cubist ideas of time/ space to the landscape were not utilized by the early modern garden designers. They did, however, position plants and shapes in such a way that individual plants produced a maximum sculptural effect.

The starting point for plant selection, of course, was the plant itself. "The twentieth century landscape, although hardly touched, even in theory, would of necessity result in the honest use of materials as in the best modern architecture and sculpture," argued James Rose late in 1938. "Plants are not applied to a preconceived ground pattern. They dictate form as surely as do use and circulation."[42] Throughout Rose's series of articles, one finds a coherent if at times imprecise argument for a "scientific" use of vegetation.

Unlike the earlier essays, the argument in "Why Not Try Science?" becomes muddled and is more open to interpretation. For one, the word "specimen" suggests horticulture and cultivation and the gardenesque use of "specimen planting." More likely, Rose uses the word for its tone of scientific rationality, which is the theme of the essay. A modern landscape results from approaching the design rationality, but tempered with the mind of an artist, as he writes elsewhere: "When we lift plants out of their little niches in an eclectic ground patern and use them as organic, structural parts of the landscape, forms will appear which are expressive of plants as material."[43] He ends "Plant Forms and Space" with a suggested listing of species suitable for the northeastern United States and modern landscape architecture, classifying them into Columnar, Horizontal, Pendulous, Broad and Spreading, Round or Oval, and Irregular and Picturesque. No value judgments are expressed; each can be used in its own "scientific way."

Like Rose, Tunnard includes a list of plants, in this case an eight-page portfolio of species appropriate to Great Britain and to the modern landscape. They have been selected for color, form, habitat, and even for their decorative effect during the winter months. But for Tunnard, any plant is part of a greater whole; its particular characteristics and "structural use" are secondary to its contribution to a coherent design. Writing shortly before Rose, he takes issue with the notion that plants must be used within the designed landscape as they grow naturally. Plants selected in isolation and applied with a "structural" order can fall short of achieving a modern landscape design, however: "To plant is but a part of landscape composition; to co-ordinate is all."[44]

Of the early landscape writers, Garrett Eckbo most precisely establishes the contribution made by plants to shaping habitable spaces. Planting design, Eckbo writes in *Landscape for Living,* is the outdoor equivalent of the spatial concerns of architecture, although it is more "varying in kind; that is, subtler, looser, less positive, less continuous, or with wider variations in the degree of continuity." William Robinson, in Eckbo's view, reversed the order of importance in selecting plants for color, texture, and mass. Instead, Eckbo believes that "Every plant, no matter how low, how prostrate, how massive, matted or solidly bushy, how fastigiate or billowing, is nevertheless a construction in space and an enclosure of space."[45] In Eckbo's own gardens, ranks of junipers form low walls; spiky specimens appear to pierce space; and grids of trunks suggest the power of the hypostyle hall. Like the slightly senior Thomas Church, Eckbo rarely used flowering bedding as the principal elements of planting plans. Shaped beds are filled, instead, with grasses or paving. In section, the mass of the plant or the shape and height of a tree canopy complements the armature provided by architecture, walls, and fences.

In spite of these authors' "structural" or "scientific" approach to plant material, the net effect in the landscape was less than radical. Was this due to the inherently conservative nature of vegetation, or to the fact that so many of the attitudes taken by the Americans had already occurred throughout history? Le Nôtre's highly structured and rational *bosquets* would appear modern in some lights, and certainly Dan Kiley's later use of the gridded bosk reinforces the connection between the regular order of the formal tradition and the centrifugal spatial order of the modern era. Trees in the English land-

scape garden, at least during the eighteenth century, were used "structurally," to borrow Tunnard's term. How else could one explain the attacks on Brown's use of "clumps"? While one may regard as shapes the patterns of Brown's stands of trees, their foremost function was to define spaces and vistas, even if these were at some remove from the main house. Thus, neither metric ordering nor the spatial use of planting was an invention of the modern landscape; each had a significant precedent in the past. Perhaps, then, a modern use of planting would be to create colored shapes or forms drawn from the new arts, although certainly the chromatic interest in plants was nothing endemic to the modernists alone.

In this sense, masters such as Roberto Burle Marx and Isamu Noguchi differ from the Californians in their handling of plants. The shapes that Burle Marx creates on the drawing board appear to be transferred directly to the ground, where free-ranging shapes are filled and delineated with low-lying plants and flowers. Single hues predominate beds seen from a distance, although the plantings are, in fact, more intricate and complex. "A garden is a complex of aesthetic and plastic intentions," Burle Marx explains, "and the plant is, to a landscape artist, not only a plant—rare, unusual, ordinary, or doomed to disappearance—but it is also a color, a shape, a volume, or an arabesque in itself. It is the paint for the two-dimensional picture I make of a garden on a drawing board in my atelier; it is the sculpture or arabesque in a garden."[46] At the suburban campus for Connecticut General Life Insurance (1953) outside Hartford, Connecticut, Noguchi planted shapes of grass, flowers, or low bushes that articulate, or are articulated by, a gravel ground. These are set pieces, internal courtyards to be viewed rather than entered. In this sense, as in the sparing use of vegetation, the correlation of Noguchi's designs with the dry Zen gardens of Japan seems obvious.

Color has always been one of the prized characteristics of plants, particularly in climates that experience dramatic changes throughout the year. The annual burst of tulips in Holland, for example, is legendary, as is the almost manic crusade to develop species of roses that would remain eternally in flower. During the later part of the nineteenth century, the play of colors and textures—so intertwined in plant selection—culminated in the combinations of the herbaceous border. Exponents such as Gertrude Jekyll (1843–1932) mixed flowers and plants so that their colors complemented and drew strength from one another, while their horticultural frailties were mitigated through judicious combinations.

In a manner that recalled the French impressionists and pointillists, Jekyll utilized the play of hues to extend the possible effects of the plant palette. Vegetation produced a heightened variety of effects through judicious combinations of colors and textures, unlike the monochromatic beds of single species characteristic of the past. Color, to Jekyll,

3–34

3–35

was itself an art: "In the old days of sixty years ago, it was simply the most garish effects that were sought for; the brightest colourings that could be obtained in red, blue, and yellow were put close together, often in rings like a target, and there would be meandering lines, wriggling along for no reason. . . . Many years ago, I came to the conclusion that in all flower borders it is better to plant in long rather than block-shaped patches. It not only has a more pictorial effect, but a thin long planting does not leave an unsightly empty space when the flowers are done and the leaves have perhaps died down."[47] She describes the shape allotted to each particular plant as a "drift," a word well chosen since ultimately the individual herbs and flowers would mesh into one another, effacing the outlines of the individual planting.

To the early modernists, the vagaries of turn-of-the-century textures and colors were a virtual anathema. Why so is difficult to ascertain in retrospect. Jekyll, for example, often collaborated with Sir Edwin Lutyens, and in gardens such as Hestercombe (1904–1909) Jekyll's wild and woolly play of color and textures complemented the basically symmetrical and rigidly architectural terraces of Lutyens's design. In this give and take between architecture and vegetation, between armature and embellishment, a striking design emerges, structured but ever-changing. Seen in critical retrospect, certain ideas advanced by the modernists could be equally applied to the parterre planting of the seventeenth-century French formal garden. Although shaped with a vocabulary more attuned with the twentieth century, their beds were normally planted to achieve a uniform color and texture, even if intended to extend the order of the architectural plan into the landscape. Fletcher Steele's rose gardens at Naumkeag incised meandering patterns upon a classical lawn; and even a radical theorist like Christopher Tunnard set flower panels of curvilinear and modernist forms into the lawn at St. Ann's Hill, continuing an essentially classical pattern. Tunnard argued forcefully against the mixed coloring of turn-of-the-century English planting. "The fear of pure structural color," he wrote, "is leading to the practice of a muddled pointillism (a general dotting and smearing of colors), a technique which accords well with fashion's matching and blending, but makes strange qualifications for garden artists in the country of all Europe in which the color garden is still the only favored style."[48] He continues by again advertising the empathetic approach, rather than the intellectual blending of color physiology, and stresses the emotive effect of mixing. Like so much of *Garden in the Modern Landscape,* the writing is itself "muddled," and to precisely decipher the meaning of "structural" and "functional" when applied to color is nearly an impossible task.

In California, color brightened and defined areas without the same reliance on shaped beds. In Church's work and that of Garrett Eckbo, flowering plants enlivened the greens of the "structural"

3-36

3-34   A landscape for living, Fraser Cole
        garden
        Oakland, California, 1941.
        Garrett Eckbo.

3-35   Garden for sculpture
        Los Angeles, California, 1950s.
        Eckbo, Dean, Austin & Williams.
        [Edwin Lang, courtesy
        Garrett Eckbo]

3-36   Courtyard, Connecticut General
        Life Insurance
        Bloomfield, Connecticut, 1953.
        Skidmore, Owings and Merrill,
        architects; Isamu Noguchi,
        sculptor.
        [Marc Treib]

plants. In general, the parterre did not prevail; a segment of lawn, perhaps shaped as a biomorphic curve, interlocked with an iridescent blue swimming pool—a low-maintenance substitute for the flower parterre. Eckbo condemned American gardeners as "color happy" and cautioned that the stronger and purer the color, the more studied must be its application. Color, like the forms and plant materials themselves, must contribute to the spatial integrity of the design: "We advocate the use of color, but we advocate its use in a disciplined and controlled fashion which will strengthen, rather than disrupt, the spatial concept of garden or park." Thus green must also be considered a color, and not just as a background: "Foliage and structure likewise have color, of considerable range: in foliage from gray, blue-gray, and brown-gray through gray-green, light, medium and dark green, to various purple and red shades, not to mention variegations of silver, yellow and red."[49] Like virtually every aspect of landscape design, the purpose of color is to strengthen and enrich the structure of the garden, its formal vocabulary, and the human uses that generated its design.

6. *Integration of house and garden, not "house-and-then-a-garden."*[50] Furthering European modernist concerns, several architects in southern California realized what Mies had proposed in his brick villa project: the complete integration of interior and exterior spaces. Frank Lloyd Wright's Millard House (1923) in Pasadena extended a pool and terraces over the ravine in which it was sited, as a planar reinterpretation of the enclosed patio common to Spanish California architecture. Building upon Wright's early investigations, two emigré Austrian architects, R. M. Schindler and Richard Neutra, produced houses in which the line between inside and outside was seriously effaced. Schindler's own house of 1922 paired inside spaces with sunken gardens in a neat play of indoor and outdoor rooms. In Neutra's Moore House (1952) in Ojai and the Goldman House (1951) in Encino (with landscape design by Garrett Eckbo), large sheets of glass and broadly overhanging roof planes extend from the structural steel frame; the patio, pool, and plantings continue through the outer wall. The influential program of Case Study Houses, sponsored by *Arts and Architecture* magazine from 1945 to 1966, continue the campaign advertising modern architecture and landscape design in southern California in the publication of these projects by designers of high caliber.[51] If architects such as those in southern California attempted to bring the surrounding garden within the house, landscape architects drew upon the spatial structure of the dwelling to design the spaces of the garden.

This last factor, more than any other, would characterize the Eckbo landscape. As the designer of over a thousand gardens large and small, Eckbo focused his efforts on the space of the lot as a whole. Realizing that to subdivide what was already limited space would reduce the perceived dimensions of the site, he allowed the site to remain fully

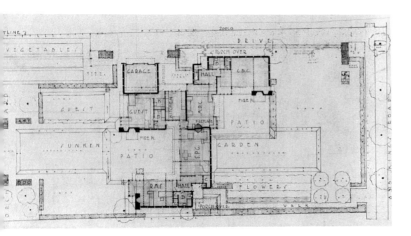

3–37

3–38

3–37   Plan, Schindler-Chase residence
Los Angeles, California, 1922.
R. M. Schindler.
[Art Museum, University of
California, Santa Barbara]

3–38   Goldman residence and garden
Encino, California, 1951. Richard
Neutra, architect; Garrett Eckbo,
landscape architect.
[Julius Shulman, courtesy
Garrett Eckbo]

3–39   Zimmerman residence and garden
Los Angeles, California, 1950s.
Eckbo, Dean & Williams.
[Julius Shulman, courtesy
Garrett Eckbo]

3–39

3–40

apparent. As early as 1937, he had described how "the rectangular area was warped, twisted, and reshaped at will, to force a forgetfulness of the hard enclosing lines. Portions of the area are partially or wholly screened, to suggest additional space by the impossibility of seeing everything at once."[52] That quality would never disappear in his work.

That the house and garden were settings for family life is also evidenced in the writings of Thomas Church, the senior figure in modern California landscape architecture. A prolific author as well as designer, Church wrote for the common person as well as the professional in publications such as the *San Francisco Chronicle* and *House Beautiful*. His *Gardens Are for People*[53] addressed future garden makers or clients by telling them to tell *him* just what they wanted. Form derived from the accommodation of the program; no two gardens should look alike, he wrote, but each should reflect the particulars of the client and the site.

Church's social polemic notwithstanding, one finds great commonalities in the hundreds of gardens that he designed and built during his long career. The gardens vary stylistically from the straightforward, which use an almost nondescript vocabulary, to those that drew upon the latest ideas borrowed from the worlds of art and architecture. Most of them, however, are tightly designed gardens in the immediate surrounds of the house, developing into an expanded view planned with a lesser degree of intervention. Paving or grass serves a functional purpose near the house, and its area is often bounded and set off from the remainder of the site by a low wall, planter, or seat. In vocabulary as well as in his office structure, Church straddled the line between tradition and modernism. Designs vary in their degree of formal innovation and in their reliance on classical structure or elements.

The garden for the Phillips residence in Napa Valley (c. 1954) typifies Church's larger gardens in its use of the swimming pool as a device to establish symmetry, to structure the garden, and to link it with the surrounding vineyards and distant mountains. From this formal axis, turned perpendicularly to the house, extend more informal garden elements: bushes, trellises, and vines. The landscape structure, anchored and wed to the tectonic structure of the house, induces a resolute feeling. And yet in the softening effect of plants and the asymmetrical development of the plan, one finds sufficient events to surprise and to sustain the user's directed attention.

In other works, often on a more restricted site or a tighter budget, Church formed the landscape to create a foil for the architecture: the sweeping curve wrapped the building, circumscribing a terrace and perhaps part of a lawn. A fence is somewhat inescapable in the suburbs, but it was cleverly exploited by Church to screen undesirable visual elements while heightening the expectation of what lies beyond. The raised planter doubles as a seat; the zigzag, the curve, the free figure of the

3–40   "The Forecast [Alcoa] Garden"
Los Angeles, California, late
1950s. Garrett Eckbo.
[Julius Shulman, courtesy
Aluminum Company of America
and Garrett Eckbo]

3–41   Phillips garden
Napa Valley, California, c. 1954.
Thomas Church.
[Marc Treib]

3–42   Donnell garden
Sonoma County, California, 1948.
Thomas Church.
[Marc Treib]

3-41

3-42

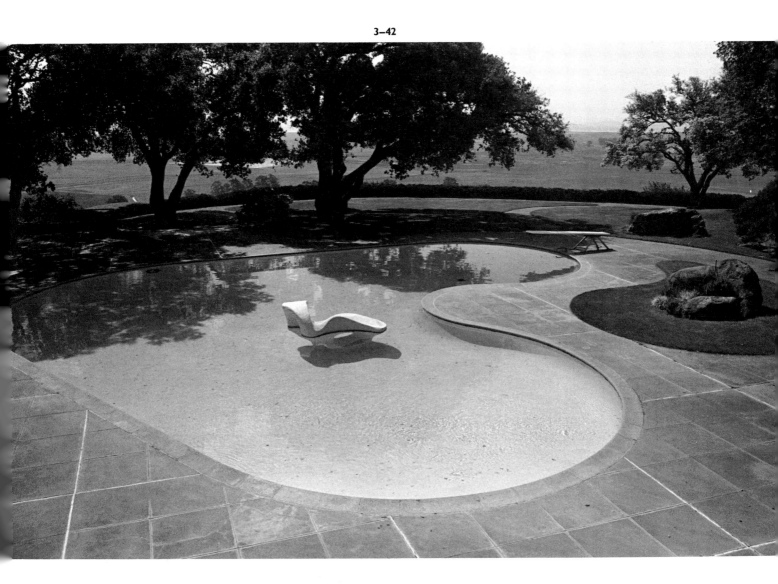

pool—all became signature elements that Church manipulated to great aesthetic and functional advantage.

Of all California gardens in the modern idiom, Thomas Church's 1948 Donnell garden in Sonoma County has become the ultimate icon. One reason, and probably the principal one, was its reliance on biomorphic forms that have become the indicators of modernity. But the Donnell garden is also quintessentially modern and Californian in other respects; for one, its preoccupation with use, that is, with living outdoors. Constructed on a site favored by the family for picnicking, the garden's realization actually preceded the house. Perhaps this explains their ambiguous relationship, adjacent rather than adjoining. A swimming pool, a lanai which is in itself a living room, and dressing rooms that double as guest quarters comprise the ensemble. A wooden deck extends out from the hillside, adding an air of floating to the experience of the pool area. If one thought of living in the benign outdoors of the Golden State, this garden would provide an ideal and idyllic setting.

A delicate balance of the indigenous ecology and horticultural importation completes the design. Church first acknowledged the existing pattern of grass-covered hillsides with their stands of California live oaks in structuring the layout. To these elements he added a line of Monterey cypresses, juniper hedges, bougainvillea, festuca, and simple lawns. Like two friends standing side-by-side admiring the view, the house and the garden share the hilltop as adjacent elements, woven resolutely together by the serpentine hedge and the informal promenade. Its look is modern; but are there any fundamental spatial developments? There are, but these are of less consequence than the pervasive feeling of contemporaneity that derives from the shapes and forms of the garden.[54] The routes by which one may traverse the garden are many, a far more modern structuring of garden space than the preferred axis of the French baroque or the meandering route of the English landscape garden.

As an entity, the Donnell garden thus epitomizes the axioms for a modern landscape. Denying the influence of historical styles and eschewing the classical axis, its vocabulary accepts the influence of modern art, not as patterns but as parts of a unified space. The composition is dynamic, and the plantings—while selected for their horticultural suitability—are used as well for their own sculptural

properties. Even the existing California live oaks were encircled with brick at their bases to incorporate them into the composition. Through its formal language and its use of extended wall planes and extensive glass areas in the lanai, the integration of interior and exterior spaces, building and garden, is nearly complete. And finally, the garden exists for people; it has been designed to be used.

III

Of course, a modern landscape architecture in the United States was neither as simply defined nor as easily created as this text might imply. Like all "movements," it is a fictional construct and coherent only in retrospect. And like any true history, the real story is far more complex than one that can be caught in a net with so loose a weave. But if the many details and many of the subsidiary works and players are missing from this cursory overview, perhaps the rudiments of the context, the reaction, the structure, and the forms of modernism may still be gleaned.

Notes

1 Sigfried Giedion, *Space, Time and Architecture* (Cambridge: Harvard University Press, 1941). The text is based on a series of lectures by the noted architectural historian, given at Harvard in 1938–1939.

2 In the revised, postwar edition, however, the role of landscape architecture in housing and town planning was greatly expanded, and Tunnard speaks equally as planner and landscape designer. By that time, the formal pronouncements of his writings had faded, and one finds, in their place, a greater affinity with the attitudes of architects than with those of the landscape architects. Christopher Tunnard, *Gardens in the Modern Landscape* (London: The Architectural Press, 1948). See also Lance M. Neckar, "Christopher Tunnard: The Garden in the Modern Landscape," in this volume.

3 Fletcher Steele, "New Pioneering in Garden Design," *Landscape Architecture* 20, no. 3 (April 1930), 162. (Reprinted in this volume.)

4 I use the term "landscape designer" because many of the landmark modernist projects, particularly in France, were designed by architects such as Gabriel Guevrekian and Robert Mallet-Stevens, or by artisans such as Pierre Legrain and the brothers Jan and Joël Martel.

5 *Style régulier* can be literally translated as the "regular style," but regular in the sense of a "regular" geometric figure. In French landscape design at the beginning of this century, the term was used to express the formality of a garden, although this need not be equated with the rigorous symmetry of the seventeenth century, for example.

6 Dorothée Imbert, *The Modernist Garden in France* (New Haven: Yale University Press, 1993).

7 Fletcher Steele, "Modern Landscape Architecture," in *Contemporary Landscape Architecture and Its Sources* (San Francisco: San Francisco Museum of Art, 1937), 24–25.

8 Fletcher Steele, "New Styles in Gardening: Will Landscape Architecture Reflect the Modernistic Tendencies Seen in the Other Arts?" *House Beautiful* 65 (March 1929), 353.

9 In her comprehensive biography, Robin Karson cites Garrett Eckbo's recollection of Steele and his characterization of him as "the transitional figure between the old guard and the moderns. He interests me because he was an experimenter, he wasn't content to keep repeating the formula—which we were still being taught was the only way to do things. . . . His vocabulary was traditional but, like any good designer, he was taking the vocabulary handed to him by the culture and manipulating it well. I was also very impressed with him as a human being. He seemed to possess great humanity, to be a leader." Robin Karson, *Fletcher Steele, Landscape Architect: An Account of the Gardenmaker's Life, 1885–1971* (New York: Harry N. Abrams/Saga Press, 1989), xix.

10 James Rose, "Freedom in the Garden," *Pencil Points* (October 1938), 639. (Reprinted in this volume.)

11 See Leo Marx, *The Machine in the Garden: Technology and the Pastoral Ideal in America* (London: Oxford University Press, 1964).

12 See Juan Pablo Bonta, *An Anatomy of Architectural Interpretation* (Barcelona: Editorial Gustavo Gili, 1975); and Wolf Tegethoff, "On the Development of the Conception of Space in the Works of Mies van der Rohe," *Daidalos* 13, no. 15 (September 1984), 114–123.

13 Kiley himself speaks of Le Nôtre as "his master." Conversation with the author, May 1991.

14 Henry-Russell Hitchcock and Philip Johnson, *The International Style* (New York: W. W. Norton, 1932), 20.

15 Traveling in 1937 with architect William Wurster, Thomas Church visited Finland and Aalto's office. It is conceivable that he reviewed the plans for the Villa Mairea then under construction, and that the pool shape of Church's Donnell garden (1948), which was to become so much an image of modern California landscape design, actually began in Finland and from Aalto's interest in cubism. The interrelation of painting and architecture is explored in Henry-Russell Hitchcock, *Painting toward Architecture* (New York: Duell, Sloan and Pierce, 1948).

16 See Martin Heidegger, "Building Dwelling Thinking," in *Poetry, Language, Thought,* translated by Albert Hofstadter (New York: Harper and Row, 1971).

17 See William S. Rubin, *Dada, Surrealism and Their Heritage* (New York: Museum of Modern Art, 1968), and Patrick Waldberg, *Surrealism* (New York: Oxford University Press, 1965).

18 See James Thrall Soby, *Salvador Dali* (New York: Museum of Modern Art, 1946), and A. Reynolds Morse, *Dali: A Study of His Life and Work* (New York: New York Graphic Society, 1958).

19 See Isamu Noguchi, *A Sculptor's World* (New York: Harper and Row, 1968); *Isamu Noguchi: The Sculpture of Space* (New York: Whitney Museum of American Art, 1980); and Isamu Noguchi, *The Isamu Noguchi Garden Museum* (New York: Harry N. Abrams, 1987). For Arp, see Herbert Read, *The Art of Jean Arp* (New York: Harry N. Abrams, 1968); James Thrall Soby, ed., *Arp*

(New York: Museum of Modern Art, 1958); and *Arp 1886–1966* (Minneapolis: Minneapolis Museum of Art, 1988).

20 Christopher Tunnard, "Modern Gardens for Modern Houses: Reflections on Current Trends in Landscape Design," *Landscape Architecture* 32 (January 1942): 60. (Reprinted in this volume.)

21 Jens Jensen, *Siftings* (1939; Baltimore: Johns Hopkins Press, 1990), 34, 38.

22 Howard Adams comments on this spatial device: "The consecutive and contemporaneous sequences of general views are reinforced with the richest details of flowers and specific textures of leaves—banishing all monotony in this large space. . . . The bifurcation of one's perceptions, moving constantly between the specific and the general, between a spray of delicate, long-stemmed orchids and a sudden panorama of the valley below, is an example of Burle Marx's carefully considered aesthetic and ecological contributions to garden art, combining the sensual pleasures of space with the equally sensual pleasures of nature." *Roberto Burle Marx: The Unnatural Art of the Garden* (New York: Museum of Modern Art, 1991), 13.

23 Eckbo, *Landscape for Living* (New York: F. W. Dodge, 1950), 46–74.

24 "As there is no horizon line nor indication of depth, they are displaced in depth. They are displaced also in plane, because a colour or a line leads fatally to a displacement of the angle of vision. Inside the large forms, small forms move." *Miro: je travaille comme un jardinier* (Paris: Société Internationale d'Art XXe Siècle, 1964), 40. The book's title, "I Work as a Gardener," refers to process rather than literal forms: "I work like a gardener or a vine-dresser. Things come slowly. My

vocabulary of forms, for example—I didn't discover it all at once. It formed itself almost in spite of me. Things follow their natural course. They grow, they ripen. I must graft. I must water, as with lettuces. Ripening goes on in my mind" (p. 44).

25 The publication of Eckbo's *Landscape for Living* was the first attempt since Tunnard to present a coherent view of modern landscape architecture, although most of Eckbo's examples are taken from his own work. Rose shared his colleague's belief that modern landscape was not a style: "It is a way of living in a world of mobility, mass production, increased leisure and mechanical facility. It has no fixed forms, and no separate entities, except for the purpose of experiment and analysis." "Gardens," *California Arts and Architecture* (May 1940), 20.

26 Garrett Eckbo, "Small Gardens in the City: A Study of Their Design Possibilities," *Pencil Points* (September 1937), 573.

27 Ibid.

28 See Geoffrey Jellicoe, *The Guelph Lectures* (Guelph, Ontario: University of Guelph, 1983). Sylvia Crowe's *The Landscape of Power* (London: Architectural Press, 1958) also reveals the landscape architect's concern for the new technologies, in this case electrical distribution.

29 *An Interview with Garrett Eckbo,* conducted by Michael Laurie, January 1981 (Watertown: Hubbard Educational Trust, 1990), 6.

30 Ibid., 10–11.

31 Garrett Eckbo, "Site Planning," *Architectural Forum* (May 1942), 263.

32 Eckbo, "Small Gardens in the City," 573.

33 Rose, "Freedom in the Garden," 642; Hitchcock and Johnson, *The International Style,* 59.

34 Eckbo, "Small Gardens in the City," 573. Eckbo's invectives against the axis continued unabated. "Axes are only the center lines of areas, and there seems no more reason for emphasizing them outdoors than in." "Sculpture and Landscape Design," *Magazine of Art* (April 1938), 205.

35 The proposal was published in the September 1947 issue of *Progressive Architecture* and later appeared in James C. Rose, *Creative Gardens* (New York: Reinhold, 1958), 16–37.

36 Several writers, like Tunnard, stated that informality versus formality was not the issue; instead a new sense of space and a new approach to landscape design were needed. In 1942 Tunnard cautioned the profession about being caught in this stylistic imbroglio: "The compromise effort to unite the two styles, 'formal' and 'informal,' [is] a last frantic move by the designers to achieve something which they fondly imagine is the right style for the twentieth century. . . . This, too, is a blind alley. *The right style for the twentieth century is no style at all, but a new conception of planning the human environment.*" "Modern Gardens for Modern Houses," 60.

37 Brenda Colvin, *Land and Landscape* (London: John Murray, 1948), 62.

38 Rose, "Freedom in the Garden," 640.

39 George Dillistone, "To Talk of a New 'Style' in Gardens is Absurd," in *Gardens and Gardening, 1939,* edited by F. A. Mercer (London: The Studio Ltd., 1939), 11.

40 James Rose, "Why Not Try Science? Some Technics for Landscape Production," *Pencil Points* (December 1939), 778. (Reprinted in this volume.)

41 Tunnard, "Modern Gardens for Modern Houses," 60.

42 James Rose, "Plants Dictate Garden Forms," *Pencil Points* (November 1939), 695. (Reprinted in this volume.)

43 James Rose, "Articulate Form in Landscape Design: People and Materials Defeat Preconceived Pattern," *Pencil Points* (February 1939), 99. (Reprinted in this volume.)

44 Tunnard, *Gardens in the Modern Landscape,* 117.

45 Eckbo, *Landscape for Living,* 95.

46 Roberto Burle Marx, "A Garden Style in Brazil to Meet Contemporary Needs," *Landscape Architecture* (July 1954), 200. That Burle Marx's landscapes were obviously of painterly inspiration is verified by the inclusion of his Burton Tremaine garden project in Hitchcock, *Painting toward Architecture,* 53.

47 Gertrude Jekyll, *Gertrude Jekyll on Gardening,* edited by Penelope Hobhouse (1924; New York: Vintage Books, 1983), 259, 266.

48 Tunnard, *Gardens in the Modern Landscape,* 109.

49 Eckbo, *Landscape for Living,* 100–101.

50 Eckbo, "Small Gardens in the City," 574.

51 See Esther McCoy, *Case Study Houses 1945–1962,* 2d. ed. (Los Angeles: Hennessey and Ingalls, 1977); and Elizabeth Smith, *Blueprints for Modern Living: History and Legacy of the Case Study Houses* (Los Angeles: Museum of Contemporary Art and Cambridge: MIT Press, 1989).

52 Eckbo, "Small Gardens in the City," 574.

53 Thomas D. Church, *Gardens Are for People* (New York: Reinhold, 1955); 2d. ed., edited by Grace Hall and Michael Laurie (New York: McGraw-Hill, 1983). See also Thomas Church, *Your Private World: A Study of Intimate Gardens* (San Francisco: Chronicle Books, 1969).

54 It is said that the shape of the pool derives from the meanders of rivers that feed San Francisco Bay, within view of the site. Whether or not this was the inspiration, the kidney shape given the pool by Church is certainly linked to its time. One colleague, whose name escapes me, ventured that Church probably got the idea for the pool "from the curtains in front of him." While a frivolous comment, it does suggest that such shapes were in the air during the late 1940s. See note 15 above.

4–I *"Aesthetic division of space imparts
distinction to this garden plan by the
author, who seeks to preserve in
materials abstract relations such as
those expressed in Picasso's* Figure"
(which was reproduced adjacent to it).

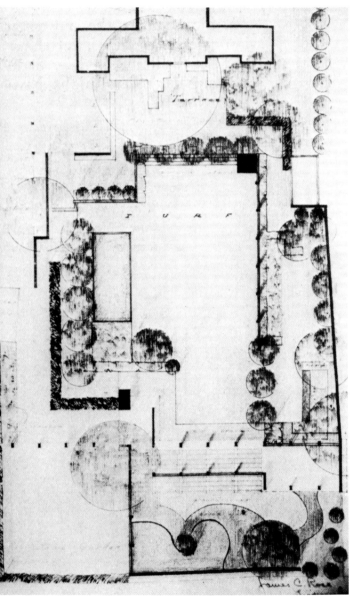

4–I

Reprinted from *Pencil Points,*
October 1938

JAMES C. ROSE: **FREEDOM IN THE GARDEN**

Landscape design falls somewhere between architecture and sculpture. Relieved of most structural and use requirements in the architectural sense, it is less purely aesthetic than sculpture because of circulation requirements. In reality, it is outdoor sculpture, not to be looked at as an object, but designed to surround us in a pleasant sense of space relations. It differs from both architecture and sculpture in several important respects:

1. Materials, for the most part, are living and growing.

2. Horizontal dimension is usually much greater in relation to the vertical, a fact that increases the difficulty in getting a sense of volume and third dimension.

3. Scale, determined by the sky and surrounding country, is necessarily larger.

4. A sense of form is more difficult to achieve because of the looseness and instability of growing material used in garden design.

In building or sculpture, shape, height, and scale are determined once and for all by non-changing elements. The variables in landscape—sky, topography, and materials—make it a subtle art, and worthy of specialized study.

II

We are told that industrial design and "so-called" modern architecture came about through the discovery of new materials and methods of construction, but that landscape design cannot change because materials and methods have not changed. We have found our final resting place. Our grave is on axis in a Beaux Arts cemetery. A monument terminates the vista, and if you approach with reverence, you can see the bromitaph authority has placed there: "A tree is a tree, and always will be a tree; therefore we can have no modern landscape design."

Painting has had no noticeable change in materials, yet how a Beaux Artist must scratch his head when he compares Picasso with Leonardo.

Sculpture seems to have undergone at least a minor revolution if you compare Brancusi and Cellini, although similar materials have been at the disposal of both.

Music achieves the most startling renovation of modern times, yet the same nine notes used by Bach are used by Stravinsky. Let us not consider what might have happened to landscape design if it had been limited to nine elements as constant as a note in music.

Perhaps the dance is the best single example of change in expression without change in material. The Ballet Russe quite obviously differs from the Greek chorus or the toe dancing of the '90s, and the human body is the only important element ever used by dancers. That must be as steadfast as a tree.

III

These changes in approach—and we can trace them everywhere from industrial design to poetry—have evolved whether or not the development of materials or methods applied directly to them. They are not changes in degree; they are not the attempt of the new generation to be different. We are told that the principles of the Renaissance are the A, B, C of design, and that we must learn the alphabet before we may talk in good company. Another beautiful bromide—but, unfortunately, to learn the Renaissance alphabet in design has about the same value as to learn the Greek alphabet if we wish to speak English. No question but that it is a scholarly thing to do, and has an historical interest; but just as we cannot assume that a professor of Greek could write a better play than Noel Coward, we cannot assume that a foundation of classic design will better equip us to do modern.

Contemporary design represents a change in kind, a change in conception, the expression of a new mentality we have derived from the effects of the industrial and economic revolutions. These revolutions have the significance for our civilization that the discoveries of Galileo, Copernicus, and Magellan had for the Renaissance. They have put a transparent but impenetrable screen between us and the past, and we find ourselves in a new mental atmosphere. We can appreciate Gothic cathedrals and Renaissance palaces, but we can no longer produce them because we have been cut off from their source of inspiration. History has no value for us unless we learn this first. The only direct stimulus we can get from the past is an understanding of how the social and psychological influences led a particular civilization to arrive at its peculiar expressions. We should do the same for our own civilization and seek to express it.

IV

Style evolves naturally from the subjective influences of the social order in which we live; fashion is the superficial manipulation of any style to produce variations that have momentary appeal. To determine the essential elements of the contemporary style, we can do no better than turn to the abstractionists. They are the great experimenters in art as Einstein and Millikan are in science. Their work is invaluable. Dissociated from context, we can see the new mentality in the raw.

The constructivists probably have the most to offer landscape design because their work deals with space relations in volume. The sense of transparency, and of visibility broken by a succession of planes, as found in their constructions, if translated into terms of outdoor material, would be an approach sufficient in itself to free us from the limitation imposed by the axial system. If you wish to consider any line of sight an axis, then you have an infinite number of axes in a garden or anywhere else, and so it should be. By selecting one or two axes and developing a picture from a given station point, we are losing an infinity of opportunities. The axial approach merely harks back to the elegant facade and two-dimensional design of the sixteenth century. Such elegance fitted the society of Louis XIV, but has no relation to our own. We no longer design buildings like Mansard. Why should we design gardens or even world fairs like Le Nôtre? No one would think of furnishing a room on the principle of the axis. You do not expect to stand at one end and find an aesthetic composition at the other. You want a sense of proper division and interest from any point. So with gardens: it is fundamentally wrong to begin with axes or shapes in plan; ground forms evolve from a division of space.

V

The Beaux Arts system—and it seems incredible that practically every landscape school in the country is bound by it—has an amazing scorn for plants. They seem to be totally dissociated from design, and a knowledge of them a matter of indifference. Plants, rock, earth, and water are the major materials of landscape; to ignore any one of them limits the possibilities. Now they are stuck in a "design" at the last minute to provide enclosure or frame a "picture," but they are seldom used for their own sake. From Brancusi we can learn the importance of qualities inherent in a material; material gives the quality to a design. Warmth, charm, and intimacy come from materials. The popular belief that the contemporary style is necessarily cold and impersonal betrays an ignorance of the style and scant feeling for the use of materials. We can use anything from adobe brick to concrete and steel, and can therefore expect all the attributes of former styles in addition to the freedom that comes with self-expression.

Plants are to the landscape designer what words are to the conversationalist. Anyone can use words. Anyone can use plants; but the fastidious will make them sparkle with aptness. At Versailles, one finds hedges and trees clipped to fit the design. The whole scheme represents that point of view which we have discarded. It belongs to the period that crowded rooms into an H-shaped plan. The contemporary landscape would require the honest use of materials and the expression of their inherent qualities.

VI

The romantic period attempted to correct the fallacy of imposed academic principles, but failed in the graphic arts because its roots were in literature and sentiment rather than form and arrangement. This single feature has been the constant war cry of the classicists against any departure from their conviction of the absolute. The informal movement, essentially destructive, offered no satisfactory alternative to the order it replaced. Informal came to mean "formless" and proved as incompatible with the evolutionary state of man as the "back to nature" philosophy of Rousseau.

Anything that has not the quality of form is amorphous and meaningless. When man arranges nature or nature arrives at an arrangement perceptible to man, the thing acquires form and meaning. The arrangement may be pleasing or ugly, it may be loose or stiff, it may be symmetrical or unsymmetrical, but if the arrangement is perceptible, it possesses the quality of form, and to that extent is "formal." Informality does not exist for us except as an effect coming from the looseness and freedom in the use of form; the "leave nature alone" attitude is complete childish romanticism, and, more important, an impossibility.

Conclusion

No absolute exists in design any more than it does in nature. It is human, perhaps, to cling to a life line, but we only do so when we are afraid. Landscape schools from New York to California cling to the Beaux Arts system, and fight because their existence is threatened. Words are of no use. Fear dissolves the intelligence and blocks the vision. These conventional instructors not only look where we look and do not see what we see, but they say what we say and do not mean what we mean.

4–2 *"The author's garden model shows how a composition of tree forms is combined with water and architecture, achieving informality without loss of form."*

4–3 *"Choosing plants to fulfill design requirements through their inherent qualities as materials, the author shows in this working model how a space composition in plant form types is achieved through definition of space, without restricting circulation. He refers to it as 'sculpture in plant materials; not in the ordinary sense of an object to be looked at, but the constructivist type of sculpture which is large enough and perforated to admit circulation.' Transparent glass brick, plant forms below eye level, and tree branches above eye level give a sense of division without obscuring the view, resulting in a three-dimensional composition."* (Used to illustrate James C. Rose, "Plant Forms and Space," Pencil Points, April 1939.)

4–2

4–3

5

Reprinted from *Pencil Points*,
November 1938

JAMES C. ROSE: PLANTS DICTATE GARDEN FORMS

It is quite common and almost a boast among some Landscape Architects that they have "never planted a seed" or "don't know one plant from another"— an "art for art's sake" attitude which puts landscape design farther and farther from contemporary life and is therefore the worst possible salesmanship. Can you fancy an architect selling a client on the basis that he knew and cared nothing about brick, wood, and concrete? Or that he was too concerned with beauty to bother about them?

Considered as materials, all plants have definite potentialities and each plant has an inherent quality which will inevitably express itself. An intelligent landscape design can evolve only from a profound knowledge of, and sensitivity to, materials. When we force materials in architecture or sculpture we are sure of at least one thing: that the form, however offensive, will be relatively constant. But with plants the struggle is endless and results in victory neither for the plant nor the man who clipped it. If the plant should win the design would be lost; and if the man should win he would succeed only in preserving something false from the beginning.

The twentieth century landscape, although hardly touched, even in theory, would of necessity result in the honest use of materials as in the best modern architecture and sculpture. Plants are not applied to a preconceived ground pattern. They dictate form as surely as do use and circulation.

II

It is only fair to mention that some Beaux Arts landscape designers have used plants for their inherent quality, but under this system they could never be more than decorative elements made to conform to an eclectic, ornamental, imposed, geometric pattern with an eye to pictorial composition alone. No striving for the picturesque has resulted in more than a superficial camouflage or facade which obscures rather than expresses the real meaning. Character develops from the actualities which have been solved rather than obscured. Otherwise, we have only the personality of a "great individual" who softens everything with a disguise of ornament to protect hothouse souls from contact with reality.

It is a vain person who believes that he is free of his own times and can create a detached "thing of beauty." The personal equation exists only as a minor part of the social equation; as society becomes interdependent its expression is social and the "great individual" passes from the scene. It is then that the elements of our own environment become integrated and virtuosity loses meaning. It is then that an expressive style evolves and design ceases to be an eclectic adaptation of ornament to provide a picturesque setting for idle people.

We cannot live in pictures, and therefore a landscape designed as a series of pictures robs us of an opportunity to use that area for animated living. The war cry is often heard that we must combine use and beauty; but by this is meant that we should develop a ground pattern of segregated, geometric areas strung along an axis in Beaux Arts relationship and separated by "embellishments" which compose a picture for the "terminal point" of each area. Something to look at!

This may be called exterior decoration, but from the standpoint of twentieth century design, it has no justification. The intrinsic beauty and meaning of a landscape design come from the organic relationship between materials and the division of space in volume to express and satisfy the use for which it is intended. From this viewpoint, the landscape "picture" fades with the "facade" and clears the deck for animated design. Now we can throw away the rubber stamp of Beaux Arts tradition and, although a continuity of style will rightly develop, the solution of each problem will acquire individuality and distinction because it is based on the organic integration of almost inexhaustible material, existing conditions, and the factors of use which could never repeat themselves exactly in all cases.

Ornamentation with plants in landscape design to create "pictures" or picturesque effect means what ornamentation has always meant: the fate call of an outworn system of aesthetics. It has always been the closing chapter of art which had nothing more to say. In one last hasty attempt to propagate, it sings the same old song with a more rasping voice and sordid emphasis. What a pity so few Landscape Architects realize the opportunity they are overlooking in not examining the possibilities of the contemporary approach. It might justify a profession which has, until now, rightly been tagged a useless luxury for the idle and not-too-intelligent rich.

6

Reprinted from *Pencil Points,*
February 1939

JAMES C. ROSE: ARTICULATE FORM IN LANDSCAPE DESIGN

6–1   *"Earth, plants, rocks, and water*
were utilized by the author to divide
space in this garden for a summer
dwelling, as the views of the
working model reveal. The house
faces east and is thus shaded from
the afternoon sun, but the landscape
was developed to the north."

Words! Can we ever untangle them? We hear talk about symmetry and asymmetry, the poetry of a curved line, the client who can't tolerate a straight line, and the endless argument whether a garden should be formal or informal.

The point misunderstood, which therefore gives rise to endless argument, is that *form is a result* and not a predetermined element of the problem. Symmetry might result from a thoroughly contemporary approach, as it does in the form of a motion picture auditorium. A curved or a straight line or the combination of both might conceivably result in any design. Something which could be labeled an axis might even develop. But when we begin with any preconceived notion of form— symmetry, straight lines, or an axis—we eliminate the possibility of developing a form which will articulate and express the activity to occur.

The objective world, rather than academic preconceptions, provides the basis (and limitations) for the development of form in landscape design. Circulation—not an opportunity for persons to find their way around within an imposed pattern but circulation as a structural part of design—is the first consideration.

Wherever man goes, we find a reorganization of nature. This fact is the sole justification for the profession of landscape design, and our job is to provide a more skilful arrangement for greater utility and for the expression of contemporary living. Unfortunately, the profession has produced a lot of aesthetic ornament which has nothing to do with the problem. This is sold to the uninitiated, who have a pathetic and naive faith in the moguls of eclecticism and who, having departed by a generation or two from the virtue of necessity, are now willing to pay for a trinket of no use for them nor they for it.

II

The materials of landscape are the second consideration opposed to any preconceived notion of form. The earth itself is a plastic medium which holds an infinity of sculptural possibilities, but according to the "rules" the landscaper must iron the earth into a series of geometric shapes, based on classic precedent, until all the original virtue of earth as a material is lost. Then only eclecticism and the arrogance of man remain.

6–1

6–2   *"Without preconceived axis,
symmetry, or asymmetry, the plan of
the 'hanging garden' was developed
from the natural contours and Rose
stresses an organic and structural
use of plants."*

6–2

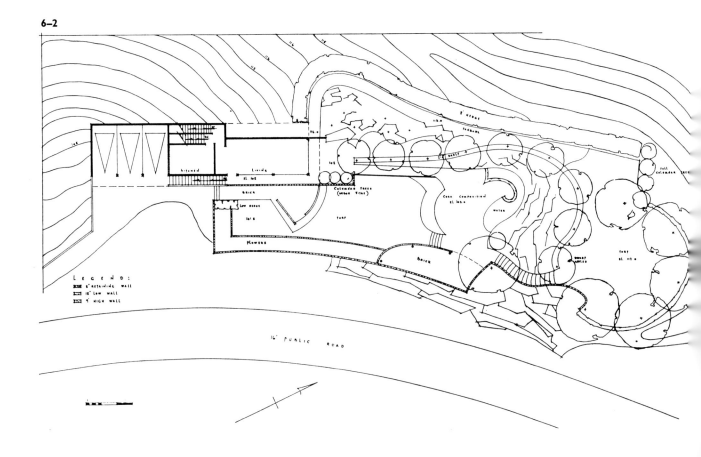

Rock materials are fundamental in both landscape and architecture. This should prove to the most skeptical the need for simultaneous development and consistency in their use. But the old school in landscape seems constitutionally incapable of breaking with tradition, while the new school in architecture seems to have practically no understanding or facility in landscape design. In this way, they can work side by side without fear of contamination or influence in form!

Plants, after all, are the saving grace of the landscaper. Because of the warm associations that are held for them, almost universally, the new movement in landscape need not suffer from the popular derision of modern as a cold, impersonal style; an opinion which the architects have not as yet succeeded in removing from the public mind. When we lift plants out of their little niches in an eclectic ground pattern and use them as organic, structural parts of the landscape, forms will appear which are expressive of plants as material.

Water is perhaps the only material in landscape which has no definite form as it depends entirely on the materials which surround it. Its fluidity permits an inexhaustible variety and fantasy in arrangement, and it becomes the interlocutor of all other outdoor forms.

III

No one with even a little insight can deny the influence of subjective preferences on the final form of a design. The greatest and most objective art always contains a symbolism in form which has no other basis than the psychology of the artist or the people who created it. This is true because we receive impressions only from the world outside ourselves, but for the reorganization of those impressions into an objective expression a period of subjective incubation is required. Who can deny that the development of form during this period of incubation is the real worth of a design? Only one thing is certain: the best designs of today will derive their subjective form from impressions of the Twentieth Century world in which we live, and not from academic archaeology which, by itself, can produce nothing but eclectic imitation.

The fundamental fallacy of the old school is an archaic conception of space which originates from the segregation of ground area instead of division in volume. That is why the members can justify themselves with the same words, and yet have an entirely different meaning. That is why we can arrive at an entirely different expression without a change in materials. And that is why we can produce Twentieth Century design while they continue in archaeological distortion.

When we permit our minds to grasp the new conception of space, and learn to use materials for their own quality, we will develop an organic style. When we consider people and circulation first, instead of clinging to the imitation of classic ornament, we will develop an animated landscape expressive of contemporary life; and catchwords like *symmetry, axis,* and *informal* will be known for their true significance . . . practically nothing.

But we have another point of view: it is expressed from the pages of the "Landscape Architecture Quarterly" of April, 1938. It is eloquent. It is authoritative. Read:

"It is perhaps to this very eclecticism—the borrowing of styles that are native to other countries and other times—that garden design in America is most obligated for its wealth of expression as an art; for in this country, there is hardly a climate or a geographical environment or an inherited American tradition to which some landscape architectural form based on European precedent cannot be appropriately adapted as a means of both utility and greater ornament." Exquisite, is it not?

7

If not openly attacked on the basis of unnecessary expense, it probably will be admitted that landscape development adds greatly to the cost of shelter. Yet, only the most unthinking architect, or the most greedy speculator, could deny outdoor space as an essential element in our environment. By the same token, one must admit that free space is not sufficient in the landscape, any more than it is in the building, until it is organized for use.

The economic organization of space depends upon an efficient system of producing materials and an expedient method of design in terms of the material produced. Landscape, as yet, has developed no system of production on which to base its design standards and keep pace with advanced methods of building. Except in a few of the newer forms, such as the highway and power dam which derive their impetus from engineering rather than tradition, science has not become an integral factor of landscape thinking.

For instance, new design problems originate with advances in horticulture, plant breeding, growth in nutrient solutions, and better control of above-ground conditions; as well as with a constantly shifting set of requirements for landscape uses. However, we do not find a corresponding invention of design forms to reflect the advances and products of science. This does not mean that science is entirely ignored, for it is possible to use almost every scientific advancement within a thoroughly eclectic design just as it is possible to use glass block and steel for the Beaux Arts building. But the result is purely ornamental because the materials are not permitted to express their potentialities in dynamic equilibrium.

II

Economy and expediency in producing useful landscapes revolve on three major factors in planning: maintenance, plant control, and grading.

When science becomes an integral part of landscape development, the very technics of control produce a definition of form and a juxtaposition of living and non-living materials which limit and reduce the maintenance. For example, some vines require special growing surfaces entirely different from others. Plants grown in nutrient solutions require a rigid set of controlling conditions. Certain activities as well as certain plants need the protection of a particular kind of wall or windbreak: others

Reprinted from *Pencil Points,*
December 1939

need exposure. Newly developed ground surfacings have infinite possibilities of form and an important relation to plant control as well as use. When any of these requirements is scientifically provided for, it automatically suggests a form, probably unprecedented, which puts maintenance on an intelligent, clear-cut basis.

One result of the application of science to environmental control is to free us of mass, and its attendant staticity. This has become part and parcel of modern architecture, mechanical locomotion, and is even found in the most progressive experiments in sculpture. Landscape design has the means with which to accomplish the same. For example, in one small particular, when plants are used as *specimens,* rather than in mass, fewer plants are required for the same control and division of space. This is partly the result of using all sides of the plant—instead of only the one side used in massing—as a design element. Conversely, more plants, more space, and more expense are required for the same utility in massing. The result is more bulk, more maintenance, and greater inconvenience.

It is only by the isolation of specimens that plants can be controlled scientifically, developed to the ultimate of their potential characteristics, and used with elastic tensility. It is the method employed in all scientific investigation in horticulture—and in the study of building materials. It cannot be entirely contrary, although it may be more flexible, while using science to produce organic form rather than producing mere camouflage.

If science has proved anything, it has proved that so-called "natural" conditions are not necessarily the best conditions for development. If experiment with materials proves anything, it proves that the greatest utility and economy per unit comes from organic use. Therefore, the theory of "massing" plants, either as an attempted imitation of natural conditions or as an antidote to "spotty" planting where specimens are used, but not organized, is essentially a negation of individual potentialities produced by the scientific method, and a denial of the economy of organic use.

Rationally, we have no basis for thinking of scientific control as anything but a means to new and fascinating possibilities in landscape design. This has been true for architecture and industrial design as well as for the other arts where science has penetrated. It is perfectly possible to use plants with the same knowledge and efficiency with which we use lumber, brick, steel, or concrete in building. And when we apply the science of growth to our landscape design standards, so that we can determine accurately the form characteristics and definitely establish growth rates for individual plants under given conditions, we will be able to use plants with the same expediency as the factory-made, modular unit in building.

Another source of expense in the traditional landscape is the grading necessary to fulfill an academic notion of segregated, geometric shapes in plan. A side slope (or, worse yet, diagonal) can absolutely ruin the pictorial grandeur of a mall. It appears, however, that it is not absolutely necessary to flatten out the earth for all types of activity, and that some variations in topography might be used as part of the three-dimensional organization. The purpose would be to develop economic ground forms for specific uses. The result would be a new dimension at considerably lower cost.

III

The advantages of an expedient and economic system for landscape control are apparent particularly in relation to housing, community recreation, and the private dwelling, where it is most needed. But who is it that keeps whispering, "You can't do that; it's not in keeping"? Could it be the architect who has just "restored" that hundred-year-old Colonial house, complete with modern plumbing and electric lights? Or is it the client who floats in chiffon across the terrace, extolling the "medieval grace of iron clothing" for the garden? Perhaps it is the landscaper who fears that we will "destroy the precious individuality of the local landscape"—the while he eats contentedly from a table set with fruits and vegetables which never would have existed were it not for the same scientific development he condemns in the landscape. What a handicap it is for those who not only think of *art* only as an "embellishment" separated from living but also put *science* in the same meaningless and unreal category.

8

All organisms seek the natural environment most favorable to the complete development of their species, and where nature fails to meet the biologic necessities, adaptation of either environment or organism must occur for life to continue. Each species produces its own forms which provide for its specific requirements in the struggle for existence. In lower organisms, the process of adaptation is so intimately related to the life cycle that it is hardly distinguishable; in vigorously motile and highly socialized organisms, the central forms are no longer individual, but are produced by the community to provide a wider adaptation to satisfy specific needs. The honeycomb of the bees and the beavers' dam are very advanced examples of such forms. Unlike the insects, however, the environmental adaptation of man is infinitely complicated by his own half-social, half-individual makeup, his uneven evolutionary development, and his distribution over every variety of geographic, topographic, and climatic conditions.

Generally speaking, man's central effort—the exploitation of all mineral, plant, animal, and insect forms for his own social welfare—has taken two forms, industrial and agricultural production. Where one of these production forms predominated, a characteristic type of environment resulted—*urban* for industry, *rural* for agriculture, *primeval* for those areas either untouched or only superficially exploited (trapping, lumbering, etc.). Although none of these environments were as socially desirable, efficient, or expressive as they might have been, they served one purpose admirably: they enormously increased man's productivity and laid the material basis for still higher forms of environment.

But as productivity rose, necessary labor time decreased: time for play as well as work became a reality for the average man. This, in turn, posed a new problem: the *absolute necessity* for and the *real possibility* of man's controlling his environment for his pleasure as well as his labor, for recreation as well as production.

This wide and expanding need of society for planned recreational environments offers tremendous new opportunities to landscape designer and building designer alike. These needs are so newly discovered, the means of meeting them so varied, and the design standards so nebulous, that it is perhaps wise to discuss the recreational needs of each type of environment relative to its dominant pro-

Reprinted from *Architectural Record,*
May 1939

duction forms, i.e., urban, rural, primeval.

Before beginning any discussion of the part of landscape design in creating such environments, a few facts about the origin of this specialized field might be worthwhile. The farmer was the first landscape designer. However remote from reality they may have since become, the great schools of landscape design sprang from the agricultures of the period. Most advances—new plant forms, new fertilizers, new construction equipments and methods—were developed to increase agricultural production, not to make possible a Tuilleries or a Kensington Garden.

The farmer has no preconceived ideas of form; he uses all available knowledge and technics to meet a given need; he plants and cultivates without abstract theories of design or beauty. He is interested in the maximum production for the minimum expenditure of time and effort. His forms are not static, but change constantly with the seasons, with advances in farming methods and plant materials. The resulting landscapes, at their best, assume a biologic, plastic quality which express man's achievements and aspirations in dramatic terms. The rice terraces of China and Japan, the wheat fields of North Dakota, the vinyards along the Rhine, are not only socially productive, they are designs which easily rival the gardens of Villa D'Este or the Alhambra.

This is not to discount for a moment the great schools of design of the past, as the English landscapist, Christopher Tunnard, has been quick to point out: "If, then, a new garden technique is to be evolved, it need not necessarily reject the traditional elements of the garden plan. Rather, its aim must be to infuse them with new life. . . . Just as the design of the locomotive, the aeroplane, and, for that matter, the modern house, is being changed by scientific invention, in a similar way science will transform the garden of the future. The latter must necessarily be influenced by new materials and their methods of application, for example, by plant importation and hybridization, and the amelioration of soil and weather conditions." This is more than ever true when the landscape designer turns from the design of the individual garden to the great recreational environments of tomorrow.

Cities Redesigned for Living . . .

"The remodeling of the earth and its cities," Lewis Mumford has said, "is still only at a germinal stage: only in isolated works of technics, like a power dam or great highway, does one begin to feel the thrust and sweep of the new creative imagination: but plainly, the day of passive acquiescence to the given environment, the day of sleepy oblivion to this source of life and culture, is drawing to an end. Here lies a new field. . . ."

Certain it is that the city today stands between man and the source of recreation, consuming his free time in traveling to and from those areas which provide a means of restoring vitality dissipated in work.

The sharp division of working and recreative worlds in today's urban areas has produced a fallacious weighting of their relative values. Work has become the dominant fact of human life—leisure and recreation a more or less luxurious afterthought which is fitted in around it. The dreary preponderance of building, the almost total absence of gardening, in our metropoli, is a direct reflection of this. Yet leisure and recreation, in their broadest sense, are fundamentally necessary factors of human life, especially in an industrial age. Recreation, work, and home life are fundamentally closely interdependent units, rather than entities to be segregated by wastefully attenuated transportation facilities, as they are today.

Since most production in the city takes place under roof, indoors, it is obvious that urban recreation must emphasize the out-of-doors, plant life, air, and light. In our poorly mechanized, over-centralized, and congested cities the crying need is for organized space: flexible, adaptable outdoor space in which to stretch, breath, expand, and grow.

Trend Toward Recreational Systems

The urban dweller requires a complete, evenly distributed, and flexible *system* providing all types of recreation for persons of every age, interest, and sex. The skeletal outlines of such systems are emerging in many American cities—New York, Cleveland, Washington, New Orleans, Chicago—although usually in a fragmentary and uncoordinated form. Of these, the combined park systems of New York City, Westchester County and Long Island undoubtedly constitute the most advanced examples.

But, aside from their sheer inadequacy—no

American city boasts even minimum standards of one-acre open space to each 100 population—these systems have many qualitative shortcomings. Public park systems are usually quite isolated: on the one hand, from the privately owned amusement and entertainment centers—theaters, dance halls, stadia, and arenas; and, on the other, from the school, library, and museum systems. This naturally makes a one-sided recreational environment. Even the largest elements—Lincoln Park in Chicago, Central Park in New York—are too remote from the densest population areas to service them adequately. And nearly all of these systems, or parts of systems, still labor under antiquated concepts of design, seldom coming up to the contemporary plane of formal expression. Nevertheless, the trend is more and more toward considering a well-balanced system essential, such a system including the following types:

1. *Play lot*—a small area within each block or group of dwellings for preschool children. One unit for every 30 to 60 families; 1,500 to 2,500 sq. ft. minimum. A few pieces of simple, safe but attractive apparatus—chair swings, low regular swings, low slide, sand box, simple play materials, jungle gym, playhouse. Open space for running. Enclosure by low fence or hedge, some shade. Pergola, benches for mothers, parking for baby carriages.

2. *Children's playground*—for children 6 to 15 years. At or near center of neighborhood, with safe and easy access. 1-acre playground for each 1,000 total population; 3 to 5 acres minimum area in one playground. Chief features: apparatus area; open space for informal play; fields and courts for games of older boys and girls; area for quiet games, crafts, dramatics, storytelling; wading pool.

3. *District playfield*—for young people and adults. ½- to 1-mile radius; 10 acres minimum size, 20 desirable. One playfield for every 20,000 population, one acre for each 800 people.

4. *Urban park*—large area which may include any or all of above activities plus "beauty of landscape." Organized for intensive use by crowds—zoos, museums, amusement, and entertainment zones.

5. *Country park and green belts*—for "a day in the country"—larger area, less intensive use, merely nature trimmed up a bit. Foot and bridle paths, drives, picnic grills, comfort stations.

6. *Special areas*—golf course, bathing beach, municipal camp, swimming pool, athletic field, stadium.

7. *Parkways and freeways*—increasingly used (1) to connect the units listed above into an integrated system and (2) to provide quick, easy, and pleasant access to rural and primeval areas.

But Quantity Is Not Enough . . .

But the types listed above constitute only the barest outlines of a recreational *system;* provision of all of them does not in any way guarantee a *successful recreational environment.* In other words, the problem is qualitative as well as quantitative—not only *how much* recreational facilities, but *what kind.* Here the element of design is vital, and success is dependent upon accurate analyses of the needs of the people to be environed. These needs are both individual and collective.

Every individual has a certain optimum space relation—that is, he requires a certain volume of space around him for the greatest contentment and development of body and soul. This space has to be organized three-dimensionally to become comprehensible and important to man. This need falls into the intangible group of invisible elements in human life which have been largely disregarded in the past. Privacy out-of-doors means relaxation, emotional release from contact, reunion with nature and the soil.

Collectively, urban populations show marked characteristics. Not only do their recreational needs vary widely with age, sex, and previous habits and customs (national groups are still an important item in planning); but they are also constantly shifting—influenced by immigration, work, and living conditions. Recent studies by Professor Frederick J. Adams of M.I.T. indicate constantly changing types of activity within definite age groups, and a gradual broadening of the ages during which persons participate most actively in sports. Organized recreation is spreading steadily downward (to include the very young in kindergarten and nursery) and upward (to provide the elderly with passive recreation and quiet sports).

In addition, the urban population uses a constantly increasing variety of recreation forms—active and passive sports, amusements, games, and hobbies. Old forms are being revived (folk dancing, marionettes); new forms are being introduced (radio, television, motoring, etc.); foreign forms imported (skiing, fencing, archery).

Consideration of the above factors imply certain design qualities for the recreational environment which are generally absent from all but the very best of current work. Design in the recreational environment of tomorrow must (1) integrate landscape and building, (2) be flexible, (3) be multi-utile, (4) exploit mechanization, (5) be social, not individual, in its approach.

1. *Integration.* The most urgent need is for the establishment of a biologic relationship between outdoor and indoor volumes which will automatically control density. This implies the integration of indoors and outdoors, of living space, working space, play space, of whole social units whose size is determined by the accessibility of its parts. Thus landscape cannot exist as an isolated phenomenon, but must become an integral part of a complex environmental control. It is quite possible, with contemporary knowledge and technics, to produce environments of sufficient plasticity as to make them constantly renewable, reflecting the organic social development. It is possible to integrate landscape again with building—*on a newer and higher plane*—and thus achieve that sense of being environed in great and pleasantly organized space which characterized the great landscapes of the past.

2. *Multiple-use.* Most types of recreation are seasonal and, within the season, can be participated in only during certain hours of the day or evening. In addition, different age and occupational groups have free time at different hours, and a great variety of recreational interests exists within the same groups. The trend toward multiple-use planning reflects needs which permeate all forms of contemporary design: decreased maintenance, increased utility, and saving of time in unnecessary travel.

3. *Greater flexibility* in building design—to provide for wider varieties of use and greater adaptability to changing conditions—can be extended into the landscape. The construction creates a skeleton of volumes which are perforated enough to permit air and sunlight for plant growth. Plants now replace the interior partitions, and divide space for outdoor use. When building and landscape achieve this flexibility, we discover that the only difference between indoor and outdoor design is in the materials and the technical problems involved. Indoors and outdoors become one—interchangeable

and indistinguishable except in the degree of protection from the elements.

Flexibility in design expresses in a graphic way the internal growth and development of society. For this reason, the great tree-lined avenues and memorial parks terminating the axes are not satisfactory, though they may have twice the open area per person above that which might be called an optimum. Once such a scheme is built, it is a dead weight on the community because it is static and inflexible. It is neither biologic nor organic, and neither serves nor expresses the lives of the people in its environs.

4. If scientific and technical advance has created the urban environment of today, it—and it alone—has also made possible the urban environment of tomorrow. This implies a frank recognition, on the part of landscape designers particularly, of the decisive importance of "the machine"; it must be met and mastered, not fled from. Indeed, the only way in which landscape design can be made flexible, multi-utile, and integral with building is by the widest use of modern materials, equipments, and methods.

As a matter of fact, this is already pretty generally recognized, though, again, in a fragmentary fashion. The great parkway systems of America are the best example of new landscape forms evolved to meet a purely contemporary demand. The sheer pressure of a mobile population forced their creation; and archaic design standards fell by the wayside almost unnoticed. The landscapings of the New York and San Francisco fairs are other examples, though perhaps more advanced in the construction methods employed than in the finished form. The use of modern lighting and sound systems, mobile theatrical units (WPA caravan theaters, Randall Island rubber-tired stages, St. Louis outdoor opera theater) is already widespread. Throughout America, advances in agriculture, silviculture, horticulture, and engineering are constantly being employed by the landscape designer.

But there are, as yet, few examples which exploit the full potentialities or achieve the finished form which truly expresses them. Nor does the use of the fluorescent light, microphone, or automobile alone guarantee a successful design. The real issue will be the use to which such developments are put. The parkway, for example, can either serve as a means of integrating living, working, and recreation into an organic whole; or it can be used in an effort to sustain their continued segregation. The theoretical 150-mile radius at the disposal of all urban dwellers for recreation is a dream of the drafting board, which, for the majority of people, is blocked at every turn by the inconvenience and cost of transportation. Only if the parkway reduces the time, money, and effort involved in getting from home to work to play, will it justify its original outlay.

In building the recreational environment of tomorrow even our most advanced forms must be extended and perfected. Man reorganizes materials consciously: their form effect is produced consciously: any effort to avoid the problem of form will produce an equally consciously developed form. Nothing in the world "just happens." A natural scene is the result of a very complicated and delicately balanced reaction of very numerous natural ecological forces. Man, himself a natural force, has power to control these environmental factors to a degree, and his reorganizations of them are directed by a conscious purpose toward a conscious objective. To endeavor to make the result of such a process "unconscious" or "natural" is to deny man's natural place in the biological scheme.

5. While the individual garden remains the ancestor of most landscape design, and while it will continue to be an important source of individual recreation, the fact remains that most urbanites do not nor cannot have access to one. And even when (or if) each dwelling unit has its private garden, the most important aspects of an urban recreational environment will lie outside its boundaries. The recreation of the city, like its work and its life, remains essentially a social problem.

Landscape—Like Building—Moves Forward

Landscape design is going through the same reconstruction in ideology and method that has changed every other form of planning since the industrial revolution. The grand manner of axes, vistas, and facades has been found out for what it is—a decorative covering for, but no solution to, the real problem. Contemporary landscape design is finding its standards in relation to the new needs of urban society. The approach has shifted, as in building, from the grand manner of axes and facades to specific needs and specific forms to express those needs.

Plants have inherent quality, as do brick, wood, concrete, and other building materials, but their quality is infinitely more complex. To use plants intelligently, one must know, for every plant, its form, height at maturity, rate of growth, hardiness, soil requirements, deciduousness, color texture, and time of bloom. To express this complex of inherent quality, it is necessary to separate the individual from the mass, and arrange different types in organic relation to use, circulation, topography, and existing elements in the landscape. The technics are more complicated than in the Beaux Arts patterns, but we thereby achieve volumes of organized space in which people live and play, rather than stand and look.

9

"There is a sentimentalism in America about 'the country' as a place to live," says Mr. Will W. Alexander in a report on rural housing. "Fresh air in the minds of many of our people—particularly city people—is thought of as a satisfactory substitute for a decent income, wholesome food, medical care, educational opportunities, and everything else which the city dwellers think of as necessary. . . ." Such a romantic attitude is all too apparent among American designers, who fail to see that the "old swimming hole" needs lifeguards and pure water, that the baseball field needs illumination, or that the farm boy may be quite as interested in aviation or theatricals as his city cousin. On the other hand, there is the danger that—once recognizing these needs—the building or landscape designer (because of his own urban background and experience) will uncritically apply *urban* design standards to a *rural* problem.

The irreducible requisite of any successful planning is that the forms developed will direct the flow of energy in the most economic and productive pattern. This is the criterion in the design of the power dam, the automobile, and the modern cotton field: it should also hold in landscape and building design, where the energy and vitality directed is that of human beings. But to organize the rural areas into the most productive pattern requires an intimate knowledge of the characteristics, rhythm, and potentialities of rural life. For if it is true that people differ little in the fundamental living needs of food, shelter, work, and play (regardless of the locality in which they live), it is equally true that the physical aspects of that locality (its topography, fertility, accessibility, exploitation, and industrialization) influence and condition the extent to which, and the method by which, it can be adapted to the needs of its people.

Homesteading and the rugged individualism of the pioneers determined the general characteristics of the rural scene. This system necessitated staking out claims and living in relative isolation to defend and improve these claims. The family became the social and recreational unit, supplemented by the school and church in the village which grew up for trading purposes. But, as Mr. David Cushman Coyle has pointed out, with changing technology and local depletion of mine, forest, and soil, we find a new type of rural population which no longer fits into the pattern of living developed by the pioneer. Recent surveys show:

Reprinted from *Architectural Record,*
August 1939

1. Mechanization of agriculture has cut in half the man labor required per bushel of wheat in 1919. In one county of western Kansas, it is cut to one quarter.

2. The nation's supply of farmland is steadily decreasing. The National Resources Board reports that as a result of soil erosion, 35,000,000 acres of farm land have been made entirely unfit for cultivation, while another 125,000,000 acres have had topsoil largely removed. A good deal of land to be inherited by farm youth is practically worthless, and will be abandoned.

3. In spite of decreasing birth rate, we have a large surplus of rural youth in proportion to farms available, and our expanding farm population is squeezed within a shrinking area of farm land. In 1920, for example, 160,000 farmers died or reached the age of 65; and in the same year, 337,000 farm boys reached the age of 18. In 1930, the surplus of boys with no prospects was 201,000. Vital statistics indicate that with the decrease in infant mortality, this surplus will increase.

4. The present and future farmer is also the victim of an accumulating drain of money from the farm to the city. He sells in a city market controlled by the buyer, and buys in a city market controlled by the seller. The farm youth is educated in rural districts, and then finds it necessary to migrate to the city to make a living. Dr. O. E. Baker, of the U. S. Department of Agriculture, estimates that this movement of population from 1920 to 1930 carried to the city human values that had cost over 12,000,000,000 dollars in private and public cash spent by rural districts.

5. The exhaustion of the farmland in some areas—such as Oklahoma or Kansas—and the simultaneous development of a highly mechanized agriculture in others—California, Texas, or Florida, for example—has meanwhile given birth to a new rural phemonenon—the migratory agricultural workers. This group constitutes a quite special and pressing problem over and above that of the rural population generally.

Special Characteristics of Rural Life

What do such trends as those listed above imply in the design of rural recreational systems? A recognition of the facts that first and foremost *the country must be redesigned for country people*—i.e., neither from the viewpoint of nor for the benefit of the urbanite. Second, in view of constantly changing social and economic conditions, that such systems should provide a plastic and flexible environment for both local and migratory farmers. Third, that such systems should be closely integrated with both urban and primeval areas, providing the greatest possible intercommunication between all three. Finally, that the following special and fairly constant factors of rural life be recognized:

1. The periods during which recreational facilities can be used by most rural inhabitants are more seasonal than daily. Whereas the city worker usually has a certain number of hours each day with a summer (or winter) vacation of short duration, the farmer has a majority of free time during winter months. This implies an emphasis on enclosed and roofed facilities.

2. Since rural labor is largely physical, and requires the use of the larger muscular system, it is reasonable to supply facilities for recreation which afford experience which is physically, mentally, and psychologically different from the major labor experience, i.e., folk dancing, swimming, arts and crafts, dramatic production, folk pageantry, etc.

3. The present relative isolation of farm families and dependence upon automotive transportation make it desirable for the entire family to seek recreation at one time. This places emphasis on the school, church, and country park as centers for recreation, and requires facilities for participation by all age and sex groups at one time.

4. Since the mobile fraternity has become such an important part of the rural scene, special facilities are necessary for the migratory laborers, the tourists, and the vacationists. It is necessary to provide for these groups, and integrate their activities with those of the more permanent residents without destroying the economic and social balance. The need here is for multiple use and flexibility in design with particular emphasis on a system integrated with the highway, shore front, waterways, and spots of scenic, natural, and historic as well as scientific interest.

Thus it can be seen that rural recreation is based on an entirely different set of conditions than urban, and it can be approached only by detailed study of specific local requirements in their relation to the region. In general, one can say that whereas in the cities the need is for *more free space* (decentralization), the rural need is for *more intensive use of less space* (concentration) to permit and provide for the social integration of a widely distributed population. But the latter does not imply mere urbanization of the country any more than the former means mere ruralization of the city.[1]

Roads Are First

The first and most essential element of any rural recreational environment will necessarily be an adequate highway system. Yet, despite the gigantic advances in highway construction in the past decade, the fact remains that most rural communities are without a road system adequate for their needs. Consciously or otherwise, the majority of federal and state construction is designed to facilitate communication between one city and the next. "With the by-pass or through-highway principle on the one hand, and the freeway or border-control principle on the other, we have the tools to adapt our future network to meet recreational needs . . . but that is only part of the highway problem. There are still the problems of local access and touring. . . . We must not only provide good trunk-highway access, but also good local-access roads. These local roads must serve directly the various cities, towns, and villages; and must open up recreational lands."[2]

Consolidated Communities Mean Better Recreation

Closely allied with the problem of transportation is that of rural housing. As long as the traditional pattern remains—thinly scattered houses, one to each farm—it is quite possible that a genuinely satisfactory recreational environment will not be evolved. In this connection, it is interesting to note how quickly *social integration* has followed *physical integration* in the new towns by TVA, FSA, and in the greenbelt towns of the former Resettlement Administration. As a matter of fact, leading agricultural economists are advocating a similar consolidation—the regrouping of farmers into villages from which they can work their land within a radius of 5 to 10 miles of them. (This type of village is of course prevalent in Europe and in isolated spots of America.) There is already a general trend toward consolidation and reorganization of schools and school districts. And the recent western projects of the Farm Security Administration—while of course designed for the landless migrants—clearly indicate the physical advantages of a similar concentration of housing facilities.

What Types of Recreation Are Required?

WPA research reveals that the average rural community needs provision for the following types of recreation:

1. Crafts and visual arts, graphic and plastic. (These might well be organized around the rapidly developing science and manual arts curricula in most rural high schools.)

2. Recreational music, including outdoor concerts, popular orchestras, group singing, etc.

3. Dancing—ballroom, folk, social square, tap, ballet, etc.

4. Recreational drama, including marionettes and puppets, plays, motion pictures, pageants, festivals, etc. The outdoor theater is recommended as an ideal form; it also encourages children in their own improvisations.

5. Children's play center, including such equipment as slides, horizontal bars, swings, seesaws, trapezes, marble courts, sand box (preferably adjacent to the wading pool with an island where children can play and sail boats).

6. Sports and athletics (conditioned by the major labor), including baseball, softball, football, basketball, tennis, archery, horseshoe pitching, swimming and water sports, snow and ice sports, hiking, camping, and nature study.

7. Other activities and special events: picnics require an area of several acres with outdoor fireplaces, barbecue pits, wood supply, and provisions for waste disposal (can also serve as a wayside camp for motorist). Occasional field days, community nights, agricultural fairs, carnivals, traveling circuses can occupy the largest free area used for sports at different seasons.

What Sort of Facilities Are Implied?

All these activities require special equipment centering around the district school, rural park, or other location designed to serve the rural inhabitants rather than the urban overflow. The usefulness is multiplied by complete and well designed flood lighting, since most outdoor activities come in the summer—precisely when the majority of rural inhabitants are busiest during the day.

Although there is perhaps no single form which meets so well the various needs of the rural community, the outdoor theater has never been satisfactorily reinterpreted as a present day recreational form in its own right. Developed as an integral part of the rural park, and in a dynamic, three-dimensional pattern, it provides for almost constant use by all age groups. Actual productions require the assistance of practically all types of craftsmanship which are physically, mentally, and psychologically different from the major labor experience. With stages at different levels, following the natural contours, and seats ingeniously arranged to accommodate both large and small audiences; with the present perfection of sound amplification; and with "scene-shifting" by spotlights instead of curtains, a type as flexible as the auditorium without its expense or intricacy is achieved. Its utility is as flexible as its organization, since it accommodates both large and small productions, festivals, pageantry, improvisations, summer-theater groups, exhibitions, meetings, picnics, and talks.

Many opportunities are overlooked by sticking too closely to arbitrary and static concepts of recreational planning. For example, the local airport is a form which deserves attention because of the interest and activity which surrounds it. Already a center of Sunday afternoon interest for many an American farm family, it orients the rural population to a larger social concept of the world outside, as well as satisfying the characteristic American interest in the technical. The same thing might be said about the old canal, the abandoned railroad engine, and the automobile junk pile—all of which hold an endless fascination for small children.[3]

Toward Scientific Landscape Design

With the exception of urban infringement in the form of summer colonies, tourist camps and hotels, and commercial recreational facilities designed mainly for the use of urban motorists, little provision for recreation exists outside America's cities. Indeed, urban invasion—in the form of commercialized amusements, billboards, suburbanization, and the "naturalism" of "preserving rural beauty" by screening out rural slums with a parkway—prevents an indigenous and biological development of rural beauty. It is thus that we handicap ourselves with a static and inflexible environment, and lose the opportunity of developing forms which express the needs of the people and the qualities of the region.

This is particularly unfortunate as concerns landscape design. The country is thought of as a restorative for the exhausted city dweller, and a land of plenty for the farmer. When help is offered by well-meaning urban societies it is, as often as not, "for the preservation of rural beauties" which look well on a post card. Another group is afraid of destroying the "delightful informality" by intelligent and straightforward reorganization of nature for the use of man. They resort to "rustic" bridges, and "colonial" cottages which will "blend" with nature. Obviously this point of view can be held only by those who do not live on the land.

We may as well accept the fact that man's activities change and dominate the landscape; it does not follow that they should spoil it. Writing on the redesign of the American landscape, Paul B. Sears has said: "Not only must the scientist of the future work in awareness of social and economic processes, but he must clear a further hurdle. . . . The scientist must be aware of the relation of his task to the field of aesthetics. What is right and economical and in balance is in general satisfying. Not the least important symptom of the present decay of the American landscape is its appalling ugliness. . . . The landscape of the United States, with its two billions of acres for a potential population of one hundred and fifty million, or even two hundred million, can be made a place of plenty, permanence, and beauty. But this most assuredly cannot be done without the aid of science. Nor can such aid be rendered by men of science unaware of the task which confronts them."[4]

Notes

1 See Garrett Eckbo, Daniel U. Kiley, and James C. Rose, "Landscape Design in the Urban Environment," *Architectural Record* (May 1939), 70–71. (Reprinted in this volume.)

2 From a paper by Roland B. Greeley read at the Outdoor Recreation Conference, Amherst, Massachusetts, March 11, 1939.

3 Recently, a recreational expert, showing some distinguished visitors in Washington the advanced planning of children's play areas in one of the greenbelt towns, was somewhat chagrined to find them quite deserted. But, as they started back to Washington, they passed the town's children playing on a dump used for fill along the roadway. One of the ladies of the party turned to the expert and inquired brightly: "And I suppose you will plan something for these children, too?"

4 Paul B. Sears, "Science and the New Landscape," *Harper's Magazine* (July 1939), 207.

10

The American people had and largely still have a natural environment which is unsurpassed in both scale and variety. But only within the last decade or so have they begun to view it as anything other than an inexhaustible storehouse of material wealth—of minerals, timbers, and furs. Farsighted Americans long ago realized the cultural, social, and scientific potentialities of the wilderness. In 1812 John James Audubon, patiently recording American wildlife while his contemporaries staked out new claims, lamented that he was not rich again, "so strong is my enthusiasm to enlarge the ornithological knowledge of my country." And later, Thoreau urged "that every community in America should have, as part of its permanent domain, a portion of the wilderness."

But such observers merely anticipated the time when the American people would awake to the fact that they faced, on the one hand, a land from which the primeval was rapidly disappearing and, on the other, a greater need for such environments than ever before. Now—with a population largely concentrated in or near an urban environment—the problem becomes one of *establishing and then controlling an environmental equilibrium*—urban, rural, primeval.

The environmental distinction implied in the word primeval is largely one of time: as such, it denotes that which came first. All habitats and life itself have their origins in the primeval. But the adaptation of the earth and its natural forces to the needs of various types of organic life has constantly developed new types of habitat, of which the human is only one. The dominance of man is predicated on his having exploited the more primitive forms of life and materials until he has developed what Benton Mackaye defines as "the habitats of fundamental human relations"—urban and rural environments.

The importance of the primeval—its integral relation and the extent to which we are dependent upon it in modern life—is apparent in both a physical (or material) and emotional (or recreational) sense. For instance, trees and other plant forms originate in the wilderness, are developed by science, and are then used in the organization of city streets, playgrounds, gardens, and for the production of fruits and vegetables. Poultry, livestock, and beasts of burden are all products of the wilderness which have been adapted and exploited by man. On the other hand, various forms of life that are not completely domesticated, such as fish, game, and

Reprinted from *Architectural Record,*
February 1940

different plants and insects, are often controlled to the extent necessary and desirable for the type of exploitation intended (sport, study, etc.).

The geographical distinction which separates man from the wilderness is produced by the cultural, social, and economic needs of his own advancement, i.e., complicated trade relations, group activity in recreation and work, industrialization, mobility. These activities fall naturally into geographical centers of easy communication and distribution (water ports, trade posts, etc.), where the urban environment develops, and into centers of agriculture, mining, lumbering (river beds, uplands, and parts of mountain regions), where the rural environment develops. The main factor which distinguishes both the urban and rural from the primeval is that, although the primeval may be exploited by him, *it is not inhabited by man*. This does not mean that it is an "untouchable" wilderness with an arbitrary fence around it. On the contrary, its intimate and tangible relation to both man and the environments which he does inhabit is apparent in the ease with which human habitats return to the primeval (Mayan cities, Stonehenge, archaeological ruins, etc.).

Design for Primeval Inhabitants

As all design of the urban environment is based primarily on the needs of the city dweller, and that of the rural environment on the inhabitants of the country, any intelligent planning of the primeval must be based on *the needs of its native "population"—beasts, birds, insects, and plant life*. It is the adaptation of the wilderness to the needs of its own "population"—either by man or nature or both—that provides its chief recreational value to man. Thus, when he controls the survival and selection of the primeval "population," he is at the same time providing for his own.

A primeval system must first establish and then control a dynamic equilibrium between man and nature. This means that we must build up the primeval itself, creating the best conditions which science can provide for the native inhabitants, and protecting them against ruthless invasion and destruction from any form or source (human, animal or insect, fire, flood, etc.).

Science Shows the Way

Recent technological advances at once reveal the complexity of the problem and indicate a trend toward more scientific control of the wilderness. For instance, scientific methods of determining food, feeding, and other wildlife habits, together with a technic for the production and distribution of forage, have in some instances completely reversed the wildlife depletion. At the same time, more than fifty million acres of swamp land, which formerly provided habitat for wild life, have been converted to farm land by advanced methods of drainage. In other sections, zoning of primeval areas has reduced the amount of arable land (particularly in lumbered and burned sections of northern Wisconsin, Minnesota, and Michigan) which can be sold for farm use. This cuts the cost of maintenance on roads to isolated and unproductive farms, and the money is used in reforestation and fire control.

The U.S. Forest Service includes silviculture, nursery and planting methods to insure forest reproduction, selection and breeding of individual trees and tree species to increase future forest values and current forest inventories, as well as sustained-yield forest management. This is undoubtedly one of the most striking examples of a technical service whose planning for primeval inhabitants simultaneously develops the recreational value of the wilderness for man, and concretely benefits both the rural (control of floods and erosion) and urban environments (development of new plant forms). A corollary is the development of new industrial technics using raw materials, one time abandoned as "waste," on a productive basis in excess of that found in their original use. For instance, 50–60% of the actual lumber grown, or available on the stump, was at one time "waste," but has lately become an important source of building materials such as wall board and plywood.

The problem of designing a primeval environment, however, is far larger than the mere development of new methods for utilizing the "leftovers," or the "economic" exploitation of raw materials with potential commercial value (salt and borax products from desert areas, for example). For, in planning the primeval, we must consider also its *interplay with the urban* (almost every stream of importance in New Hampshire has been impaired for recreational use by industrial sewage) and the rural (destruction of the western grass lands equals dust storms in the Mississippi Valley).

Clearly, it is not enough to "establish monuments and reservations" and "preserve the natural scenery." As already pointed out, it is neither possible nor desirable to put a fence around an environment that is a result of complicated and delicately balanced reactions of natural, ecological, and biological forces. Since the primeval is really a distinction of time, what is satisfactory for today may disturb the environmental equilibrium of tomorrow, unless it is shifted and modified to meet new elements in the balance. Even a thoroughly scientific and rational technic can destroy the balance if it considers only one objective.

Man in the Primeval

Even the fragmentary coordination of technics in the attempt to establish an equilibrium for the plant, animal, and insect life fulfills its purpose, in a qualitative sense, to a greater degree than the specific planning for human enjoyment of the primeval. The majority of our "resort" areas and too many of our parks, although planned to provide man with *access* to the primeval, actually defeat their own purpose—the primeval *retreats* before this advance.

As Lewis Mumford points out, the purpose is "to make the region ready to sustain the richest types of human culture and the fullest span of human life—offering a home to every type of character and disposition and human mood, creating and preserving objective fields of response for man's deeper subjective needs. It is precisely those of us who recognize the value of mechanization and standardization and universalization who must be most alert to the need for providing an equal place for the complementary set of activities . . . the natural as opposed to the human . . . the lonely as opposed to the collective. A habitat planned so as to form a continuous background to a delicately graded scale of human feelings and values is the genuine requisite of a cultivated life."

As a start toward this end, the Recreation Committee of the National Resources Board has divided the primeval into four classes to meet the varying needs of the population. The following types of activity are recommended to go with the classification:

DEVELOPED—specific areas especially equipped for concentrated human use. This is the link which integrates urban and rural with the primeval wilderness. It is the last point designed exclusively for the needs of human activity (and the point from which man goes deeper into the areas designed to satisfy his own subjective and objective need for contact with nature). It includes such recreational types as:

1. camping and picnicking (with facilities provided for both day and vacation needs);

2. summer sports (swimming, diving, boating, beach activities, etc.), including instruction and facilities;

3. winter sports (skiing, tobogganing, bobsledding, iceboating, etc.);

4. recreational drama, including music, play, and festival organization, amateur and professional productions, summer companies, etc.;

5. arts and crafts, including woodcraft skills such as fire lighting and lean-to building, as well as horseback riding, archery, pistol practice, etc.

SCIENTIFIC—areas which contain special zoological, botanical, geological, archaeological, or historic values especially developed as natural museums or collections for the enlightenment of interested groups or individuals or students of the natural sciences.

MODIFIED—areas where man has made alterations with emphasis on the needs of the native population, and some provisions for travel and communication. This includes such activity types as:

1. nature tours, group and individual;

2. camping, with and without facilities provided;

3. practice of arts and crafts, with restrictions;

4. some sports, including hunting, fishing, hiking, cross-country skiing, etc.

PRIMITIVE—mainly unexplored or partially explored areas with conditions of transportation as well as vegetation or fauna unmodified by man. The main types of activity are: scientific investigation; study and collection of natural species valuable in cross breeding for the development of new forms; exploration; and satisfaction of the last degree of subjective and emotional need for contact with the primitive.

Design Implications . . . Access

It is true that the primeval resources and their ultimate value to man depend upon scientific control, but the extent to which the recreational value thereby created can be used by man depends upon its accessibility. "This does not mean," says Lewis Mumford, "that every type of environment should be equally available to every type of person, and that every part of the natural scene should be as open to dense occupation as the concert hall of a great metropolis. This vulgarization of activities, that are by their essential nature restricted and isolated, would blot out the natural varieties of the habitat, and make the whole world over into a single metropolitan image. In the end, it would mean that one must be content with only one type of environment—that of the metropolis . . . a degradation in both the geological and human sense."

There is, however, a discrepancy between the distribution of population and the accessibility of primeval recreation which cannot be overlooked. For instance, although 45% of the population in the United States lives within 55 miles of the sea and Great Lake shores, only 1% of this area is available for public use. Inland primeval areas are also insufficiently accessible to urban and rural populations—partly due to occupational shifts and the difficulty and cost of transportation. The situation has been somewhat alleviated by legal processes such as zoning and the right of eminent domain, donations from individuals, public subsidy of transportation, and programs of the state parks.

Toward "the Remodeling of the Earth"

But the problem is more qualitative than quantitative since wholesale invasion of the wilderness is by no means desirable. On the other hand, access which is necessary to make the primeval useful in satisfying the varying degrees of human needs can not be camouflaged out of existence by "styles" of architecture which are supposed to retain the "feeling" of a particular section, or by "rustification" which is supposed to "blend" with nature, and simulate the honest craftsmanship of the pioneers. There is no reason for abandoning the scientific and rational methods of building and construction simply because we come close to nature. The clean cut, graceful forms of the T.V.A. constructions are certainly less destructive of nature than the heavy, often purely ornamental forms used mainly for their

association with primitive technics, rather than because they are the best solution of the problem. The result of such affectation is usually a mutilation of nature which has nothing in its method that is common to that of the pioneer. It cannot be justified even on the aesthetic basis of "harmonizing" with nature. Harmony is the result of contrast: opposites that complement one another.

Thus, we come back to the biological conception of environmental design as found in scientific agriculture, and as exemplified by the life cycle and group habits found in many of the lower organisms. Man's forms must be designed to meet his biologic needs. His social and scientific as well as cultural advancement have placed him in an evolutionary position where he can no longer survive without the protection from the natural elements which science has provided. He has also found that the so-called "fittest of the species" which survive in a struggle on an elementary plane are not always the most desirable, and that the "natural" environment is seldom the best for the optimum development of desirable human, plant, animal, or insect species. Through the application of science he has the means of developing those species which will benefit his own existence and controlling those which do not, and by that method he will retain dominance.

The design principles underlying the planning of the urban, rural, and primeval environments are identical: *use of the best available means to provide for the specific needs of the specific inhabitants; this results in specific forms.* None of these environments stands alone. Every factor in one has its definite influence on the inhabitants of the other, and the necessity of establishing an equilibrium emerges. To be in harmony with the natural forces of renewal and exhaustion, this equilibrium must be dynamic, constantly changing and balancing within the complete environment. It is this fact which makes arbitrary design sterile and meaningless— a negation of science. The real problem is the redesign of man's environments, making them flexible in use, adaptable in form, economical in effort, and productive in bringing to individuals an enlarged horizon of cultural, scientific, and social integrity.

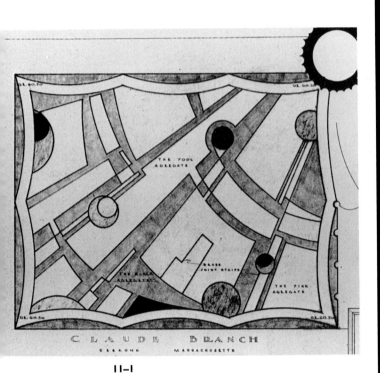

11-1

Dorothée Imbert holds advanced degrees in architecture and landscape architecture and is the author of *The Modernist Garden in France* (1993). Her research centers on modernism in European architecture and landscape design.

While they denied—or borrowed selectively from—historical precedents, early twentieth-century architects frequently cited parallel artistic currents to define the modernist movement as witness to the transformation of society. The emerging generation of American landscape architects—which included the noted trio of Garrett Eckbo, Daniel Kiley, and James Rose—also sought a formal expression in a modernism truly rooted in its time. As students in the late 1930s, they analyzed cubist and constructivist compositions, drew architectural lessons from Walter Gropius, and looked toward Europe for a model of the new garden.[1] Almost a decade before the English landscape designer and critic Christopher Tunnard defined his precepts for gardens in the modern landscape, Fletcher Steele had publicized French projects in a pair of articles published in American periodicals, thus bringing these works to the attention of the young designers.[2]

Where Tunnard argued didactically and topically, Steele's definition of the "new styles" and "new pioneering" in landscape design swayed between ambiguous concepts of "modern" and "modernistic," illustrated by a higgledy-piggledy collection of new French gardens. Despite the somewhat repetitive nature of his commentary, his articles nevertheless insightfully surveyed one of the most significant periods in the history of twentieth-century garden design. The impact of Steele's testimony was reinforced by the almost complete absence of contemporary criticism and theory in the field of landscape design, an absence perhaps due to the fact that these gardens were seen as belonging to an architectural ensemble, rather than as part of the landscape.

Although his journalism reads at times as cautious, ambivalent, even contradictory, Steele maintained both an open eye and an open mind toward radical garden design.[3] His own work was too rooted in Beaux-Arts *données* of estate planning to provide a new landscape idiom; in the few instances in which he attempted to apply modern concepts to his landscape designs, the results looked like old structures revamped with modern fragments. Thus Steele's principal contribution was as an informant and provocateur rather than as a model.

The "real impetus to gardening in the new manner," wrote Steele, emerged from the Exposition des Arts Décoratifs et Industriels Modernes held in Paris in 1925.[4] While significant modern gardens were designed both before and after the exposition, this event placed the gardens within the stylistic, cultural, and social currents of the interwar years. The myriad of publications that accompanied and followed the fair also exerted a critical influence on the development and perception of the field of garden design. Originally planned to take place in 1915, the Paris exposition was modeled on a 1902 predecessor in Turin in that only original and aesthetically innovative submissions were to be admitted.[5] The program prescribed design products arranged in real-life settings, whether at the scale of the book or that of the street. To extend the architectural ensemble to the spaces between pavilions, a section was dedicated to the *art du jardin* for which several gardens were specially designed.

The products of garden design were placed within the densely planted areas on the *rive droite,* or displayed on the barren Esplanade des Invalides, across the Seine. Although planned to infill the open space between the pavilions, the landscape exhibits seldom bore any formal relation to the architecture they accompanied, whether controversial like Pierre and Charles-Edouard Jeanneret's Pavillon de L'Esprit Nouveau and Konstantin Melnikov's USSR Pavilion, or more typical like those structures dressed in *Art Déco appliqué.* The styles and degree of innovation of the gardens also varied widely. Some were presented as mere vegetal decorations, others as aesthetic statements in their own right; they ranged from Mediterranean courtyards, to aviaries and pools attempting to evoke Moorish precedents, to exterior showrooms for ceramic and porcelain, to sculptural shapes. As the landscape architect-in-chief, Jean-Claude Nicolas Forestier coordinated the outdoor spaces and the garden projects as well as ensuring the safety of the existing trees. He encouraged the various designers, not without some hesitancy, to "unbridle their imagination."[6] For an immediate effect, the gardens had to be built quickly, at times in less than ten days, and needed to remain vivid for six months. Realized within these constraints were two extremely bold and innovative submissions—which I would term "instant gardens"—that would substantially expand the limits of French garden design in the succeeding decades. Exploiting new materials such as concrete, new horticultural varieties, electricity, and a renewed formal vocabulary, their authors challenged gravity, the relation of time and motion, and the preconceived notion of nature and garden as a symbiotic system.

11–2

11–1   Paving of the West Terrace, Claude Branch Garden
Seekonk, Massachusetts, 1929.
Fletcher Steele, landscape architect.
[Suny ESF Archives]

11–2   Rendering, Garden of Water and Light, Exposition Internationale des Arts Décoratifs et Industriels Modernes
Paris, 1925. Gabriel Guevrekian, architect.
[Éditions Charles Moreau]

11-3

The architect Robert Mallet-Stevens joined the sculptors Jan and Joël Martel to plant a pair of sunken lawns with four perfectly identical "mature" trees whose foliage consisted entirely of articulated concrete planes. It is not clear whether these cast elements were intended to be covered with vines, as Steele claimed, or were simply an expression of the morphological and structural capabilities of concrete.[7] Forestier attributed the unusual nature of these planted specimens to the designers' quest for a perfection attainable through construction rather than horticulture: "When the garden was built, it was not possible to plant four trees identical in shape and size, as the layout demanded. The designers resolved the problem with reinforced cement. Very simply and without attempting a puerile copy of nature, they expressed the material's characteristics with the implied silhouette and volume of a tree. The result was undeniably interesting".[8] In its suggestion of nature, the Garden for Modern Living stretched the limits of acceptance and comprehension for many a visitor at the exposition; it caused "hilarity and bewilderment."[9]

The *Jardin d'eau et de lumière,* located on a small triangular site along the Esplanade des Invalides, appeared as the counterpoint to the Mallet-Stevens garden. There, Gabriel Guevrekian, an Armenian-born Persian architect, created the paragon of a *tableau-jardin* as an enlarged icon painted with grass, flowers, and glass. Tilted banks of lawn and brightly colored ground covers were fitted to the triangular geometry of his "Simultaneism"-influenced pictorial landscape vignette. To be seen but not entered, the Garden of Water and Light was an *exercice de style* in morphology and chroma. The triangular motif was found simultaneously in plan, elevation, and perspective, forming respectively pools, glass fences, and inclined planes of flower beds. With blue-white-red circles painted on the bottom of its tanks by Robert Delaunay, the three-tiered pool reflected a patriotic air. The large-scale floral harlequin pattern opposed orange pyrethrum to the complementary blue ageratum, and in turn the green of the banked lawn was cast within the deep red of the "flamboyant" dwarf begonias. In the two-and-a-half-dimensional *Jardin d'eau et de lumière,* time and motion were expressed by the revolution of the faceted glass sphere, the water jets, and more subtly by the optical vibration of the complementary color planes. Its geometries and hues would be explored again two years later, in Guevrekian's triangular *tableau-jardin* for the Villa Noailles in Hyères.

The *Art du Jardin* section was also represented within the galleries of the adjacent Grand Palais. There, Jean-Charles Moreux exhibited his contemporary interpretation of the classical *gloriette,* or garden pavilion, as a furnished room complete with fabrics by Sonia Delaunay and a bas-relief by Henri Laurens, while André and Paul Vera submitted images of their own garden at La Thébaïde in Saint-Germain. Another exercise in modern classicism, the Vera garden translated the lines of the

11–4

11–3   Garden, Exposition Internationale des Arts Décoratifs et Industriels Modernes
Paris, 1925. Robert Mallet-Stevens, architect; Jan and Joël Martel, sculptors.
[Éditions Albert Lévy]

11–4   Parterre, garden at La Thébaïde
Saint-Germain-en-Laye, c. 1921.
André and Paul Vera, designers.
[*L'Architecte*]

French formal landscape into the confines of modern scale, simplified and reduced, with orthogonal boxwood parterres, a formal flower garden, and a gilded concrete statue. Displayed with these designs in the Grand Palais were the plan and photographs of a garden that would later be considered an icon of French modernism.

Between 1909—the date at which he contributed illustrations to Paul Iribe's periodical *Le Témoin*—and his death some twenty years later, Pierre-Émile Legrain achieved considerable notoriety as a designer of furniture and bookbindings. Inventive in his geometries and combinations, he also rethought the use of sumptuous as well as mundane materials in various applications. With Macassar ebony and palm woods, leathers, corrugated cardboard, metals, mother-of-pearl, parchment, silver-plated glass, or oilcloth, he assembled interiors "where the art of the Far East appeared to be coupled with the most modern cubism."[10] He incised the same "discreet search for sumptuousness" of these ensembles on the yellow China shark, "Galuchat," and lacquered leather with which he bound 1,236 books.[11] While his sense of craft was consistent regardless of medium, Legrain displayed eclectic interests that included designs for a piano encased in glass, a car, a cigarette case, and even one for a camera; dresses, stage sets—and a garden. To some critics, Legrain's furniture pieces appeared excessive in their unusual materials and forms. The bookbindings he designed, on the other hand, were unanimously celebrated and frequently imitated. It is therefore curious that Fletcher Steele would write in 1930: "Pierre Legrain died recently. He was perhaps the greatest loss that modern garden design could have suffered."[12]

In fact Pierre Legrain's contribution to landscape architecture appears to be limited to a single garden that earned him a silver medal at the Exposition.[13] The photographs and plan he presented there—recorded in Joseph Marrast's publication *1925 Jardins*—featured a garden design for Jeanne and André Tachard, in La Celle-Saint-Cloud.[14] While it brought Legrain recognition for its "cubistic" and "modernist manner," the landscape design was in fact the extension outward of an interior design. At La Celle-Saint-Cloud, Legrain composed the ultimate ensemble, ranging from the design of a door handle to the grading of the site's earth.

The plan submitted at the 1925 fair was only a partial representation of the garden, itself a remodeling of an existing picturesque landscape. The previous structure was undiscernible beneath the new design, however. As the architectural footprints and hedges were rendered in the same technique, the house appeared as a mere graphic element in the overall composition of the grounds. Legrain balanced poché surfaces and geometric shapes to achieve a design that substantially departed from any garden tradition. Seen in plan or from the air, the refurbished landscape resembled one of Legrain's bookbinding designs. Order reigned but symmetry was banned. For the Tachards, Legrain

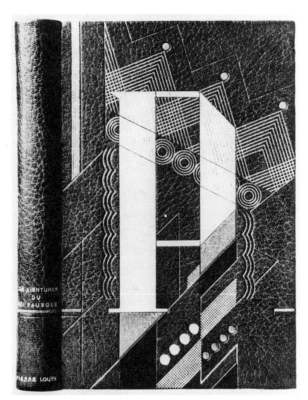

11–5

11–5   Book cover, *Les Aventures du roi Pausole* (Pierre Louÿs, 1911)
c. 1924. Pierre-Émile Legrain, designer.
[Auguste Blaizot]

11–6   Plan, garden for Jeanne and André Tachard
La Celle-Saint-Cloud, c. 1923.
Pierre-Émile Legrain, designer.
[Éditions Charles Moreau]

11–7   Annotated plan, Tachard Garden

1. Corridor
2. Salle fraîche
3. Sunken lawn room
4. Dining room
5. Kitchen garden
6. Corridor (the "lost axis")
7. House

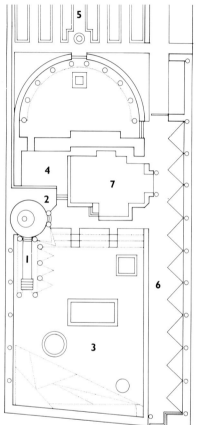

11–7

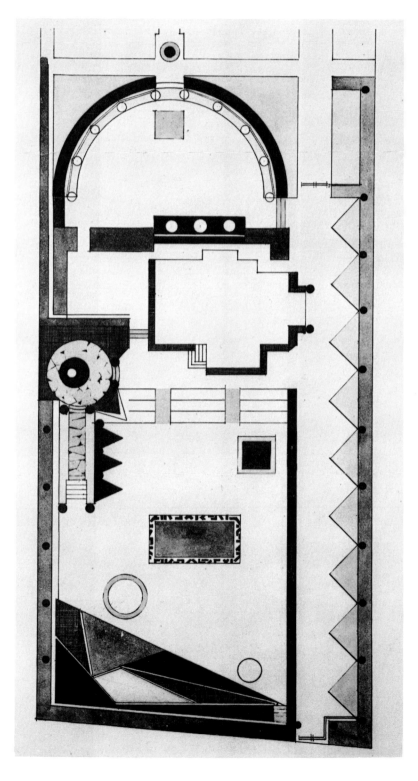

11–6

diverted vegetal materials from their traditional use to create a garden as an enlarged book cover, with lawn replacing morocco leather, the flower beds and earthworks protruding slightly like gilding, and the zigzag lateral allée acting as the volume's spine.[15] He was described as a designer who had "learned from Cubism and the expressionist schools the arrangement of geometrical forms in asymmetrical patterns to symbolize a mood or attitude"; in his only essay in landscape design Legrain resorted to a formal vocabulary of triangles, circles, and squares that fit comfortably within his repertoire of bookbinding figures.[16] Functionalism did not completely yield to graphic concerns, however; the "immutable" evergreen structure was overlaid with seasonal colors and textures to create an outdoor apartment of green corridors (1), boudoir/salle fraîche (2), sunken lawn room furnished with concrete elements (3), dining room (4), and kitchen garden (5).[17]

Extremely formal, the Tachard plan followed the geometric premise of the *style régulier,* with which André and Paul Vera and Guevrekian shaped their exposition gardens. This comparison remains superficial, however. As a modern adaptation of a classical formalism, the design of the brothers Vera for La Thébaïde relied on a more traditional axial balance, and Guevrekian himself composed the extreme geometries of his triangular tableau within the axioms of symmetry.[18] The elements of the Tachard garden, on the other hand, were arranged, wrote Fletcher Steele, according to an "occult unsymmetrical balance."[19] That is a form of balance, continued Christopher Tunnard, that depends "on the interplay of background and foreground, height and depth, motion and rest."[20] Legrain's landscape design formed a homogeneous ensemble despite the eclecticism of its parts. The sober rows of an orchard and vegetable garden led to a precious semicircular rose garden above the house. Below, a sunken expanse of lawn was etched with tiers and wedges, its surface punctuated by a variety of trees edged with concrete bands. To further distend the appearance of the regular structure of the upper part of the plan, a peripheral path played the rigor of a sheared allée of horse chestnuts against its sawtoothed base.

As if to illustrate Theo van Doesburg's take on "symmetry and repetition," the parts of the Tachard plan balanced each other in their dissimilarity.[21] The dissonant silhouettes of the trees planted across the expanse of lawn either distorted or reinforced the sense of perspective, depending on the angle from which one viewed their contrasting scale and branch structure. Arranged like rocks in a dry Japanese garden, it was virtually impossible to see all the trees concurrently. Like a distorted mirror image of the broad tiers of lawn on which the house sat, triangular wedges of grass terminated the picture; their spiraling up toward a corner of the site eluded the predictable focus of a frontal vanishing point while implying a continuation of the garden beyond.

II–8

II–9

II–8   Detail of lawn steps with begonias, Tachard Garden
Pierre-Émile Legrain, designer.
[*L'Amour de l'Art*]

II–9   View across the lawn, Tachard Garden
Pierre-Émile Legrain, designer.
[*Jardins et Cottages*]

11–11

11–10

11–10 The "lost axis," Tachard Garden
Pierre-Émile Legrain, designer.
[Éditions Charles Moreau]

11–11 Sketch from a photograph of the
"lost axis," Tachard Garden
Garrett Eckbo.
[Courtesy Garrett Eckbo]

The tangential access to the Tachard villa—severed from the pleasure, as well as the functional, grounds—appeared as an independent gallery with its own furniture. The path was lined on one side by a clipped hedge and on the other by a wall of vegetation layered in a highly articulated sequence of textures and planes. The sheared horse chestnut trees created a mass of foliage hovering above the finer-grain partition of a clipped hedge, itself resting on a smooth plane of lawn. The tree trunks rhythmically divided both the length of the hedge and the somber elongated void between the two linear masses of vegetation, in whose shade the site boundaries disappeared. The asymmetrical balance of this allée, which led to an off-center gate, was further unsettled by the vibrating effect of a zigzag band of lawn. In this section of the garden, Legrain continued to apply the precept he had proposed for the interior arrangement of the villa. Seeking an overall harmony without any single dominant note, he achieved a composition in which no detail overwhelmed and from which no detail was omitted.[22]

The plan as well as the period photographs convey the garden's fragile equilibrium. The relation between the various elements was intangible and yet ineluctable, as if any change, however minimal, would transform the dynamic quality of the design into a static banality.[23] All the parts appeared to be on the brink of falling into place: the geometrical concrete planters hovered on the lawn, held only by the tension between their respective circular and square shapes; the concentric circles wrapped around a tree trunk were set hypnotically off-center; and the zigzag edge of the allée vibrated, distorting the perception of apparent depth.

In his account of the garden at La Celle-Saint-Cloud, which could easily apply to numerous more conventional designs in the *style régulier,* Legrain did not specifically describe the saw-toothed path.[24] This was ironic, as that one feature was to become for many a landscape architect and critic the essential signature of the Tachard garden.[25]

Fletcher Steele's "New Pioneering in Garden Design" reported on the 1925 Paris and the 1929 Barcelona expositions, and he described the work of Tony Garnier, André and Paul Vera, Albert Laprade, Robert Mallet-Stevens, Jean-Claude Nicolas Forestier, Gabriel Guevrekian, Le Corbusier, and André Lurçat. A single article was thus able to present, if only briefly and sometimes inaccurately, the primary protagonists of the French landscape movement. In this introduction, Steele established the principal connection between France and the United States. In depicting all ranges of modernism in garden design, his contribution was essential, as even the writings of Achille Duchêne, Forestier, and André Vera remained within a more traditional and at times visionary framework. Steele's selection of projects must have appeared radical to the young designers in light of the textbook examples of Beaux-Arts planning provided by Hubbard and Kimball. Even if hazy in places, articles such as

11–12

11–12 Detail of model, Griffin Garden San Francisco, California, c. 1936. Thomas Church, landscape architect. [*Contemporary Landscape Architecture,* 1937]

Steele's placed France on the map of modern landscape design. If to Garrett Eckbo English was Tudor, Italian evoked Renaissance, and Spanish rhymed with Moorish, French was bound to be modernistic.[26]

Both Eckbo and Daniel Kiley cite Steele's article as the source of their interest in Legrain's landscape design. It appears however, that the influence it exerted upon their work was due to a photograph of the garden rather than its description.[27] The definition of a formal element—the zigzag—recurring throughout the modernist American landscape[28] was thus based on the illustration of the "lost axis" from the Tachard garden.[29] Eckbo traced an overlay of the photograph to study its composition. The serrated edge became a motif that variously assumed form as benches, retaining walls, and bed shapes, imprinting its shape upon several compositions by Thomas Church. If Eckbo literally applied this elemental figure onto his early designs, he later derived from its shattered formalism a more flexible geometry of informal curvilinear systems.[30]

While one could argue that the sawtooth line enlarges the perimeter, its success was more probably linked to its cubistic, and thus modernistic, allure. In fact, both the *Jardin d'eau et de lumière* and the Tachard garden applied a cubistic aesthetic to their patterns, relying on segmented lines, juxtapositions of faceted planes, and optical effects uniting foreground and background. A journalist found the geometrical motifs alive and well among decorative arts as clearly deriving from the deceased artistic movement of cubism.[31] Legrain was himself adequately positioned in the wake of cubism, as he not only successfully adapted the imagery of painting to interior and exterior design but also understood the principles of cubism as potential generators of new forms and spaces.[32] The influence it exerted on the design of gardens in America toward the end of the 1930s evidences the delay with which landscape architecture records ideological and morphological transformations occurring in other artistic domains.

In crediting Pierre Legrain as one of the initiators of the modernist movement in landscape design, Eckbo also inadvertently revealed the power of photography.[33] A single image of this garden created by a bookbinding/interior designer would foster numerous progeny in France and abroad. In 1942, an architectural critic pointed out how photographic representation influenced the development of modernist architecture—a tyranny still exerted today. He argued, however, that landscape design did not benefit from the halftone system of reproducing black and white photographs. "One hindrance to the spread of modern garden design," he wrote,

> is the difficulty of describing a modern garden by photographs, drawings, or written specifications. The bird's eye perspective—invariable in the old-line landscape plans—shows all but shows nothing, due to its artificial viewpoint. The photograph taken from eye level usually describes

only a single detail, for modern garden design is often too dispersed, and above all too continuous, for photographic description, unless by a movie camera in a series of tracking shots.[34]

Photography, however, by illustrating a considerable number of French modern gardens, was the prime vehicle for promulgating new ideas in landscape design.[35] Relying essentially on planes and geometry, these gardens—the work of architects—were barely three-dimensional entities and thus benefited from an aerial perspective.[36] Legrain's garden was no exception, as the strength of its solid geometries was best revealed in plan or from the vantage point of an airplane. The aviator Tachard could have readily perceived the strict linear composition and read its forms as that of an enlarged bookcover.[37] But the existing vegetation being simply encased within the formal structure, the garden avoided the rigor and stilled aspect of the contemporaneous *tableaux-jardins,* and appeared as a volumetric landscape as well. Of the photographs published in *1925 Jardins,* the representation of the zigzag edge was the most noticeable and the most noticed, becoming within a decade an emblem for modernist landscape design.

The 1925 exposition has signaled the debut of a garden whose renewed formalism reflected the exchanges among the fields of architecture, decorative arts, and landscape design. At the Exposition Internationale des Arts et des Techniques dans la Vie Moderne held in Paris in 1937, practically all traces of innovation had disappeared from the garden section. The *tableau-jardin* of the 1920s proved Steele's point that "horticulture as such is important, not for the love of plants, but for what one can do with them."[38] The compositions of the 1937 fair, on the other hand, seemed to prompt Tunnard to write, "The fact that garden making is in part a science does not free it from the duty of performing an aesthetic function—it can no more be turned over to the horticulturist than architecture to the engineer."[39] Quietly, the discipline of garden design had rejoined the ranks of floral decoration: Jacques Gréber, the chief architect of the exposition, praised the dahlia section and the displays of perennials, cacti, conifers, and roses, whose picturesque ensembles he saw as providing the perfect frame for the architectural variety of the fair.[40] This retreat from innovation is fully revealed in the comparison between the collection of gardens presented in *1925 Jardins* and that of *Jardins Modernes,* the account of the 1937 garden section. As he had evaluated the landscape submissions of the Decorative Arts Exposition, Fletcher Steele reviewed the work illustrated in *Jardins Modernes.* He saw

> the latest French gardens at the *Exposition Internationale de 1937* . . . [as] exhibit[ing] the dangerous tendency of all but the greatest modern art. Sharp, thin, and anaemic, they quite fail to make up in originality what they lack in charm and elegance. There has always been a certain stiffness and precision about good French par-

11–13

11–13 Martin Garden
Aptos, California, 1948. Hervey
Parke Clark, architect; Thomas
Church, landscape architect.
[Rondal Partridge, courtesy
Thomas Church and Associates]

11–14 Detail, Zwell Garden
Los Angeles, California, c. 1950.
Garrett Eckbo, landscape
architect.
[William C. Aplin, courtesy
Garrett Eckbo]

terres. It was appropriate to the design. The horticultural variety was brilliantly arranged. In these new parterres one is persuaded that everything is forced and an attempt to be merely original replaces soundness of plan. . . . Some of the earlier modernistic gardens by Guévrékian, the Veras, Pierre Legrain, etc. done ten years or more ago, seemed to promise a great future along lines that had scarcely been developed hitherto. We can only feel disappointment in knowing that these strong, fine new ideas withered before they came to flower.[41]

James Rose regarded 1937 as a pivotal year in the development of modern landscape design for the [misdated] publication of Tunnard's *Gardens in the Modern Landscape,* the special issue of *Architecture d'Aujourd'hui* on gardens, and the international exposition and the first international congress of garden architects, both held in Paris.[42] The absence of the United States from both the critical and design arenas was striking.[43]

In his report at the Premier Congrès International des Architectes de Jardins, Achille Duchêne described the art of gardens as evolving as a function of the economic and political situation. As the collective organization gradually replaced the art patron, the uniqueness of the *tableau-jardin* gave way to the public realm of utilitarian landscapes such as a park for recreation or a productive vegetable plot. *"The Art of Gardens,"* sighed Duchêne, *"is dying away."* New designs, however, should sum up "logic, order, clarity, and hierarchy," in order to accustom the working class to beauty, "to refine its senses and develop its contemplative or critical abilities, and be given the impression of serenity and order."[44] If modernist architecture drew its force from an almost utopian social program, perhaps it was achieved to the detriment of garden design, which, ultimately, remained a luxurious artifact.

Rose condemned the French modern garden as retaining "a static, highly formal, non-functioning, artistic self-consciousness."[45] It is thus ironic that a zigzag, itself a transformation of a cubistic cliché and uprooted from a photograph of an extremely decorative garden, was distilled to become a recurring element in the "functional" gardens of modern American landscape architects. If at times simplistic, elitist, and "show[ing] an utter lack of interest or understanding of plant life,[46] the French gardens of the 1920s and 1930s nevertheless challenged the definition of what modern landscape architecture could be. Even as images, or perhaps especially as images, these designs are still relevant, not for any answer they might provide but for the questions they ask.

11-15

11-15 Detail, Thomas Garden
southern California, c. 1950.
Garrett Eckbo, landscape
architect.
[William C. Aplin, courtesy
Garrett Eckbo]

Notes

Parts of this essay are based, to some degree, on material presented in Dorothée Imbert, *The Modernist Garden in France* (New Haven: Yale University Press, 1993).

1 "Architecture was upstairs. . . . [With the arrival of Walter Gropius in 1937] the atmosphere in the Graduate School of Design was charged, controversial and exciting. . . . Dan Kiley, Jim Rose and I were so turned on by the new ideas upstairs that, on our own, we began to explore new forms and arrangements which might reflect the new design ideas. In our experience at Harvard, we did learn about earlier efforts in Europe, particularly by Christopher Tunnard in England and Pierre LeGrand [sic] in France." Garrett Eckbo, cited by Elizabeth K. Meyer, "The Modern Framework," *Landscape Architecture* (March 1983), 50, 52.

2 Christopher Tunnard published a series of articles between 1937 and 1938 in *The Architectural Review*, collected thereafter in the book *Gardens in the Modern Landscape*. Fletcher Steele wrote "New Styles in Gardening: Will Landscape Architecture Reflect the Modernistic Tendencies Seen in the Other Arts?" for *House Beautiful* (March 1929), and "New Pioneering in Garden Design" for *Landscape Architecture Quarterly* (April 1930); both are surveys of French gardens from the 1920s. ("New Pioneering in Garden Design" is reprinted in this volume.)

3 Steele's opinions are a bit more caustic in the first article ("New Styles in Gardening"). There the design for the vicomte de Noailles by André and Paul Vera is described as "mere surface covering" that would affect "fundamental matters of design no more and no less than wallpaper affects the design of a room" (353). "New Pioneering in Garden Design" sees the same Vera landscape as displaying a parterre in a "frankly modernistic design," while the mirrors along its boundaries appear as signs of a "real innovation" (164). If Steele initially considered Legrain's landscape design as failing "to look much different from anything the rest of us might do," a year later he mourned the death of the designer who "was perhaps the greatest loss modern garden design could have suffered" ("New Styles in Gardening," 354; "New Pioneering in Garden Design," 172).

4 Steele, "New Pioneering in Garden Design," 165.

5 For a study of the 1902 Prima Esposizione Internazionale d'Arte Decorativa Moderna in Turin and its rules, see *Torino 1902: polemiche in Italia sull' Arte Nuova,* ed. Francesca R. Fratini (Turin: Martano, 1970).

6 J. C. N. Forestier, "Les Jardins de l'Exposition des Arts décoratifs," *La Gazette Illustrée des Amateurs de Jardins* (1925), 24.

7 "As a matter of fact, with vines all over them, as was intended, the concrete trees would not be one whit less absurd than a Redcedar trunk with stubby branches sticking out in all directions to catch climbing roses which one can see in many a New England garden." Steele, "New Pioneering in Garden Design," 166. Or for another interpretation: "One garden of the exposition had trees of concrete in cubist lines. They were not originally intended but had come about because the ground was not ready when the trees ordered arrived; so they died and could not be replaced at that season. Something had to be substituted in a hurry and a sculptor designed these amusing concrete trees." H. Morgenthau-Fox, "J. C. N. Forestier," *Landscape Architecture Quarterly* (January 1931), 98–99.

8 Forestier, "Les Jardins de l'Exposition des Arts décoratifs," 24.

9 ". . . où les frères Martel, hélas! avaient élevé des arbres en béton armé" (Raymond Fischer, "Les Jardins," *La Liberté,* March 5, 1930). "Mallet-Stevens probablement avec une arrière-pensée de blague, voulant à toute force des arbres, les a imaginés en ciment armé" (Marcel Weber, "Les jardins," in *Exposition Internationale des Arts Décoratifs et Industriels Modernes* [Paris: Librairie Larousse, 1925], 60). "Il faut bien en parler cependant, ne serait-ce que pour le succès d'hilarité et d'effarement qu'ils ont eu" (Ch. Risler, "Les objets d'art à l'Exposition des Arts Décoratifs," *L'Architecture* [1925], 418).

10 Gaston Varenne, "Quelques ensembles de Pierre Legrain," *L'Amour de l'Art* (1924), 406–407.

11 Jacques Doucet, a collector and fashion designer, commissioned Legrain to create covers for his collection of avant-garde manuscripts. See *Pierre Legrain Relieur: Répertoire descriptif et bibliographique de mille deux cent trente six reliures* (Paris: Librairie Auguste Blaizot, 1965), "Galuchat" is a process perfected around 1770 that consists of smoothing and coloring the calcified ruggedness of the shark skin. See Raymond Bachollet, Daniel Bordet, and Anne-Claude Lelieur, *Paul Iribe* (Paris: Editions Denoël, 1982), 124.

12 Steele, "New Pioneering in Garden Design," 172.

13 Steele praised Legrain's "landscape design*s*," and an obituary published in *Art et Décoration* (August 1929) cited him as a "meublier et dessinateur de jardin*s*"; I have been unable, however, to trace any other of his designs related to landscape. For the list of awards in the category "Art du Jardin" see *Exposition Internationale des Arts Décoratifs et Industriels Modernes, Paris 1925: Liste des récompenses* (Classe 27) (Paris: Imprimerie des journaux officiels, 1926).

14 I have not as yet established a precise date for the Legrain garden. The earliest reference appears to be Gaston Varenne's article "Quelques ensembles de Pierre Legrain," published in 1924.

15 Robert Bonfils described a bedroom designed by Legrain for the Vicomte de Noailles as another enlarged bookcover. The walls were stretched with white oilcloth inlaid with irregular patterns of cork, set off by a snakeskin bed and metal tables. See "Pierre Legrain Décorateur Créateur" in *Pierre Legrain Relieur,* xxxvii.

16 Phyllis Ackerman, "Modernism in Bookbinding," *Studio International* (November 1924), 148.

17 "Axiomes: un jardin ne doit pas vivre de tel mois à tel mois pour mourir dans la période froide. Aussi, emploi intensif du gazon, des troènes, des ifs, des cyprès, araucarias. Ceci formera la base immuable, viendra ensuite la robe de printemps, puis celle d'été par les fleurs, mais le corps restera intact." Pierre Legrain, "La Villa de Madame Tachard à La Celle-Saint-Cloud," *Vogue* (June 1, 1925), 68.

18 Steele, "New Pioneering in Garden Design," 164, and Steele, "New Styles in Gardening," 354.

19 Steele, "New Pioneering in Garden Design," 172.

20 Tunnard, *Gardens in the Modern Landscape,* 84–85.

21 "In place of symmetry the new architecture offers *a balanced relationship of unequal parts* . . . The equality of these parts rests upon the balance of their dissimilarity, not upon their similarity . . . 12. *Symmetry and repetition.*" Theo van Doesburg, "Towards a Plastic Architecture," in *Programs and Manifestoes on 20th-Century Architecture,* edited by Ulrich Conrads (Cambridge: MIT Press, 1970), 79–80.

22 "Le but est atteint lorsqu'aucun détail ne s'impose particulièrement. Il faut réaliser un accord dont aucune note ne soit dominante, par conséquent aucun détail ne doit être négligé." Legrain, "La Villa de Madame Tachard," 68.

23 Steele compared the garden to the beginning of a movie in which "we expect each part to walk over to its familiar place; bias lines to straighten, the old order to return, habit to be satisfied, and boredom enthroned." "New Pioneering in Garden Design," 177.

24 "La Villa de Madame Tachard," 68.

25 See Steele, "New Styles in Gardening," 354, and "New Pioneering in Garden Design," 172, 177; Fletcher Steele, "Landscape Design of the Future," *Landscape Architecture Quarterly* (July 1932), 301. Another American critic and designer saw the modernist landscape architect as "provid[ing] interest with certain harmonious relations produced by repetition (sometimes too much), or by sequence (sometimes harshly, as in the famous example of the saw-tooth edged path), or by balance (occult preferred to symmetrical)." Leon Henry Zach, "Modernistic Work and Its Natural Limitations," *Landscape Architecture Quarterly* (July 1932), 293.

26 "English Tudor, Italian Renaissance, or French modernistic, or Spanish-Moorish." Garrett Eckbo, "Small Gardens in the City: A Study of Their Design Possibility," *Process Architecture* (August 1990), 117.

27 Conversations with the author.

28 Although the zigzag pattern imprinted the projects of other designers, such as the Belgian landscape architect Jean Canneel-Claes, it was marked as belonging to Legrain's repertoire.

29 Steele illustrated the Legrain garden with the plan and a photograph of the saw-toothed allée that was captioned "Excellent Formal Composition on a Lost Axis." "New Pioneering in Garden Design," 177.

30 "This may look innocuous today, but this sawtooth border to me was a revolution in the way you look at a garden walk. That is, instead of just a straight walk in which you proceed through from one end to the other, you have a series of interlocking connections with the forms to the side. I think I may have done one or two or three sawtooth walks in my designs, but I never really imitated or copied. It was just a great inspiration and challenge." Garrett Eckbo in an interview conducted by Michael Laurie, January 1981. *An Interview with Garrett Eckbo,* edited by Karen Madsen (Watertown, Massachusetts: The Hubbard Educational Trust, 1990).

31 "There remain strictly ornamental arrangements. I need not insist here on the prevalence of geometrical motifs in modern decoration, a conception deriving from Cubism, the survival of which—although extinct in the realm of painting—continues in the decorative arts." Georges Cretté, "Distinctive Designs in Hand-Tooled Book-Bindings," *The Studio* (1930), 379.

32 Varenne, "Quelques ensembles," 407–408.

33 "Initiated in California by Tommy Church in the early 30's—following still earlier efforts in Europe by Pierre Le Grand [sic] and others, and in England by Christopher Tunnard, and at Harvard Graduate School of Design by Dan Kiley, James Rose and me, [modern landscape design] spread vigorously across the country and around the world." Garrett Eckbo, "American Gardens 1930's–80's," *Process Architecture* (August 1990), 111.

34 Geoffrey Baker, "Equivalent of a Loudly-Colored Folk Art Is Needed," *Landscape Architecture Quarterly* (January 1942), 66.

35 Therese Bonney's photos, for example, successfully conveyed the modernist aspect of garden design across Europe, England, and the United States.

36 "Some of the bizarre effects may be due to the fact that, more often than not, the designers are architects. Surely this is in part the reason for . . . the over-plentiful use of architectural and geometric forms: excessive indulgence on paper of the T-square, triangle, and compass. It is surprising, after seeing a plan of a given design, how much the third dimension has been considered on the ground" (Zach, "Modernistic Work and Its Natural Limitations," 293). "Herein lies an analogy between the painter and the architect, the sculptor and the landscape architect. [The architect] express[es] his ideas as a series of related planes on a sheet" (Robert Wheelwright, "Thoughts on Problems of Form," *Landscape Architecture Quarterly* [October 1930], 4).

37 The Tachard grave in the Paris cemetery of Montparnasse, "Tombeau pour un aviateur" (Tomb of an Aviator), was sculpted by Henri Laurens in 1924.

38 Steele, "New Pioneering in Garden Design," 166.

39 Christopher Tunnard, "The Functional Aspect of Garden Planning," *The Architectural Review* (April 1938), 197.

40 *Jardins Modernes: Exposition Internationale de 1937* (Paris: Éditions d'Art Charles Moreau, n.d.). Jacques Gréber was a renowned landscape designer himself.

41 Fletcher Steele, review of *Jardins Modernes, Exposition Internationale de 1937,* in *Landscape Architecture Quarterly* (January 1938), 117–118.

42 James Rose, cited by Marc Snow (said to be a *nom de plume* for James Rose himself), *Modern American Gardens* (New York: Reinhold, 1967), 12.

43 The United States did not participate in the 1925 Paris exposition either. Herbert Hoover, then Secretary of Commerce, had declined the invitation on the grounds that America was incompetent in the field of modern decorative arts. See the 1926 *Report of Commission Appointed by the Secretary of Commerce to Visit and Report upon the International Exposition of Modern Decorative and Industrial Art in Paris 1925.*

44 Achille Duchêne, *Premier Congrès International des Architectes de Jardins,* (Paris: Société Française des Architectes de Jardins, 1937), 1,2. I wish to thank Caroline Constant for bringing this report to my attention.

45 Rose, *Modern American Gardens,* 13.

46 Steele, "New Styles in Gardening," 354.

11–16 *Tombeau pour un aviateur (Tomb for an Aviator)* Cimetière Montparnasse, Paris, c. 1924. Henri Laurens, sculptor. [Dorothée Imbert]

12

FLETCHER STEELE: NEW PIONEERING IN GARDEN DESIGN

Perhaps the reader never acted foolishly as a child. The writer did. I liked sunsets and would watch them with a certain passion until the glow began to fade all too soon. Anything to bring it back! For a moment the miracle could be accomplished by standing on my head to look at it upside down. The paling colors glowed again like a cooling horseshoe returned to the forge.

Looking at the sunset upside down was but a naïve discovery of the familiar optical commonplace,—the nerves of the eye soon tire when used with concentration and are refreshed by changing the viewpoint. There seems to be an analogy here with our subject, though the sunset daily does waste away and art never. The glow of much old beauty is fading before our hungry eyes from the very excess of our interest and the inevitable changes in our modern life and thought. We must search a new point from which to view art.

We are handicapped, moreover, by that which was false or in any way untenable in our inheritance. Victorian art in America tried to soften edges until "modulation" seemed unduly important. It gave prominence to what was elegant, genteel. It made unpleasant things as agreeable as euphemism allowed, slurred over the inelegant and ignored naked or unpalatable facts. It opened its eyes to nature once a year in the White Mountains and called it perfect all the year round. In a word, it lived in a Fool's Paradise,—saw beauty only where it wanted to find it and truth all too rarely.

At the same time the scientific world was going all round everything in the effort to learn what things really are. Still we go round everything, under everything, through and over everything, looking through microscopes and telescopes. Ever more powerful, ever more quick. Yet the answer is not there. The mind of man no more than his heart is satisfied with what can be determined by science. Man wants to know eternally what a thing *is*, not merely what it looks like from the outside. For example, consider the crude problem of a mere material object like a stone. You see and feel its surface and that's all. Cut it in two and still you're seeing only surfaces, and so *ad infinitum,* to the last jumping electron.

We know from science not only how things look but what they will do. Yet we never get any farther that way either, in knowing what they are. Religion helps, but with vague, grand generalities when it comes to everyday definitions. There lies a

Reprinted from *Landscape Architecture,*
October 1930

great field between what science can teach us about things and faith which explains their spiritual meaning and place in life.

It is that great field into which it is human and proper to inquire that can be covered only by the artist, be he musician, poet, painter, or builder. Ouspensky outlines this whole matter in saying, "The mystery of life dwells in the fact that the . . . hidden meaning and the hidden function of a thing, is reflected in its phenomenon. It is possible to know the . . . [hidden meaning] by the phenomenon. But in this field the chemical reagents and spectroscopes can accomplish nothing. Only that fine apparatus which is called the soul of the artist can understand. *We* do not notice those differences between things which cannot be expressed in terms of chemistry or physics. But art is the beginning of vision" (*Tertium Organum,* p. 161). "In art we have already the first experiments in a language of the future" (p. 83).

Just what terms artists will use to show us the inner meaning of things, only artists and time will show. They have done much in the past. They never go more than one step at a time, any more than the rest of us. They are doing the best they can. In what they are doing now, so poorly termed "modernism," what interests most is the expanded sense,—not a new sense but the expansion of our old sense of dimensions, space, relativity, call it what you will. Artists don't turn things inside out (though some of their results look as though they would like to). Rather they help us to imagine ourselves part of the thing they are describing in an almost abstract sort of way. For painting Mr. Barr has touched on the idea in his foreword to the first catalogue of The Museum of Modern Art. "While we study a Cézanne we feel these planes shifting forward and back, taking their appointed distances until after a time the painted world into which we are drawn becomes almost more actual than the real world. The grandeur of a Poussin is perceived, is read, remains as it were at arm's length. But a great Cézanne is immanent; it grows around one and includes one. The result is at times almost as hypnotic as listening to great music in which strength and order are overwhelmingly made real."

Certainly this states a new viewpoint toward art on the part of the observer, and implies a definite expansion of the average man's sense of dimension.

Groping in new directions is common to all the arts. During the last week or two I have picked at random such remarks as the following. About a writer, James Joyce: "M. Marcel Brion suggests that *Work in Progress* represents a carrying-over into human life and human language of the modern scientific conception of time, as seen in the fact that if one could move away from the earth at a speed faster than that of light, the events of history would unroll backwards before one's eyes, and if one could shoot through space at an infinite speed, one would see everything almost simultaneously. Briefly, Mr. Joyce shuttles back and forth incessantly at this infinite speed."

In music the intangible, new technique is described by one critic who says: "One listens to this music and that of others like Hindemith with two selves; an analytic self, which buries its head in its hands and hears clearly every voice streaming along its course, but gets no connection between the voices, and a synthetic self, which leans back in its chair and gets a total result, but without any clear idea of how that result came, and there seems to be at present no bridging of these two, as there was with the classics."

Speaking in general of the new movement, Bell remarks: "It would bring back to the plastic arts—that mysterious, yet recognizable quality in which the art of Raffael excels—a calm disinterested and professional concern with the significance of life as revealed directly in form, a faint desire, perhaps, to touch by a picture, a building, or a simple object of use some curious over-tone of our aesthetic sense."

One artist attempts the new understanding through color, another through form, another by new and strange uses of materials, another through pattern, or by new proportions and aspects of old familiar things. All use the principles of balance, rhythm, and harmony that artists cannot and would not be deprived of. The results make one feel (when the works are masterpieces) that one *has* a new understanding, if not of a woman or chair, then of movement, color, vibration, space, or what not. Who will say that movement, *per se,* is not just as concrete a thing as a church tower, and quite as legitimate for the artist to paint if he has the mind to try? It's his business to explain things to us, not ours to sneer at him for trying.

New concepts of mathematics identifying space and time, asserting that parallels meet and that a straight line is *not* the shortest distance between two points, demolish all known laws of common sense with scarcely a whimper on our part while poor old art is fallen upon by highly respectable gun-men of culture whenever it pokes its head out for a bit of fresh air.

What a modernistic garden may be is everybody's guess. The reason is that it does not yet exist as a type. We gardeners have always been behind other artists in adopting new ideas. At heart we are a conservative lot, sure that the perfect garden does not depend on new and strange things, but on the perfecting of what we already know. We do believe, however, in fitness. When the architect has built a new-fangled house filled with new-fangled furnishings, when all styles have changed and the youngsters complain, "Why don't you do something with the stupid old garden?", we wake up. When we once start to bring things up to date, we do it thoroughly. The Villa d'Este is essentially one hundred years behind Peruzzi's beautiful Roman houses in point of time, and the gardens of Le Nôtre were done only after many a fine palace had been finished in France. So it may be with modernistic gardens. When they do come, I believe they will bring a new meaning into the whole contemporaneous movement of thought and art, for the field of gardening is peculiarly adapted to interpreting these ideas, and to making all of us conscious of new aspects in materials, colors, and dimensions.

Among the first and most able pioneers in the new tradition was Tony Garnier. From the gardener's point of view, his most interesting work was done on his own villa years ago. In the architecture there is hardly a trace of strangeness to those who are familiar with the appearance of Mediterranean buildings in general. Horizontal lines are stressed and moldings largely omitted. There is every likelihood that the houses in Pompeii looked much like his house. House and garden are not separated, as we usually see them, but each are obvious parts of a unified whole,—which is a return to the best traditions of the past, rather than a new thing. Nothing is more fantastic than can be found in many a favorite painting of Maxfield Parrish. In that part of the place which is predominantly garden, there is only a trace of the new. The main feature is started with a strong axial feeling, which is maintained throughout, although in detail the symmetry is dissolved

and only balance is left. This is so cleverly done as nowhere to be conspicuous. In this is the beginning, however, of the strong modern trend away from symmetrical axial treatment. The forms are everywhere kept architectural, what in gardening we know as "formal." The occult balance of "informal" (ghastly word excellently describing many an amorphous work of landscape architecture) design seems to have little interest for contemporaneous designers. Yet their formal lines and masses are in fact occultly balanced on an axis which is broken again and again, although rarely entirely lost. This results in a marked vibration and quite a new interest culminating in the garden plans of Pierre Legrain, of which more later.

Véra is another of the earlier garden pioneers. His book *Le Nouveau Jardin,* which appeared before the war, was stimulating to designers. In 1919, he published *Les Jardins,* somewhat further advanced. At first sight, much that he plans seems quaint and new, but, for the most part, at first sight only. His plans are soundly French, in that he maintains the minutest, the most meticulous orderliness and compactness of design. His houses stand in the open facing the gardens, which are strongly bounded by masses of trees just as is the case at Versailles. To be sure, the design in detail has a more fantastic modern note, but at bottom the whole order is maintained largely because of an absolutely symmetrical axial balance throughout.

When it comes to actually carrying out a scheme, however, M. Véra is capable of much more original feeling than his books would seem to promise.

The best known perhaps is his garden for the Vicomte Charles de Noailles in Paris. It is built on a small triangular lot, on one side of which is the house, the other two being bordered by streets. In the usual French fashion high walls were built on the two street sides effectually cutting out the highways. Both inside and outside the walls, high trees entirely conceal all the neighboring buildings in summer. The center of the area is left open and is covered with a parterre in frankly modernistic design, which is particularly happily adapted to filling in odd shapes. The strong bands of which it is composed are cleverly worked out and keep the eye distracted from the all too close boundaries. While a certain amount of horticulture is used in working out the bands, yet grass, blue lobelia, or what not, are of no importance except as one of a series of materials like colored gravel and marble, of which the different parts of the pattern are composed.

The real innovation of M. Véra lies, however, in the use of mirrors lining the street walls on two sides. Obviously, the reflections from mirrors inside the triangle are unexpected. So cleverly are they installed that, in connection with the parterre pattern, one quite loses consciousness of the definite boundaries of the place, and seems to see off toward indefinite distances through and over partitions and subdivisions of area. In this case one's sense of immediate dimension is lost in a thoroughly justifiable illusion.

The real impetus to gardening in the new manner came with the Paris Exposition of 1925, where many experiments were tried. Then for the first time appeared the great importance of light as an element of the future garden.

It is both in the use of light and in building up his gardens with new dimensional vistas that M. La Prade is conspicuous. He suggests volume through emphasis on geometrically shaped banks and mounds of earth. In his general schemes, he has stuck to symmetrical axes, but in placing and connecting lines and masses and in the exaggerated sizes of details (for instance, artificial flowers ten feet in diameter floating on pools) he introduces quite new possibilities.

Until recent developments in Barcelona, however, one did not go to Europe for the most advanced ideas on the subject of lighting. The most important results had been worked out near Wilmington by Mr. Pierre du Pont, where, especially in his water theater, the constantly changing numbers, shapes and sizes of the fountains, lighted from beneath by constantly modulating color, were very much the finest that had been done, and are still the best on any private place, so far as I know. The great fountains at Barcelona are amazing as *tours de force*, but lack the interest that any public place lacks.

Another architect whose gardens were conspicuous in the 1925 Exposition was M. Mallet-Stevens. Like M. La Prade he is primarily an architect, yet he did the most talked-of garden there. This was largely because of his use of concrete trees. I have it on the authority of M. Forestier, who had a great deal to do with all phases of the landscape design, that the original intent was to have real trees trained and clipped to predetermined shapes. It was impossible to get just what

was required without more time and money than was available, yet something had to be done. Half a dozen minds and hands working together produced the concrete trees, and, unfortunately, at the same time, a norm by which unthinking people judged the whole effort as merely a trick on the part of artists to attract attention by eccentricity. As a matter of fact, with vines all over them, as was intended, the concrete trees would not be one whit less absurd than a Redcedar trunk with stubby branches sticking out in all directions to catch climbing roses which one can see in many a New England garden. M. Mallet-Stevens was also one of the first to develop marked vertical elements in his garden beds.

Even more startling in its geometrical forms, resulting in an utterly new quality and design in gardening, was the little triangular area developed by M. Guevrekian. As a matter of fact, this little place was chiefly interesting because of the frankness with which he tried experiments in color and material.

Everything was whipped into the severest of geometrical shapes. This makes the pattern three-dimensional rather than two-dimensional. Water in the pools lies at different levels. The beds are not flat, but pyramidal or tilted at various angles, so that the usual loss of interest in a flat pattern in perspective is minimized and a way indicated by which vertical dimensions may play a major part in future garden design. Materials whether water, concrete, earth, or plants are frankly used for their aid in carrying out the artist's idea. The mirror globe turning slowly to reflect lights is rather a night-club trick than a serious attempt at garden decoration. But it is completely successful in focusing the interest and relieving by its unexpected location what would otherwise be an altogether stiff pattern. Horticulture as such is important, not for the love of plants, but for what one can do with them.

M. Guevrekian designed one of the gardens at a villa in Hyères, designed by M. Mallet-Stevens, which is really remarkable. He is extremely modest about it, warning me that it is not to be considered typical in any way, but only a special solution of an exceptional problem. As a matter of fact, is this not true of all design? In this tiny triangular corner, M. Guevrekian felt that almost complete seclusion was desirable, because elsewhere from the villa glorious Mediterranean views lie spread before one in every direction. Here he wanted close enclosure and attention directed to artifice, yet without confinement. Converging walls and floor hold one tight yet as in a funnel, because, at the small end, the walls break down. Interest is concentrated in the outlet where a statue with strong outlines is silhouetted against the sky. Repeated vertical breaks in the checkerboard floor pattern are emphasized by pyramidal garden beds along the side walls. Looking from and toward the house (which lies at the base of the triangle), the effects are original and amusing. Here and there the garden beds climb right up the side walls on concrete supports. There is no slightest attempt at softening or modulation by vines or other horticultural qualifications. It is obvious that M. Guevrekian feels and visualizes, and hence designs in three dimensions. He thinks in terms of volume. In garden designers this ability is all too rare.

Another most interesting work by him is a small suburban house in Neuilly, surrounded by very limited ground. Everything is done in the modern manner, but with a restraint and charm that make it quite the most livable of the modernistic houses which I happened to see. From our point of view, it is particularly interesting, because, so far as I know, the first in which the roofs and terraces all over the house are designed as integral elements of the garden, whether on the ground or on the roof. On each floor are terraces outside the rooms. The uppermost level is for the children and there is even a tiny grass plot about six by twelve feet on the topmost roof with a shelter nearby for nurse and infant. In style and feeling it is as much a part of the garden as the pool outside the dining-room window. The ground garden on an axis which turns two corners is composed of several small areas, on slightly different levels sharply separated from one another by low barriers. In several places are other features which are frequently enough found to justify the term modernistic tendencies,—ceilings over parts of the garden areas supported from the building in the background practically without posts, so that one gets a strong sense of the garden boundary over one's head because of the contrast between such ceilings and, elsewhere, the open sky. This again emphasizes three-dimensional volume outdoors in buildings.

One of the important architects in the modern style is M. Le Corbusier. He has strikingly original ideas on the subject of planting and architecture, and has written interesting books on the subject of modern design, in which he particularly emphasizes the importance of thinking in terms of volume. In his gardens, however, he becomes banal. There is no evidence (save as an occasional use of the ceiling out of doors) that he considers that the volumes of garden areas and their surfaces would come under his own rules. To be sure, he makes odd patterns of concrete walks, which are pleasant, but they fail to tell because two-dimensional patterns fail always to tell in perspective interrupted by trees and bushes. Otherwise his solution of landscape problems by using new patterns is hardly different from what has been done elsewhere for centuries. It is only in his architecture and in problems where architecture and landscape meet that he is sure to find unusual solutions.

M. André Lurçat is a young man whose work is more and more in demand. He belongs to the contemporary school, yet is very far from being an extremist. At times his matter-of-fact use of the motives and elements that are emotionally combined by M. Le Corbusier, seems almost to lack originality. This is far from being the case. He solves his problems in his own way every time. Being young, and being born to the tradition, he uses the modern elements as part of his natural alphabet and lets it go at that. In his gardens, as with his buildings, he achieves picturesqueness through simple, yet careful, relation of all details. He makes use of the intimate relations between garden and house that is common in the best of the new buildings. He uses his terraces to plant on when there is no room on the ground. These terraces are integrated in the garden scheme. His patterns do not follow the old conventionalized lines, yet, on the other hand, they rarely show the more extreme complications of certain of the modernists.

Horticulture plays a large part in M. Lurçat's gardens, but the selection and arrangement show the utter lack of influence of our common English and American traditions of grouping and arranging plants. Even his vines grow in different patterns on the walls. In much of the modernistic work in France, one finds what would be expected,—that in the new, the French point of view with regard to the placing and importance of flowers and horticulture remains as in the old. When the new design becomes common with us, it is inevitable that our greater interest in plants and flowers will continue as in the past and mean quite a different racial use from what is seen in France. The same difference has existed always between old French and old American gardens.

Pierre Legrain died recently. He was perhaps the greatest loss that modern garden design could have suffered. We feel the importance of his influence mightily, although the bulk of his efforts turned rather to furniture, book bindings, and so on, than to gardens. We have the plan of one of his landscape designs, however, which is striking to the professional eye,—indeed, as a study in abstract design, to any one. In general layout and details the best tradition in garden design is clearly evident, yet new blood courses through it all. The position of the long walk next the building might be inspired by our own Colonial prototypes. A small semicircular front yard lies before the house. Behind is a house terrace, and below it an open lawn well enclosed. From the description alone it might be the most ordinary of American suburban designs,—certainly nothing bizarre or untraditional in spirit, even to us. Yet how unexpected in detail! The long path neatly hedged in on one side is cut in triangles across the way. The semicircular front lawn is no new thing. Nothing new in the rear lawn,—nothing save the relation of the parts and the use of what we formerly called formal elements arranged in occult unsymmetrical balance. In fact, the most arresting feature is the manner in which the main axis of the composition has been shattered and the cross axes diminished. It looks like the beginning of an animated movie, and we expect each part to walk over to its familiar place; bias lines to straighten, the old order to return, habit to be satisfied, and boredom enthroned. The surest proof of the life in this design is its power to provoke again and again question and answer, "Why?" and "Why not?" Balance is achieved, new relations are established, and the dead axis of the past has come to elusive vibrant life. We are made to think and to feel whence must come understanding.

13–1

Thorbjörn Andersson holds a master's degree from the University of Agricultural Sciences in Alnarp, Sweden, and is the founding editor of *Utblick Landskap,* the National Review of Swedish Landscape Architecture. He maintains his professional base at the office of FFNS Architects.

13–2

13–3

13–4

An often-published landscape photograph shows a certain park, its framework of oak trees apparently several hundred years old. Other aspects of the landscape suggest that this is not just any natural meadow. A man-made pond dominates the photograph's composition; children splash joyfully in the water. A girl sits on a bench in the shade of a tree's leafy canopy, watching the scene, gently rocking her infant brother in a baby buggy. In the background, apartment houses tell us that this is not a country scene but a real-life stage set in an inhabited quarter, possibly an urban neighborhood of significant population density. On first viewing the scene appears unspectacular, but in spite of its simplicity it conveys a remarkable ambience of tranquility and harmony.

The photograph, which shows the children's pond in Fredhäll, Stockholm, was taken in 1946 by the well-known Swedish photographer K. W. Gullers. Almost single-handedly, this picture secured an international reputation for the so-called Stockholm School of park design, which was to become famous among landscape architects the world over. Rarely before had park designers worked in such an informal manner, creating actual country landscapes in the middle of the city. Seldom before had landscape architects so consciously decided to take nature's own expressions as their artistic point of departure.

Although the Stockholm School at times appears similar in form to the English landscape garden, the two have only limited characteristics in common. The eighteenth-century landscape garden emanated from the work of landscape painters and created a living three-dimensional painting from the two-dimensional dream of an artist. But the Stockholm School had little to do with an imaginary Arcadia, nor with design rules such as the "waving line of beauty."[1] Instead, it took its aesthetic point of departure from regionality; from the characteristics of the place as such; from the forms of the local landscape, which were then stylized and reinvested in the site. Its ideological base derived from political and social circumstance rather than from the academic minds of a wealthy elite, which explains why the designs of the Stockholm School always resulted in public parks, whereas the English landscape tradition first found its principal expression in gardens for the private use of a relatively small group of people.

In Sweden, the 1940s were a happy and optimistic time, a period of economic expansion and so-

---

13–1 The children's pond in Fredhall Stockholm, designed in 1937 by Oswald Almqvist. As the Director of the Department of Parks from 1936 to 1938, Almqvist established the lines for what would become the Stockholm School.
[K. W. Gullers, courtesy Nordic Museum]

13–2 The inland lake with forested hills,
13–3 the birch grove, and the
13–4 archipelago were some of the landscape archetypes that the Stockholm School collected inspiration from.
[Thorbjörn Andersson]

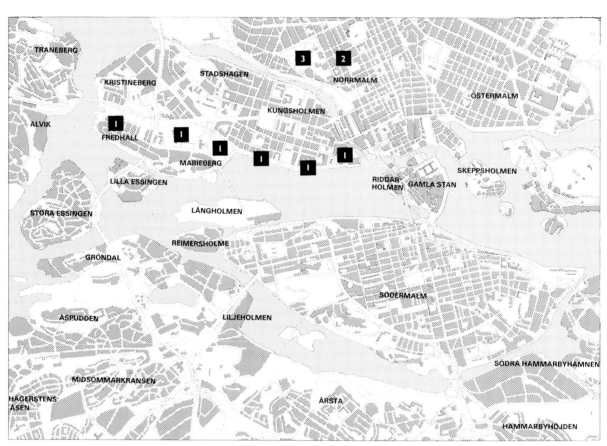

13–5

13–5 Map of Stockholm showing locations of parks designed by Erik Glemme
(1) Rålambshovsparken with Norr Mälarstrand. The linear park stretches from Fredhäll in the western outskirts of the city to the terrace garden fronting the centrally located City Hall. (2) Tegnérlunden, originally an 1890s park, modeled by Glemme in 1941. (3) Vasaparken, remodeled by Glemme in 1947.

13–6

13–7

13–6   Hagaparken
Stockholm (1781–1786), by
Fredrik Magnus Piper. An
internationally known park in the
English landscape style.
[Thorbjörn Andersson]

13–7   Drottningholm
West of Stockholm, by Nicodemus
Tessin the Younger (1681). This is
a formal garden in the French
baroque style. The palace and
garden are now the permanent
residence of the royal family.
[Thorbjörn Andersson]

ciety's belief in the promise of the future. The
country had been spared from the ravages of war
and was thus given a chance to lay the cornerstone
of what was to become known as the "Swedish
model": a welfare state whose aim was to benefit
the ordinary citizen. With only very few interrup-
tions, the Social Democratic Party had enjoyed a
strong majority in the Swedish parliament since
1917, and thus possessed the power to promulgate
ideas and laws that affected society on all levels, including the making of landscape architecture. The
functionalist movement in Scandinavian architecture—and landscape architecture—stood at the
peak of its popularity, driven by a considerably
stronger political ideology than its counterparts in
the United States. In Sweden, functionalism was
more than an architectural style; it was a gospel
and a scheme for building a society.

In spite of its progressive social program,
which would influence many international proposals
for postwar society, Sweden remains a remote
country of small population, geographically removed
from most of the world. Thanks to the Gulf Stream,
the climate is comparatively mild despite its northern latitude, making possible a long tradition of
landscape architecture. Sweden possesses at least
one baroque garden of international fame, namely
Drottningholm, some fifteen kilometers west of
Stockholm on Lake Mälaren. Nicodemus Tessin the
Younger, who designed the chateau as well as the
garden (c. 1681), is known as one of the more tal-
ented disciples of André Le Nôtre, and Drottningholm is regarded as his largest and most important
work. The estate was given all the typical features
of the French baroque garden: allées, star-shaped
bosks, box parterres, and cascades, all symmetri-
cally organized along a central axis. In addition, one
of Europe's finest parks in the landscape style is
found in Haga, north of Stockholm, designed by
Fredrik Magnus Piper from 1781 to 1786. Piper returned from a five-year study assignment on the
Continent but spent the majority of his time in
Great Britain, where he was greatly influenced by
the park at Stourhead. He designed the park at
Haga as the setting for a new chateau planned as a
country residence for King Gustav III. Although
major projects such as Hagaparken and Drottningholm acquired recognition in Europe and Scandina-
via, neither of these classic parks displayed the
same originality or importance as the parks of
Stockholm School, realized during the 1940s and
1950s. In spite of the skill with which they were designed, the parks at both Drottningholm and Haga
followed international styles rather than creating
new ones.

During the eighteenth century, France
provided the prototype for Swedish cultural life,
and French was the language spoken in the royal
salons. In spite of this early French cultural hege-
mony, however, Swedish parks of the late nineteenth and early twentieth century were heavily
influenced by German tradition. In a time of stylistic uncertainty in garden art, the geographical

proximity to Germany, with Denmark serving as a bridge, was sufficient reason for Swedish landscape designers to adopt the patterns of their neighbors in the south. Among garden historians the German tradition, often executed by gardeners or amateurs, is considered aesthetically to be a degenerate branch of the English landscape garden.[2] Maintaining the social pattern of the late nineteenth century, parks from the early decades of this century were intended as strolling grounds for the bourgeoisie. The design language was coerced by a fascination with geometrical patterns expressed in undulating paths determined by the templates of the designers rather than the contour of the landscape. Stress was also placed upon the horticultural expressions of individual plant specimens. The features of these parks were often contrived and sentimental to a point of parody, with replicas of antique sculptures and ready-made ruins made to populate the planted landscape. The design of the parks mirrored a bourgeois political system nearing its end; the functionalist park on the other hand came to express a social system at its birth.

During the first decades of this century, Swedish landscape designers were commonly trained in Germany, due to the lack of professional educational programs in their own country.[3] The impetus to change the prevailing static language came not from the entrenched landscape profession but from design professionals in other fields. From the beginning of the 1910s Rutger Sernander (1866–1944), professor of botany at Uppsala University, began to argue for a new type of park more in accord with the form of the existing landscape. For example, Sernander criticized the design for St. Erik's park in Stockholm (1918) for its lack of attention to the natural assets of the site: "Such careless intrusions [upon the land] deprive the future [citizens] of existing natural values that can not be recreated."[4] Sernander promoted the creation of a stylized landscape of pasture and grove that integrated the features of the local landscape with plant material sympathetic to the existing characteristics of the site. Parks following Sernander's model were created on the outskirts of Uppsala, for example Stadsskogen (1916). But only when it took root in the middle of urban Stockholm did this park idea find acceptance—and heavy protests—among Swedish landscape architects.

Sernander was not the only person to protest against the rigidity of contemporary park planning. Lorentz Bolin (1887–1972), a well-known cultural personality and an enthusiastic and prolific author on landscape topics, declared his love for meadow and pasture late in his life (1947):

We have now endeavored to let nature slip into the city again, after times when we tried to destroy most of it. Stockholm can serve as an illustration of this attitude, although this city is not a representative terminator of nature's values, thanks to its given beauty, its extraordinary location, and the assets of many open watercourses that preserve much of the landscape's originality

and freshness. However, only during the most recent times has there been a firm intention to let nature blossom in the pastures and meadows within the city's environs. Nowhere else is this more visible than along the Norr Mälarstrand shoreline promenade.[5]

Norr Mälarstrand is a long, narrow waterfront park that connects without interruption the inner city of Stockholm with its perimeter. It is the masterpiece of all Stockholm parks from the period. It was constructed on what had been, practically speaking, wasteland, and in this respect the park and its designer actually refuted Sernander's words about the impossibility of recreating naturelike settings in the city.

Erik Lundberg was Professor of Garden Art at the Royal Institute of Technology in Stockholm, where a certain Erik Glemme also served as a tutor. Lundberg has described the ideas that underlay the designs of the Stockholm School in unrivaled clarity, and in so doing he simultaneously defined the very basis of the functionalist movement:

We have two clues to go by when it comes to realizing the full potential of beauty that lies within reach for the Art of the Garden. One of them is to listen to the possibilities of the place, to care for what may already exist, to enhance these aspects through emphasis and simplification, to augment the allure of natural beauty by picking and choosing. The other clue is always to return to the practical demands and requests that are the purpose of the work as a whole: What do we want to obtain? How is life going to be lived at the chosen spot? What comforts, recreation, and pleasures are to be won in this, our paradise-to-be?

These are the two positions one has to acknowledge when examining design work. Each landscape design has to issue from its own internal conditions. It is these conditions that challenge the designer, through inherent difficulties and hidden possibilities, to find the right solution for any particular assignment.[6]

William Kent had seen that "all nature was a garden," as Horace Walpole wrote in the middle of the eighteenth century. The functionalist park movement in 1930s Sweden inverted this dictum, rephrasing it as "all gardens are nature." But it was not just any nature; neither was a garden any surviving natural area spared from exploitation. The sites selected for the new parks were often inaccessible marshlands or rough, mountainous terrain at first perceived to be of little recreational value. The designers of the Stockholm School recreated, in enhanced form, features of the regional landscape within the city parks: the rocky terrain of the archipelago, the aromatic pine forest, the flowering meadows, deciduous groves, forest ponds, and mountain streams. These and other natural landscape ingredients served as the natural archetypes to be reformed and reestablished within the context of the urban park. The city's buildings and parks were thus cast in a fruitful dialogue, a dialogue that in time came itself to constitute the city body and that elevated the urban fabric of central Stockholm to the beautiful state in which most parts still remain.

In the early postwar years, the profession of landscape architecture in Sweden was structured differently than it is today. Many cities had powerful park departments whose own landscape architects were given the responsibility for almost all the important design work. A strong organization was necessary to implement the new ideas, ideas that in fact constituted a radical change of direction in Swedish landscape design. Strong political connections were also necessary for influencing decision makers to allocate the necessary funding. Several cities tried to take the step, among them Malmö, Karlskoga, and Uppsala. But the city with the strongest personalities and the most explicit design and planning strategy was the capital: Stockholm. The first to establish the new design method was Oswald Almqvist, an architect with visions and ambitions, Director of the Stockholm Department of Parks from 1936 to 1938. During his short term in office Almqvist established a firm foundation for what would follow in later years. Pushing himself recklessly in order to transform conceptual ideas into reality, he vividly participated in all levels of the work at the park department. His interventions ranged from the design of a single park bench to formulating a greenbelt system for the entire metropolitan area. Almqvist's high ambitions and urge to personally handle all tasks in detail soon overwhelmed him and he repeatedly encountered trouble meeting project deadlines. Though he resigned after only a brief period as director, during his tenure a new era had begun. Almqvist was the first Director of Parks to formulate a cohesive park program of both broad policy and specific designs, and his ideas remained as guidelines for the activities of the Stockholm Park Department for many years thereafter.

The man who was to perpetuate Almqvist's ideas, refine them, and eventually instigate what was to be called the Stockholm School was Holger Blom. An architect with six years' work experience at the Office of City Planning in Stockholm and for Le Corbusier in Paris, Blom became the second youngest director of Stockholm parks when he assumed the office in 1938 at the age of 32. Blom remained director for an unprecedented term of 34 years, and when he retired in 1971 he could look back upon a life of achievement without equal in the history of Swedish landscape architecture. Blom was the perfect park director. He had a strategic talent that seldom failed him. He realized the importance of public relations and maintaining good connections with the press. He succeeded in attracting the ear of influential politicians and was extremely persuasive in arguing the case for excellence in park design. He was a smart negotiator when budget issues were discussed. He had energy and he had a goal.

13–8

13–8   Erik Glemme
May 27, 1905–January 20, 1959.

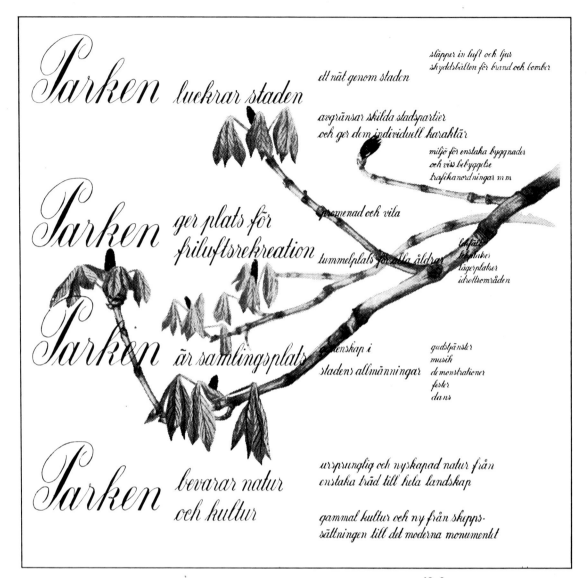

13–9

13–9 Holger Blom's park program as
condensed in one picture
This was often used as an
argument to persuade politicians.
The image clarifies in a simple
manner the more complex ideas of
the complete park program.

Blom also understood the need to employ able collegues, and many skilled landscape architects were given the opportunity to work under his directorship. Some of these would become major figures in Swedish landscape architecture, among them Sven A. Hermelin, Ulla Bodorff, Walter Bauer, and, possibly the most gifted among them all, Erik Glemme.[7] Glemme used his abundant ideas and design skill to transform the features of the local landscape into landscape architecture at the highest level.

Blom worked eagerly to realize his goals and make them visible. He refined the park program of his predecessor Almqvist, using it to increase the impact of urban parks on the lives of Stockholm's citizens. Blom condensed the complexities of the entire park program into one coherent picture that was provocative and easily grasped and communicated.[8] The picture he proposed was an artwork in itself, made to appeal to the public as well as to the politicians. The branches of a horse chestnut form the background for simple mottoes, written in elegant letters. The mottoes translate thus:

The park breaks up the unrelenting flow of urban construction. Taken as a group, parks can form a network in the urban fabric that provides citizens with necessary air and light. They can create borders between different parts of the city and provide each district with an individual character and identity.

The park offers to citizens of all ages space for recreation, for promenades and rest, for sport and play.

The park is a place in which to gather: for concerts, demonstrations, parties, dance, and even religious services.

The park preserves both nature and culture: existing nature and newly created; old traces of culture as well as modern additions.

Among other cultural institutions generated by Blom's scheme was the Park Theater, an ambulatory performance group sponsored by the city that traveled among the parks presenting plays in the summertime without charge. The Park Theater still exists five decades later, performing from May until September, moving their stage sets every night from park to park. The social program also offered supervised park play for children in day care centers open to all. Here, children could be left under the guidance of preschool teachers, or participate in the activities with their parents. Public art programs sponsored site-specific sculptures created by leading Swedish artists; these were set in appropriate landscape surroundings, improving the aesthetic qualities of the parks and squares. The Västertorp square, situated in the southern part of the metropolitan area, is a good example. On and around the square stands a collection of public art that any art museum would envy, from nationally renowned artists such as Bror Marklund to international celebrities such as Henry Moore.

The park program thus reflected the *Zeitgeist* of the era: the city was to be a truly democratic institution; the parks belonged to everyone. Although Blom never confessed any particular political leanings, his ideas were clearly sympathetic to those professed by Social Democratic politicians who held a firm majority in the city council. But a social and design program for the parks would have been of little value without a staff of highly skilled landscape architects to implement it. The Park Department, in fact, served as a nursery for ambitious young designers in Sweden who wanted to work with the best masters available. Erik Glemme, born 1905, had been hired by Almqvist in 1936. He remained at the Park Department as its chief designer until 1956, just a few years before his death. The unmistakable mark of Glemme's pencil lies behind most of the masterpieces that came to comprise the Stockholm School. The current Director of Parks, landscape architect Anders Sandberg, describes Glemme's accomplishment: "In very small areas, often at the scale of the miniature, Glemme created a very rich experience of nature, not just for the eye but an experience that affects all the senses and leads one to imagine a still deeper resonance at a point where the mind fails to find words to describe it."[9] Glemme had a natural facility for every task he undertook. As a personality he was somewhat shy and timid, but he tended to be easygoing nonetheless, and his weakness for the circus frequently appeared in his perspective drawings, which were often made with a festive air.[10]

If Glemme appeared to be a light-hearted pragmatist, he also possessed a mystical side. Interested in foreign philosophy and religion, he might sometimes blend exotic patterns with those of the locally derived Stockholm School—an odd mixture that strangely enough still worked. Glemme's interest in foreign cultures may have been the origin of his predilection for vivid ornamentation, which was otherwise close to a taboo during the functionalist era. His urge to sketch graffiti and abstract patterns was nearly pathological; on every scrap of paper, every cigarette package, and along the edge of every drawing were small and peculiar graphics from his pencil. One of his students at the School of Architecture and an eventual colleague, Torsten Grundberg, describes a situation that suggests the dimensions of Glemme's personality:

One lecture was introduced by an hour-long wait in complete darkness with maritime music as the only ambience. Our astonishment increased when a somewhat sleepy Harry Martinson entered the room and began to tell sailors' stories in his slow southern accent. Martinson finished by talking about the great sailing ships, comparing them to Gothic cathedrals. After an additional wait the sketch problem was distributed. We were to design a tattoo for the body.[11]

Stockholm has uncountable markings of Glemme's sensible elegance: from the design additions to Kungsträdgården, the city's most central and probably most important open space, to any little streetcorner arrangement in some suburb; from the cast iron ornaments of a staircase railing to the design of the conference table in the commissioners' room of the City Hall. Glemme sensed no borders between indoors and outdoors, or between the design of details and site planning. Four projects may illustrate the characteristic qualities of Glemme's work and of the Stockholm School: Norr Mälarstrand with Rålambshovsparken, the Tegnér Grove, and Vasa Park.

Norr Mälarstrand with Rålambshovsparken

The lakeshore promenade along Norr Mälarstrand is probably the most significant of all the Stockholm School projects. Less a single space than a sequence of parks, it forms one long green finger that stretches from wooded countryside to the heart of Stockholm, a green corridor that begins in Fredhäll on the western outskirts of the city and ends in the neoclassical garden terrace of City Hall. The promenade is about four kilometers long and runs undisturbed by any cross streets along its full length. At its starting point in Fredhäll, the scene of the photograph described earlier, the pond beneath the crooked oak trees appears as a natural setting that one could easily encounter when hiking in the surrounding countryside. Moving toward the city, one eventually reaches Rålambshovsparken, which meets the waters of Lake Mälaren in a spectacular way. Vegetation and other landscape elements are pushed toward the perimeter of the space, creating an open center that joins the vast sheet of water that is Lake Mälaren's surface. On the south side, a stylized forest pond accompanies a huge amphitheater for public gatherings, concerts, and plays. The theater, which holds 5,000 people, has a rustic air, with seats of wood and with boulders and low pine shrubs used as transitions between the angled rows. In materials and arrangement the amphitheater reflects the elements of the archipelago landscape outside Stockholm.

The highway that crosses the site at the entrance to Rålambshovsparken is elevated on columns some 65 feet (20 meters) above park level to avoid any conflict between traffic and pedestrians and to promote visual transparency. At the opposite point, Rålambshovsparken narrows quickly into what becomes Norr Mälarstrand, a park strip containing a world of features although never more than 40 feet in width. This slender segment of the park includes a softly curving footpath, seats of various kinds, places to bask in the sun, boat landings, sculpture settings, bridges, ponds, a little café, playgrounds, and smaller garden rooms for individual meditation or a conversation in small groups. In places, Glemme pulls the shoreline into a loop and thus allows a small bay to break the path, only to traverse it with a slender bridge, allowing the stroller to experience the full presence of the water.

13–10

13–11

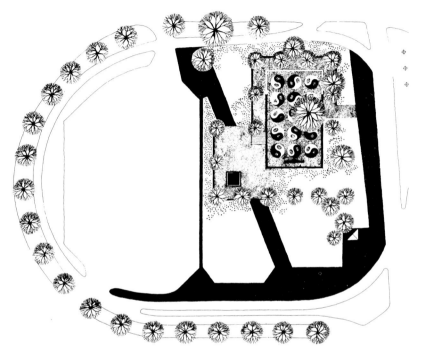

13–12

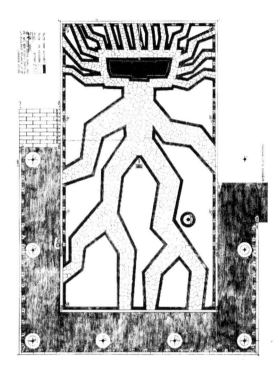

13–10 Section of Norr Mälarstrand looking
toward Rålambshovsparken
Stockholm, 1941. Perspective
sketch by Erik Glemme.

13–11 Proposal for an open-air theater in
Bellevue Park
Stockholm. Several open-air
theaters were built in the
Stockholm parks, fulfilling the
concept of the park as a social
place for parties and gatherings.
Perspective sketch by
Erik Glemme.

13–12 Proposal for Norra Bantorget
Stockholm, plan by Erik Glemme,
1950. The floor pattern at left,
where yin and yang symbols cover
the walled space, shows Glemme's
fascination with foreign cultures.
The plan at right shows the
situation as realized. Far Eastern
religion is switched to Nordic: the
stone pattern now depicts the tree
Yggdrasil, in medieval mythology a
symbol for the world.

13–13 Section of Norr Mälarstrand
Stockholm, designed in 1941–1943
by Erik Glemme on formerly
unusable ground. The narrow
lakeshore promenade winds
through clumps of hazel, birch, and
other native trees and shrubs. The
sandbox fence is designed in scale
with a child.
[C. G. Rosenberg]

13–14 The hop hut at Norr Mälarstrand
1941, by Erik Glemme. Hop poles,
common in Swedish farms where
the vine's flowers are used as a
spice in beer brewing, are here
used as an element of design. The
vine-covered poles create a
sloping, transparent roof over the
tiny walled space.

13–15 Plan of Rålambshovsparken and
Norr Mälarstrand
Designed by Oswald Almqvist and
Erik Glemme (1936–1953). This
park uses Lake Mälaren as a
backdrop to increase the sense of
the water landscape upon which
Stockholm is built.

13–13

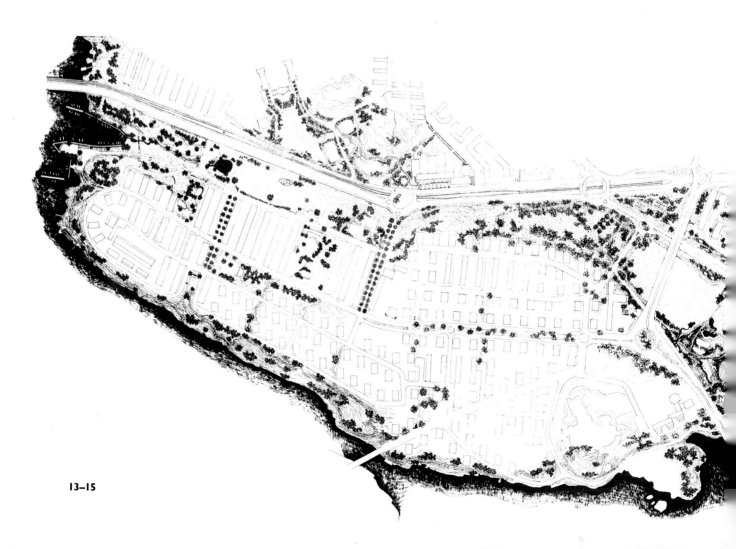

13–15

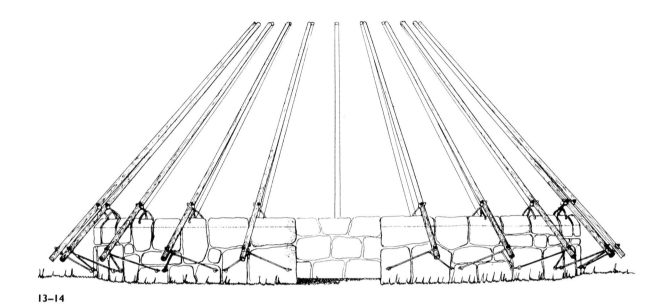

13–14

13-16   13-18

13-17

13–16 Norr Mälarstrand
Erik Glemme. Parks at this
northern latitude are bound to
have a meaningful winter aspect.
The shoreline café, in summertime
disguised in lush vegetation, steps
out to become a major viewpoint
once the leaves have fallen.
[Thorbjörn Andersson]

13–17 Norr Mälarstrand
To stress the presence of Lake
Mälaren—with a natural quality
that Glemme fully understood how
to use—the shoreline here was
curved inward to form a little bay
that breaks the route. Delicate
detailing, as shown in the bridge
railing, is characteristic of the
Stockholm School.
[Thorbjörn Andersson]

13–18 Detail from Norr Mälarstrand
Wooden platforms with benches
stretch out over Lake Mälaren to
form a series of splendid
viewpoints across the water.
[Thorbjörn Andersson]

13–19 Detail from Rålambshovsparken
The outdoor theater is frequently
used for concerts and plays.
Wood, boulders, and low pine
trees are used to blend the large
structure into the landscape.
[Thorbjörn Andersson]

Glemme regarded this lakeshore promenade
as only one edge of the park; its complement was
to be found on the opposite shore. In his mind, the
floor of the park was created by the water surface
itself, a recreational park that could be used for
swimming, boating, skating in the wintertime, ca-
noeing, windsurfing, and fishing—the favorite leisure activities of Stockholmers. Norr Mälarstrand
is transformed into a stone quay as it approaches
the central city and culminates in one of Stockholm's more delicate outdoor spaces, the garden
terrace on the south side of the stolid City Hall.[12]
Norr Mälarstrand was built from 1941 to 1943,
when Europe was closed to Sweden by the war.
Perhaps this imposed isolation catalyzed the call for
a thoroughly regional landscape architecture. In
Norr Mälarstrand, not only its very idea but every
single straw and herb is of native origin.

13–19

13–20

The Tegnér Grove

The Tegnér Grove, one of the so-called mountain parks, lies embedded in tight urban development, located in rough terrain deemed impossible to use for building purposes. The design history of the site dates from the 1890s, and its form clearly mirrored the ideals of this past time when Glemme began remodeling it in 1941. At that time, the park had a rather formal layout crossed by a complicated geometrical system of footpaths; it was a handsome park but not very useful, although it possessed a solid structure formed by mature trees. A renovation of the park landscape was seen as the answer to contemporary demands that the park should serve primarily as a social spot, providing opportunities for play and recreation. Glemme reduced the footpath system in order to increase the areas of turf and added small secluded corners to give character to this formerly rather anonymous landscape. The hilly terrain of the Tegnér Grove has two significant peaks, one near the center of the site and the other to the east. On the latter was placed the Strindberg monument[13] by Carl Eldh, one of the group of artists with whom Glemme frequently collaborated. On the other peak Glemme situated a small pavilion. Beneath its six-cornered shingle roof, surrounded by a circle of lindens, a small spring was created. The pavilion also serves to mark the most important viewpoint of the park. Water from the spring spills into a lively brook that bounces down the hillside, held in place by rounded boulders and surrounded by water-loving perennials. The falling water finds its place of rest in two pools built with curving shorelines, disposed on two levels.

The Blossom Garden was an invention of the Stockholm School and was implemented for the first time here in the Tegnér Grove. As formulated by its designers, the idea was to create a small garden room with a large variety of flowering shrubs, perennials, and herbs that blossomed through all the seasons of the year. In its form, it reacted against earlier attitudes that planted few species of plants formally composed in extensive flower beds in order to create a mass effect. A second idea behind the Blossom Garden was to inspire visitors with practices they might use in their own gardens, or simply to provide a surrogate for those citizens who could not create a garden of their own. The pergola and benches were built in round timber, a wood-building tradition drawn from the anthroposophic movement, with which Glemme had ties.[14] The Tegnér Grove demonstrates Glemme's ability to read and transform the existing qualities of a given site. By restricting his design efforts to a few spots in the park where they would have the strongest impact, he succeeded in enhancing the character of the existing park, improving both its aesthetic impression and its possibilities for use.

13–20   The Tegnér Grove
Stockholm, remodeled by Erik Glemme in 1941. The man-made run of water takes different aspects along its length: the spurting spring beneath the pavilion; the trickling brook; and eventually the quiet pool at the foot of the hill.
[C. G. Rosenberg]

13–21   Plan of the Tegnér Grove
The additions to this nineteenth-century park were essentially three: the shingle-roofed pavilion with its spring and brook, the blossom garden, and the Strindberg monument.

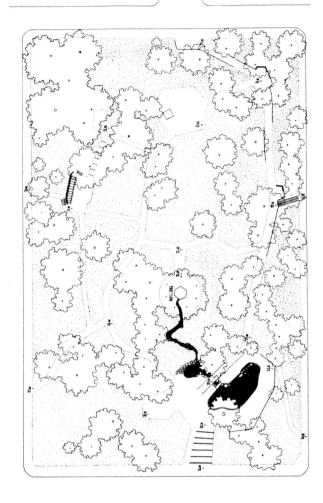

13–21

Vasa Park

The large Vasa Park, laid out in one of Stockholm's most densely populated areas, dates from the turn of the century. This district of Stockholm is plotted on an orthogonal grid; the park fills four square blocks, or about 12 acres (5 hectares). The park's eastern side is rather flat and open, with trees that frame a slightly sunken lawn area used as a playing field. In contrast to this sunny openness, the shaded western part is more hilly, with jagged rock outcroppings and thick vegetation. The main walkway in this wilder part leads through what can best be described as a canyon that ends in a steep cliff. This western edge of the Vasa Park was demolished in the beginning of the 1940s when the new street of Torsgatan was cut through the rock. Heavy blasting work was required, leaving in its wake an untreated wall, 65 feet (20 meters) high, as an exposed scar. It was Erik Glemme's task to heal this wounded segment of the park, and it resulted in one of his most intricate works, the Rock Gardens in Vasaparken, begun in 1947.

Glemme's strategy was to play the antagonists against each other. A strict geometrical pattern of three square shapes was situated with an almost chaotic, demolished landscape. The park's small-scale square rock gardens confronted the huge face of the blasted cliff, while the tranquility of the small, walled rooms engaged the dramatic wildness of the hilly site.

The exposed hillside, a few pine trees, and a considerable heap of blasted rock were the available resources and what were taken as the main ingredients for executing the design. Glemme started his work by establishing a new frontier against the intrusive moat of Torsgatan. A low wall of worked stone almost 300 feet (100 meters) long was built on the extreme edge of the park to establish a firm and precise border. The wall ends in a little curved bastion from which one gains an excellent view over the traffic below, which in the 1940s was still regarded as an attraction rather than a liability. Behind the wall, and all along the hillside, extend black rocks arranged to form paths and steps while creating a landscape scene slightly rough and mystical.

The three rock gardens rise from this disturbed slope, straight-edged and orderly, contrasting with the nearly complete irregularity of the landscape. The rock gardens are placed on three different levels to emphasize the slope of the site; perfectly square in shape, they are a man-made geometrical form inserted into the rugged landscape. The exterior faces of their granite boundary walls are left irregular, whereas their insides are surfaced with a concrete facing that rises above the outside granite as slender double columns supporting a series of horizontal beams. These beams as a group suggest a roofline that contributes to the feeling of enclosure within the terrace, a feeling reinforced by the climbing vines that cover the vertical columns. The largest of the three rock gardens, still no more than 40 by 40 feet (12 by 12 meters), is also the most subtle. Its floor is nothing less than

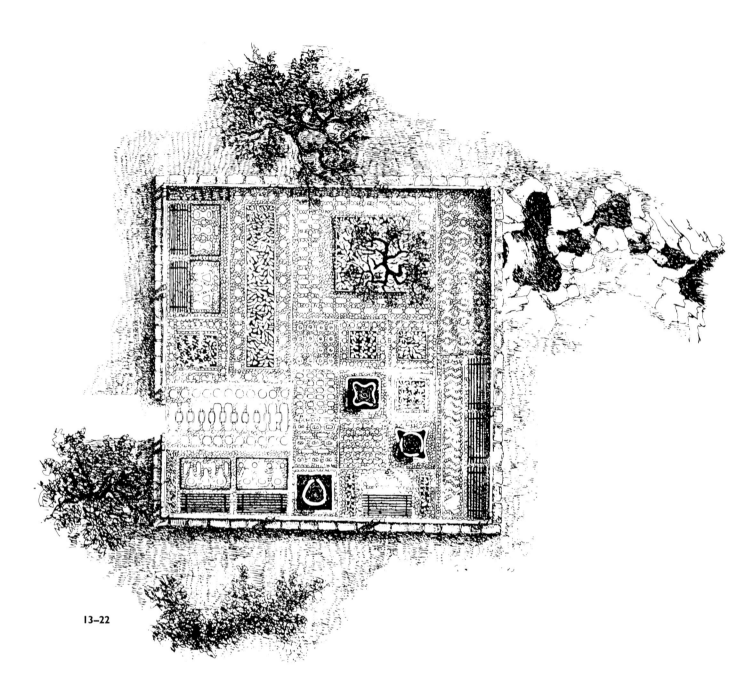

13–22

fasad mot söder

a graphic artwork of high complexity, executed in tailor-made precast concrete slabs in varying shapes, divided by lines of pebbles. A group of three fountains replaces the stonework in front of the park benches. Water again, but with a different temper, also springs from the outside of the boundary wall and continues as a creek down the hillside. One of Glemme's sources of inspiration for the project was the enclosed monastic garden of medieval times, and a similar calm is found here in the uppermost rock garden, adjacent to a natural hillside which it helps to render more dramatic.

***

In every work by Glemme's hand one can trace the humanistic attitude he applied to the task of design. Truly convinced of the social significance of his work, his vocabulary varied from the organic to the mathematical; regardless of the specific form, it was always carried through with temperance, variation, and social concern. For Glemme, the fascination of landscape architecture resulted from the experience of the soul as well as the senses.

The Stockholm School emerged in a golden moment in the history of landscape architecture in Sweden. It was a powerful moment because professionals as diverse as landscape architects, city planners, botanists, cultural geographers, and nature conservationists for once shared the same basic belief, in spite of their varied backgrounds. In this respect, the Stockholm School was more a synthesis of ideas than a single conception. Nevertheless, this conception of a landscape within the city became the strongest contribution that Sweden has made to the course of landscape architecture.[15] Moments of equal strength do not occur very often and have not been seen in Swedish landscape architecture either before or since that time.

Over time, the work of the Stockholm School lost much of its boldness. The peak years were from 1936 to 1958, when the International Federation of Landscape Architects congress was held in Stockholm.[16] After 1958, the decline became more apparent, a dissolution also felt in other aspects of Swedish society; the happy days had reached an end. In the beginning of the 1960s thousands of Swedes migrated to Stockholm and other urban centers for better job opportunities. A political program was adopted whose specific aim was to build one million apartment units in the short period of ten years—an extremely high building pace by Swedish standards. The goal was achieved, but the price for this achievement was the typical semi-urban zone of monotonous suburbs constructed in cheap, prefabricated materials. Landscape architecture also suffered from these so-called rational production methods. The preexisting characteristics of the landscape, for example, were eliminated in order to provide easy access for construction cranes. And the new landscape consisted of vast deserts of grass—good for maintenance if poor for the people—and rationally organized playgrounds designed

13–23

13–22 Plan of the central piece of the three cliff gardens in Vasa Park Drawn in 1947 by Glemme. The small formal garden dramatizes its natural setting. The intricate stone pattern reveals the designer's interest in ornament.

13–23 The cliff gardens in Vasa Park Stockholm. This was an addition to the nineteenth-century park, designed by Glemme in 1947. The worked stone walls are put in dialogue with the natural shapes of the raw cliff.
[C. G. Rosenberg]

13–24

in the manner of the straight line. In the heart of the city radical interventions took their toll. The Klara quarter, a dense downtown district, charming but troubled by sanitary problems, was torn down to the last brick; the ridge that Klara once climbed was leveled in favor of what was considered a flat, modern city. And there it now stands, with bank palaces, office buildings, and desolate, windy plazas. The demolition of the Klara district is often considered something like the urbanistic crime of the century, and both landscape architects and architects must carry their share of the blame. These persons were, in many cases, the same design professionals who only a decade earlier had seen the Stockholm School at its apex. The new, late modernist direction that replaced a regional sensibility was, ironically enough, true to the teachings of Holger Blom's former master Le Corbusier: to tear down the old, to reject local traditions, to regard the city as a machine. It worked, significantly, in complete ignorance of the potential in the landscape.[17]

In spite of this later decline in the quality of the Stockholm parks, several of the best examples of Glemme's work and that of others of the Stockholm School still exist to be seen. Their vegetation has now reached maturity, their open spaces are preserved; Stockholmers of today benefit from a unique intersection of design talent and opportunity, many would say the apex of Swedish landscape design.

13–24 Plan of the western part of Vasa Park
The cliff gardens are shown in the lower right corner. The dotted lines are sight lines, connecting important sections of the park. Glemme thus felt free to use a design tradition derived from the eighteenth-century landscape garden.

Notes

The author wishes to express his gratitude to Marc Treib who has helped revise and edit the text, and who has been critical in a most supportive way. The photos by C. G. Rosenberg and K. W. Gullers are published through the courtesy of the Park Department of Stockholm, the Museum of Nordic Culture, Stockholm, and the Museum of Swedish Architecture, Stockholm. Susanne Nylén prepared the manuscript.

1 William Hogarth, *Analysis of Beauty* (1753).

2 Christopher Thacker, *The History of Gardens* (London: Croom Helm, 1979).

3 The first training program in landscape architecture in Sweden was started in 1933 in Alnarp with Sven A. Hermelin as teacher. The program received academic status in 1960.

4 Rutger Sernander, *Stockholms Natur* (Uppsala: Almqvist & Wicksell, 1926).

5 Lorenz Bolin, *Vackert och fult i det svenska landskapet. Städernas exempel* (The Beautiful and the Ugly in the Swedish Landscape: The Example of the Cities) (Helsingfors: Tilgmanns Tryckeri, 1947); and Lorenz Bolin, *Det föränderliga landskapet* (The Changing Landscape) (Linköping: Studiefrämjandet, 1969).

6 Erik Lundberg, *Trädgårdskonst* (Garden Art) (Stockholm: Natur och Kultur, 1948).

7 Walter Bauer, born 1912, is a landscape architect who has gained an international reputation for his restorations of historical gardens. Among his more well-known projects are the restorations of Gunnebo, Mölndal (1949) and Drottningholm, Stockholm (1969). See Walter Bauer, *Parker, trädgårdar, landskap* (Parks, Gardens and Landscapes) (Lund: Signum, 1990).
     Sven A. Hermelin (1900–1984) was a leading landscape ar-

chitect in private practice from the 1930s to 1970s. Important works by Hermelin include the Marabou Park, Sundbyberg (1937–1943) and Grevagården, Karlskrona (1975). See *Utblick Landskap,* no. 1/85.
     Ulla Bodorff (1913–1982) was the first woman landscape architect in Sweden to maintain a private practice (1937). Her most important project is Reimersholme, Stockholm (1942–1946). See *Utblick Landskap,* no. 3/89.

8 Holger Blom, "Gröna ytor i Stockholm" (Green Spaces in Stockholm), *Byggmästaren,* no. 16/46.

9 Anders Sandberg, "Landskapet i staden" (The Landscape in the City), *Utblick Landskap,* no. 2/88.

10 Glemme lectured on circuses at the Royal Institute of Technology, talking not only about the tent as a structure but also about light, music, and clowns.

11 Torsten Grundberg, "Med naturlig lätthet" (With Natural Grace), *Utblick Landskap,* no. 2/88. Harry Martinson (1904–1978) was a Swedish novelist and playwright; he was a Nobel laureate in literature in 1974.

12 Ragnar Östberg (1866–1945), architect and Professor at the Royal Academy of Arts, Stockholm, designed the City Hall (1911–1923) in what has been termed the national romantic style.

13 August Strindberg (1849–1912) was a Swedish novelist and playwright.

14 The anthroposophic movement was founded by the Austrian writer Rudolf Steiner in 1913. The Swedish branch of the movement developed a strong consciousness for landscape design. During the period that Glemme taught at the Royal Institute of Technology he often chose the anthroposoph Erik Vesterberg as his assistant.

15 In the 1964 catalogue accompanying an exhibition at the Museum of Modern Art in New York, Sweden's contribution is divided between the Stockholm parks and Gunnar Asplund and Sigurd Lewerentz's Woodland Cemetery in Enskede (1915–1940). Carl Milles's Millesgården on Lidingö island is the sole additional project, represented by a single image. Elizabeth Kassler, *Modern Gardens in the Landscape* (New York: Museum of Modern Art, 1964; revised edition, 1984).

16 City Commissioner Yngve Larsson made a study tour to the United States in 1936. He returned enthusiastic about American park design as carried out by Frederick Law Olmsted, among others. Larsson's impressions possibly helped trigger the Stockholm School. For instance, both the "emerald necklace" of Olmsted's parks in Boston and Central Park in New York use greenbelt zones to structure the city—as does the Stockholm School.

17 When Le Corbusier participated in a city planning competition for downtown Stockholm (Norrmalm) in 1933, his question to the jury was which buildings should be *spared* from demolition—an unusual, if ironic, attitude toward this historical city for the time. Le Corbusier's entry allowed only half a dozen structures to remain, the Royal Castle and the Opera House among them.

14

This essay addresses some moments in the dialogue of modern landscape architecture with its past; it grew out of an invitation to consider some verbal statements of professional landscape architects.[1] One of the most conspicuous themes to emerge from a scrutiny of those published pronouncements was an uneasy and uncertain knowledge of historical developments in landscape architecture at that very moment—the late eighteenth century—that constituted the watershed of modernism.

At the center of any modernist art form is likely to be articulated that art's relationship with its own past; this is true at whatever period a modernism is studied—for let us not forget that while "modernism" is a term habitually reserved for a certain phase of twentieth-century culture, there have been earlier moments of similar modernist self-consciousness (consider, for instance, the Italian Renaissance or the early eighteenth-century English garden). Any modernism has always wanted at the same time to "Make it new"—as Ezra Pound's slogan had it—and to execute complicated treaties with its predecessors: complicated by Judas-like denial, studied neglect, disrespectful and slighting allusions, cavalier or irresponsible borrowings, or inventive reworking. But I think it is true to say that the historical traces were always a strong presence, even if they were taken to be a threat, a challenge, or a tedious bore, as they have also been at the center of any good critical assessment of them. If you made it new, you had to know a deal about the old. Indeed, an anxiety of influence (to use the now-famous title of Harold Bloom's book) is one of the very subjects or obsessions of modernism, more substantially even, albeit less explicitly, than in postmodernism.[2]

Now one of the most striking aspects of modern landscape architecture is its ignorance of history. When Mrs. Bliss inaugurated her program of studies in landscape architecture at Dumbarton Oaks in the 1960s she planned to entice practitioners to learn about the history of their discipline; only when she discovered they were not interested did she open the program to historians. Landscape architecture in Europe and the United States has come to its phase of modernist self-consciousness very late, long after some of the other arts. Maybe in this belated discovery of modernist zeal it was difficult not to confuse knowledge of history with historicist design which it rightly wished to reject.

John Dixon Hunt is Academic Advisor to the Oak Spring Garden Library in Upperville, Virginia, editor of the *Journal of Garden History,* and the author of *Gardens and the Picturesque* (1992). He was previously Director of Studies in Landscape Architecture at Dumbarton Oaks.

One particular moment of history that Anglo-American modernist landscape architecture should perhaps have taken on board, but which—in its wholesale disregard of the past?—it did not, was a moment of French modernism.[3] In this it was strikingly dissimilar to the attitudes of T. S. Eliot and Ezra Pound, Americans whose serious and enthusiastic attention to modern French poetry transformed their own.

In all of this Christopher Tunnard is typically Anglo-Saxon, publishing his *Gardens in the Modern Landscape* in 1938 with a ludicrously cavalier treatment of history. This included an ambiguous and absurdly eclectic account of the English landscape garden, highlighting eccentric if interesting moments like the Painshill grotto in a photo essay and laying out the portraits of the eighteenth century's main gardeners—Kent, Brown, Repton—in unchronological order. His account of what he fondly calls "romanticism" was even more sloppy and useless.

This ignorance or cavalier disregard of history is part of a larger poverty of discourse. Of all the modern arts none has displayed such a meager command of analytical, including rudimentary philosophical, language as landscape studies. Steven R. Krog is surely right when he stigmatizes landscape architecture as "a discipline in intellectual disarray," with a "deficiency of theoretical discourse."[4] Although I am concerned with some of the central English-language texts of landscape modernism—Fletcher Steele's, Percy S. Cane's, Christopher Tunnard's, and others—it is also worth noticing that this poverty of discourse is still widespread. What was one of the first attempts to codify landscape architecture modernism and is still kept in print, Elizabeth B. Kassler's *Modern Gardens and the Landscape* of 1964, evinced little historical discrimination.[5] This lack of critical sophistication in historical matters and in overall explanatory skills—the two are connected, of course, in the verbal inefficiency of explaining its place in history—is one of the reasons why landscape architecture has been a particularly inhospitable field for modernism.

The lack of historical knowledge per se is not, of course, worrisome: by all means ignore history, if you want to. But it is ill-advised to do so when you are engaged in formulating a modernist aesthetic that takes up its position vis-à-vis a past that is either grotesquely misrepresented or lamentably ill understood; or, perhaps, when you are at work in such an atavistic art as that of gardens. Again, one may accept that revolutions (and modernism has always seen itself in revolutionary terms) need to distort the past in order to clear enough space to do—and gain appreciation for—their own thing. But it is also arguable that the inadequacies of landscape architecture's historical grasp have also contrived that it fail to attend to essential *ideas* of garden and landscape.

The historical ignorance mostly concerns that watershed of landscape design, the late eighteenth century and early nineteenth. Since it was to England during that period around 1800 that the rest of Europe looked and to that time in England to which, say, A. J. Downing would look back in the United States, I shall focus upon England. The late eighteenth century was a watershed in landscape architecture for a variety of nonartistic reasons, and since then there has really been no comparable change in social, political, aesthetic, and psychological attitudes: we still exist in a world that was determined by what happened around 1800. Yve-Alain Bois has convincingly argued that "the rupture of modernity actually took place in the eighteenth century," a convincing dating that seems far more historically nuanced than the more usual ascription of the watershed to circa 1900.[6]

Let me state seven simple truths about that period that seem to be wholly obscured by modern landscape architecture writings.

First, garden design was quite suddenly taken up by a much increased section of the population. There had always been small gardens, vernacular plots, but now far more landowners than before had the chance to invoke fine-art treatment of their property; landscape architecture invaded the suburbs and their villas, the public park, the burial ground. As a consequence, not only did the amount of landscape design increase but now more kinds of design were called for (though not necessarily delivered). Further, with the work of Humphry Repton and John Claudius and Jane Loudon, the art of garden design with all its new modes and styles was codified and broadcast through printed texts and journals (by contrast, their two foremost predecessors, William Kent and "Capability" Brown, had issued no theoretical or practical texts).

Secondly, this considerable growth in the gardening public coincided with a breakdown of the public claims of the fine arts (to which landscape gardening at that time aspired). This breakdown as it concerns painting has been set out recently by John Barrell;[7] his admirable and cogent account should be studied by everyone interested in seeing why, quite suddenly toward the end of the eighteenth century, many arts gave up their service to some general, collective public will and fragmented into instances of personal expression. This certainly includes the art of garden design.

Third, what Barrell explains in political, ideological ways may be tracked also in terms of psychology. The legacy of John Locke throughout the eighteenth century[8] culminated in the romantic privileging of the individual. Each man or woman could enjoy—nay, could only have—his or her own perspective, mental set, sensibility, and (by extension) response to everything around them, including gardens, parks, and the wilderness. This latter became fashionable precisely because it occasioned highly personal experiences of sublime *frissons* in opposition to the old socially engineered and sanctioned attitudes available within landscape parks and gardens.

Fourth, at the moment of the social expansion of landscape architecture, freed of its public art functions and now appealing to and encouraging the taste of whomever chose to invoke it, style became available as if in some mail order catalogue. Style for the generation of early landscape gardenists—those who designed Castle Howard, Stowe, Stourhead, among others—had been a matter of ideology; medium was message.[9] When William Kent featured Gothic (what we may now term "Gothick") and/or classical buildings, he was able to assume that for a small circle of cognoscenti their codes were readable. Forty years on, Humphry Repton did not encode his architectural styles; instead he offered his clients straightforward visual options. Style was, quite suddenly, simply a formal choice, and if say "Gothick" had meanings, or more likely something as vague as associations, these were local, personal, and not obviously encoded in the visible style.

My fifth point is a consequence of this diversity of styles, Chinese, Turkish, classical, Gothic (and within the picturesque camp you could also opt for models in the style of Claude, Dughet, Poussin, Teniers, or Hobbema, and so on).[10] Given also the surrender by the arts of any viable public role, taste became a term each person constructed for himself or herself. Whereas in the early eighteenth century the invocation of Taste largely still meant the taste

of a small elite, confident and secure about its values (political, social, and aesthetic), now it was a notion up for grabs. Journalists vied to convince readers that their aesthetics and taste were right, but a community of right judgment in these matters had become a matter of opinion and fashion. Eclecticism of styles—the Victorian garden was a splendid exhibition ground of this—joined with an eclecticism of taste, visual values, and notions of what was beautiful in landscape architecture. We still inhabit this world of relative taste.

Sixthly, the landscape architect could no longer count upon any normative value for Nature. Everybody now had their version of nature, just like the formal eclecticism we have canvassed. From the Renaissance to, say, Alexander Pope, though the term *Nature* had a congeries of meanings there was some agreement about their interpretation. And equally, when garden design sought to represent nature there was some unanimity as to what was being represented and how. By 1800 the word *Nature*—always a portmanteau term—was invoked by different individuals or social groups for varied purposes. Even in the limited meaning of the physical world of earth, water, vegetation, and so on, different natures were possible depending, perhaps chiefly, upon the situation of the speaker. Nature had always taken its meaning in some structural relationship with other concepts—hence, I think, that tripartite arrangement of sixteenth- and seventeenth-century gardens where three distinct areas presented different ratios of control to wilderness.[11] But by 1800 its possible meaning had enlarged precisely according to the alternative structures opened to human experience: if somebody had traveled, say, through the Alps, they had a standard of "nature" quite different from somebody who had never left the Home Counties.[12] We can explain the different emphases of Uvedale Price and Richard Payne Knight in the picturesque controversy at the end of the eighteenth century precisely by the relative wildness of their estates, Foxley and Downton. We still live with this structuralist determination of nature: to say that a person craves the wilderness depends very much where on the scale of urban-rural-primeval that person is habitually situated.

The picturesque in its heyday around 1800 was one way of coping with this various and fluid natural world "out there." Whatever the small print of its seemingly interminable debates—precisely those journalistic skirmishes to win public support for one particular point of view noticed above—its main concern was how to process the unmediated wild world, how to control it or make it palatable for consumption by sanitizing it with art. Given different needs, the picturesque could invoke different styles of picture to format the raw materials of the natural scene. If you were more timorous, Claude or a homely Dutch style would serve; stronger spirits could find nature via Ruisdael or Salvator Rosa; but whatever you did, nature out there was recycled for civilized use and consumption.

One further aspect of the picturesque concerns this discussion. It became programmatically opposed to other styles: to the so-called formal or regular styles of garden design, most obviously; but also even to the most refined vision of the landscape garden, the Capability Brown representation of natural materials in their ideal, perfected forms. These were deemed too bare, too boring, largely because their aesthetic purpose was lost to sight. In their place was promoted the fuzzy, busy, colorful, endlessly textured picturesque. Long since denuded of the older assumption that picture meant human story, a strenuous version of the picturesque in which the likes of Alexander Pope and William Kent had still believed,[13] the picturesque from around 1800 to this very day became the style to fill any landscape vacuum. Just as picturesque taste had been popularized by invoking the busy texture of engravings, where lines and scratches must fill all the surface of the image, so the picturesque in garden design has crammed space with materials, kept the eye endlessly busy. Even when, say, in England the National Trust is bold enough to restore something of an old formal or regular garden, they cannot resist (or they cannot disappoint a public that seems to crave) picturesque distraction from clean geometry.

Now, how do these radical alterations of the theory and practice of landscape architecture around 1800 affect or fail to affect the pronouncements of modern design? In the most general terms, few writers appreciated that those alterations were significant or indeed that they had even taken placed when they did (circa 1800); further, it does not seem to have been realized that these cultural changes were significantly orchestrated by nonartistic factors. Let me try, as far as possible, to address the modernist stance vis-à-vis the seven specific points already canvassed (some of the

seven overlapped anyway and will be further elided now).

An obsession with one kind of garden—basically the English landscape garden of the upper and middling landed gentry—seems to have prevented theory from addressing the many other types of site that the modern world has called for since that watershed of 1800. The grounds of some English country estate provided the model for all nineteenth-century developments: the cemetery, the public park, the golf course. And the fixation on that one type doubtless partly explains some of the great missed opportunities of the twentieth century—airports, the highways, the railroad.[14] Messrs Eckbo, Kiley, and Rose did discuss the new possibilities of school and other community landscaping, urban spaces, and wilderness parks in a series of articles in the *Architectural Record* of 1939 (reprinted in this volume), and in so doing they were effectively aiming to recover the lost ground of art's dedication to politics that John Barrell has shown was abandoned by the early nineteenth century. But British writers like Percy Cane and Tunnard were still locked into thinking of landscape design as a question of private house + garden + (almost certainly) a larger terrain. It never occurred to them to ask whether all modern clients or projects can indeed be treated like English Georgian squirearchy; indeed, there is a telling rebuke to Tunnard by Fletcher Steele in 1942 when the expatriate Englishman is urged to get to know the vernacular American way of life better before he sounds off on ideal design.[15]

Yet more astonishing have been the bungled responses to the essential privatization of art experience. Whether that is traced, as John Barrell does, to the breakdown of a public, political role for the arts, or to psychological and epistemological causes, the 1800 watershed meant, at its simplest, that no imagery—whether medium or message—could be counted upon to have a wide, shared, public appeal. There were many causes of this, many effects, none of which seem to have registered in the literature of landscape architecture.

One effect, as early even as 1800, was that designers abandoned meaning for medium. Individual clients during the nineteenth century could prescribe some local, private iconography; public park authorities in northern British cities also worried about what popular imagery was apt. But design largely retreated to matters of style. And because it did not address the question of what meanings were possible within garden space, modernist landscape architecture, such as it was, sidetracked itself by coveting the formal effects of other arts rather than considering what its own medium could achieve.[16] An example, indeed, would be Guevrekian's Garden of Water and Light of 1925. Fascinated with the formal properties of flat cubist geometry and yielding an exciting design on paper, Guevrekian yet loses on the ground the essential experience of analytical cubism. He is perhaps an extreme example of that strange and widespread tendency to substitute modernism of graphic presentation for modernist content. (A study urgently needed is how the modernist presentation of drawings was or was not adequately translated into three-dimensional structures.)

Another professional bias toward medium at the expense of message is an obsession with materials, especially modern ones; this was most notable in the frequent irritation with the lack of cooperation from plant materials. These biases, together with merely formal debates for and against axes, for or against "picturesque," ensured that designers circled without daring to grasp the whole business of meaning in gardens. The problems of meaning in modern gardens are not negligible, not the least of them being the very meaning of "meaning," which deserves an essay in itself.[17] However, what I intend by the term is not just sensual pleasure from colors and forms, but experience that is susceptible to and translatable into a discourse also available in other zones of human culture. That such experience may often receive verbal expression perhaps explains Fletcher Steele's typical refusal of what he oddly called "literary content" in design.[18] Yet despite the absurdities of much belletristic commentary that the modernists were right to distance themselves from—typical of which is the suggestion that meanings be researched in "the small cottage gardens of Renaissance Europe"[19]— the verbal articulation of meaning in a garden alerts one to a range of experience that concentration upon mere forms wholly marginalized.

From 1800 each person notionally, even ideologically, felt free to register his or her own meaning, to do his or her own thing, and indeed probably did want something unique after the manner of the really brave spirits of romanticism. Yet what prevented a marvelous flourishing of ad hoc, idiosyncratic, or vernacular gardens was the nervous

bourgeois temperament that wanted to do the right thing, that wanted to know whether the gardening periodicals authorized this or that. Gardening, in short, had entered the consumer society. An immediate consequence was the pervasion of bland uniformity of design: keeping up with the Joneses meant looking like the Joneses and sharing their values and meanings. Exceptions, predictably, were the occasional independent-minded Victorian, perhaps some new, northern industrialist who had the guts to go the whole hog and have what he wanted and damn taste or public opinion.[20] *Plus ça change, plus c'est la même chose:* this uniformity of mass-produced taste and its corollary, the bizarre but infinitely more refreshing juxtaposition of divergent individual tastes, have been everywhere apparent. And we should note that, while beauty continues to be a source of appeal, there is little consensus on aesthetics—if you find yourselves in agreement with somebody about a beautiful design, this happy accident can be explained in more cases than not by a shared class background or education rather than by any examinable philosophical criteria. Maybe if there was a more determined attempt to study and debate aesthetic questions, modern landscape architecture would benefit.[21]

Modern designs, perhaps to escape this double bind of solipsistic meanings and judgments, have insisted both upon design as problem solving and specifically upon designing for groups or the community. These were, and still are, the shibboleths of modernism. Fletcher Steele in 1941 wrote that "from kindergarten to old man's home, we join the crowd."[22] Eckbo, Kiley, and Rose in their 1939 articles were wholly concerned with community spaces; Tunnard in an article two years later turned toward this too, though not sufficiently to placate the American zeal of Fletcher Steele. Yet modern designers have not sufficiently bothered to find out what people really want of private or public gardens.[23] Granted that meanings (significances, cultural topics) that pleased and enthralled late eighteenth-century garden users have lost relevance, it cannot be beyond the wit of man or woman to establish a new agenda of meanings for the garden, an agenda that offers plurality, variety, and not simply formal maneuvers. Some of these meanings, I know, will be long established, archetypal if you like: it is a topic that I do not have time to explore here. Yet none of the modernists writing about garden design in the 1930s and 1940s bothered to confront this aspect of their subject and some even tried to eliminate long-standing gardenist experience. Sometimes blending with, sometimes striking out independently of archetypal experience, other meanings will be local, either geographically or politically. Some of the most intriguing recent designs that I have seen recently exploit locality—whether Warren T. Byrd's Virginia tidewater garden, Terrance Harkness's midwestern plains or the wild horses of Williams Square, Las Colinas, Texas; or, the intricate proposals for the new Tuileries that Bernard Lassus has conceived out of a strongly poetic attention to that one site.[24]

As far as modern private gardens are concerned, there seems little escape from the sterility of homogenized, packaged "good taste." It takes a bold patron to strike out. The theorists of the 1930s and 1940s never dreamed either that public and private imagery might be radically different from each other or that one feasible modernist strategy was to let every person really do their own thing. Fletcher Steele invoked the American vernacular to admonish the immigrant Tunnard, but he himself never took up that radical challenge.[25] Even Tunnard actually allowed as how "gardening, after all, is one of the oldest of the folk arts," but seemed unable to do anything with that strikingly modernist perception.[26]

Fleeing from problems of meaning, modernists have relied almost exclusively upon the discussion of formal or stylistic effects. A special feature of this use = form equation, though it gives the illusion of a quest for meaning, is the call to designers to discover the "innermost idea" of plant materials,[27] a strange romantic obsession that we may actually track from Linnaeus to Blake and Erasmus Darwin, to Ruskin, Hopkins, and James Joyce. This romantic quest for *quidditas* (inherent thingness or quality) had underpinned Clive Bell's zest for significant form, which Fletcher Steele triumphantly cites;[28] but in practice it abandons any philosophical rigor to slide quickly into a concentration upon formal elements, perhaps the most striking and depressing feature of modernist landscape architecture writing.[29]

This is of course a direct legacy of post-1800 emphases, but it ignores a whole chapter of previous garden history in which style was informed by content or meaning. In the first edition of *Gardens in the Modern Landscape,* Tunnard could attack rightly the "medley of styles" in the nineteenth cen-

tury without registering how it had come about or what the plethora of styles represented (what, if you like, they encoded); yet in the preface to his second edition he actually pleaded for eclecticism of styles, still without pausing to ask about their cultural basis or determination, even though he had somewhat enhanced his treatment of Victorian design.[30] In the same year as Tunnard's first edition, 1938, James C. Rose found abstract art his best inspiration in landscape design simply because it addressed matters of style that were devoid of content.[31] Yet we might note that in other modernist arts, formal preoccupations did not neglect content: cubism or Pound's *Cantos,* for example, need a subject matter in order to explore new formal means. Perhaps the vitality of those arts is that medium and message once again were melded after some inert alliances of the late nineteenth century.

By limiting his backward glances to the nineteenth century at best (in his second edition)—the gestures toward the eighteenth century are still risible in 1948–Tunnard effectively cut himself off from considering the strategies of periods before what T. S. Eliot called the "dissociation of sensibility."[32] This disjunction separated not only form and content but thought and feeling, beauty and use. It is, indeed, striking, how that dissociation of sensibility was accepted uncritically by landscape architects: Fletcher Steele seems ignorant of the classically derived bonding of *utile* and *dolce* in Renaissance aesthetics.[33] Even the more historically and culturally experienced authors of the recent *Poetics of Gardens* completely misunderstand the seventeenth-century mind when they say of Oxford Botanical Garden that it was "made for the intellect rather than for the senses."[34]

The stress upon formal matters has been widespread, the rage against axes and symmetry particularly vociferous.[35] It occurs to none of these modernist writers to ask why axes and symmetry were invoked and on what occasions, what they articulated of human concerns and views (the notion, for example, that symmetry holds a deep appeal to the human mind is never raised, even by Fletcher Steele who objected strongly to Tunnard's rejection of the axis by invoking its native American precedents; he might have considered how its order suited a people struggling against a wild continent).[36] Such, indeed, is the fear of formality in any of its historical manifestations (and the shortsighted association of it simply with the Beaux-Arts traditions) that modernists have rather pinned their faith upon some version of picturesque, even though they should have spurned its messy and sentimental lures, rather than commit themselves to geometry. Christopher Tunnard was perhaps the shrewdest, rejecting both "picturesque or romantic effect" and "formal" or axial planning; but after discarding both suits of imperial clothes he was left naked and retreated to town planning and problem solving.

Essentially what a concentration upon formal matters has done is to bypass the whole matter of garden experience in its fullest emotional-imaginative-intellectual range. The authors of the recent *Poetics of Gardens* are to be congratulated for their insistence upon garden art involving "the emotions and mind of the spectator" in its creative process and upon gardens as memory theaters, exercise grounds for the "adventures of the imagination."[37] Otherwise, while we still hear much of design structure, of design vocabulary, the structure and syntax of garden experiences and significances (note the plurals) are missing. Again, this is a dismal legacy of 1800: eclecticism of styles marginalizes any consideration of how gardens appeal to their users and how creators/users express themselves or represent much of their total experience in gardens. The craze for picturesque, surprisingly (as I have noticed) not fully rejected by modernism, was also a dedication to the thin end of that particular cult, to its formal qualities and not to the careful blend of mental associations with visual stimuli that had marked its heyday.

Landscape architecture needs to recover a desire and a capability of addressing experience. It need not be a question of iconography, though that is an obvious way forward and one that I will not take up here. More subtly, we need to recover a sense of gardens as expressions or representations[38] of a culture's position vis-à-vis nature. This was not lost after 1800, though it always tended to get submerged beneath stylistic concerns. Personally, I find uncongenial what has been called the "born-again language of fundamentalist ecology."[39] But it is a dominant aspect of our culture and its expression in garden art may come to be judged as *the* mark of this phase of contemporary gardening.

But one of the serious disabilities of the ecological tradition from William Robinson's *The Wild Garden* of 1870 to Ian McHarg's *Design with Nature* of 1969 and beyond is that it failed to expose a fallacy it inherited from that 1800 watershed. The fallacy consists in our supposedly being offered a choice between nature and art; yet these are not at loggerheads, and they derive their meanings in terms of each other, in structural tension that differs at every period and in different countries. Nature is not a stable, objective norm against which art is assessed (and vice versa); rather each derives local and historical meaning from their relative places on a scale—a scale that after 1800 tended to be ad hoc, eclectic, idiosyncratic. Failing to register this, modernist landscape architectural theorists lost their way.

What we need to do is put back into our thinking a proper attention to where each individual instance of private or public landscape architecture locates itself in the discourse of culture vis-à-vis nature. In this context city gardens are a particularly vexed question. The needs of urban inhabitants have changed over the last two hundred years, as have the views of the authorities who decide what public parks and gardens are appropriate. These have been working-class escapes from urban oppression, or elegant promenades for the bourgeoisie.[40] And they become different experiences, even within cities, when density of population forces apartment blocks skyward and shrinks garden space to roof terrace or window box. They were different, too, and therefore occupied another point on the nature-culture scale, when more and more of urban populations had access, by road or television, to (let us call it) the wilderness. Man-made settings then seemed negligible or displayed, in a new structural tension with nature, either more artifice or more ambiguity. Perhaps where the modernists went wrong is that they tricked themselves, like all would-be modernists, into thinking it was a battle of past/art versus present/nature; in fact, it was another replay of nature (not versus but) vis-à-vis culture.[41]

Notes

1 Before the conference Modern Landscape Architecture [Re]Evaluated, Marc Treib circulated various texts to the speakers, inviting some response to them. I chose to do so directly, partly to draw upon my own literary training with texts, partly because it had always been with theoretical formulations of aesthetic and design principles that I had worked as a garden historian. Some of those texts are reprinted in this volume; others are cited in my notes.

2 As T. S. Eliot put it in his essay on "Tradition and the Individual Talent," our predecessors are "precisely . . . that which we know."

3 I am referring to cubist designs and some theory of the 1920s, on which see the forthcoming book on *The Modernist Garden in France* by Dorothée Imbert (New Haven: Yale University Press, 1993).

4 Steven R. Krog, "The Language of Modern," *Landscape Architecture* 75, no. 2 (1985), 56.

5 For instance, her biased and overgeneralized notion of Renaissance and baroque aesthetics—"man's triumph over nature" (p. 5)—or her characterization of the nature/art dialectic in the English landscape garden (pp. 9ff.). See also Garrett Eckbo's brief paragraph on eighteenth-century garden designs in his "Pilgrim's Progress" (published in the present volume).

6 Yve-Alain Bois, "A Picturesque Stroll around Clara-Clara," *October* 29 (1984), 61.

7 John Barrell, *The Political Theory of Painting from Reynolds to Hazlitt* (New Haven and London: Yale University Press, 1986).

8 See for an excellent account of this Ernest Tuveson, *The Imagination as a Means of Grace: Locke and the Aesthetics of Romanticism* (Berkeley and Los Angeles: University of California Press, 1960).

9 I have discussed this variously elsewhere: for a brief account see "Style and Idea in Anglo-Dutch Gardens," *Antiques* (December 1988), 1354–1361; for more extended accounts see either *Garden and Grove: The Italian Renaissance Garden in the English Imagination* (Princeton: Princeton University Press, 1986), especially chapter 11, or *William Kent: Landscape Garden Designer* (London: Zwemmers, 1987).

10 The availability of different models was a staple argument among the picturesque theorists: see the selection from Richard Payne Knight's poem *The Landscape*, reproduced in *The Genius of the Place*, John Dixon Hunt and Peter Willis (rev. ed., Cambridge: MIT Press, 1989), 342–344.

11 Shaftesbury's use of these descending orders of control in a garden is discussed by David Leatherbarrow, "Character, Geometry and Perspective: The Third Earl of Shaftesbury's Principles of Garden Design," *Journal of Garden History* 4 (1984), 332–358.

12 See, for example, George Cumberland at Hafod in picturesque Wales after his travels abroad, though interestingly his patriotism lets him adjust his scale to allow Welsh scenery still to be sublime: see his *An Attempt to Describe Hafod* (London, 1796), vi–vii.

13 See my essay "Ut Pictura Poesis, Ut Pictura Hortus, and the Picturesque," reprinted in *Gardens and the Picturesque: Studies in the History of Landscape Architecture* (Cambridge: MIT Press, 1992).

14 The neglect of railroad landscaping everywhere is one of the appalling failures of the profession, as Richard Schermerhorn noted in "Landscape Architecture—Its Future," *Landscape Architecture* 22 (1932), 286.

15 *Landscape Architecture* 32 (January 1942), 65: "but when Mr. Tunnard has been longer among us, when he has had time to acquaint himself with the people and the pattern of life in our villages and on our rich farms . . ." One of the few modernist voices to speak out against the model of the English landscape garden was, unsurprisingly, French: André Vera, in *Le Nouveau Jardin* (Paris, 1912), writes that he is against not the park but only "le Jardin paysager" (p. iii).

16 See Fletcher Steele eyeing the other modernist arts in *Landscape Architecture* 20 (1930), 161.

17 See the useful collection of essays addressing this essential topic, *The Meaning of Gardens*, edited by Mark Francis and Randolph T. Hester, Jr. (Cambridge: MIT Press, 1990), and the special issue of *Landscape Journal* 7, no. 2 (1988), guest-edited by Anne Whiston Spirn and entitled "Nature, Form, and Meaning." See also Sunderland Lyall, *Designing the New Landscape* (London: Thames and Hudson, 1991).

18 Fletcher Steele in *Landscape Architecture* 22 (1932), 301.

19 Ralph H. Griswold in ibid, p. 298: that the absurdity of this remark—the idea that "cottage gardens" were somehow a Renaissance style and not in fact invented by the romantic period—is still unappreciated is further indictment of a wholly inadequate sense of history in the profession. At the conference where a first version of this essay was read nobody thought Griswold's remark either odd or even funny.

20 Any casual survey of illustrations in recent books on Victorian gardening will quickly show that the order of the day was unadventurous uniformity, from which a few gloriously improbable examples stand out. See also Michael Waters, *The Garden in Victorian Literature* (Aldershot: Scolar Press, 1988).

21 I notice that Laurie Olin also seems to make the same plea indirectly when he criticizes the current "anti-cultural stance that eschews aesthetic concerns" (*Landscape Journal* 7 [1988], 150).

22 Fletcher Steele, "Private Delight and the Communal Ideal," *Landscape Architecture* 31 (January 1941), 70. To which one might reply, with E. M. Forster, that we are also born alone and die alone. See also Steele in the same journal, 22 (1932), 299.

23 Compare the research that has been done into how people want their office spaces designed, which is by no means the same as getting users to do the designing. However, see the excellent results of Mark Francis's research, an interim report of which makes heartening reading: *Gardens in the Mind and in the Heart: Some Meanings of the Norwegian Garden* (Center for Design Research, University of California, Davis, 1989).

24 Bernard Lassus et al., *Le Jardin des Tuileries de Bernard Lassus* (London: The Coracle Press, 1991).

25 See Robin Karson, *Fletcher Steele, Landscape Architect: An Account of the Gardenmaker's Life, 1885–1971* (New York: Harry N. Abrams/Saga Press, 1989).

26 "Modern Gardens for Modern Houses: Reflections on Current Trends in Landscape Design," *Landscape Architecture* 32 (January 1942), 58.

27 Kassler, *Modern Gardens*, p. 14. Where else but in landscape architecture theory would an appeal to "the 'back to nature' philosophy of Rousseau" have seemed adequate intellectual history, as it did to James C. Rose, "Freedom in the Garden: A Contemporary Approach in Landscape Design," *Pencil Points* (October 1938), 643.

Even the far more cogent essays of Eckbo, Kiley, and Rose in the *Architectural Record* of 1939 and 1940 are flawed by showing little depth of history—what is "new" to them is often déjà vu to a longer historical perspective. I continue to be struck by the inadequacy of their historical thinking—I am grateful, though, to Garrett Eckbo for sending me the text that he did not choose to read at the Berkeley conference but which is printed here. For readers of this volume I would locate our substantial difference of position in his lumping together of "history, tradition, and a preconceived vocabulary" (see Garrett Eckbo, "Pilgrim's Progress," below): to know history and tradition does not necessitate preconditions.

28 Fletcher Steele in *Landscape Architecture* 20 (1930), 162.

29 See, for instance, James C. Rose, "Freedom in the Garden," *Pencil Points* (October 1938), 639ff.

30 See Lance Neckar, "Strident Modernism/Ambivalent Reconsiderations: Christopher Tunnard's Gardens in the Modern Landscape," *Journal of Garden History* 10 (1990), 237–246.

31 Yet he claims that "style evolves naturally from the subjective" without pausing to ask what informs style: Rose, "Freedom in the Garden," 642.

32 Eliot addressed these matters in his 1921 essay "The Metaphysical Poets." See also the entry on "dissociation of sensibility" in the *Princeton Encyclopedia of Poetry and Poetics* (enlarged ed., 1974), 195–196.

33 See the fuzzy thinking on this theme in his "Fine Art in Landscape Architecture," *Landscape Architecture* 34 (1934), mainly pp. 177–178. It is perhaps the very brevity of his essay (was this supposed to be in a functional, modernist spirit?) that disables his

thinking. It is a fault, incidentally, that continues to disturb much current writing on landscape design.

34 Charles W. Moore, William J. Mitchell, and William Turnbull, Jr., *The Poetics of Gardens* (Cambridge: MIT Press, 1988), 113.

35 A whole article could and should be written about the modernist obsession with axes: Fletcher Steele is muddled and ambiguous in his attitudes (see *Landscape Architecture* 20 [1930], 177), Ralph H. Griswold sentimentally hostile to straight lines laid on a rolling landscape (what else is Vaux-le-Vicomte?)—ibid., 22 [1932], 294), and so on. See also in this volume Garrett Eckbo's castigation of axial design as "arbitrary habit," surely a blind refusal to recognize a deep-seated human need for various kinds of order.

36 This is a point well made by Barbara Sarudy in her discussion of eighteenth-century gardens of the Chesapeake: see *Journal of Garden History* 9, no. 3 (1989), passim.

37 Moore, Mitchell, and Turnbull, *Poetics of Gardens,* 81, 217, and 188 among other places.

38 Laurie Olin calls this "translation": see *Landscape Journal* 7 (1988), 149 (abstract).

39 Ibid., 150.

40 For brief glimpses of these perspectives see J. C. N. Forestier, *Gardens* (New York, 1924), 8, 11; Garrett Eckbo, *Landscape for Living* (New York: F. W. Dodge, 1950), foreword; and Ian McHarg's account of his childhood as a preamble to *Design with Nature* (Garden City, N.Y.: Natural History Press, 1969).

41 These complicated matters are taken up in my *The Greater Perfection: A Theory of Gardens,* to be published in 1993 by Thames and Hudson.

15

15–1

*1940   September. . . . Halprin
reads Christopher Tunnard's book,*
Gardens in the Modern Landscape
*. . . and becomes aware of the signifi-
cance of design in the environment.
Decides on the spot to study design in
architecture, with emphasis on landscape design.*

Lawrence Halprin: Changing Places,
1986

Lance M. Neckar is Associate Professor of
Landscape Architecture at the University
of Minnesota and a practicing landscape
architect. His research interests include
American and early modern landscape
design, and their application to
contemporary practice.

When Christopher Tunnard (1910–1979) completed
Gardens in the Modern Landscape in 1938, he led
the way to a "brave new world of landscape."[1] Certainly modernist gardens had been designed and
constructed in the previous decade, but little had
been written in the English language to suggest
that there was a bona fide way of thinking about the
garden in the context of modern conditions. In his
book Tunnard put forward three approaches to the
problem of the modern garden: the functional, the
empathic, and the artistic. He executed landscape
architectural commissions in England in the late
1930s for several modestly scaled country houses,
attempting to apply his approaches as experimental
formal devices in this traditional realm of British
garden design. He further suggested that landscape
architecture, in order to be a potent problem-solv-
ing agent in the modern world, must transcend its
confining historical and horticultural conditions and
move into the wider landscape. He had ties to the
architectural community, particularly architect
Raymond McGrath and the Modern Architectural
Research (MARS) Group. The MARS Group, Britain's contingent of the Congrès Internationaux
d'Architecture Moderne (CIAM), focused on social
problem solving through design and planning, and
specifically concentrated on the interwar housing
problem.[2]

Tunnard's ideas detonated the accepted nineteenth-century canons of the arts and crafts garden
and the residual gardenesque in England, and the
blast reverberated across the Atlantic. Tunnard
himself emigrated to the United States in 1939 to
teach amid the modernist experimentation initiated
at the Harvard Graduate School of Design by Walter Gropius, himself only recently emigrated from
Germany via England. By direct exposure and the
osmotic learning inherent in the studio method,
young designers who would dominate the modernist scene of postwar America absorbed the three
approaches. The result was a rich profusion of
modernist work at virtually every scale. In 1945 he
became an assistant professor of city planning at
Yale University, and although he taught a course in
landscape architecture, he himself had leapt the
garden wall into a broader landscape. With him he
brought the difficult baggage of history and horticulture, burdens with which he had wrestled in England and would continue to wrestle for the
duration of his later career in the United States.

The Making of a Modernist: The Three Approaches

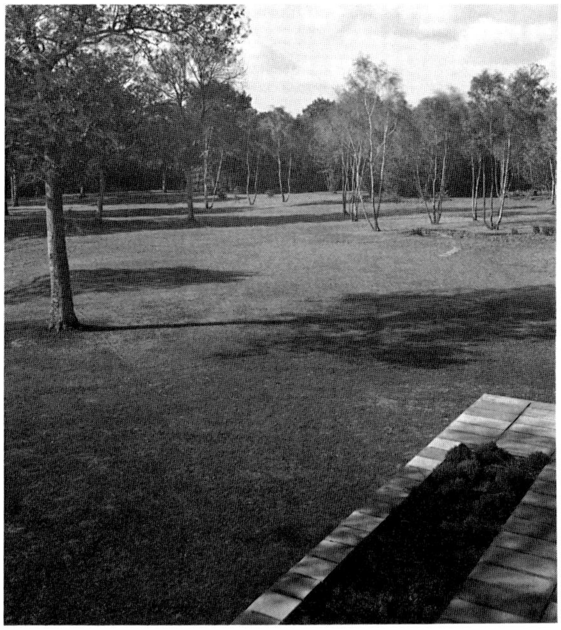

15–2

Tunnard was born in Victoria, British Columbia, Canada. He received his advanced education at Victoria College, University of British Columbia, and later at the College of the Royal Horticultural Society at Wisley, England (diploma, 1930) and the Westminster Technical Institute, England, where he took building construction courses in 1932. From 1932 to 1935 he was a garden and site planner in the London office of Percy S. Cane, one of the preeminent garden designers in the arts and crafts tradition of Gertrude Jekyll, Thomas Mawson, J. D. Sedding, and others.[3] Cane, who thought of his work as "modern," was responsible for inculcating a kit of design ideas from which Tunnard would later draw freely, keeping and embellishing some and disdainfully discarding others as passé. For example, with Cane he shared an admiration for the Japanese garden.[4] Many of Tunnard's ideas about the empathic merely elevated Cane's understanding of Japanese gardens to the level of an approach. Both scorned the fussy gaudiness of the Victorian garden, but Tunnard was quick to break from Cane's neomedieval idea of the garden for the modern world.

Within a year of his independence from Cane, Tunnard had become closely embroiled with the avant-garde in modern British art and architecture.[5] In 1937, with several projects under way in his office, he initiated the series of articles in *Architectural Review* that would be recast the following year as *Gardens in the Modern Landscape.*[6] In the book Tunnard hit upon the idea of the three approaches (functional, empathic, and artistic) as a way of organizing his developing thoughts into a synthetic modern landscape aesthetic. Looking back today, we may find that the approaches derived almost entirely from contemporary ideas in art and architecture, as did most of the gardens that Tunnard used to illustrate their application in the book. Regardless of their derivative character, images of these gardens served to jolt the polite English garden.[7] The work of Jean Canneel-Claes in Belgium and the iconic Hyères garden in France, designed by Gabriel Guevrekian, had already inspired similar minimalist and "boxed" schemes in Britain by architects A. E. Powell and Oliver Hill.[8] The modernist social agenda had been expressed in a few landscape schemes for multiunit developments such as Frank-

15–1 Bentley Wood
Halland, Sussex. A prospect of the house in its landscape setting, including the thinned wood.
[Dell and Wainwright, courtesy *Architectural Review*]

15–2 Bentley Wood
Halland, Sussex. The thinned woods.
[Dell and Wainwright, courtesy *Architectural Review*]

furt-Römerstadt, Neubühl near Zurich, and Garrett Eckbo's early work for the Farm Security Administration camps in Texas. Tunnard also admired the well-publicized scheme for Bos Park in Amsterdam, a project that he saw as the quintessential functionalist recreation grounds.

In Tunnard's mind, function was the fundamental consideration of the modernist garden. The functional became the overarching approach of the three. Derived directly from his reading of Adolf Loos and Le Corbusier, functionalism in the garden would free landscape design from sentimentalism and romantic nature worship to satisfy rational human needs such as "rest and recreation. [The functional garden was], in effect, the social conception of the garden."[9] Tunnard's garden was rooted in a nonornamental aesthetic, a crisp low-maintenance landscape that would enable social change via efficiency and ease of care. The question of using the garden for sustenance was less clearly addressed, since it was only modern to assume that means of mass production would, in fact, more satisfactorily put food on the table; yet the argument in favor of food directly at hand could hardly be denied, as some of Tunnard's design work demonstrated. Tunnard's functionalist approach can be clearly seen as a close relative of similar intentions in architecture, where formal and substantive design moves were made in the name of convenience and hygiene, such as in the Le Corbusier's Villa Savoye at Poissy, which was illustrated in the book.[10]

Functionalism's expressive handmaiden, the empathic, would necessarily be freed from formal tyrannies, particularly that of symmetry, so closely associated with the most despotic regimes of garden design. Tunnard encouraged experimentation with the compositional tool of occult balance.[11] Occult balance, for Tunnard, was, in part, a formal device for relating the designed landscape to the cubist and constructivist schemes of modern architects. In practice it could be applied to the landscape in either geometric or curvilinear schemes, but in no way, Tunnard cautioned, should it be seen as imitating the forms of nature. The empathic approach engaged nature on a completely different level of materials and their direct spiritual impact. He illustrated these ideas primarily with examples from Japanese gardens, especially the contemporary work of Sutemi Horiguchi.[12] Tunnard postulated empathic effects in a minimalist atmosphere where the landscape expressed itself directly through the placement of plants and stones, the management of contours, and the use of water.

This direct expressiveness was broadly related to trends in modern art, the third of the approaches.[13] Tunnard celebrated nonrepresentational art, especially sculpture. In the garden sculptural effect would convey the honesty of the materials by virtue of its nonrepresentational character. Even in the 1930s Tunnard (among others, including Gropius) realized that no one designer could fully comprehend the range of technologies necessary to build in the modern world. Socially responsible design would, therefore, be attained through collaboration among artists.[14] For Tunnard, such an art in the landscape would efface, once and for all, the disguises and lies of hobby gardeners, nurserymen, horticultural journalists, and contractors.[15] His examples of the artistic approach ranged broadly from the inclusion of modern sculpture in gardens to the appropriation of ideas from modern art in the making of architectonic space and form. Specific examples included the *objet vertu* works of British sculptor Paul Nash; the 1929 Barcelona Pavilion by Mies van der Rohe; experimental walls and garden sculptures from various French and German gardens; and the mysteriously unattributed Alexander Calder sculpture that appeared on the last page of his chapter entitled "Towards a New Technique" in *Gardens in the Modern Landscape*.[16]

The Approaches in the Landscape

Together with these examples, Tunnard put forward his own commissions as flashpoints for a modernist garden. The actual number of his projects in England between 1936 and 1939 was small, and it is, therefore, difficult to discuss this work chronologically as a body of developing ideas. Not only was the time period short, but the projects had interrupted and overlapping schedules that make their tracking, in the absence of office records, nearly impossible.[17] Probably more significant, in any event, were Tunnard's variations on the approaches as they became primers for his American readers and students. These designs, to a greater or lesser degree, also demonstrated the considerable hold that the tradition of garden design had on Tunnard. First, there was the matter of the unwelcome inheritance of the nineteenth-century scale of the garden itself (i.e., simultaneously too small and too big); second, there was the omnipresent and heavily accreted burden of British history; and finally, there was all of that excessively English horticulture. In theory, Tunnard broadly finessed these problems by appropriating a pre-nineteenth-century idea: the indeterminate edge of the eighteenth-century English landscape garden was, in its time, avowedly modern.[18] Tunnard embraced the wider scale of the contemporary landscape in a manner that made direct and indirect references to this other archetypally English garden. Even the title of his book bore the mark of this implicit recollection. By making what had once been conceptually modern again modern, he held at bay history and horticulture.

Bentley Wood, a house in Halland, Sussex, was designed in 1935 by architect Serge Chermayeff for his own occupancy.[19] When the design was presented to the Uckfield Rural District council in that year, the Council objected to its flat roof and clapboard facade. Pointing to the local precedents of brick and tile construction, the Council delayed the project for some time. Tunnard was brought onto the project to suggest a landscape setting for this bumptious house. Chermayeff and Tunnard

15–3

15–4

15–3 Bentley Wood
Halland, Sussex. The straight-on view shows the relationship between the house and the terrace.
[Dell and Wainwright, courtesy *Architectural Review*]

15–4 Bentley Wood
Halland, Sussex. The terrace and Moore's *Recumbent Figure,* gazing across the Downs.
[Dell and Wainwright, courtesy *Architectural Review*]

15–5

15–5   St. Ann's Hill
Chertsey. The aerial view that
shows the difficult junction
between the new house and the
stable and Dutch kitchen garden.
[courtesy RIBA Library]

used the period of delay to prepare the site. They thinned the dense woods that dominated one corner of the property and planted a color field of daffodils ranging from deep yellow in the foreground to near white in the rear.[20] While the color field reversal might be esteemed as a modernist painting of landscape, this design also shows Tunnard's debt to the eighteenth century in its control of larger landscape prospects. Yet the naturalizing of daffodils was an idea that undoubtedly could have been observed in any number of English gardens, and almost certainly at Kew, the botanic garden of the Royal Horticultural Society.[21]

The design of the terrace at Bentley Wood, illustrated in *Gardens in the Modern Landscape*, represented a direct and elegant expression of Tunnard's approaches. The extension of the interior dining space of the house through then-innovative sliding glass doors to a terrace of rectangular pavers expressed a spare functionalism. Walled on one side, the length of the terrace was terminated by a light, ten-part rectangular timber grid that enframed the changing prospect to the landscape beyond. Modern art had an explicit, if brief, presence in 1938. As the house was completed, Henry Moore's *Recumbent Figure* rested near the grid, on a plinth opposite the longitudinal wall and next to a short flight of steps.[22] By the following year, Chermayeff had resolved to emigrate to the United States, and he asked Moore to take the sculpture back. The photographs in *Architectural Review* and in Tunnard's book, however, show the figure distinctly in its position of occult balance, looking, in Moore's words, "out across a great sweep of the Downs, . . . her gaze gather[ing] in the horizon." Sensing the human role in the difficult connection between the hard-edged house and the resilient landscape, Moore added, "The sculpture . . . had its own identity and did not need to be on Chermayeff's terrace but it so to speak *enjoyed* being there, and I think it introduced a humanizing element. It became mediator between modern house and ageless land."[23]

The Bentley Wood scheme bore a striking resemblance to that portion of the January 1938 MARS Group exhibition devoted to the dwelling in the landscape. Under the banner "Architecture—Garden—Landscape" was a small terrace that terminated a long vista with an open frame. In words that might have been Tunnard's the exhibit text proclaimed: "The architecture of the house embraces the garden. House and garden coalesce, a single unit in the landscape."[24]

This difficult unity of house, garden, and the wider landscape would be the principal motif in the design of Tunnard's own dwelling, St. Ann's Hill, Chertsey (1936–1937).[25] The best documented of Tunnard's projects, indeed of any project in *Gardens in the Modern Landscape*, the house was designed by Australian architect Raymond McGrath. Built of reinforced concrete, it was conceived as an eroded cylinder with a highly fenestrated garden wing. The spaces made by the erosion of the pure

form became occasions for the sprawling terraces that edged, somewhat uncomfortably, the larger landscape. Tension with the accretion of history on the site was present in every prospect; the new scheme was overlaid upon a landscape that had developed from the late seventeenth century forward. In its more recent incarnations, the landscape bore the imprint of the mid-eighteenth-century designs in the manner of Capability Brown, or, according to Tunnard, Charles Hamilton, the landscape gardener of Painshill.[26] Tunnard grafted his new *parti* onto the older landscape and made it modern again by the new additions. Distant views of the house showed it to be a dramatic tour de force gesture in a mature and beautiful landscape, a gleaming machine in the garden.

Up close and in detail, however, the resistance of the approaches to the grafting process, at least in Tunnard's hand, revealed itself. The intellectual stiffness of the forced-perspective axial garden along the face of the wing was palpable. The ingredients—the open, prospect-rendering garden wing wall; a polite, almost unrecognizably asymmetrical layout; the honest chunk of Hopton stone floating, in defiance of gravity, in a not-quite-modern pool; the end wall, unfolding like a drawing rolled too tight—were all carefully placed. Another terrace leapt away from the house in a daring circling maneuver to flank the spread of a gigantic *Rhododendron ponticum*. Tunnard swept around this venerable clump of evergreen with a crescent-shaped terrace and pool that spilled uneasily over the sloping terrain, confined by its rigid planometric conception and denied the possibility of a looser biomorphic gesture that might have more deftly adapted the scheme to the landform. The unwieldy siting of the new house in relation to the existing buildings on the estate was only revealed in a few photographs of the project. Tunnard's inability (unwillingness?) to shed the burden of history reveals itself in a straight-on photograph of the house. The image shows the cupola of the old stable peaking over the wing of the new house like an uninvited country cousin. The preservation of the stable occasioned old and new, round and rectangular forms conjoining in an uncomfortable embrace in the entrance courtyard. Another formal anomaly is revealed only in the aerial photograph. The Dutch-inspired formal kitchen garden of the early eighteenth century was retained by Tunnard as part of the scheme but was not showcased as a modern resolution of the problem of sustenance, even though such gardens seemed to crop up again in his later projects. If today the landscape at St. Ann's Hill seems quintessentially British, dignified, momentarily dramatic, but ultimately reserved to the point of near dryness, in its time it was quite bold.

This project for his own house, more than any other, gives insights into Tunnard's personal aesthetic struggle (though this may not have been visible at the time, for Tunnard never identified St. Ann's Hill as his own house in any of the publications that featured it). By way of contrast, in *Gar-*

15–6

15–7

15–8

15–9

15–6 St. Ann's Hill
Chertsey. The house in the wider landscape from below the lower pool terrace.
[Robert Felton, courtesy Norman McGrath]

15–7 St. Ann's Hill
Chertsey. The straight-on view of the house, with the stable to the rear, reflected in the curving pool below.
[Robert Felton, courtesy Norman McGrath]

15–8 St. Ann's Hill
Chertsey. The architectonic terrace at the garden wing.
[Robert Felton, courtesy Norman McGrath]

15–9 St. Ann's Hill
Chertsey. The view from the roof terrace of the rhododendron and pool composition.
[Robert Felton, courtesy Norman McGrath]

15–10

15–10 **The Week-end House**
Cobham, Surrey. Probably an
unexecuted design, attributed by
Tunnard to Raymond McGrath.
[sketch by Gordon Cullen, from
Gardens, 72]

15–11 **Galby**
Leicestershire. The Dutch garden.
[sketch by Gordon Cullen, from
Gardens, 75]

15–12 **Galby**
Leicestershire. A Japanese effect
with water, stones, and plants.
[sketch by Gordon Cullen, from
Gardens, 91]

dens in the Modern Landscape he illustrated a small
project for a weekend house designed for a site in
Cobham, Surrey. Whether it was the avowedly
recreational program or the lack of residue on the
site, this scheme was the simplest illustration of his
three approaches and the most like the California
gardens that it both mimicked and inspired. Biomorphic in form, casual and broadly Japanese in
feeling, the garden was "frankly planned as a
playground and for low upkeep cost."[27] The simple
lyric of the project, apparently unfettered by personal or historical leitmotif, yielded a lighthearted,
easy-on-the-mind composition.

On most projects, however, Tunnard was
rarely free of the responsibility that came with his
knowledge of history and horticulture, and this responsibility was inseparable from the intrinsically
reserved demeanor of Tunnard the man, always
counterbalancing the rage of Tunnard the modernist. In *Gardens in the Modern Landscape,* for example, he presented an extraordinary hypothetical
project designed to preserve the large expanses of
the landscape garden of Claremont, designed in the
eighteenth century by Kent and Brown. He appropriated a chunk of Le Corbusier's Radiant City, or,
more accurately, the 1935 scheme for a London
high rise, Highpoint I, designed by Ernst Lubetkin
of Tecton.[28] This he plopped onto one corner of the
Claremont site, thereby saving the remainder from
the "Butcher Method" of subdivision. If St. Ann's
Hill represented one kind of merging of modernist
and historicist agendas, this *parti* represented another. In other examples of his executed projects at
Walton-on-the-Thames and at Galby, Leicestershire, he combined historicist and modernist ideas
in the same design move.[29] In these instances, he
appropriated the Dutch formal kitchen garden (perhaps from St. Ann's Hill), combined it with a dash
of Canneel-Claes's cubism, and folded the modern
garden into the larger landscape. Both designs involved formal rectilinear masses of planting marching out from the house in an occultly balanced
relationship to the rest of the scheme. Ultimately,
in part because of their large scale and profusion of
plants, these geometric gardens seem, however,
not to have had the crispness of Canneel-Claes's
work or of the Bentley Wood terrace.

That crispness, driven by the twin necessities
of economy and a small site and by the responsibility of higher social purpose, reemerged in a project
unencumbered by either plants or history. The All-
Europe House, designed in collaboration with architect Elizabeth Denby in 1939, was the consummate
social project of Tunnard's early career.[30] Tunnard
and Denby were members of a MARS-sponsored
team to plan for the growth of London. The team
was led by the German emigré planner Arthur Korn
and included Gropius's London partner, Maxwell
Fry.[31] The MARS scheme was wildly idealistic from
a social planning perspective and emphatically based
in the formal vocabulary of the Radiant City. The
Tunnard-Denby collaboration on the All-Europe
House may, in one sense, be seen as a subset or

piece of the broader MARS plan. In another sense, it represented a British version of design for social responsibility that had dominated modernist architecture and planning on the continent.

Tunnard's design envisioned separate private gardens for horticultural use, including the cultivation of vegetables for the table, and a common garden beyond. The whole scheme was simply and elegantly staged by Denby's building, a jagged row scheme that surrounded the garden spaces with a fully enclosed block. (For purposes of demonstration at the 1939 Ideal Home Exhibition only one unit was constructed.) The private gardens were similarly laid out, with small terraces set into the spaces made by the angular setbacks of the individual dwellings. Paving blocks were carried along one fenced (or hedged) boundary of the yard to the vegetable garden. Here the path turned 90 degrees to the midpoint of the yard, where it again turned 90 degrees to separate the vegetable garden from the flower garden and to lead to the shared toolshed and the gate to the common garden. It was an extraordinarily simple spatial organization of everyday rituals.

The entire *parti* was described in detail in the *RIBA Journal* (June 1939), hailed as a socially responsible contribution by British designers to the problem of housing an expanding European population of minimal means. The scheme was developed in considerable detail, one specific point of which was the rationale of providing such housing as a part of a mixed development with flats at a density of 20 dwelling units to the acre. This standard, undoubtedly derived from the MARS research work, was substantiated in terms of comparable densities in Regency period terrace cottages, the only such "historical" reference made in this project.

In 1939, as Tunnard was in the process of supervising the construction of the All-Europe garden, he must surely have been preoccupied by the rumblings of war and the incipient tumult that would dash the social dreams of the modernists and any possibility for an All-Europe design ethos. Tunnard made a dramatic move. Realizing that the war would end his opportunities to pursue his ideas for collaborative design in the wider landscape, and spurred by an invitation from Walter Gropius to teach at the Harvard Graduate School of Design, he emigrated to the United States. Tunnard recalled, in a paper delivered in 1962 to the Society of Architectural Historians, that he joined Gropius's studio with fellow critics Martin Wagner and Hugh Stubbins. He also taught a course in site planning that covered, in his words, "everything from the TVA to residential densities."[32]

His teaching and his commissioned work remained generally allied to the formal and social principles of modernism. Building on his Harvard and Gropius connections, he executed a small number of residential gardens in the Cambridge and Lincoln areas of Massachusetts. In the absence of substantial records that would illuminate this period, it seems that few of these projects, however, involved the social agendas and larger landscapes to which the All-Europe and the MARS planning effort had turned his work in 1938 and 1939.[33] At Harvard he had the extraordinary opportunity to shape some of the ideas of the principal progenitors of modern design in the postwar era, including his friends Garrett Eckbo, Dan Kiley, and James Rose and his students Lawrence Halprin, Philip Johnson, and Edward Larrabee Barnes.[34]

The Unmaking

As modernism began to lose its social edge in the 1940s, Tunnard became more and more disillusioned with its mannered practice, particularly in architecture.[35] As a member of the architecture faculty at Harvard, he had been immediately set at odds with many of the old guard of the landscape architectural profession, who stubbornly held to more traditional design ideas.[36] He had made substantial enemies among the mainstream of American landscape architects with his unruly declarations. In 1942 Tunnard wrote an article for *Landscape Architecture* entitled, "Modern Gardens for Modern Houses."[37] Three respondents to the article, Fletcher Steele, Geoffrey Baker, and William Strong, were less than warm in their review of Tunnard's ideas.[38]

Tunnard was suddenly drafted in 1943. He served briefly in the Royal Canadian Air Force and lost one eye in a non-combat-related accident. Discharged, he returned to the United States on a Wheelwright Fellowship and found his way to a tenure-track position at Yale in 1945. The position was in city planning, and although he taught at least one landscape architecture course, he never returned to the fold of that profession. In the meantime the history of urbanism had completely fascinated him. His first book in this vein was *The City of Man* (1953) which included "The City of Shadows," a stinging graphic critique of Le Corbusier's Ville Radieuse by Gaston Bardet.[39] By the 1970s Tunnard was a well-known activist in historic preservation circles in New Haven, Connecticut—where he was a founder of the local landmarks commission—and around the world as a member of the International Committee on Monuments and Sites (ICOMOS).

In 1958 Ian McHarg, Professor of Landscape Architecture at the University of Pennsylvania, was about to embark upon the regional planning and design work that would culminate in *Design With Nature* (1969). In preparation for the work ahead, McHarg wrote to ask Tunnard for references to writings that would be "most indicative of the path toward design of open space appropriate to 20th century society." He added: "Your own book, 'Gardens in the Modern Landscape', still remain[s] the best thought on the subject."[40] Tunnard retained no record of his reply, but he must have been similarly at a loss. With the exception of Eckbo's *Landscape For Living* (1949), there was precious little of theoretical weight from which to draw.[41] It was as if the

15–13

15–13 All-Europe House
A simply conceived garden for people of modest means.
[sketch by H. F. Clark, *RIBA Journal*]

15–14 All-Europe House
The plan and aerial view shows the jagged setback scheme and the basic layout of private and common gardens.
[sketch by H. F. Clark, *RIBA Journal*]

15–14

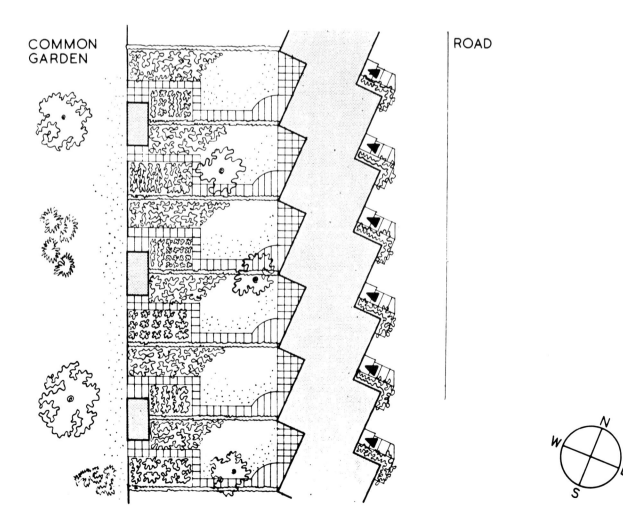

COMMON
GARDEN

ROAD

problems of the designed landscape had become so self-referential and urgent (or banal?) that no one could be attracted to their serious study. In the meantime, modernist formal solutions had overtaken the studio, even at Harvard, where Hideo Sasaki had assumed the chair of the Department of Landscape Architecture.

Tunnard and the Lost Legacy to Modernism Today

For all of the shortfalls of Tunnard's work, designed and written, it constituted the most significant critical mass of inquiry in landscape architecture in the late 1930s. That he dropped out of the discourse in landscape architecture in the late 1940s constituted a critical loss to the development of the discipline. One might argue, in fact, that for many landscape architects today, modernism as a whole has been a phenomenon detached from its original thinking. Nearly all landscape architects today have been affected by modernism in practice, but few have a sense of why or how it came to be the mainstream aesthetic of the discipline. Fewer still can point to a modernist approach or method.[42]

Certain ironic losses to the present state of landscape architectural theory cannot be ignored. These losses were made manifestly clear when Bernard Tschumi formulated his polemical exposition of ideas that would guide the design of the Parc de La Villette in Paris (1984).[43] This park, said Tschumi, would be about culture, not nature. It would be perceived as a meaningless (or mad?) series of three-dimensional images/spaces, the *cinegramme folie*. These spaces would be made as a discontinuous building deployed onto the landscape via a formal sandwich of three autonomous geometric slices: points, lines, and surfaces. When the scheme was published, many landscape architects and others were irate about the formal autonomy of the park and the indeterminacy of the method by which it was designed. There should have been no cause for alarm. The whole idea was, in fact, remarkably old hat.

In 1924 Frederick Etchells, a vorticist painter turned architect, translated Le Corbusier's book *The City of Tomorrow* into English.[44] On page eight, facing the title page of the "First Part: General Considerations," appeared a chart of *lignes, surfaces,* and *solides.* This chart, as the caption noted, was printed on the backs of copybooks issued to the elementary schools of France. Le Corbusier had added the declaration, "This is geometry." Tunnard had read *The City of Tomorrow,* or at least he cited it in *Gardens in the Modern Landscape.*[45] Tunnard offered the sole methodological clue as to how one would actually apply the three approaches to a design problem on the same page of his book as he placed the illustration of Corbusier's Villa Savoye. He wrote:

> The plan . . . [is] an organizing factor [that] would help to make . . . functional garden planning a reality. The plan as coordinator must be

translated into three dimensional terms—those of plane, line, and mass, the first denoting the spatial values, . . . the second, the linear values . . . and the third, mass values of inanimate and living material.[46]

Neither Tschumi nor perhaps anyone else has noted this rather obvious methodological connection to an earlier modernism. Like a half-remembered catechism, Tschumi has recited this simple old trinity of architectonic geometry as if it were a new canon of formal elegance. Substantive comment about the formal expression of social (cultural) agendas at La Villette and what connection they may have to the similar agendas of another time has been markedly absent from landscape architectural discourse. What does this situation say about our reconsideration of modernism in landscape architecture? If few can either connect Tschumi's geometric sandwich to any earlier canon or remember Tunnard's three approaches, it probably says that we have not retained too terribly much of the modernist formal idea base. It may also say that we have lost any clear connection with the social agenda inherent in the best applications of the approaches. In the last analysis this fact should not be surprising since, in part, our perforated knowledge clings to slender strands of recent history, including one that we hold to the provocative, troubled, and, finally, truncated, landscape architectural career of Christopher Tunnard.

Notes

1 The phrase is from a review by G[eoffrey] A. Jellicoe, "The Dynamic Garden: *Gardens in the Modern Landscape*, etc.," *Architectural Review* 85 (March 1939), 152. Tunnard's *Gardens in the Modern Landscape* was published in 1938 by the Architectural Press, London; a second edition, with an interesting foreword in which Tunnard reflected upon his changed ideas about modernism, appeared in 1948. Much of the present essay's biographical material can be more specifically tracked in Lance M. Neckar, "Strident Modernism/Ambivalent Reconsiderations: Christopher Tunnard's *Gardens in the Modern Landscape*," *Journal of Garden History* 10 (1990), 237–246.

2 David Dean, *Architecture in the 1930's: Recalling the English Scene* (New York: RIBA/Rizzoli, 1983), 112–113.

3 R. Webber, *Percy Cane: Garden Designer* (Edinburgh: John Bartholomew & Son, 1975), provides an overview of Cane's life and work including his writings.

4 Ibid., 149, 173.

5 See particularly Jane Brown, *The Art and Architecture of English Gardens* (New York: Rizzoli, 1989), 178–185. Brown mentions connections to Henry Moore, Barbara Hepworth, and Bernard Leach. Of this group, Leach's name appeared in the acknowledgments in Tunnard's *Gardens in the Modern Landscape;* this connection may offer another explanation for Tunnard's interest in Japan. Only Moore's work appeared prominently in Tunnard's book. Tunnard was apparently close enough to J. M. Richards, associate editor of the *Architectural Review,* to have his articles on landscape design published; this fact is notable because it underscores a clear relationship between Tunnard's work and the modernist editorial stance of the *Review.*

6 The principal contents of the book were printed in *Architectural Review,* October 1937 to September 1938. The book was published by the in-house arm of the magazine, the Architectural Press, and was advertised in the *Architectural Review* 84 (December 1938), cxv.

7 Jellicoe, "The Dynamic Garden," 152.

8 The Powell garden, illustrated in Tunnard's *Gardens* (1948), 71, literally repeats the boxed imagery of the Guevrekian garden. Much was made of such boxed schemes; Oliver Hill had designed a boxed scheme for his British Pavilion at the 1937 Paris Exhibition, documented in a special supplement, "The Paris Exhibition," *Architectural Review* 82 (September 1937), pl. iv.

9 Tunnard, *Gardens,* 80.

10 Ibid., 79.

11 Ibid., 83.

12 Ibid., 89.

13 Ibid., 99. Tunnard seems to have personally favored the work of Paul Nash, a somewhat more conservative presence on the modern scene than Moore or Hepworth; see ibid., 95.

14 Christopher Tunnard, "Walter Gropius at Harvard," typed manuscript of lecture given at the Annual Meeting of the Society of Architectural Historians, Boston, 27 January 1962; Tunnard Papers, Manuscripts and Archives, Yale University Library.

15 The phrase is mine, but Tunnard says that these people "killed" the garden (*Gardens,* 93), a similarly strong point of view.

16 Ibid., 106.

17 Tunnard Papers, Manuscripts and Archives, Yale University Library.

18 See Horace Walpole, *Essay on Modern Gardening* (Strawberry Hill, 1785), and Thomas Whately, *Observations on Modern Gardening* (London[?], 1770), cited by Tunnard in *Gardens,* 179 and elsewhere.

19 "Modern Architecture in the Sussex Landscape" and "House near Halland, Sussex," *Architectural Review* 85 (1939), 61–78. I have purposefully avoided crediting Tunnard with the design of the terrace at Halland because Serge Chermayeff (interview with the author, October 1989) claimed that Tunnard only made suggestions about the thinning of the trees that occurred as part of the site preparation. Brown, *Art and Architecture,* similarly skirts this issue in the absence of persuasive evidence one way or another.

20 Related in author's interview with Chermayeff and generally described in the *Architectural Review* articles cited above.

21 I have no personal knowledge of Tunnard's exposure to the technique of naturalizing bulb plants, but he most probably would have seen it in the course of his horticultural training or just on a visit at Kew.

22 The title of the work was not given by Tunnard in *Gardens* but is identified and documented by Brown, *Art and Architecture,* 181.

23 Brown, *Art and Architecture,* 181.

24 "MARS Exhibition," *Architectural Review* 83 (March 1938), 116. The subtitle in the text read "Architecture: Garden Landscape."

25 The fact that the house was Tunnard's own was not mentioned in *Gardens,* but is documented in Dean, *Architecture in the 1930s,* 39, and Jeremy Gould, *Modern Houses in Britain, 1919–1939* (London: Society of Architectural Historians of Great Britain, 1977), 31.

26 "House in Surrey," *Architectural Review* 82 (October 1937), 117. I have presumed that the attribution

to Charles Hamilton was Tunnard's own, and that part of the reason that Painshill (or Pain's Hill, as Tunnard spelled it) was featured so extensively in *Gardens,* 27–33, related to his discovery of some connection between Hamilton and his own property.

27 Tunnard, *Gardens,* 72.

28 Ibid., 148–157, especially 154. See also Kenneth Frampton, *Modern Architecture: A Critical History* (London: Thames and Hudson, 1980), 252–253, and Dean, *Architecture in the 1930s,* 53–56.

29 The house at Galby, near Leicester, was designed for Sir Charles Keene; it is mentioned in Gould, *Modern Houses in Britain,* 47 (who also calls it "Norton Gorse"), and is partially documented in "Galby, Leicestershire, House," *Architectural Review* 90 (November 1941), 132–134.

30 "The All-Europe House: Designed by Elizabeth Denby, Garden Layout and Planning by Christopher Tunnard," *RIBA Journal* 46, series 3 (1939), 813–819.

31 The MARS effort is chronicled by Dean, *Architecture in the 1930s,* 72, 112–114, and Maxwell Fry, *Fine Building* (London: Faber and Faber, 1944), 86–114, among others. There are some relevant documents (notes) in the Tunnard Papers, Manuscripts and Archives, Yale University Library.

32 Tunnard, "Walter Gropius at Harvard."

33 Ibid. In the 1948 edition of *Gardens in the Modern Landscape* some of the smaller gardens are illustrated, such as the garden at 4 Buckingham Street, Cambridge, with architects Stone and Koch. The garden featured objects after the work of Paul Nash. As a student, I walked past this walled garden nearly every day for two years without knowing its connection to Tunnard.

34 Tunnard, "Walter Gropius at Harvard." Tunnard made a great deal of the collaborative atmosphere at the GSD, an atmosphere that he credited to Gropius's presence. The Tunnard Papers at Yale are, at this writing, very minimal and disorganized with respect to his experiences in England and Harvard. See Benjamin Forgery, "Lawrence Halprin: Maker of Places and Living Spaces," *Smithsonian* 19 (December 1988), 160–170, for the Barnes, Johnson, and Halprin connections.

35 Tunnard, *Gardens* (1948), 7.

36 This assertion is borne out in commentary by Garrett Eckbo in an interview with the author, 23 January 1989, and by a perusal of *Landscape Architecture* in the period.

37 Christopher Tunnard, "Modern Gardens for Modern Houses," *Landscape Architecture* 32 (January 1942), 57–64.

38 See particularly Fletcher Steele, Geoffrey Baker, and William Strong, "Comment: The Voice Is Jacob's, but the Hand . . .; Equivalent of a Loudly-Colored Folk Art Is Needed; and It Is Modern if It Cares Well for Basic Necessities," *Landscape Architecture Quarterly* 32 (January 1942), 64–68.

39 Christopher Tunnard, *The City of Man* (New York: Charles Scribner's Sons, 1953), 227.

40 Tunnard Papers, Manuscripts and Archives, Yale University Library.

41 Garrett Eckbo, *Landscape for Living* (New York: F. W. Dodge/ Duell, Sloan and Pearce, 1950), presents the most developed case for landscape architecture in book form other than Tunnard's *Gardens in the Modern Landscape.*

42 Many commentators have noted a lack of discursive literature in landscape architecture in this period; certainly Thomas Church's *Gardens Are for People* (New York: Reinhold Publishing, 1955) and James Rose's *Gardens Make Me Laugh* (Norwalk, CT: Silvermine Publishers, 1965) are written not only at a very practical level, but also in an extremely self-referential manner.

43 Bernard Tschumi, *Cinegramme Folie: Parc de La Villette* (Princeton: Princeton Architectural Press, 1987).

44 Le Corbusier, *The City of Tomorrow and Its Planning* (Cambridge: MIT Press, 1971), is a reprinting of the 1929 edition translated by Etchells.

45 Tunnard, *Gardens,* 58.

46 Ibid., 79.

16

During the last ten years a number of private houses of modern design have been built in the United States. There is a scattering of them throughout the industrial East, in New England, and in and around New York and Philadelphia. There are some in Michigan and in the vicinity of Chicago; Frank Lloyd Wright was building there in the 90's houses which are modern in construction and planning. In California, where the architects Richard Neutra and R. M. Schindler have been working since 1925, there is probably more evidence of modern architecture than in any other section of the country. Since the advent of the administration of 1933 modern houses have also been built by the government. The town of Greenbelt, near Washington, D.C., and some of the communities started by the Farm Security Administration are good examples. With the exception of large areas of the South it is impossible to travel through the country without being made aware that a new and growing architecture exists, even though your trip should include such seemingly unlikely places as Long Island and the Olympic Mountains.

These houses are being built by progressive architects of varying individual talents. Some are distinguished men of established American or European reputations like Frank Lloyd Wright or Walter Gropius; others are young graduates of the architectural schools embarking on their first job. All are united by a belief in a method of building which avoids the shams of stylistic "good taste" and offers a form of shelter suited to a modern way of life. Their clients have discovered that apart from the aesthetic banality of much contemporary work, a "pretty" house does not even offer good value for money. The plan is seldom flexible enough to allow for varying family activities or to make the most of the sun and air at the proper seasons. The modern house, on the other hand, is planned for multiple uses and easy expansion; it acknowledges the land and the elements by ingenious siting and orientation. In other words, it is a product of the circumstances which determine its growth, not a preconceived, picture-book thing, into which the owner must fit his personality like a servant into his master's cast-off clothing.

Modern houses are not uniformly well planned, of course. Who would expect an experimental architecture to be exemplary from the beginning? But much of the criticism of the new building is unreasonable or based on deep-seated

Reprinted from *Landscape Architecture,*
January 1942

prejudices. One of the commonest of these is that modern architecture is cold-looking, hard in outline, and unrelieved by decoration which might break up its plain wall surfaces. People who make this comment have either had their aesthetic sense debased through years of unquestioning perusal of the fashionable magazines or have failed to realize that architecture cannot be judged apart from its environment.

In the first case they have ceased to be alive to the beauty of materials, to the satisfaction of clean continuing lines and of regular but unsymmetrical masses, in which a delicate balance or bold tension holds the eye more surely than the meaningless fancies of half-timbering, Colonial plans, and Classic detail, which are used by architects and speculators alike as concessions to taste. In the second case, these critics may have seen houses suffering from an unsympathetic treatment of the surrounding land. The organic nature of modern building demands that architecture does not stop with the house, but continues out into the landscape. That is not to say that the landscape shall be stiff or necessarily "formal," but it does imply that a tree on the terrace, for instance, shall have as much real importance as any structural support within, and that there shall be no incongruity in scale between the arrangements for outdoor and indoor living space. You would think that this was a logical and inevitable process for all concerned with house and garden making.

"Modern gardens for modern houses?" What else would you have? Unfortunately there is at the present time an almost complete lack of designers skilled in the technique of planning for modern architecture, or even aware of the implications of this new movement. People who are used to the conventional methods of axial composition or of naturalistic arrangement of plant material just haven't the right approach to the problem of the modern garden. An architect would rather tackle the grounds himself with the help of a horticultural expert than call in a landscape architect unsympathetic to his ideas. Can you blame him? And can you wonder that a perfect relationship of site and shelter is not always achieved?

This unfortunate state of affairs can only be remedied by a return to fundamentals on the part of designers and an understanding of the demands of modern living by professionals and lay people alike. Collaborative work on the home and its surround-

ings can in future only be successfully undertaken by those who understand the significance of the whole field, although they may be specialists in just one part of it. If, as is the case at present, there are few landscape designers who understand what modern architecture is all about, we cannot expect too many good gardens for modern houses. You do not after all expect to find the most up-to-date models in a second-hand furniture store, and second-hand designs have for years been used to furnish the gardens of Europe and America. Our gardens desperately need new ideas. The first of these ideas most be the understanding that *modern landscape design is inseparable from the spirit, technique, and development of modern architecture.*

It is easy enough to find reasons why the gardens of this country have failed to keep up with the times. One is that many people use them to express their sentimental attachment to the past. Another requires a more detailed explanation.

For many years there has been a great deal too much insistence on an arbitrary ground pattern in garden planning. This is the "design" which has always been such a mystery to the man in the street; he thinks, and reasonably, that a garden "grows," and that design, perhaps, is not the most important thing about it. The most important thing, possibly, in his opinion, is that a garden lives and breathes, contains organic elements which change with the seasons, which expand, grow, and reproduce themselves in a way that he can order and enjoy. This is probably his greatest pleasure in the art of gardens, that of productive cultivation. Gardening, after all, is one of the oldest of the folk arts. If this average man is an expert organizer he will plan his garden to provide room for himself, his family, and his friends, as well as for plants, and he will arrange things so that the outdoor activities of the family are taken care of without conflict or interference with the life of the garden itself. He may also, if he is mindful of the community in which he lives and the landscape of which it is a part, so organize or control the elements of his garden that they bear a good relation to the activities of the neighborhood and achieve at least a nodding acquaintance with some features of the land beyond. None of this is concerned with design as he knows it from the picture books and magazines, where, if the fundamentals are considered at all they are inextricably mixed up with pattern-making for the sake of picturesque or romantic effect.

I think our friend will be very lucky indeed to avoid reproducing design clichés which have been accumulating through the centuries and have become part and parcel of the garden planner's technique. He may one day turn over the pages of a book of garden plans, an error which can prove fatal to the uninhibited garden maker. Here he will learn about vistas, axes, and such things as oval lawns, all the elements of pattern-making left over from an age when the garden was enjoyed as a picture and not as an experience. He will be told that gardens begin on paper, and not realize perhaps that the arbitrary, preconceived design is a result of tradition (or laziness, as we now define it) or of sheer emptiness of mind. He will be encouraged by his reading to copy the ideas of other people, designing for other purposes and other situations—he will be perpetuating the styles. Hence the similarity in garden plans and details all over the country. Just as in the tedious repetition of architectural styles, we have the same plans for rose gardens and pools, we use the same sculpture and the same fashionable plants. The keynote of the garden for years has been, not space division for use, but detail of this sort, applied in patterns, with more regard for mass than for volume when these factors are considered at all. Picture-book planning is a far cry from the gardens of folk art or from their fundamental modern equivalents.

It would seem obvious that it is better not to start planning a garden with a lot of half-formed ideas about the shape of a flight of steps, the pattern of beds in an iris garden, or the style of outbuildings you would like to have. Yet frequently that is just the kind of equipment the designer brings to his job, together with a set of rules which preclude any freedom of choice such as our average man might exert. One of these rules is concerned with the enframement of views. It is required that at some point or points in the scheme you must accent a feature of the house (the door onto the terrace, maybe) by planting or by ornament of some kind to create a vista from it. Echo this planting at some distance from the house in a straight line and you can create an axial view. This is one of the unfortunate fixations which prevent the conventional designer from accomplishing anything but a rigid dullness when confronted with the problem of the modern house, which may not have a garden door to accent, nor indeed any door or other emphatic feature on the garden side. The very walls may be

of glass, avoiding any visible barrier between inside and outside space. The technique of the axis line, standby of designers in America since 1893, is thus rendered completely useless.

What is to be done?

Let me try to indicate some of the changes that have been taking place in gardens since the advent of the new architecture and the consequent modern approach to its surroundings. I can think of at least ten factors that are important to an understanding of the new gardening, and that they are no less applicable to large-scale design in the landscape makes them of some additional value as points of departure for study. They can scarcely be more than enumerated here; even so, I believe that they point to an inevitable conclusion: that garden planning is about to change, and change rapidly from its archaic methods and sentimental attachment to the past to something contemporary in spirit, a manifestation of the times in which we live.

The first change, as I have already hinted, is concerned with the idea of outdoor space. If you examine the plan of a typical present-day garden you will find its space divisions are determined largely by stylistic convention. If the design is of the "formal" kind that is often associated with Georgian or Colonial style houses, for instance, there may be a wide terrace under the house windows, but it is unlikely that this will be an inviting place for modern outdoor living. There will be a lawn beyond it, perhaps, nicely proportioned and surrounded by shrubbery and cut through by an axial vista to a figure reflected in a pool, a summer house, or other focal point usually considered necessary in this type of plan. With all its variations it is a set design, tied up in a bundle and delivered ready for use, and seems to me the kind of thing you would quickly tire of. Everything about it is perfectly obvious; there is nothing unusual; nothing to violate good taste. All the spaces are neatly confined, the boundaries are well screened, and everything is in its proper place. But we are not still living in the eighteenth century. Does this type of design offer us the freedom we demand in our modern way of life? It would seem, unfortunately, that the designer has been far too occupied with tricks of diminishing perspective on the main axis and drawing broad stylism to think about the human uses of the plan and its deadening effect on the human mind.

Neither does the opposite type of plan, the naturalistic or "informal" treatment, offer a better solution. Here is apparent the dying breath of the romantic age, long since broken down and already discarded by the sister art of architecture. The compromise effort to unite the two styles, "formal" and "informal," in a last frantic move by the designers to achieve something which they fondly imagine is the right style for the twentieth century, is already recorded in the most recent histories of landscape art. This, too, is a blind alley. *The right style for the twentieth century is no style at all, but a new conception of planning the human environment.*

In the modern garden an attempt is made to let space *flow* by breaking down divisions between usable areas, and incidentally increasing their usability. It is a truly three-dimensional composition planned in model form or on the site, rather than as a pattern on paper. Here, too, there may be a terrace under the house windows, but the modern designer is not bound by convention to make it a uniform width. He is free to vary its direction and to provide width where width is needed. He realizes that the space enveloped by surrounding plant and architectural forms is as important as the forms themselves. And when you consider that gardens, like houses, are built of space, you will perceive that there need be very little difference in our approach to the planning of the indoors and the outdoors, which under modern ways of life have become parts of a single organism.

Related to the question of space change is that of integration and grouping, which the styles have hitherto forbidden. There is a fine tradition in this country of the open site, in both urban and rural communities, in which grounds have been landscaped to the street and to the neighboring properties without visible barriers. Some authorities suggest that this tradition developed in the friendly, pioneer days; perhaps it was also due in part to the influence of the English Landscape School. It is certain, however, that the idea is dying out to some extent. There are economic reasons for the wall and hedge complex of today, but a more obvious influence in this direction hails from Beaux Arts stylism. French and Italian gardens are essentially gardens of enclosure, and so enclosure gets approval.

New modern architecture is not offered to the public as a style so much as a method. That method is a means of providing necessary shelter for large numbers of people in centralized, workable communities, at low cost. This form of shelter is eminently suitable for integration in rows, terraces, or other simple groupings, which occupy a small land area and thus provide greater outdoor freedom for all. The row houses in the town of Greenbelt, Maryland, and, on a smaller scale and for a different income group, a community of houses by Carl Koch on the hills of Belmont, Massachusetts, are good examples. Schemes of this kind demand a revival of the tradition of open land, and their effect on the garden proper is considerable. The latter becomes a series of units—terrace, lawn space, flower borders, perhaps—which not only are integrated with the house, but with neighboring houses and the common landscape. Sometimes one of these units serves for two or more families, or the whole group may share one communal facility, like tennis courts or a swimming pool. You can easily imagine the differences that must exist between the old concept of private gardens on land subdivisions and these new areas for people who exert some form of group control and share much of their outdoor living space.

The next change on the list is concerned with materials, including that most important of all garden materials, the plant. The romantic tradition of planting dies hard. Who is not familiar with the massed collections of shrubs and trees which make up the woody plant border? It is not really very different from the old-fashioned shrubbery, wherein one plant was used to hide the deficiencies of the next and none could attain its full beauty. Now there is something inherent in the structure of every plant which makes it suitable for some particular purpose in the garden, and that purpose is seldom just display. It is true that certain plants can be grown closely together in masses, but these are usually hedge plants, ground covers, or herbaceous subjects cultivated more for their flowers than for their form or outline. In other cases plants need freedom, sometimes complete isolation, to take their place in the scheme. Selection, not massing for picturesque effect, is the requirement of the modern garden. I shall have more to say about plants under another heading.

Other materials are creeping in, notably for screening. To take one example, it is only recently in a garden for a house by the English architect, Wells Coates, that I saw the first interesting use of asbestos sheeting for a screen and vine support.

Previous to this I had seen the same material molded under pressure to make plant containers for a roof garden, where its cheapness, lightness, and durability have proved a source of satisfaction to the owners. Glass in its many new forms for walls, pools, and fountains, reinforced concrete for ramps and bridges, and weatherproof plywood for shelters are all unfamiliar but usable materials for the modern garden, as tests have already proved. Their use opens up possibilities for exciting new plant groupings and lighting effects; unhappily a public which can view these things with pleasure in the gardens of a World's Fair does not readily pursue the same adventurous ends in the surroundings of its homes.

At this point we must note briefly the changing attitude toward nature, a philosophical concept which has made possible developments like the ones already mentioned. It is only recently that men have gotten over their fear of wild nature. Eighteenth-century landscaping bears witness to the fact that at that time men were no longer in awe of their surroundings, or thought, like Cicero, that it was agreeable to live only in safe, pastoral valleys; but even up to the middle of the last century certain aspects of nature, such as swamps and prairies, were considered horrible by those who were forced to make their living on the frontiers. Thoreau reacted against this feeling when he cried, "Give me the ocean, the desert and the wilderness!" In his time the material conquest of nature by the railroad and by industrial exploitation generated a new feeling in man, a desire to escape to wild nature and enjoy the freedom it afforded. This was a complete reversal of the Greek and early Christian attitudes.

Ironically enough, by the end of the nineteenth century there was very little wild nature left; the lumber, fishing, and mining industries had seen to that. There is still less today, when we have increased facilities for transport in the automobile and airplane, an increased population, and an increasing adaptation of nature to man's needs. The latter process is necessary and inevitable; many people are now for the first time beginning to face that fact. The changing attitude to nature is bound up in the acceptance of the part that man must play in ordering the natural environment, tempered by the necessity for keeping the balance by an understanding of the natural processes and evolutions. This involves not conservation so much as experi-

mentation, something more productive and less sterile.

When you translate this attitude into terms of modern landscape and garden planning it becomes a matter of controlling nature, but not imposing on the natural scene an unproductive or wasteful design. The designer becomes a forester when he deals with woods, an agriculturalist when he encounters fields, a horticulturist in the orchard. That which is productive, balanced, and orderly, like the latter, he is apt to leave alone, so that instead of the old-fashioned landscaped estate you are likely to find a modern house in its meadows, or its woods, or its cornfields, without much apparent change in its surroundings, except in the immediate vicinity of the house. This requires restraint on the part of the designer, who may have been used to lining his drive with an avenue of trees and shrubs instead of letting it wind unassumingly through the meadows. A white wooden gate is likely to take the place of the massive wrought-iron affair of the twenties. The monastic exclusiveness of the great landscaped estates is disappearing. We have partly to thank the great architect Le Corbusier for this change in thinking. He would have cattle grazing as near as possible to the dwelling, and bring agricultural areas up to the outskirts of his vertical cities. A humanized landscape is now the aim of all serious and progressive designers in the physical planning field.

Two other changes in gardens result from an acceptance of this thesis. One is concerned with economy of design—an aesthetic economy, let us say. In an ordered landscape we can surely be content with less insistent order in our private grounds. Freedom and flexibility of design, but not a loose naturalism, can be obtained in the simple arrangement of a path, a plant, a tree. Somewhere a well-cultivated plot produces flowers, fruit, and those vegetables we care to grow rather than buy. There need no longer be any attempt at show or picturesque composition.

The second point involves the question of orientation and views. With the changed attitude to nature, which has banished fear, there need no longer be any dislike for the urban view. Of course prejudices die hard. I well remember my surprise at seeing, in New York City, an apartment building of comparatively recent construction which turns its back on the East River. Only the kitchens and the bathrooms look out on what must be one of the most magnificent prospects in the world. But it is all man-made, and therefore must be considered ugly. Some of it is, considered in units, but as a whole a more lively and stimulating panorama could hardly be found. Far too much of our landscape technique has been devoted to screening smoke-stacks and silos, garages and garbage cans, instead of making some effort to encourage better design and siting of these necessary objects. Prejudice prevents our being able to look at them squarely and accept them for what they are.

Yet we make our own contribution to confuse when we build houses in irregular lines along a new street, turning them as best we can to make the most of the sun and air. The design of the street, the whole pattern of communities and large cities, is in the same chaotic state. A coordination of interests, however desirable in theory, does not suit the policies of the speculative builder; and as yet it is only in certain government and cooperative projects that total order has been achieved.

Next on the list of changes are the new appreciation of form and the new understanding of color. Here we can return again to the discussion of plants. It is a subject surrounded by fetishes. How many gardeners can look at a plant nowadays without thinking of its rarity, its sentimental value, or its temperamental ways under cultivation? I have known presidents of garden societies whose places are veritable plant museums, kept up to date with the latest introductions from abroad, and yet whose appreciation of forms and composition is relatively small. At least that is what their gardens indicate.

I am inclined to believe that study ("worship" would hardly be too strong a word) of the individual plant has led to a state of affairs in gardens comparable to that existing in the art world, where museum appreciation has tended to deaden creative power. A return to a vigorous folk art is needed in both cases. A poetic appreciation of plants would be preferable to the historical attitude which now prevails. At the same time it is possible to perceive in the development of modern thought, and through its practical applications in plastic design, a new appreciation based on structural and textural qualities which is affecting the use of plants in modern settings. We can even go back as far as Ruskin and find that distinguished critic making an attempt to classify plants for art students according to habits of growth, which he classified as "sword-shaped," "fan-shaped," and so on.

Nowadays it is enough for us to perceive structure without giving it a label, and I think we are beginning to appreciate natural forms with a different understanding, something akin perhaps to the Oriental manner. But we have not yet arrived at the Oriental's simultaneous mastery of technical and aesthetic values. We can appreciate dogwoods, for instance, not because of their fine blooms alone, but because of the way they are displayed in their native woods, on long arching branches appearing against the gloom of their background like dismembered thrusting arms of an incredible whiteness. Yet we are quite likely to dig up the tree and transport it to a position on the lawn in full sunshine, where it quickly makes new growth and becomes a massive affair quite unlike its natural form. It is still dogwood, and that is enough for some of us, but the aesthetic quality gained in its woodland habitat has gone. To understand the character of plants and to use those which can supply a formal quality of their own, without insisting on size of bloom or certain fashionable shades of color, is the aim of the modern garden-maker.

The massing and blending of colors is a Western habit long overdue for investigation. William Bowyer Honey has some interesting remarks on this subject in his book, *Gardening Heresies and Devotions*. Speaking of popular tastes in flowers he says: "Crudities are shown in a preference for the largest and most double flowers, in a fondness for merely startling combinations of color, however muddy in distant effect, and for casual or ill-considered massing in beds and borders, 'a blaze of color' is the familiar cliché. These are typical failings to which the trade purveyors constantly pander." It is the responsibility of all of us to remedy this state of affairs.

It may be necessary to fall back on certain unfamiliar and merely incidental uses of color, such as the Rembrandtesque technique of light coming out of darkness which can be managed quite well in the placing of certain plants, or of concentration on foliage rather than flower effects. It is necessary to remember the part played by light outdoors, that changing quality which can make the conventional color border appear drab at certain times, and at others throw the most carefully planned scheme entirely out of balance. This seems to hint that color schemes are not a worthy end for gardeners' aims, and that color composition gets too much of its share of attention from the expert. However, restraint in the use of showy flowering plants, which often lack the quality of form due to unthinking hybridization for color, is a noticeable tendency among discriminating gardeners of late, and is, I think, a feature of the modern movement not entirely unconnected with the discriminating tendencies of modern painters and sculptors.

Decoration is usually left to the end of any treatment of the subject of garden planning, and here it is in its usual place. It deserves better treatment than it usually receives from lovers of incidental or applied ornament. Enthusiasts for the modern garden are much more concerned with the quality of inventiveness than of added decoration. I have already spoken of the appreciation of materials in architecture and the pleasure that can be gained from contemplation of simple forms and flowing lines. At the Swiss building of the Cité Universitaire in Paris, Le Corbusier invented a stone wall with wide and smoothly pointed interstices which serves as a decorative motif for the whole of one façade. Near it he planted poplar trees with leaf forms which echo curiously the shapes of the stones in their setting. This composition has given new life to an ancient form of building, yet how many can appreciate it as an act of decoration?

Fewer than those who raise their hands in horror at the introduction of modern sculptural art into the garden. This is as organic in its way as the decoration of the wall, because modern sculptors design for the outdoors rather than for museums and galleries. Their scale is the scale of the open landscape.

A Calder mobile sculpture in a garden at Farmington, Connecticut, is of a scale comparable to that of a fair-sized tree, and as you watch it reveal its form, turning slowly in the breeze, you realize that nothing man-sized would have served the purpose. Certainly not only of those sentimental reproductions in stone, lead, or bronze which pass under the name of sculpture in the studios. They have their appointed niches in the gardens of yesterday for which they were created. Since then, the modern arts of painting, of sculpture, and even of engineering, make possible a form of expression which is significant for the modern landscape and for man, who is a watcher there and also part of all he sees.

So much, then, for some of the new ways of approach to the old problem of garden design. As in every time of renaissance, the influences which are changing the old order come from the contempo-

rary background, and not from the medium itself. Architects and engineers were pioneers in the creation of the modern aesthetic; the integration of site and shelter and the physical conquest of space are no mean contributions to the planning art of recent times. Painters have accomplished the mastery of space in another way, through the abolition of perspective in abstract art, and sculptors have discovered that space can be described without the necessity of capturing it and holding it fast. Social reformers in housing and kindred occupations have indicated new ways to develop outdoor space, based on researches into human leisure needs and desires.

Because of these advances I would risk any accusations of irresponsibility in saying to those interested in modern garden planning: Do not go to the fashionable gardens for design inspiration. Go out and study the design of orchards, of truck gardens and experimental grounds, where plants are grown scientifically. Gardening is not a fine art: it is an art of the people. In the planning of these useful areas you will discover true organization. Go out and study nature's living structures, the detail of a woodland scene, the balance held within a community of plants; there you will learn about materials. Study the larger works of man to gain a sense of scale: new forms of shelter, the gigantic sculptures of the oil derricks, the simple pattern of a fish hatchery. Watch how water flows from a big dam, how steam shovels cut the mountainside in search of gravel for the roads. Books, studios, and dictated standards of beauty can never supplant the faculty of observation in design: this faculty can only feed on what is significant and real. And reality lies in the world between today and tomorrow, the realm of the modern movement in science and in art.

17

MICHAEL LAURIE: THOMAS CHURCH, CALIFORNIA GARDENS, AND PUBLIC LANDSCAPES

17–1

Michael Laurie is Professor of Landscape
Architecture at the University of California
at Berkeley, where he has taught since
1962. He is author of *An Introduction to
Landscape Architecture* (second edition
1986) and editor of the revised edition of
Thomas Church's *Gardens Are for People*
(1983).

It is a commonly held belief among garden historians that California was the center of a school of landscape design that broke new ground in the post–World War II years. The garden was the medium through which new concepts were expressed; it reflected aesthetic developments in art and architecture and a new social order. The modern California garden has been described as an informal outdoor living room filled with deck chairs, tables, and swings, more social than horticultural in its intention.[1] Similarities with the relationship of the Islamic house and garden or with the austere restraint and occult balance of a Japanese garden have been suggested.[2] Finally, the California garden has been described as "one of the most significant contributions to landscape design since the Olmstedian tradition of environmental planning in the second half of the 19th Century."[3]

Even if there is no real consensus about the California school of landscape design, it is clearly identified in the literature, often referred to as the California style, the Quality California look, or in other similar terms. And names are named: Thomas Church, Garrett Eckbo, Robert Royston, Theodore Osmundson, Douglas Baylis, and Lawrence Halprin, for example. Thomas Church is commonly credited with originating the new approach to garden design; the prewar publication of his work is supposed to have made him the informal leader of the school. But Church and Eckbo were equally strong in their innovative contention that the garden, in California at least, could be more or perhaps less than a collection of plants, more than an imitation of historical styles, and that it could be, once again, an art form, expressive of its place, time, and people.

The climate and landscape of California were essential to the new garden prototype. The coastal areas of the state have a Mediterranean climate. Temperatures range from the 50s F in winter to the 70s in summer, hotter in the south, cooler in the north, rarely dropping below freezing. Rainfall is limited to the winter months from November to April and typically amounts to 20–30 inches, often less. Crops and gardens must be irrigated in the summer. Predictable patterns of rainfall, warm temperatures, sunny skies, low humidity, and a dearth of flies and mosquitoes result in a climate conducive to outdoor living and make a swimming pool a worthwhile investment provided there is no shortage of water.

The relatively new geology of the Coast Ranges that run from San Francisco through Los Angeles provided sites for urban and suburban homes on steep hillsides with views. Native vegetation, such as evergreen oaks, madrone, ceanothus, and chaparral, and the introduced Australian eucalyptus cover the hills. This landscape of slopes, views, and existing vegetation was embraced as counterpoint by the designers of the modern California garden.

The historical garden tradition in California differed from that of the eastern and midwestern United States. Spanish settlement in the second half of the eighteenth century introduced mission architecture, the arcade, and the courtyard to the Pacific coast. These forms were adopted on a domestic scale by the Mexican ranchos, where patio gardens were surrounded by the rooms of the house and a connecting covered walk. Containing herbs and vegetables as well as flowers, the gardens were also places of work. By contrast, the Anglo-Victorian house of the late nineteenth century denied the benign climate and focused family life indoors. At best, a porch well off the ground would provide a protected place to sit on warm evenings. Around the house would be a landscape garden comprising a collection of exotic plants.

In the early 1900s, Henry and Charles Greene introduced a new form of domestic architecture to Southern California that responded more appropriately to the climate. Their houses reflected the concern of the arts and crafts movement for simplicity, the promotion of craftsmanship, and a back-to-nature lifestyle. The Gamble House in Pasadena (1907–1909), for example, included porches and terraces related to the rooms of the house to encourage outdoor living. The popular California bungalow, which proliferated in subsequent years as a one-story, easily maintained house type for families of modest income, was based on similar principles. A garden, though small, was considered an essential element of the home.

In the 1920s, in common with other prosperous areas, California experienced the eclectic revival in architecture and garden design. Large houses often based directly on models from Italy and Spain were surrounded with Renaissance-style terraces, clipped hedges, and classical fountains. Blind copies and excessive though these may have been, the traditional loggia facilitated an easy transition between indoors and out, by then a prescribed

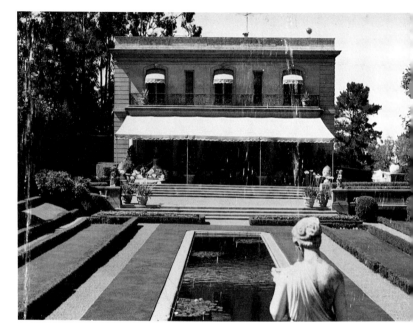

17–2

17–1   Camulos Ranch
Piru, Ventura County, California,
c. 1853.
[*Gardens of Colony and State*,
1931–1934]

17–2   Villa Rose
Near Burlingame, California,
c. 1915. Lewis P. Hobart,
architect.
[*Stately Houses of California*,
1915]

attribute as people increasingly enjoyed being outdoors in the California climate.

By the late 1930s, a simpler lifestyle led to the new problem of the small garden, usually but not always in town, that would provide maximum delight and use with minimum maintenance. The small garden could not be natural if it was to serve as an extension of the house, nor could the heroic proportions of the classic formal garden fit into the limited area available.

The postwar years saw the full flowering of the informal California lifestyle. Californians had always been obsessed with the outdoors, having spectacular landscape easily accessible and the Sierra Club to remind them about its virtues. A tradition of eating out of doors dating back to the rancho barbecue, and the informal entertaining that it inspired, was a major theme of *California Sunset* magazine, whose readership included new immigrants from the East and Midwest with young children: mobile, active, and interested in sports and leisure. The garden came to be considered an extra living room for the shrinking middle-class family house.

The modern California garden evolved in the '40s and '50s as a prototype from a distillation of the master works of Church, Eckbo, and others, photographed and published in popular magazines such as *House Beautiful, House and Garden,* and *Sunset.* A primary characteristic of the prototype is its small size or compact form, even where plenty of land is available; for example, half an acre of designed garden in the country, and town gardens as small as 1,000 square feet. Other typical features include direct indoor-outdoor connections and a predominant use of hard surfaces adjacent to the house for garden furniture; grass, if any, confined to a small irrigated area; on sloping sites, wooden decks to extend usable level space and provide views; swimming pool, barbecue, and provision for other recreational pursuits: fences, walls, and screens creating privacy and hiding utilities and neighbors with immediate effect (essential for mobile families); shade provided by inclusion of existing trees into the design or by a constructed overhead trellis; car parking space, especially in the country, often exceeding the size of the house in area; and of course plants, the quantity and variety depending on the owners' interest—a lemon in a pot, espaliered fruit trees, geraniums, or special collections.

Although each garden was different in style, reflecting site, architecture, owners' preferences, and designer's approach, these were the basic characteristics of the California garden. It was an artistic, functional, and social composition, every part of it carefully considered within the context of climate, landscape, and lifestyle. As such, it was a reflection of time, place, and people.

Born in Boston in 1902, Thomas Church spent his childhood in the Ojai Valley of southern California. There he learned to love the native landscape and to appreciate the advantages and limita-

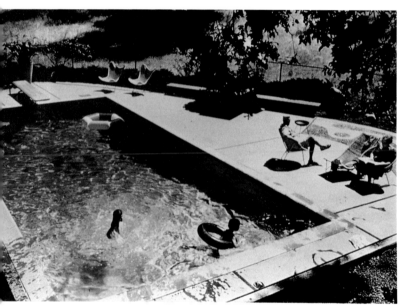

17–3

17–3　A generic modern California garden
Designer unknown.

17–4　Pasatiempo Garden
Santa Cruz, California, 1930.
Thomas Church, landscape
architect.
[courtesy Thomas Church and
Associates]

tions of the climate and its great potential for outdoor living. His adolescence was spent in Berkeley, where at the age of 12, Dolliver (the middle name by which his family called him) made his first garden for his mother on an open lot adjacent to their home. The young gardener terraced the sloping site, built steps, seeded a lawn, and planted roses and privet hedges.[4] But his route into landscape architecture was not clearly marked. As a student at the University of California at Berkeley, he was expected by his family to major in law. However, a course in the history of garden design, offered by the fledgling division of landscape design in the College of Agriculture, intrigued him so much that he changed his direction and graduated with a degree in landscape architecture in 1922.

On the West Coast in those days, the landscape profession was dominated by a few professionals, most of whom were educated in the East and whose practice involved adapting eastern landscape or classical garden concepts to the California landscape and climate. By 1920, Los Angeles, Santa Barbara, and to a lesser degree San Francisco all had houses and gardens built in the Italian and Spanish traditions, often within an English landscape garden setting. Evidence indicates that as a student at Berkeley, Church was fascinated by this work. To expand his skills, based until then on his study of garden history and horticulture as well as keen observation, Church enrolled as a student of landscape architecture at Harvard University's Graduate School of Design, where the subject had been taught since 1900.

Even more important to his development, however, was the opportunity to travel in Europe. As a recipient of the Sheldon Travel Scholarship, Church spent six months in Italy and Spain. On his return to the United States in 1927, he submitted a master's thesis that drew parallels between the climates and landscapes of the Mediterranean region and California. Church interleaved pictures of houses and gardens in Santa Barbara with descriptions and photographs of the villas and gardens of Tuscany and Frascati, which he found "delightful and livable because of scale and imagination—not magnificence." He compared sixteenth-century Italy and twentieth-century California in terms of the number of wealthy patrons who aspired to comfort, luxury, and beauty, concluding, "As in Italy and Spain, the pleasure of living out-of-doors, the need of shade, and the conservation of water are all problems which the California gardener must meet and answer."[5] Climate that made outdoor living a constant and central aspect of home life was to become a major influence on Church's approach to garden design. The need for irrigation in summer necessitated simple planting plans, small symbolic areas of lawn, and the use of native and other drought-tolerant plants. Above all, Church believed that the cultivated garden area should be compact and clearly defined.

Church returned to the Bay Area in 1929 and was soon at work on Pasatiempo, a planned com-

17–4

17–5

munity near Santa Cruz. His contribution was the siting of individual houses in the natural landscape and the design of patio gardens suited to the Spanish rancho-style architecture. The gardens were carefully separated from the surrounding landscape by clipped hedges. Distant views were created or maintained by selective pruning of the coast live oaks and madrones, within which the houses were set for shade and wind protection. The simplicity of these outdoor rooms, the use of paved surfaces and low-maintenance planting, and the careful preservation of existing mature trees characterize Church's early style and much of his later work.

Until the late 1930s, Church's designs could be described as quite conservative; although not replicas of historical models, they were clearly based on traditional principles. After another European trip in 1937 to study the work of Le Corbusier and the Finnish architect and designer Alvar Aalto, as well as that of modern painters and sculptors, Church began a period of experimentation with new forms. Two small gardens designed for the 1939 Golden Gate Exposition marked the beginning of this new phase. They demonstrated the possibilities for the evolution of new visual forms in the garden while satisfying all practical criteria. The central axis was abandoned in favor of multiplicity of viewpoints, simple planes, and flowing lines. Texture and color, space and form were manipulated in a manner reminiscent of the cubist painters. A variety of curvilinear shapes, textured surfaces, and walls were combined with a sure sense of proportion, and the gardens incorporated some new materials such as corrugated asbestos and wooden paving blocks. Stylistically these gardens were a very dramatic advance on all previous designs in the United States.

The new house and its small garden, he argued, "must go to work for us, solving our living problems while it also pleases our eyes and our emotional psychological needs." The new kind of garden did not arise from arbitrary whim or designer's caprice; it evolved naturally and inevitably from people's requirements. Out of the solution to these requirements came a whole new visual aesthetic, and "since the garden is being designed more and more to be seen from several parts of the house, the plan of it cannot be rigid, and set with a beginning and an end. The lines of the modern garden must be moving and flowing so that it is pleasing when seen from all directions both inside and out."[6] This notion suggests the influence of cubism on Church's aesthetic thinking about the garden. Similarly Stephen C. Pepper, professor of philosophy and aesthetics at the University of California at Berkeley, suggested in 1948 that the arts had rediscovered space; "the creation of a garden in this new light becomes something halfway between the making of a painting and the making of a house. It is as if the landscape architects were composing an abstract painting for people to live within."[7]

Church had arrived on the landscape scene at a time of transition. He was traditional enough to

17–6

17–5   Exhibition garden
17–6   San Francisco, California, 1939.
       Thomas Church, landscape
       architect.
       [courtesy Thomas Church and
       Associates]

17–7

see value in the old, open enough to consider the new, and sensible enough to know that each, to be good, must be the product of a thorough knowledge of the principles on which it was based. Thus, Garrett Eckbo, a younger and equally distinguished colleague of the California school, has described Church in conversation as "the last great traditional designer and the first great modern designer."

The variety to be found in the approximately 2,000 gardens designed in 40 years of practice not only substantiates this claim but also illustrates Church's respect for the unique qualities of every situation.

The gardens of the late '40s indicate a continuation of Church's exploration of new forms: curvilinear pools, zigzags and piano curves, trompe l'oeil, and false perspective; but always with respect for context. Nevertheless, Church did not reject other styles that his clients might have preferred; "formal or informal, curved, straight, symmetrical or free, the important thing is that you end up with a functional plan and an artistic composition."[8] More specifically, his approach to design sought direction from three major sources: the site, the architecture of the house, and the client's personality and preferences.

The best plans and the greatest designs depend on attention to detail, both in execution and after the project is completed. In this Church was preeminent, carefully selecting materials and colors, personally designing corners and edges, employing historically proven forms or inventing new ones. In the garden for the Aptos beach house (1948), for example, diagonal redwood decking extended the house into the site, its powerful zigzag with nautical lockerlike seating challenging the flowing wavelike curves of other edges. The central space, which in other situations would have been a lawn or swimming pool, was filled with sand from the beach.

The very small San Francisco town garden for the Kirkhams (1948) utilized the same curve and zigzag motifs at a different scale and for different purposes. Wood and concrete surfaces provide space for outdoor living, sheltered from view and winds by fences, flowery planting, and a grove of birches. The diagonal is emphasized to create an illusion of space.

At the Mein garden at Woodside (1953), Church experimented with forced perspective in the shapes of the brick terrace next to the house and a swimming pool that combines straight edges with arc and circle. Existing trees were carefully integrated into the design, which reflected the sloping site and desired southern orientation for the house.

Regardless of their purely visual characteristics, Church's gardens typically embodied several basic concepts. These include: careful *siting* and orientation of the house with regard to sun, views, exposure, existing trees, and topography; a distinct *sequence* of arrival including entrance drive, parking area, and front door; a *direct connection* between

17–7　Beach house garden
Aptos, California, 1949. Thomas Church, landscape architect.
[courtesy Thomas Church and Associates]

17–8　Town garden
San Francisco, California, 1948. Thomas Church, landscape architect.
[Rondall Partridge, courtesy Thomas Church and Associates]

house and garden, including provision for outdoor living; a *defined edge* for the garden, separating and at the same time joining it to the surrounding landscape; *provision for functional spaces*—parking, garage, work area, kitchen garden, doghouse, etc.— plus ease of maintenance; *a selection of plants* that would reinforce the structure of the garden and the objectives of the plan.

All these concepts are clearly demonstrated at the Donnell garden in Sonoma (1948). A long winding drive leads the visitor from the main road through the hilly landscape to a spacious parking area sheltered by California live oaks near the top of the hill. A diagonal concrete arrival terrace is angled on the front door and runs straight through the main public room of the house and out through sliding doors to the garden, with framed views of the river, bay, and San Francisco skyline in the distance. The house is nestled into the live oaks. The extent of the garden is limited to three paved areas, one with a terazzo dance surface. A thin lawn and the entire south edge of the garden are defined by a broad low juniper hedge. Following this to the top of the hill, one arrives at the much-photographed swimming pool, guest house, and lanai complex once again integrated with land form and existing trees for wind protection. A deck extends the pool surround where the land begins to slope away; trees protrude through its wooden slats. There is an extensive service area hidden behind the house, including garage, cutting garden, vegetables, compost, etc. In this exceptional place at a quite grand scale can be seen all the components of the ideal, but some aspect of each can be traced in all Church's gardens of whatever size or style.

Although garden design was always Church's chief interest and the principal source of his reputation, he is also known as the landscape architect of record for several major large-scale projects completed in the postwar decade. The reason for this may lie in the friendship and trust of William Wurster, a noted West Coast architect who, as Dean of Architecture and Planning at MIT (1944–1950), moved in the widest and highest architectural circles. A word from Wurster put Church on the design team, and eventually, as his reputation grew, a design team without Church was like a crown without a diamond. The depression and the altered priorities of war may also have led him by necessity into public and corporate projects. Church's contribution at this scale was of two types: first, as a consultant—visiting sites, talking to architects and planners, and making recommendations; and second, as a designer and site planner in association with architects for specific buildings in context, for which he produced working drawings and built forms.

The Valencia Public Housing project in San Francisco (1939–1943), an early collaboration with Wurster, was published as a completed project in the 1948 "Landscape Design Exhibition" at the San Francisco Museum of Modern Art. It was voted by

17–8

17–9

17–10

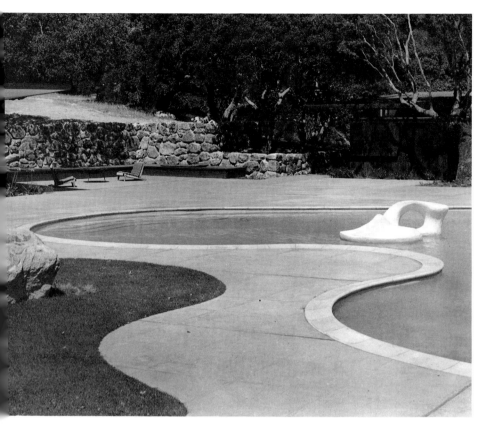

17–11

17–9 Garden at Woodside, California
1953. Thomas Church, landscape
architect.
[Ernest Braun, courtesy
Thomas Church and Associates]

17–10 Henderson garden
Burlingame, California, 1959.
Thomas Church, landscape
architect.
[courtesy Thomas Church and
Associates]

17–11 Donnell garden
Sonoma, California, 1948. Thomas
Church, landscape architect.
[Rondall Partridge, courtesy
Thomas Church and Associates]

the Museum of Modern Art as one of the most out-
standing housing projects in the United States. The
sunny courtyards were paved with exposed aggre-
gate to the base of the three-story buildings and
furnished with raised lozenge-shaped lawns framed
by brick seat walls, tree clumps, and animal sculptures by Benjamin Bufano. It was an extremely
clean design in which "planting and maintenance
[were] reduced to a minimum without sacrificing
aesthetic standards."[9]

The huge and innovative Park Merced (Metropolitan Life) middle-income housing development
in San Francisco (1941–1950) was based, according
to Robert Royston, very much on Church's concept.[10] Here, streets radiating out from a central
plaza produced pie-shaped lots with interior garden
courtyards surrounded by two- and three-story du-
plex rental units of varying size (later tower blocks
were added). Sheltered from the wind, the courtyards contained a children's playground and communal landscape. Each ground level apartment had
a screened patio linked by paths to the garage,
which was a separate element of the plan. Strong
planting helped to achieve a clear pattern of public
and private use areas, and the predominantly low-
rise development with varied architectural treatment and nonrectangular layout contrasted favorably with Stuyvesant Town in New York by the
same developer.

There is less certainty about Church's role at
the General Motors Technical Center (1949–1959)
outside Detroit with its 22-acre artificial lake and
four islands of weeping willows, two spectacular
fountains, and tall shining water tower, which came
to be known as GM's Industrial Versailles. Here
Church's relationship with Eero Saarinen was that
of consultant, and in this capacity he attended
meetings and spent a lot of time in the field.[11] The
resultant massive tree planting reinforced the rectangular plan and produced a sense of total unity
between the 25 high tech buildings, the massive reflecting pool, and the site. It is a fine example of
Church's capacity for bold understatement.

A similar situation can be imagined for his
work with Edward Durrell Stone on the Stanford
Medical Center (1959). Dubbed by the *Architectural Forum* "Medicine's Taj Mahal," it was a garden hospital that did not look like a hospital. Low-
rise buildings were arranged on the site of gnarled
oaks and towering eucalyptus; courtyards, galleries, balconies, terraces, and lacy grills ensured that
every room looked out onto a sunny garden, intended to heal the soul as well as the body. At the
entrance, in the center of a 10-acre quadrangle,
Church designed a massive fountain pool with circular islands and Italian cypress, a theatrical gesture
in keeping with the architecture and spirit of the
place.

Another kind of large-scale landscape architecture in which Church played a significant role
was campus planning for Stanford University and
the University of California at Berkeley (1962) and
Santa Cruz (1962). Louis DeMonte, campus archi-

17–12

17–13

17–14

17–12   Valencia Public Housing Project
        San Francisco, California, 1939–
        1943. William Wurster, architect;
        Thomas Church, landscape
        architect.
        [courtesy Thomas Church and
        Associates]

17–13   Park Merced
        Metropolitan Life Housing
        Development, San Francisco,
        1941–1950. Schultze, architect;
        Thomas Church, landscape
        architect.
        [courtesy Thomas Church and
        Associates]

17–14   General Motors Technical Center
        Detroit, Michigan, 1949–1959.
        Eero Saarinen, architect; Thomas
        Church, landscape architect.

tect, tells of Church's contribution to the Central Campus Landscape Plan for Berkeley, in which Church identified those spaces and elements essential to its unique visual quality and those areas where a formal architectural quality should prevail and be encouraged. Working on the master plan, Church was "a key part of the team."[12] Church was also responsible for siting and integrating 10 major new buildings at Berkeley whose details (lighting fixtures, benches, kiosks, and bold retaining walls) established an appropriate design vocabulary for the campus.

At Santa Cruz, Church was involved with initial proposals for a new 2,000-acre campus in a redwood forest. His recommendations warned of the potential impact on the forest and consisted of an aesthetic charter for the campus that stressed the importance of land, site, and landscape qualities and the siting of buildings determined by topography and groves, not as a preconceived diagram.[13] Although mistakes have been made in their realization, these concepts have guided development of the campus as a unique synthesis of architecture and landscape. His design work for campus urban places shows an understanding of scale and use. The College Avenue entrance to the Berkeley Campus (1964) and the White Memorial Plaza at Stanford (1964) both look best filled with students. Both have fountains as focal points but there is no formula applied indiscriminately. Sensitivity to the different architectural and landscape contexts led Church to design asymmetrical space in the first instance and a strong axial layout for the second.

Other large-scale projects included recreation facilities for prosperous new companies such as Hewlett Packard in Palo Alto (1960) and the Stuart Chemical Company in Pasadena (1958). For the latter, working again with Edward Durrell Stone, the "tropical" architecture was enhanced by Church with floating planted islands and hanging gold saucer gardens. A garden court and dining lounge were connected to the recreation area with an oval swimming pool, pool house, and other facilities for the employees.

Using a particular style—modern or traditional—never seemed to be an issue for Church. In almost all his public work and many of his later private garden designs, there is a classical approach that draws strength from the architecture. The San Francisco Opera House courtyard (1935) is the most obvious example, but others like Stuart Chemical only barely conceal the axiality of the design with flamboyant planting and unusual materials.

The influence of Thomas Church in the development of a modern landscape design to accompany modern architecture was powerful and widespread. His rapport and successful collaboration with major architects and publication of their projects in *Architectural Forum* and *Architectural Record* brought him professional recognition and high visibility. He was awarded the Fine Arts Medal of the American Institute of Architects in 1951. The frequent publication of many of his 2,000 gardens in the popular press and magazines illustrated with his own photographs established his reputation as a designer of innovative yet sensible gardens. His *Gardens Are for People,* published in 1955, compiled his ideas and designs to date in one volume. In addition, his office nurtured a set of younger landscape architects who would in turn contribute to the California school: Robert Royston, Douglas Baylis, Theodore Osmundson, and Lawrence Halprin all started their careers there.

Church's success and fame were a result of his skill in combining the rational with the romantic; his ability to produce form related to the site and to the purpose of the place; his concern for materials and details; and above all, his relationship with his clients who were willing participants in the process.

17–15

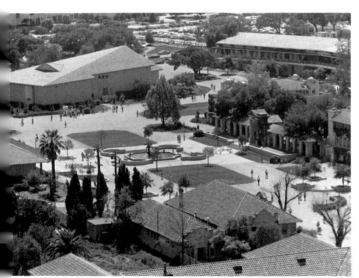

17–16

17–15 Medical Center
Stanford, California, 1959. Edward
Durrell Stone, architect; Thomas
Church, landscape architect.
[courtesy Visual Art Services,
Stanford University]

17–16 White Memorial Plaza
Stanford University, California,
1964. Thomas Church, landscape
architect.
[courtesy Department of Special
Collections, Stanford University
Libraries]

Notes

1 Christopher Grampp, "Gardens for California Living," *Landscape* 28, no. 3 (1985), 40.

2 Sylvia Crowe, "Garden Design," *Country Life* (London, 1958), 75.

3 David Streatfield, "Where Pine and Palm Meet: The California Garden as Regional Expression," *Landscape Journal* 4, no. 2 (Fall 1985), 61.

4 Elizabeth Church, in Thomas D. Church Oral History Project, The Bancroft Library, University of California, 1978, p. 374.

5 Thomas Dolliver Church, "A Study of Mediterranean Gardens and Their Adaptability to California Conditions," master's thesis, Harvard University, 1927.

6 Thomas Church, "The Small California Garden," *California Arts and Architecture* (May 1933), 16.

7 Stephen C. Pepper, in *Landscape Design* (exhibition catalogue, San Francisco Museum of Modern Art, 1948), 5.

8 Thomas Church, *Gardens Are for People* (New York: Reinhold, 1955), 53.

9 *Landscape Design* (exhibition catalogue, San Francisco Museum of Modern Art, 1948), 34.

10 Robert Royston in Thomas D. Church Oral History Project, The Bancroft Library, University of California, 1978, p. 219.

11 Ibid.

12 Louis DeMonte in Thomas Church Oral History Project, The Bancroft Library, University of California, 1978, p. 273.

13 Jack Stafford in Thomas Church Oral History Project, The Bancroft Library, University of California, 1978, p. 625.

18

To treat history as an accumulation of garden features . . . is to leave us here in the middle of the twentieth century with a horrible potpourri of Egyptian pyramids, Babylonian hanging gardens, Roman atriums and Spanish patios, Medieval cloisters, Renaissance terraces and parterres, English landscape gardens, Colonial box gardens, Chinese pagodas, Japanese lanterns and rocks, American alpine beds. What do we do with it? What principles of organization must we establish to wade through this eclectic hash and determine a clear, clean, and beautiful way of solving our own problems on their own terms with the materials we have at hand? That is the objective of this book—to point a way out of the swamp of eclecticism and sentimentality in which the leaders of landscape architecture and horticulture have left us.

Landscape for Living, 10

Reuben M. Rainey is Associate Professor of Landscape Architecture at the University of Virginia, where he teaches history and theory. Before entering the field of landscape architecture, he taught history and philosophy of religion at Columbia University and Middlebury College.

Garrett Eckbo's *Landscape for Living* exhibits all the verve and fervor of a manifesto while denying the pretension of being one. It depicts the profession of landscape architecture in North America as mired in a Slough of Despond like John Bunyan's famous Pilgrim. According to Eckbo's precise chemical analysis, the stagnant waters of that slough are a solution of bizarre eclecticism, a rigid and inappropriate set of a priori design formulae, a simplistic dualistic vocabulary of "formal" and "informal," a bag of irresponsible "juke box tricks," a penchant for static pictures rather than space, and an over-emphasis on artistic intuition at the expense of the rigor of empirical science. Further analysis reveals additional pollutants—a general neglect of the specific needs of twentieth-century human beings, an erroneous understanding of the relationship of the built landscape to the world of nature, and a copy-book view of historical precedent rooted in a measured-drawings approach to the great works of landscape architecture.

This sharp polemic is a prelude to a positive vision of a rejuvenated profession, one Eckbo charges with the mission of creating a more humane environment, in concert with architects, planners, and engineers. Written in the halcyon days of American economic prosperity after World War II and first published in 1950, *Landscape for Living* exudes the optimism of an era rife with visions of a new world order based on democratic government and the enlightened application of scientific knowledge to human welfare. It quickly became one of the classics of landscape architectural design theory. Addressed to a North American audience of professionals and lay people alike, it was the first comprehensive theory of modern landscape architecture to be written in the postwar period.[1] While exhibiting a sense of humor rare in the literature of design theory, it laid no claim to final answers. It opened *a* way, not *the* way out of the "swamp of eclecticism." It intended "to begin discussion not to end it."

That discussion was both immediate and prolonged. *Landscape for Living* quickly replaced Henry Hubbard and Theodora Kimball's authoritative *An Introduction to the Study of Landscape Design* (first published in 1917) as the most influential work on design theory in American professional schools and remained so through the '50s and '60s. In the immediate postwar period, "Hubbard and Kimball," as the book was usually referred to, was perceived as dated and narrow by many practicing professionals and academicians, but no comprehensive replacement had yet appeared. *Landscape for Living* was widely read and favorably received. Many landscape architects who were in school or just beginning practice in the 1950s recall the sense of intellectual excitement generated by its appearance and its prolonged influence on their thinking about design.

In a manner reminiscent of Sigmund Freud's case studies, *Landscape for Living* was written in the heat of a busy professional life in the firm of Eckbo, Royston and Williams, Planning Consultants and Landscape Architects. The context for that practice was Los Angeles and San Francisco, which at the time were tearing down, building, and expanding at an unprecedented rate. The book was illustrated exclusively with the work of Eckbo's own firm. This was not an act of hubris. Rather it was as if Eckbo were saying, "This is how my firm is addressing basic questions of landscape design, and I invite you to find your own voice, keeping in mind the fundamental issues I have discussed."

What were those fundamental issues? A good way to explore them is to look at several specific works of landscape design, comparing some that Eckbo found lacking with those he offered as effective alternatives in the illustrated portions of *Landscape for Living*. Revolutions in politics or art are best understood by examining what they negate, what they affirm, and the relationship between the two. In the case of landscape architecture, examples from Hubbard and Kimball can represent the *ancien régime,* or as Eckbo often called it, the "Beaux Arts" approach. For the sake of clarity I will focus on their examples of residential site planning, although their book addresses a variety of project types, including gardens, residential communities, and urban parks. A comparison of their site plans with some of Eckbo's own in *Landscape for Living* will lead us into the heart of Eckbo's thought and reveal the fundamental contours of his modernism. Hubbard and Kimball is an appropriate choice, given its pervasive influence and the fact that Eckbo was quite familiar with it as an assigned textbook when he was a graduate student at Harvard. In fact, the marginal notes in his student copy take issue with most of the book's fundamental tenets and contain the seeds of many of his more developed ideas in *Landscape for Living*.[2] However, it would be simplistic to view the latter merely as a

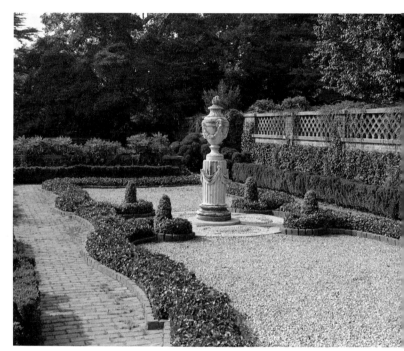

18–1

18–1   The Urn Terrace
Dumbarton Oaks, Washington,
D.C., designed by Beatrix
Farrand, one of the best surviving
examples of the Beaux-Arts
garden design tradition repudiated
by Garrett Eckbo.
[Dumbarton Oaks Research
Library and Collections,
Washington, D.C.]

18–2

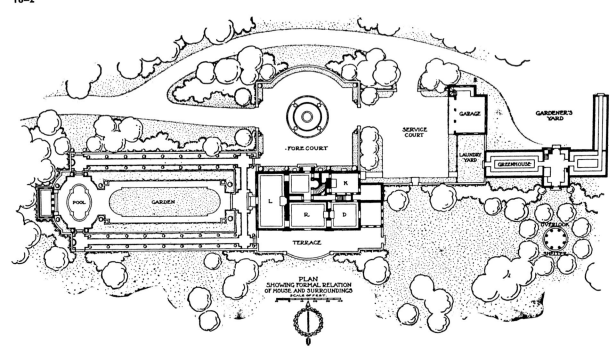

PLAN
SHOWING FORMAL RELATION
OF HOUSE AND SURROUNDINGS
SCALE OF FEET.

18–2 A characteristic Beaux-Arts
residential site plan
Hubbard and Kimball. With entry
court, garden terrace, lawn, and
separate service precinct.
[from *An Introduction to the Study
of Landscape Design*]

reaction to Hubbard and Kimball, since *Landscape for Living* takes into account a wider range of theoretical literature not only in landscape architecture but in architecture and planning as well.

Figure 18–2, a typical residential site plan illustration from Hubbard and Kimball, is based on a host of underlying assumptions concerning the nature of landscape architecture as a "fine art," the use of historical precedent, certain fundamental design principles, and an understanding of the relationship between professional and client. These assumptions are carefully explicated and meticulously documented; to do them justice requires an exposition of some length.[3]

Landscape architecture for Hubbard and Kimball is a "fine art," and, like all fine art, its most important goal is to create "an effect of pleasure in the mind of the beholder." Of course the plan must also address functional and economic needs, but its ultimate aim is to produce a pleasurable response from the client, whose specific tastes and aesthetic needs must be carefully considered. The capacity to experience aesthetic pleasure is "born in the human mind," which is another way of saying it is innate, although it can be developed and refined by the study of great examples of design work.

Thus the goal of design for Hubbard and Kimball is primarily a "psychological effect." Such pleasure is produced when we experience certain *forms* arranged in *unified compositions.* Our perception of such unity and the "emotional" pleasure this perception evokes is "beauty." Beauty is not intrinsic to these forms themselves; it is a quality we attribute to them because their unity pleases us. There is no absolute canon of beauty—it is often perceived differently by different individuals.[4]

Thus the ultimate success of a residential site plan *as a work of art* will be judged in terms of whether or not it elicits a sense of pleasure from those who participate in it. Such a feeling is known as a "landscape effect"; it can result from the experience of either a work of art or a natural landscape untouched by any sort of intervention. While "pleasure" is the predominant effect, such experience can also include various "moods," such as melancholy or gaiety, depending on the character of a given landscape. For the designer, it is important to understand that landscape effects are stimulated primarily through the sense of sight and more indirectly through the sense of touch, which includes the bodily sensation of moving through a design. Other sensations, such as taste, smell, and hearing, are of lesser importance.

Hubbard and Kimball also assert that our experience of pleasure is far from simple. It is a rich and complex state composed of three distinct types of pleasure, that of *sensation, perception,* and *intellection.* In the immediacy of our experience, we are unconscious of these three distinct forms, but analysis after the fact reveals their existence. The pleasure of sensation is stimulated by an intense, direct, simple, and unreflective sensing of an object or group of objects. For example, the garden to the

east of the terrace in figure 18–2 may dazzle us with the emerald green of its turf parterre, and we simply revel in the intensity of the pleasure without further reflection. The pleasure of perception occurs simultaneously with that of sensation. It involves perceiving the orderly arrangement of objects in space and remembering similar images from past experience. One may even be inspired to create new configurations of similar forms in the imagination. For example, gazing at the same garden, we take note of its symmetries and how its corners are marked by elegant statues. We are reminded of a similar garden we once visited in Tuscany and may even engage in a pleasant reverie of designing such a garden for the estate of a friend. Indeed much of the pleasure of perception resides in association, which differs from individual to individual. Finally, we experience intellective pleasure as well, which is essentially conscious and rational reflection on the specific qualities and properties of objects. For example, we might admire the carefully crafted stonework in the garden's retaining walls or their skillful buttressing and economic construction.

Thus the pleasure we experience from a "beautiful" work of landscape architecture engages many capacities of the human psyche, ranging from immediate sensation, to memory and creative fantasy, to rational analysis. Although a genius may be able to create a design that includes all three intuitively, we lesser mortals will be assisted in our work if we consciously take all three into account. Hubbard and Kimball will have nothing to do with design cookbooks; following pat rules will not *guarantee* good design, nor will studying historical precedent. Furthermore, "no esthetic theory is final" and "most of the essential fire of emotion in . . . design" is "forever untranslatable into written words." Yet conscious reflection on design principles and a knowledge of the design excellence of the past can be of considerable assistance if used properly as tools for exploration and creative adaptation.

For Hubbard and Kimball the critical ingredient in this threefold experience of pleasure is a perception of "unity" in the design. Such unity is essentially "completeness of organization," which is achieved primarily by designing a site as a series of self-contained, well-ordered visual compositions or scenes that are clearly connected either by axes or a processional path. The various elements of these compositions—primarily shapes, colors, and textures—are to be structured according to the design principles of sequence, balance, and repetition. The particular manner in which such unity is expressed is known as "style." Style is based in large part on an "ideal"—a prototypical example, or "composite photograph," of a class of objects that manifest "exceptional" unity. As a designer my first question in approaching a project should be "what is my ideal?" That is to say, which prototypical image of aesthetic unity should I apply to this particular situation? By studying the styles of past generations, I can de-

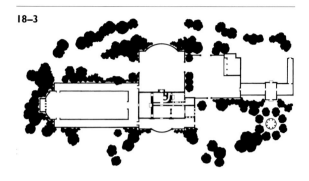

18–3

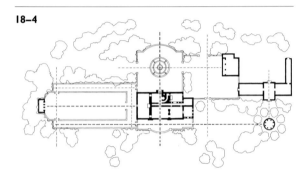

18–4

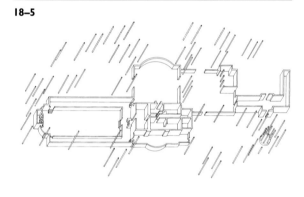

18–5

18–3 Figure and ground in Hubbard and Kimball's typical residential site plan
The plan structures the site around well-defined spaces that enframe views frequently terminated by focal points.

18–4 Axis diagram of the typical residential site plan
A central axis and secondary cross axes link the various indoor and outdoor spaces.

18–5 Axonometric of the typical residential site plan
The plan consists of a hierarchy of well-defined spaces arranged along sight lines. House and site are designed as a totality.

velop my own "taste," which is the ability to perceive such ideals. This enables me to accumulate a treasure trove of design precedents, or prototypical stylistic ideals, such as the Italian Renaissance garden or the eighteenth-century English park. In the case of the garden in figure 18–2, its ideal is most likely derived from sixteenth- and seventeenth-century Italian gardens. This is clearly a typological approach to design that relies heavily on the adaptation of historical precedent to present conditions.

Hubbard and Kimball warn, however, that we must not be mere "copyists" or archaeologists. Rather, we must creatively adapt the styles of the past to the tasks of the present. Originality in design is basically the imaginative application of proven precedent. We should also bear in mind that styles are the products of particular cultures and their physical environments. If I am designing in climatic and functional conditions similar to certain historic styles, then I am justified in adapting one or more of those stylistic ideals. For example, an interpretation of a Moorish patio would be appropriate for a townhouse in Tucson but not in Anchorage. Some cases are not so clear-cut. An exact replica of a sixteenth-century Italian villa might be inappropriate for the Boston suburbs, but if it were "interpreted" in local materials and plants hardy to the region it would probably be suitable, especially if the owner was a professor of Renaissance history or an ardent traveler to Italy for whom this particular style had many positive associations.

Hubbard and Kimball claim that the whole of the history of landscape architecture can be distilled into two predominant styles—the "humanized" or "formal," and the "naturalized" or "informal." The formal style expresses the control of humans over the natural world. It arranges clear geometrical forms in carefully orchestrated relationships, often making use of axial spatial organization. Informal design expresses humanity's understanding and reverence for the organization of nature and the pleasure to be derived from this. It strives to express not the dominance of human will but "the complete expression of nature's self." It employs the complex forms of the natural world and eschews the axial spatial organization and pristine Euclidian geometry of the formal tradition. Hubbard and Kimball contend that one should have a good command of both of these styles and on occasion can even combine them in a design, as they have done in figure 18–2—where the formal style is embodied in the house plan, the terrace, the garden, and the entry court, while the perimeter of the site is treated in an informal style reminiscent of English eighteenth-century parks. The lawn serves as a transition between the two. (See figure 18–6.) Both the formal and the informal style have their appropriate context, but in some passages Hubbard and Kimball seem to imply a preference for the informal style as a "higher art" that is more "subtle" and can enrich human life by bringing it into close association with the ordered world of natural processes. (The influence of Frederick Law Olmsted, Sr., obviously looms large here.)

Having set forth the basic tenets of their theory of aesthetics, Hubbard and Kimball proceed to outline a multitude of specific design principles to guide the practitioner in planting and the use of various structures and materials. They also provide, with great assurance, minutely detailed guidelines for the design of various project types—gardens, residences, subdivisions, and nature preserves. While our concern is specifically with their residential guidelines, it is important to note that these share an aesthetic point of view with their guidelines for other project types. Whether we are designing a park or a residential complex, the project should be structured by carefully orchestrated views and embody either formal or informal style or a judicious mixture of the two.

The site plan in figure 18–2, which has served to illustrate Hubbard and Kimball's general theory of aesthetics, can also provide examples of almost all their specific guidelines for the design of residential properties. They do not indicate whether this plan is a hypothetical example or a real design, but for our purposes this does not matter. (It bears a striking resemblance to the work of Charles Platt, whom Hubbard and Kimball greatly admired.)[5] The site is a gently sloping forested hillside with a panoramic view and a highly desired southern exposure. The plan includes Hubbard and Kimball's typical elements for a residential site plan—house, entry court, service buildings, garden, terrace, entry road, service road, sweeping, tree-studded lawn, and ornamental structures—arranged in a series of compositions linked by various major and minor axes (figures 18–3, 4, 5). The major north-south axis extends from the forecourt through the house's entrance hall and reception room to the main terrace, which opens to the panoramic view across the extensive lawn. A series of secondary east-west axes establish a variety of additional views that serve as counterpoints to the terrace vista (figures 18–7, 8, 9).[6] The formal garden is set apart as a distinct unit, carefully enclosed and clearly revealing itself as a work of human artifice. One can view it as a single unit from its raised entry stairway on the east side; it is terminated by the focal point of the pavilion, which is carefully set against the dark wall of the surrounding forest (figure 18–8). The garden itself is structured on three axes, the central of which aligns with the door to the living room on the west facade. Thus the plan treats house and garden as a single unit. The garden's walkways define the other two axes. The southernmost of them directs one's view east across the terrace to a small temple sited in a circular bosk (figure 18–9). Two additional main east-west axes extend from the forecourt to the garage and from the greenhouse through the garden service building. These axes do not serve to structure views; rather they establish an orderly relationship among the various service buildings and entry court.

18–6

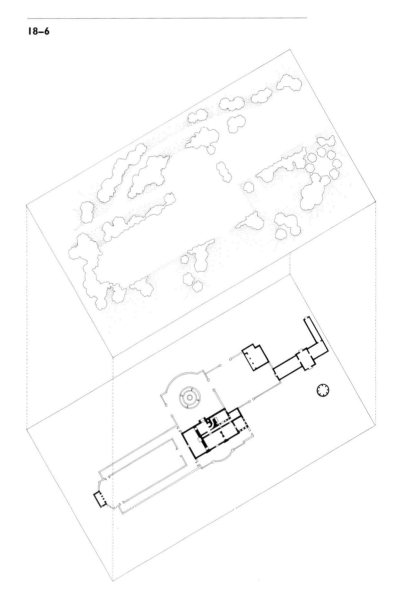

18–6   A diagram of formal and informal elements in the typical residential site plan
The "informal" treatment is mostly confined to the perimeter of the site, while the "formal" is basically an extension of the interior of the house into the landscape.

The site plan carefully relates all of the views to the various rooms of the house. The most important room, the living room, is provided with the garden view. This garden serves, as all gardens should, as an "outdoor living room," a place of "calm" and "repose" where one is brought into close association with the processes of nature. A garden, according to Hubbard and Kimball, should be designed as a three-part composition—a ground plane, enclosing walls, and various individual objects, primarily structures and ornaments. This garden's "floor" is predominantly a simple turf panel providing a quiet foreground to the view west to the pool and pavilion. (A more elaborate parterre would have destroyed the unity of the view by competing with the more distant focal points.) All of the views or compositions are distinct, well-enclosed units, illustrating another of Hubbard and Kimball's basic tenets. One discovers them by moving through the site. Each is different in character, adding up to an ensemble of rich but highly unified counterpoints: the panoramic sweep of the lawn (figure 18–7), the crisp, serene geometry of the formal garden (figure 18–8), the dark and intimate bosk enclosing the circular temple (figure 18–9). These views are carefully screened from all service facilities and they are not crossed by either the entry or the service road, which would spoil their unity and character.

The plan is also an excellent illustration of Hubbard and Kimball's emphasis on zoning for functional efficiency. The house plan provides private living quarters on the second floor and semipublic spaces for entertaining and family living on the first floor. Entry road and service road are carefully separated. A clearly defined forecourt provides ample parking for guests. All service facilities are clustered conveniently near the kitchen, which is located in the northeast corner of the house to avoid cooking odors in the main suite of rooms.

The various compositions of this plan were probably intended to conjure up pleasant associations—the formal garden, for instance, perhaps served as a reminder of the family's last junket to Vicenza or Verona, or their love of classical art. Yet nothing in this site plan is an *exact* copy of a historical design. Rather we have, as Hubbard and Kimball advocate, an interpretation of historical precedent articulated in local materials and adapted to this particular site. The skillful use of sequence, balance, and repetition in the various compositions would have produced a "landscape effect" of "serenity" and "calm" befitting a country house, which should be a "retreat" from the "noise and hurry of the outside world."

Other examples of Hubbard and Kimball's residential site design reveal how these guidelines can be adapted to a wide variety of site conditions—an oceanfront site (figure 18–10), a rural site with somewhat complex topography (figure 18–11), and a sloping suburban site (figure 18–12).[7] The oceanfront property is designed around four major views structured by axes. The kitchen is canted to

18–7

18–8

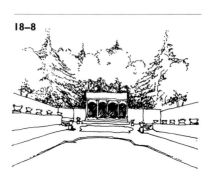

18–9

18–7 View of the lawn from the terrace in the typical residential site plan
This parklike vista contrasts with the "formality" of the garden.

18–8 Formal garden view in the typical residential site plan
The middle ground is deliberately understated so as not to conflict with the pavilion, which serves as a terminus to the view.

18–9 View of the temple in the typical residential site plan
A characteristic view with terminal focal point, intended to contrast with the garden and lawn views.

open up the northern vistas for the dining room. Service and entry roads are carefully separated, and most of Hubbard and Kimball's other principles pertaining to residential site planning are much in evidence. The rural site plan reveals these same principles adapted to somewhat more complex topography necessitating extensive terracing. Here the undulating slope to the south dictates more informal shrub and wild gardens, which are set apart as distinct compositions. The living room is provided with the best vista, and strong axial organization is again in evidence. In the suburban site plan the various views are still the structuring elements, but in this context they are more contained in order to provide privacy and to clearly articulate property lines. The curved entry drive on the east is sited so as not to obtrude on the main view from the front of the residence across the sloping lawn. The addition of a small, enclosed, informal private lawn on the west side provides a much-needed Olmstedian respite from urban congestion. The planting plan is vintage Hubbard and Kimball. Massed flowering shrubs and herbaceous borders abound in what is obviously a high-maintenance scheme emphasizing seasonal color. Strong mixed plantings of evergreen and deciduous trees enframe the various vistas, and ornamental conifers distributed about the lawn provide a note of variety. This residence, like the other examples, is obviously the abode of a very affluent family that can well afford a staff of gardeners and house servants.

These examples are typical representations of the *ancien régime* or Beaux-Arts approach in landscape design applied to residential site plans. Until the 1940s this approach, in various permutations, reigned supreme in professional degree programs throughout the United States. It had filled the portfolios of aspiring Rome Prize applicants and the brochures of professional offices. It had produced a rich array of residences from Newport to Beverly Hills for those who could afford them. (Their numbers declined mightily after the Great Depression.) Beatrix Farrand's masterpiece, Dumbarton Oaks, is probably its greatest surviving example. Fragments of it still echo in studio instruction across the country when students are taught to choose between "formal" and "informal" designs or to structure their work around carefully modulated vistas.

The Beaux-Arts tradition was characterized by clear and comprehensive design principles. It told you what beauty was and how to design for specific landscape effects. It stressed the perceptive analysis and careful application of proven formulae rather than brilliant originality. As such it could draw sound work even from designers of average talent. Yet Garrett Eckbo viewed this tradition as a formidable menace to the future of landscape architecture. He knew it quite well. As Melanie Simo has shown, he had been taught a more flexible and pragmatic approach to design in his undergraduate days at the University of California, Berkeley, but when he arrived at Harvard as a graduate student he was given a heavy draft of

Beaux Arts theory in its Hubbard and Kimball vintage.[8]

Why did Eckbo find such fault with this tradition? Did he find anything of value in it? And, most importantly, what did he propose as an alternative?

Eckbo's critique is comprehensive and detailed. It centers on three main issues: the nature and scope of landscape architecture; the correct use of historical precedent; and the proper expression in built form of humanity's relationship to nature.

On the nature and scope of landscape architecture, Eckbo agrees with Hubbard and Kimball on a few points but differs on more.[9] Eckbo prefers to speak of "landscape design," since this "implies a three-dimensional relation between materials and people." The more traditional term "landscape architecture" suggests an "integration" with architecture that no longer exists. Landscape design is a "conscious rearrangement of the elements of the landscape for use and pleasure." As such it is an "art," but Eckbo also refers to it frequently as a "discipline." Its primary task is to respond to human needs with built forms that embody democratic values and express a proper relationship of humans to the natural world. Hubbard and Kimball share Eckbo's emphasis on landscape architecture as an art that meets human needs, but they lack his vision of it as an embodiment of democratic values.

Eckbo's democratic humanism resounds throughout *Landscape for Living:* "The product of [the designer's] efforts and inspiration is not, finally, magnificent space and beautiful enclosure, but the people who expand and grow and develop within it."[10] Such design is "a democratic discipline" based on "the brotherhood of man as a necessity of life" and "a clear vision of the magnificent continuity of free spatial order which we can bring to our world." Designs embodying democratic values are scaled to the needs of humans, "simple" and "practical in detail," and "flexible" in plan. This emphasis on a formal expression of democratic values grounds Eckbo in the tradition of Thomas Jefferson and Frederick Law Olmsted, Sr., who also viewed their design work (at the University of Virginia and Central Park, respectively) as statements of democratic values. It also links Eckbo with Walter Gropius and other European modernists who placed their architectural theory in the context of a political vision. Eckbo, however, claims that twentieth-century culture has yet to find a way to embody convincingly its democratic values in the built environment. Rather it continues to rely on design vocabularies derived in large part from the autocratic cultures of the past. A major task of landscape design is to pioneer such democratic expression.

For Eckbo, landscape design is based on two pillars: the rigor of scientific analysis and the "intuition" of the artist. He contends that the Beaux-Arts approach to design overemphasizes artistic "intuition" and "romantic" or "mystical" feelings about the power of nature at the expense of lucid scientific data. Artistic intuition has its place, indeed

18–10

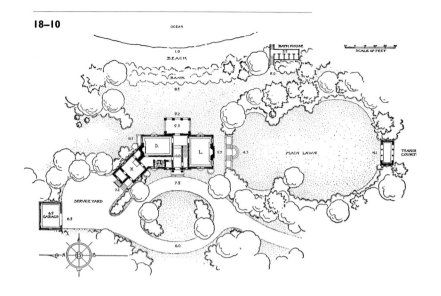

18–11

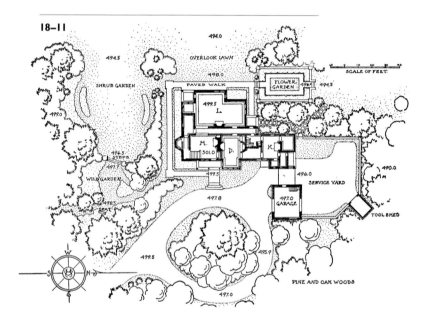

18–12

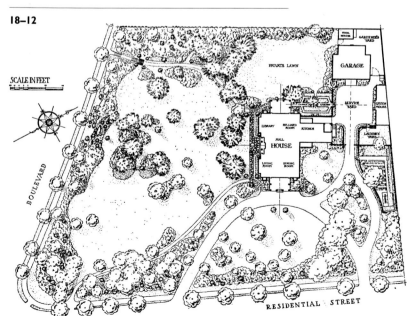

18–10 An oceanfront residence
Hubbard and Kimball. The site
plan is structured around four
views; the kitchen is canted to
open up the north view from the
dining room.
[from *An Introduction to the Study
of Landscape Design*]

18–11 A rural residence
Hubbard and Kimball. The rolling
topography has suggested a more
"naturalistic" treatment of the
ground plane of the shrub and wild
gardens.
[from *An Introduction to the Study
of Landscape Design*]

18–12 A Boston suburban residence
Hubbard and Kimball. In a
suburban context, the views that
structure the plan are more
restricted, but otherwise the
design is very similar to those of
the rural residences shown in
preceding figures.
[from *An Introduction to the Study
of Landscape Design*]

even science makes use of it, but it often leads to fuzzy thinking or inappropriate a priori design solutions that fail to take into account the particularity of a given context. For Eckbo a design problem has not one but many solutions, and those solutions should grow out of our open-minded understanding of the program and site, assisted in no small part by scientific analysis—a concern with "stylistic ideals" is simply irrelevant. Science for Eckbo includes both the natural and social sciences, and his call for scientific rigor in design process foreshadows today's widespread emphasis on ecology and human behavioral studies as important determinants of design form.

Eckbo envisions an art of landscape design of immense scope. It encompasses "that portion of the landscape which is (1) developed or shaped by man, (2) beyond buildings, roads, or utilities and up to wild nature, (3) designed primarily as space for human living—not agriculture, forestry, etc."[11] Landscape design is also by nature interdisciplinary. One aspect of its mission is to combine forces with architecture and engineering to create the field of "site-space design." Such overlap and cooperation with other kindred disciplines is healthy for all. Eckbo's vision of an ideal design school would house under one roof not only architecture, planning, landscape design, and engineering, but all the fine and dramatic arts (including film, television, and radio), with industrial and fashion design included as well. Hubbard and Kimball do not envision such a rich cross-fertilization of design ideas.

Landscape design's responsibility among its kindred disciplines is a crucial one. Its task is "to serve as the final integrating element which gives continuity to our physical environment." As such it serves as a "social barometer" of the quality and stability of our society. Its major frontier in the immediate future will be "urbanism," meaning the interdisciplinary design of cities.

Eckbo conceives of modern landscape design as comprised of four major emphases: "the space concept," "the materials concept," "the social concept," and "climatic regionalism." The "space concept" emphasizes "three-dimensional space form" as the primary medium of landscape design. This differs markedly from the Beaux-Arts concentration on the unified arrangement of objects or the creation of static stereometric "compositions." The "materials concept" stresses the intrinsic qualities of materials and their primary use as definers of space. Eckbo will have nothing to do with such Beaux-Arts conceits as the faking of materials (wood for marble, etc.) or their embellishment with extraneous decoration. The "social concept" focuses on the priority of meeting specific human needs through the creation of "space for living." "Climatic regionalism" acknowledges the specific constraints and opportunities offered to design work in temperate, tropical, and arid zones. It does not attempt to force solutions appropriate to one zone on another and respects the particularity of regional plants and materials without succumbing to

a dogmatic view that only native vegetation is legitimate.

There are some traces in Eckbo of Hubbard and Kimball's notion that a "good" design is one that elicits a pleasurable response. Eckbo generally agrees that "good" design is a source of pleasure, but he does not proceed, à la Hubbard and Kimball, to dissect that pleasure's finer nuances. Neither does he explicitly define beauty, although he refers from time to time to the "beauty" of various "pleasing designs." Eckbo makes it quite clear, however, that the basic stimulus for our pleasure in a design is not the statically composed *views* of Hubbard and Kimball but the "lyrical experience" of well-ordered yet dynamic *spaces*.[12]

Eckbo differs markedly from Hubbard and Kimball in his understanding of historical precedent. We might well expect him to reject historical tradition altogether in a manner reminiscent of Hannes Meyer and Sant'Elia, given his fierce polemic against the "hash" of eclecticism and the dogmatic copybook mentality of the Beaux-Arts. Yet Eckbo is no iconoclast, despite his prophetic thundering against irrelevant historical pastiches lacking coherence.[13] For him historical tradition is of immense importance if one understands its dynamic and protean nature and one's responsibility to improve and develop it. Of course Hubbard and Kimball, too, were against exact copying. Yet for Eckbo, their insistence on adapting "stylistic ideals" to local circumstances made it all but impossible for landscape designers to deal decisively with the needs of contemporary society. To him their approach was lazy, too rigid, and closed to the realities of twentieth-century culture's advances in the arts and sciences. He cites approvingly Le Corbusier's dictum—"the styles are a lie"—and is aghast that landscape architecture has developed no new design vocabulary since the time of Repton.

How, then, does one come to terms with historical precedent? For Eckbo, "History is the body of tradition from which we start. The purpose of creative design in any field is to continue the life and vitality of the tradition by developing it and expanding it."[14] Thus we are not the "slaves" of history but its "heirs." Eckbo agrees with most of his modernist cohorts in architecture that the styles of the past reflect unique circumstances of time, place, and social pattern, and that one can certainly admire their greatest expressions. Indeed, their role "is to stimulate us to produce things as great in quality, but expressing in their specific form our own time, place, people, and technology." The most fruitful approach is to totally immerse oneself in both the traditions of the past and the dynamic vitality of one's present culture—one must freely open oneself to the many pleasures of the *Zeitgeist*. Those "who express only themselves" have little to offer.

On what shall we base our forms? Where shall we find them? And the answer is, in the world which is around you in space, and behind you in time. If you understand it and love it and enjoy it

18–13

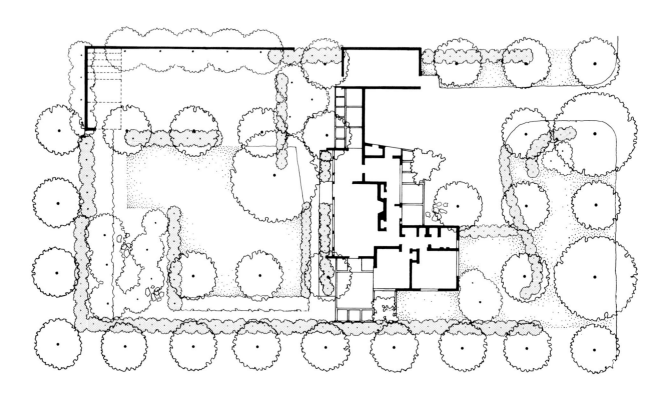

there is your inspiration. The more you are a part of your world the more inspired you will be.[15]

For Eckbo, that world ranges from Picasso's cubist paintings to the power dams of the TVA; from the design of "women's hats" to the virtuosity of "New Orleans jazz" and the natural beauty of Yosemite National Park.

Furthermore, Eckbo believes the Beaux-Arts tendency to view design tradition almost solely in terms of specific works that are either "formal" or "informal" is far too narrow. He posits instead "a rich and manysided octagon" of precedent comprised of (1) the formal design traditions of Islam, Renaissance Europe, baroque Europe, as well as creative and less rigid expressions of this approach in ancient Greek and High Gothic traditions, (2) the informal "romantic" traditions of eighteenth-century England and of Japan and China, (3) scientific horticulture with its emphasis on "plants for their own sake," (4) the conservation movement with its stress on the beauty and value of the wilderness landscape and the need for urban parks, (5) the urban and regional planning movement with its insights into the design of towns and cities and the relations between buildings and open space, (6) "the modern movement" in architecture, the arts, and landscape design dating from the mid-1930s, (7) rural agricultural traditions of land use, and finally (8) folk garden traditions, especially those of the twentieth century.[16]

Eckbo's work draws from all of these, especially from the modern movement. Although it is not my intention to trace these influences on his designs in any detail, I can cite some examples. The organization of his Menlo Park residential site plan (figures 18–13,14), which is a spatial continuum of overlapping hedge planes played off against an orchard grid, is clearly reminiscent of Mies van der Rohe's Barcelona Pavilion (figure 18–22). The spatial organization of rural agricultural landscapes also profoundly affected his work. Eckbo's description of such landscapes, which he calls "the basic democratic landscape pattern of the world," could serve as an apt caption for many of his residential site plans, especially figures 18–13 and 18–29:

> In the rural landscape we find innumerable definite three-dimensional space forms produced with both structural and natural materials: . . . trees in rows or belts forming planes; the regularity of orchards; straight lines of untrimmed hedgerows . . . ; free-standing clumps of trees forming natural pavilions; intersecting planes of these lines of trees and hedges and walls forming a fragmentary organization of space. It is space which is seldom completely enclosed; always there is a suggestion of its continuity, something to follow, the stimulating impossibility of seeing all the space at once.[17]

Eckbo's discussion of the proper relationship of human beings to the world of nature and the implications of that bond for landscape design is perhaps the most original and challenging aspect of his

18–14

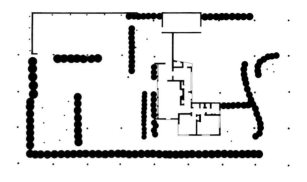

18–15

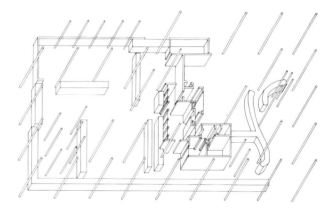

18–13 Garden in Menlo Park, California 1940. Garrett Eckbo. The lot was situated in an existing pear orchard.

18–14 Figure and ground in the garden in Menlo Park
The plan is structured around a series of well-defined, layered spaces, which provide a multiplicity of views and discoveries. House and garden are designed as a totality.

18–15 Axonometric of the garden in Menlo Park
Eckbo's alternative to axes and focal points in the design of the garden is a spatial continuum of overlapping vertical planes.

18–16

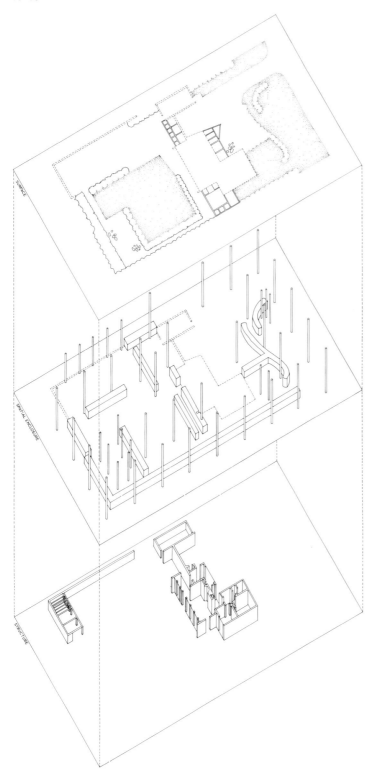

18–16 Enclosure, ground plane, and structures illustrated in the Menlo Park garden
Eckbo's characteristic tripartite approach to designing a site. The repetition of orthogonal forms strengthens the unity of the plan.

18–17 Tree plan in the Menlo Park garden
Eckbo preserved most of the original grid of orchard trees (shown in gray) and augmented it with selected specimen trees.

18–18 Layering diagram for the garden in Menlo Park
The tree canopy (shown in gray) and the shrub understory (shown in black) provide a rich layering of the site both vertically and horizontally.

18–19 A garden view in the Menlo Park garden
Drawing by Garrett Eckbo. The garden cannot be seen in its entirety from any one point but reveals itself gradually from a multiplicity of views.
[from *Landscape for Living*]

18–20 A second garden view
Eckbo uses plants in their natural habits so their organic structure can be appreciated.

18–21 Garden view from the pergola, garden in Menlo Park
Eckbo's garden structures are usually highly transparent and emphasize space rather than mass. Their austere geometry contrasts with the lushness of the plants.

18–19

18–17

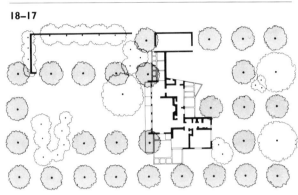

18–18

18–20

18–21

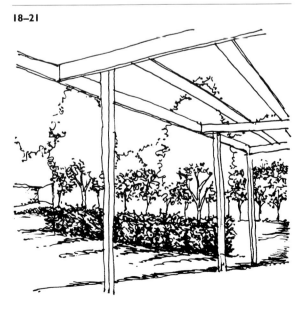

thought. His polemic against the "styles," eclecticism, and typological design of the Beaux-Arts had been voiced previously by several architectural and landscape architectural theorists, such as Walter Gropius and Le Corbusier, James Rose and Christopher Tunnard. His call for landscape design based on space, truth to materials, the fulfillment of human needs, and climatic regionalism is essentially an application of central concerns of architectural modernism to the profession of landscape architecture in order to bring it up to speed with its kindred discipline. However, in broaching the issue of humanity's relationship to the natural world, Eckbo returns to a perennial issue of landscape architecture and treats it afresh.[18] The result is far more than the adaptation of previously developed modernist theory to landscape architecture. What emerges is a concerted attempt to develop a new design vocabulary—one that transcends the old formal/informal split while expressing a harmonious relationship between humans and the world of nature.

Eckbo's discussion of this relationship and its implications for landscape design reveals the full scope of his humanism.[19] He asserts that humans are endowed with a natural capacity to improve their environment through the application of reason and artistic imagination. This activity is "natural" in that humans are a part of nature—they are not some sort of alien force outside of it. Whereas preliterate societies lived a relationship of harmonious reciprocity with natural forces, modifying them for human benefit but preserving them intact, in today's industrial, capitalist society we are almost totally alienated from these processes and consequently are destroying the earth's ecosystems at an unprecedented rate.

For Eckbo, the task of landscape design in the last half of the twentieth century is to "integrate" human beings with nature, not through a nostalgic return to a simple primitivism but by establishing a relationship of "unity and solidarity," one that finds directive in centuries-old agricultural landscapes, the last vestiges of a harmonious reciprocity with the natural world. Landscape designers will fail miserably if they continue to offer responses couched in the sterile and erroneous Beaux-Arts dichotomy of "formal" and "informal" design. This dichotomy is a *symptom* of our alienation from nature, not its *solution*. It forces us to make an untenable choice between designs that express either human domination of the natural world or mystical subordination to it. There is simply no way to express in built form a viable reciprocity between humanity and nature within the confines of this schizophrenic formula.

What is the cure for this "neurotic" alienation? (Eckbo is fond of images from psychotherapy.) Landscape designers must stop making copies of nature in a vain attempt to redeem human beings through "mystical" experiences of scenery. They must cease apologizing for the intervention of their art in the natural world and team up with engineers, architects, and planners to produce comprehensive "site-space" designs that will address human needs and yet respect the constraints and opportunities of the processes of nature. Such work must be based in large part on a precise and well-documented *scientific* understanding of the natural world and the potential consequences of our intervention in it.

Eckbo thus anticipates some of the concerns of Ian McHarg's *Design with Nature,* which was to become the preeminent statement of landscape architectural design theory in the 1970s. Unlike McHarg, however, Eckbo in *Landscape for Living* does not provide any detailed discussion of the contents of environmental sciences and their precise implications for design. He is more interested in outlining the contours of a new design vocabulary to express a harmonious relationship between human beings and the natural environment. Fletcher Steele had observed as early as 1937 that a hallmark of "modern" landscape architecture was a concerted attempt to transcend the formal/informal dichotomy and develop a fresh design vocabulary.[20] However, Steele did not go on to link this attempt to the issue of humanity's relation to the natural world. *Landscape for Living* provides the first detailed and comprehensive theoretical reflections on this issue in modern landscape architectural writing.

Eckbo develops only the general principles of this new vocabulary, which he refers to as "organic form in the humanized landscape." This new design vocabulary should be a creative synthesis between the dynamic forces of nature, which embody "growth" and "change," and the rational geometries of humans, which express "organization for a purpose." Design work expressing this vocabulary will serve as "a bridge between man and nature." Those who employ this approach will no longer ask the superfluous and erroneous question, "Should my design be formal or informal?", but rather the pertinent question, "How will my design serve human needs in this particular context?" Eckbo sketches the outline of this new vocabulary as follows:

> The character of nature is expressed in the pyramidal forms of earth and the angular or rounded forms of rock, the gravity relation of water, and the bursting growth of plants. It results in accidental space patterns—sometimes strong, often weak or unnoticeable. The character of man is expressed in specific space organization for use and pleasure. These characters must meet and collaborate, losing neither the wayward movement of natural elements through human arrogance or fussiness, nor the imaginative form and pattern of man through subjective mysticism about subservience to nature, apologies for intrusion into the natural landscape, . . . etc.[21]

For Eckbo, there were some good things about the old formal tradition—order, "clarity, proportion, rational planning," and "the free expression of human creativity." The new vocabulary must preserve these. The informal tradition had its strong points as well—a recognition of the power and beauty of the natural world and the understanding of humanity's need to live in simple, unostentatious settings. It also exposed the irrelevance of bilateral symmetry, which it correctly perceived as boring, static, and symbolic of an autocratic political order. These insights must also be heeded and combined with those of the formal tradition in "endlessly varying proportions and combinations."

This is not some new kind of eclectic "hash." Neither is it an insipid compromise or banal "golden mean" that destroys the integrity of these two traditions. Rather,

> it means quite the contrary: that we have *both* together, reinforcing each other, bringing each other to life, developing strength, clarity, coherence, integrated contrast, organic geometry, with a richness and flexibility beyond the capacity of the standard sterile static academic clinging to one or the other oversimplified pole. It means that man and nature . . . meet, merge, and dance together in ever-shifting . . . patterns that are truly the reflection and the fit environment for the dance of life itself.[22]

Eckbo assures us that these principles are not intended to license the arbitrary carving up of the landscape into intricate self-referential geometries. One must always take into account the context and the scale of a project. Our design work always occurs on a spectrum from the urban landscape to the "primeval" landscape, with the agricultural landscape in between. Our design work must carefully heed these various contexts. For example, if we are designing a regional park adjacent to a wilderness area, our park should respect the natural beauty of its context and bear a resemblance to its neighbor. If, on the other hand, we are working on a highly enclosed house-garden complex in an urban setting, we may have more freedom to experiment with complex and dynamic geometries. Also, the larger the site, the more clear and simple our forms need to be to preserve the unity of the design.

Claudia Lazzaro has observed how Italian Renaissance gardens were understood in the fifteenth and sixteenth centuries to be a combination of nature and artifice that produced a "third nature." In such a "third nature," "Nature and art are united into an indistinguishable whole, in which nature . . . shares the essence of art. Together they produce something that is neither one nor the other, and is created equally by each."[23] Eckbo's synthesis of formal and informal design traditions is reminiscent of this tradition of a "third nature"—although his specific design vocabulary differs markedly in certain respects from that of Italian Renaissance gardens in that he does not make use of bilateral symmetry, imitate landscape scenes, or use sculpture in an allegorical fashion. This vocabulary can best be discussed by examining several of his residential site plans.[24]

A house-garden complex in Menlo Park, California, expressing many of his principles was a joint project of 1940 with architect Frederick L. Langhorst. The site was a medium-sized flat lot approximately 85 by 165 feet, situated in an existing orchard that was rapidly being converted into a residential development. In the middle of the lot was a one-story house that, with its horizontal redwood siding, massive central chimney, and generous overhanging eaves, to some degree recalled the Prairie houses of Frank Lloyd Wright. Ample picture windows in the living room and dining room provided views of the rear garden and distant hills.

Eckbo prefers to break a site plan down into three interrelated component parts: enclosure, ground plane, and structures (figure 18–16). (Hubbard and Kimball followed a similar procedure.) A hallmark of all Eckbo's designs is clear spatial definition. At the Menlo Park residence he achieves this in several ways. In keeping with his emphasis on context, he takes as his point of departure the existing orchard grid of pear trees, which he preserves almost intact. The exception is the center of the garden, which he opens up to accentuate an experience of spatial volume (figures 18–13,14). This "open center," which is found in almost all of Eckbo's design work, contains no objects or focal points. It is enlivened by people, who are the "terminal features," the "final vitality of any spatial enclosure one may create." All sides of the lot are given strong boundaries, variously composed of hedges and redwood fence reinforced by pear trees. The street boundary is a row of alternating walnut and pear trees backed by a row of pears, thus providing a layering of the space that furnishes a screen for privacy.

Eckbo's intention in all of his design work is to create spaces that are ordered and unified yet avoid being boring and static, manifesting a "balanced, dynamic stability" that "expresses life" and "the needs of life." He believes this can be achieved in part by employing "strong, clear, and coherent forms" embodying either the pull of gravity or the stability of the horizontal plane. Also it is necessary to provide contrasts of line, color, texture, and form that produce "vision in motion"—our eye will be persuaded to roam freely about the design as if scanning a cubist painting. Hence he provides no static focal points or one-point perspective compositions in the Menlo Park garden, presenting instead a multiplicity of views and discoveries as we move about the site enjoying the "lyrical experience of space," which for Eckbo is one of the greatest of human pleasures. This spatial dynamism is achieved primarily by a series of orthogonally structured understory hedges that establish a sequence of overlapping planes playing off against the canopy and trunks of the orchard grid and bosk (figure 18–18). Eckbo characterizes this design as "a kind of free-rectangularity, reminiscent of de Stijl–van der Rohe planning" (figure 18–22).

The ground plane is designed as a series of clearly etched rectangles of varying size that define "zones of use": an open lawn, a "color border," a bosk, and a badminton court. He delineates each zone with a different material—soil, sand, turf, and crushed stone—in keeping with his notion that different functional zones be defined by different ma-

18–22

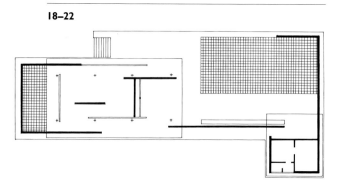

18–22 Plan of the German Pavilion,
Barcelona International Exposition
1929. Ludwig Mies van der Rohe.
The spatial organization of Eckbo's
Menlo Park garden is quite similar.

terials. The red crushed brick of the badminton court contrasts with the deep emerald lawn and the multicolored flower border, enhancing the dynamism of the space and inviting our eye to move from one precinct to another. However, we cannot see the entire ground plane from any single viewpoint as we can in the typical Beaux-Arts garden. The ground plane of the lot adjacent to the street also manifests a dichotomy between the cool green of the roughly textured ground cover and the smooth gray surface of the drive. Furthermore, Eckbo delineates the "walls" that partially enclose the various ground planes in contrasting plant materials. He frequently recommends such a differentiation of vertical and horizontal planes by the use of different materials, but he refuses to make it into a rigid dogma. The use of contrasting geometries to enhance the visual dynamism of a space is another of his principles. Two overlapping curvilinear hedges define the edge of the drive and provide contrast with the layered grid of pear and walnut trees as well as the orthogonal geometry of the rear garden.

Nowhere at Menlo Park is there a transition from one design vocabulary to another similar to the Beaux-Arts transition from "formal" geometry in the vicinity of the house to "informal" geometry on the site's perimeter. Rather the space is designed as one consistent fabric. (This is true of some of Eckbo's larger-scaled residential work as well. The plan of a large ranch in the Central Valley [figure 18–29] abruptly interlocks with the contrasting pasture—there is no gradual transition.)[25] He does not attempt to reflect the style of the house in the garden. He does relate his design to the scale of the house and its regulating lines, but he will have no truck with Beaux-Arts period gardens or stylistic adaptations. This is also characteristic of his work. The Beverly Hills house shown in figure 18–23 is Spanish colonial, but he makes no attempt to reflect its materials or stylistic traits in the garden design.

The structures in this garden are unpretentious, functional, and elegant, reinforcing the spatial structure of the garden and linking it with the house. Eckbo sites the small wooden pavilion in the right rear of the garden so as not to form a static focal point or obtrude into the space (figure 18–16). It is light and transparent, emphasizing space, not mass, and its finely milled members contrast with the luxuriant growth of the plants (figure 18–21). In contrast, Hubbard and Kimball's garden structures serve as focal points and are designed to accentuate mass (figures 18–8,9). Eckbo on occasion has designed structures in new industrial and prefabricated materials. In his own garden in the Hollywood Hills he even experimented with pergolas of prefabricated aluminum but did not repeat this elsewhere because of the expense of the material and lack of client interest. The fence of the Menlo Park garden is constructed of simple vertical redwood posts. Its quiet continuity of surface directs our attention to the volume of the space, illustrating Eckbo's emphasis on simplicity, continuity, and subtle rhythm in the planes that define his spaces.

Eckbo's planting plan reflects his principle that plants should be used primarily to define space. They are "structural, not plastic" elements. This means they should not be arranged in the amorphous massings prescribed by the Beaux-Arts tradition (figure 18–12). Rather they should be expressed in their natural habits of growth so we can appreciate their organic structure and individual qualities. They are "anti-gravity" elements, defiers of gravity, like structures built by human artifice. Their upward-thrusting dynamism contrasts with the quiet stability of the horizontal plane.

Eckbo uses numerically fewer plants than does the Beaux-Arts tradition, but he sees no virtue in a short list of plant species. In fact, his planting schemes usually have a lush, well-ordered complexity, and they are much easier to maintain (figures 18–19, 20). The Menlo Park garden has approximately thirty-eight plant species, some of which are planted as individual specimens to enhance the variety of the design, such as the sycamore in the garden and the purple beech and red jar maples in the front of the house. Eckbo places great emphasis on texture as a unifying element in planting design; many of the plants in the Menlo Park scheme are of "rough" texture with glossy leaves.

While Eckbo rejects the Beaux-Arts notion of stylistic or historical association, he does allow that plants and rocks evoke significant associations with natural processes. Plants remind us of the power and beauty of the natural world expressed in dynamic growth, and rocks engender reflection on the structure of the earth and the dynamics of soil formation. Rocks are also a "gravity material," manifesting the pull of the earth's core, and they add stability to a design. In the Menlo Park plan, Eckbo sites rocks at the entrance to the house and on the sand floor of the garden's bosk (figure 18–13).

The entire design also clearly embodies Eckbo's notion of "organic form in the humanized landscape," that careful synthesis of the best qualities of the old formal and informal traditions that expresses a harmonious reciprocity between humans and nature. Its layered vertical planes and the functional zoning of its surfaces speak of human use and intention. The presence of nature is expressed by the lush growth of plants in their natural habit and their contrast with the finely wrought structures. (One is reminded of fourteenth-century Moorish planting design at the Alhambra.) This synthesis is carefully attuned to the surrounding middle agricultural landscape of orchards and fields (soon to disappear under a blanket of tract housing). Eckbo recalls this vanishing landscape in the old pear orchard matrix that is kept partially intact in the new plan and enriched with additional spatial elements. It is an archaeological trace of a former landscape that expressed a valid relationship between humans and nature. Eckbo now sets it anew in a space that strives to express the same harmonious reciproc-

ity. Thus the rich layering of the Menlo Park design is both temporal and spatial. The overall plan also expresses Eckbo's criteria for "democratic" design in that it is scaled to human need, "flexible in plan," and "practical in detail." This plan is a compelling example of Eckbo's new approach and is the first case study of his work to appear in *Landscape for Living*. Without question, it embodies a fresh language when compared with the old formal/informal dialect of Hubbard and Kimball. Eckbo has supplanted their emphasis on the pleasure derived from static harmonious pictorial "compositions" with the intense delight of dwelling in and experiencing harmonious yet dynamic spaces.

Eckbo's "pool garden" in Beverly Hills, California, designed six years later in collaboration with "structural consultant" Jack Zehnder, manifests many of the same design strategies of layering of space, contrasting geometries and textures, clearly delineated zones defined by use, and plants expressed in their natural habits. As at Menlo Park, Eckbo sites the structures of the Beverly Hills garden to reinforce the experience of space (figure 18–25). He locates the curvilinear brick bathhouse in the corner and partially covers it with the perimeter fence so it will not become a focal point. He sites the pool at the rear of the garden so as not to create a "canyon effect." The pergola is a light, delicate structure whose pipestem columns obtrude as little as possible into the space (figure 18–27). The crossed diagonals of its two-by-eights mirror the paving pattern of the patio as the line of its roof form resembles the shape of the swimming pool, further unifying the space. Even the circular concrete stepping stones along the west and north side of the garden tie in with the arc of the pool's perimeter and the serpentine brick wall along the east border. The pool itself is carefully integrated with the overall geometry of the ground plane and is its dominant element; its glasslike surface mirrors the sky and provides an atmosphere of deep tranquility reminiscent of Moorish gardens. Throughout this design Eckbo is striving to achieve a unity of clear, strong forms that walk a razor's edge between boring simplicity and disordered complexity.

The Beverly Hills garden expresses one design principle not found in the Menlo Park garden: Eckbo believes it is appropriate to channel sight lines by means of the geometry of the ground plane. He points out how the diagonal edge of the patio, which is echoed in reverse by the diagonal of the north edge of the swimming pool, reflects "outlook directions" derived from the "form" of the house. Thus these two edges are not arbitrary but work in concert with the sight lines from the interior of the house to establish a strong link between house and garden. In this instance Eckbo is clearly composing a "picture." Indeed, he acknowledges, "It is true that spatial experiences and the sensation of space are compounded of pictures."[26] Yet this is not a static Beaux-Arts composition of bilaterally symmetrical elements, but one articulated by ever-shifting diagonal views of "strong," "clear,"

18–23

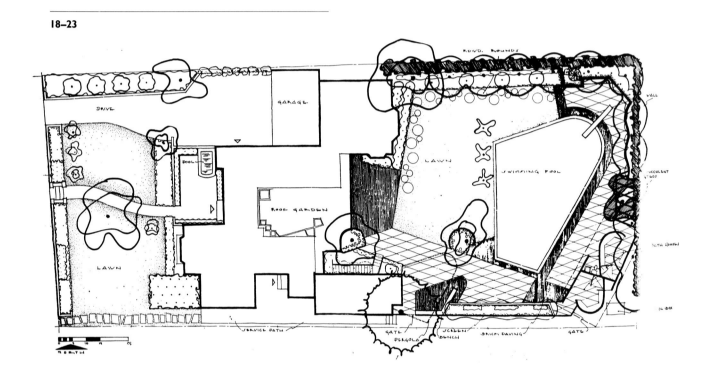

18–24

18–23 Pool garden in Beverly Hills,
California
1946. Garrett Eckbo. In the walled
confines of a suburban garden,
which is by nature self-referential,
Eckbo experiments with more
complex interlocking geometries.
[from *Landscape for Living*]

18–24 Figure and ground in the pool
garden
The layering of the garden space is
less pronounced than in the Menlo
Park plan. Note the contrast of
curvilinear and rectilinear forms.

18–25 Enclosure, ground plane, and
structures in the pool garden
The diagonal edges of the pool and
patio define sight lines from the
interior of the house. The form of
the pool and pergola are similar.

and "dynamic" forms. In the walled confines of a suburban garden that is by nature self-referential, Eckbo allows himself to experiment with more complex geometries than in the Menlo Park estate, with its surrounding grid of orchards.

A third example of Eckbo's work reveals yet another response to context. He conceived the design for a 10,000-acre "ranch home" in the Central Valley of California in 1945 in collaboration with architect Mario Corbett (figure 18–29). Eckbo likens the scale of the design to "baroque France" and describes it as "a pattern in three dimensions developed to combine a sense of enclosure and security with that of radiating integration with the great space around, and the view across thirty miles of flat land to the Coast Range hills." He expresses the same design principles here as in the much smaller Menlo Park and Beverly Hills gardens: the layering of space on the vertical and horizontal planes and an interlocking "strong" geometry of arcs and tangents (figures 18–30,31). The L-plan ranch house with extensive porch interlocks with a circular "open center," which is the point of departure for multiple radii of trees and hedges that direct the eye to the distant views—another example of Eckbo's coordination of geometry with sight line. Trees planted along the arc of these radii to the south of the house layer the space by forming a series of concentric overlapping planes. Eckbo plays off the rectilinear rows of trees north of the house against the circular forms to the south, creating a dynamic tension in the design. A reverse arc of trees south of the pool provides an additional note of contrast. He zones the site functionally in vintage fashion to include a children's play area, an orchard, and a swimming pool–court games complex. An arid cattle pasture interlocks with an oasis-like extension of the circular lawn on the north and south side of the house. Two bosks set in sand balance one another on the north and south sides of the site and provide much-needed shade in the blistering summer heat (which can exceed 100°).

Here again all plants are expressed in their natural habits, and the plan even includes a working orchard. The predominantly curvilinear geometry of Eckbo's site plan would contrast sharply with the surrounding orthogonal grid of the Central Valley's crop land. (This grid does not appear on the plan, which is not of sufficient scale to include it.) He has offered a fresh restatement of a middle agricultural landscape; forming a visual counterpoint to its surroundings, it sharpens our awareness of them.

Thus while the Menlo Park and Beverly Hills projects differ in scale and context from the Central Valley ranch, all three manifest a consistent application of similar design strategies that depart substantially from the Beaux-Arts tradition. For Eckbo they are meant to suggest how one can preserve the best of the old formal and informal traditions in creating "space for living" that embodies "organic form in the humanized landscape."

A comprehensive critique of Eckbo's design theory and its specific manifestation in his work

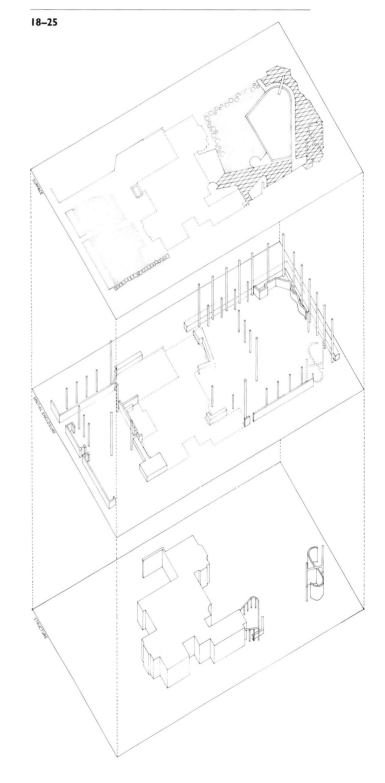

18–25

18–26

18–27

calls for a separate study of some length. Yet at the end of this historical investigation, I would like to offer some brief critical observations.

Landscape for Living is now a mature 42 years old, the age when most humans are said to be at the height of their creative and intellectual powers. Can we consult it as a wise counselor whose insights have been vindicated time and time again? Or is it more like those rather sad individuals who peaked years ago and, though charming, are rather out of touch with contemporary life?

Without question, it is still a wise counselor, one that landscape architects can greatly profit from in the coming decades as they struggle to address exceedingly complex and daunting problems of environmental design.

Eckbo rightly reminds us, lest we lose our way in the labyrinth of specialization, that landscape architecture is primarily a *design* profession concerned with the expression of democratic values and a harmonious relationship between humans and the natural world. It is not art for art's sake, but an art that blends scientific rigor and artistic discipline to serve the needs of people. It is also by nature interdisciplinary and cannot deal with the tasks of the present without understanding and working closely with architects, planners, engineers, and environmental scientists. It is at its best when it opens itself to the quickening influence of a vast range of human cultural endeavors—avant-garde art, folk culture, literature, architecture, engineering, fashion design, etc. Yet it must preserve its identity as a *design* profession and continually build upon and improve its own heritage.

Eckbo's initial definition of the profession helped lay the foundation for today's large-scale corporate practice and the curriculum of many of our professional design programs. It is as sound today as it was then. Yet how far we still are from his comprehensive vision, especially in academia. Eckbo called for a kind of new Bauhaus of interdisciplinary study. Yet fragmentation is too often the hallmark of today's academic departments. Witness, for example, the poor relationship between architecture and landscape architecture departments that is all too common throughout the country.

Peter Walker has rightfully called for today's landscape architects to develop a "new modernism, that is more sympathetic to land use, to historic-fabric and to the Earth itself."[27] One will find wise counsel for that new modernism in *Landscape for Living*. Eckbo insists that we design in accord with the most rigorous principles of the environmental sciences and be fully aware of the impact of our work on the ecosystems of the earth. He grounds design work in four sound principles—the primacy of space, truth to materials, the fulfillment of human needs, and climatic regionalism—and provides comprehensive and detailed discussions of each of them. Furthermore, he envisions a dynamic relationship with historical precedent that rejects sterile copying in favor of the creative application of the

18–28

18–26 Bathhouse and wall screen in the pool garden
The continuity of surface and quiet rhythm strengthen our spatial perception, and the constantly changing shadow patterns enliven the space.
[Julius Shulman, courtesy Garrett Eckbo]

18–27 Pergola and fence in the pool garden
The light, delicate structure of the pergola seems to hover over the ground without support. The crossed diagonals of its roof mirror the paving pattern.
[from *Landscape for Living*]

18–28 Curvilinear bathhouse wall in the pool garden
The bathhouse is sited on the corner and partially shielded by a fence so as not to become a focal point. Its form is echoed in an adjacent serpentine wall (see figure 18–24).
[Julius Shulman, courtesy Garrett Eckbo]

18–29

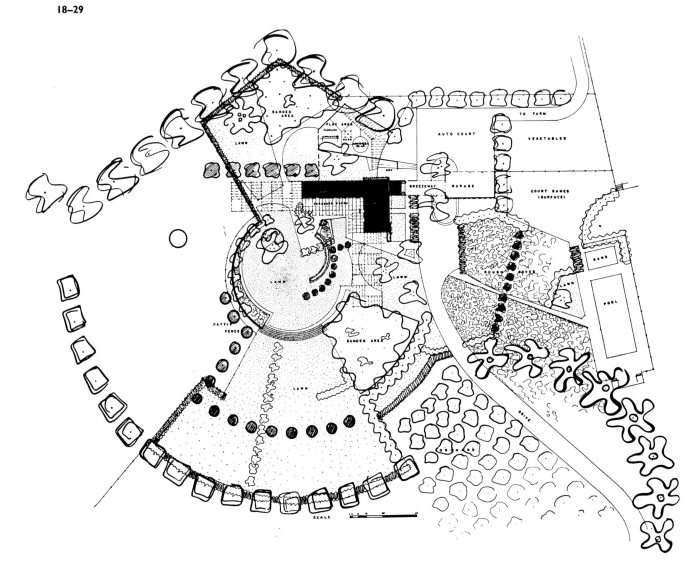

18–30

18–31

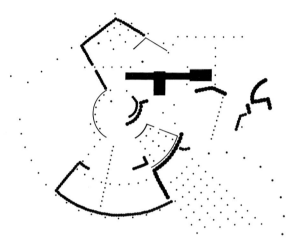

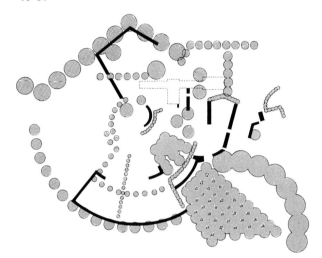

18–29 Ranch home in the Central Valley of California
1945. Garrett Eckbo. In this plan for a 10,000-acre ranch, Eckbo plays off the rectilinear rows of trees north of the house against the circular forms to the south to create a dynamic tension. The plan contains no transitional geometries but simply interlocks with the surrounding cattle pasture to the west.
[from *Landscape for Living*]

18–30 Figure and ground, Central Valley ranch
Eckbo employs a radial geometry of overlapping planes with a characteristic open center.

18–31 Layering diagram for the Central Valley ranch
This large-scale site plan, with its sweeping arcs of trees and extensive understory, manifests a rich layering of the vertical and horizontal planes similar to the Menlo Park garden.

design excellence of the past to the tasks of the present. Finally, he correctly insists that past must include the recent past—the creativity and insight of one's immediate predecessors. One should not hark back exclusively to Olmsted, Repton, and Le Nôtre.

Eckbo is a bit rough on the *ancien régime* of the Beaux-Arts. It shared his concern for the meeting of human needs, and its pictorial compositions required well-defined spaces. It too was against literal copying of past precedent. Eckbo is quite correct in his critique of its rather glib stylistic approach and its sterile formal/informal dichotomy. However, we may take issue with him over his rejection of the axis and bilateral symmetry as legitimate tools of design; in fact that rejection smacks a bit of the design dogma he warns us against. To be sure, many a pompous static scheme has resulted from the use of bilateral symmetry, but in certain contexts it is a legitimate ordering principle, as Daniel Kiley has aptly demonstrated in his work. Also we may question Eckbo's rejection of the Beaux-Arts notion of historical association. One does not have to be a copyist or embrace rigid typologies to recognize that in certain contexts one's designs may legitimately interpret (not copy) a historical style. Such contexts would include sites where the existing buildings were either authentic historical structures or period revivals of a certain style. Such a response would enhance the unity of the designs as well as respect the historical and cultural associations they might evoke.

What about Eckbo's own specific design vocabulary? It is often criticized as too busy and lacking in contextual sensitivity. I hope that my analysis of three of his design projects has dispelled these misconceptions, revealing their subtle unities and their heeding of context. Eckbo's plan view drawings often make his work appear more visually complex than it is when constructed. A visit to an Eckbo garden (and they are vanishing fast) usually impresses one with the abundance and lushness of its plants, which define the space and serve to unify the sometimes intricate geometries of the ground plane or structures. Photographs fail to convey an accurate impression—for Eckbo's work lacks the striking one-point perspectives so beloved of design magazines. Like Mies's Barcelona Pavilion, his designs are not facades but must be experienced within as a spatial continuum *in their specific regional context.* Today's younger generation of designers sometimes speak as if they had rediscovered contextualism via "site-specific" environmental art. Eckbo, in his emphasis on climatic regionalism, never departed from contextualism.

Of course, one may quibble for various reasons with this constructivist arc or that cubist layering or biomorphic form in Eckbo's work. But they are hardly the principal design issues. Eckbo has rightly raised that central issue and asked us to resolve it for ourselves. He reminds us that a major role of form in landscape architecture is to express a proper relationship of human beings with the natural world. We as heirs of the environmental movement are still searching for that expression. Eckbo's "organic geometry in a humanized landscape" is but one possible response. Other contemporary landscape architects have offered promising alternatives as well: Lawrence Halprin's challenging abstractions of processes of nature, Richard Haag's creative synthesis of Japanese and European classical traditions as well as prospect-refuge theory, Daniel Kiley's fresh restatement of classicism, Peter Walker's suggestive explorations of iconography and the boundaries between nature and artifice, and A. E. Bye's subtle abstractions of natural landscape compositions that produce moods. Eckbo invites us not to mimic him or anyone else, but to find our own vocabulary to resolve this issue—to experiment, to take risks, and not to be bound by traditional prejudices.

Laurie Olin has aptly remarked that individuals "have made whole careers out of the fragments of [Eckbo's] thought."[28] It takes only a brief encounter with *Landscape for Living* to find out why.

Notes

The author wishes to thank Garrett Eckbo for providing a copy of his annotated student edition of Hubbard and Kimball's *An Introduction to the Study of Landscape Design,* and Mitchell Glass, who drafted the numerous analytical drawings and provided the sketches used in this essay.

1 The most influential book on modern landscape architectural theory prior to *Landscape for Living* (New York: F.W. Dodge, 1950) was Christopher Tunnard's *Gardens in the Modern Landscape,* first published in 1938 and revised in 1948. James C. Rose had also published a series of influential essays in *Pencil Points,* four of which are reprinted in this volume.

2 I am indebted to Melanie Simo for calling my attention to Eckbo's annotated copy. Also, several themes in *Landscape for Living* were prefigured in Eckbo's essays published in the late 1930s and early '40s. The more important of these were "Small Gardens in the City: A Study of Their Design Possibilities," *Pencil Points* (September 1937), "Outdoors and In: Gardens as Living Space," *The Magazine of Art* (October 1941), and three articles coauthored with James Rose and Daniel Kiley and published in the *Architectural Record*: "The Urban Environment" (May 1939), "The Rural Environment" (August 1939), and "The Primeval Environment" (February 1940).

3 The following exposition is based on chapters 1–7 of Henry Vincent Hubbard and Theodora Kimball, *An Introduction to the Study of Landscape Design* (New York: Macmillan, 1927).

4 Hubbard and Kimball's understanding of beauty is quite similar to the one developed by George Santayana in *The Sense of Beauty, Being the Outlines of Aesthetic Theory,* first published in 1896.

5 See *Monograph of the Work of Charles A. Platt, with an Introduction by Royal Cortissoz* (New York: The Architectural Book Publishing Company, 1913).

6 These perspective sketches are conjectural, based on the plan view drawing in Hubbard and Kimball (drawing xxx).

7 The following plan view drawings are from Hubbard and Kimball, drawings xxxi, xxxii, and xxxvii.

8 See Melanie Louise Simo, "The Education of a Modern Landscape Designer," *Pacific Horticulture* 49, no. 2 (Summer 1988), 19–30.

9 The following exposition of Eckbo's ideas on the nature and scope of landscape architecture is based primarily on chapters 2, 8, and 15 of *Landscape for Living.*

10 Eckbo, *Landscape for Living,* 254.

11 Ibid., 5.

12 Ibid., 59, 109.

13 Today Eckbo levels the same critique against many examples of so-called postmodern landscape architecture.

14 Eckbo, *Landscape for Living,* 10.

15 Ibid., 59.

16 Ibid., 57.

17 Ibid., 41.

18 Of course, the theme of humanity's relationship to nature was also a major concern of many modern architects, especially Frank Lloyd Wright, Le Corbusier, and Richard Neutra, all of whom Eckbo respected.

19 The following exposition of Eckbo's ideas on the relationship of humans to the natural world is based on chapters 3–7 of *Landscape for Living.*

20 Fletcher Steele, "Modern Landscape Architecture," *Contemporary Landscape Architecture and Its Sources* (San Francisco: San Francisco Museum of Art, 1937).

21 Eckbo, *Landscape for Living,* 42.

22 Ibid., 51.

23 Claudia Lazzaro, *The Italian Renaissance Garden from the Conventions of Planting, Design, and Ornament to the Grand Gardens of Sixteenth-Century Central Italy* (New Haven and London: Yale University Press, 1990), 9.

24 In the following commentary, all of the design principles discussed are explicitly mentioned by Eckbo in various chapters of *Landscape for Living.* I have simply applied these principles to the three residential designs discussed below. Eckbo's own commentary on these three designs is quite brief.

25 Eckbo did attempt a transitional geometry in the project illustrated in *Landscape for Living* entitled "Country Home in Westchester County, New York, 1945" (fig. 93 in the book). He describes the transition as follows (caption 88–94): "The old problem of relating the large house to the open landscape, with the new content of the widespread low informality and openness of modern architecture. In general a progression from refined living terrace through rougher play terraces and lower terraces (abstractions of meadow elements) to the wild site."

26 Eckbo, *Landscape for Living,* 68.

27 Peter Walker, "Prospect," *Landscape Architecture* 80, no. 1 (January 1990), 124.

28 As quoted by William Thompson in "Standard Bearer of Modernism," *Landscape Architecture* 80, no. 2 (February 1990), 89.

19–1

Garrett Eckbo is Professor Emeritus and former Chair of Landscape Architecture at the University of California at Berkeley, and a preeminent figure in modern landscape architecture. He is a Fellow of the American Society of Landscape Architects and was awarded an Honorary Doctorate of Fine Arts by the University of New Mexico in 1992.

19–1   Model, "Small Gardens in the City"
Garrett Eckbo.
[*Pencil Points*, September 1937.]

Art, design, and culture have always lived in an uneasy balance between tradition and innovation, precedent and new concepts, preconception and imagination. This has been true in varying degrees throughout history. It was not surprising that the Industrial Revolution—the biggest and most shaking event since the Agricultural Revolution—should generate the most startling responses in art and architecture. In the modern era, painting and sculpture—the most stable of arts—were quickly taken over by impressionists, cubists, surrealists: Picasso, Braque, Matisse, et al. Architecture fell to Wright, Le Corbusier, Mies, Gropius, Aalto, Neutra, and many others. These were all brilliant and sensitive innovators who saw quickly and clearly the implications of industrialism. Creative responses came first in Europe, where industrialism began.

Landscape architecture—most traditional, earth- and nature-bound of the environmental arts—developed garden and park responses in Europe in the '20s, as Dorothée Imbert has shown.[1] Although Frank Lloyd Wright was producing American modern architecture early in the century, his tragic break in career left the stage open for Joseph Hudnut, Dean of the Harvard Graduate School of Design (GSD), to introduce modern architects Walter Gropius and Marcel Breuer to North America in 1937. Earlier, in New York, the Armory Show had introduced modern art to our frontier society.

This was the background into which I, an innocent westerner, moved in 1936. Born in New York State but raised in northern California, I had graduated from the University of California at Berkeley with a degree in landscape design in 1935. During a year of work for a large nursery in southern California, designing about 100 gardens, I took and won a competition for a scholarship to the GSD at Harvard.

In southern California I found myself in a new world. I had grown up (1915–1929) in the San Francisco Bay region; specifically in Alameda, a large flat island city in the bay, just west of Oakland. Before World War II brought military worker congestion, it was a pleasant green community of middle-class suburban commuters, who rode ferries across the bay to work in San Francisco. Alameda was a relatively safe and comfortable city in which to grow up in the '20s, but position made it vulnerable to moisture, fog, and wind that came through the Golden Gate, creating a cool, humid, and misty environment. The fact that I was a poor boy in an affluent community did not make life any more pleasant.

Southern California was a major change and a sharp contrast, particularly in the inland Pomona Valley where I lived and worked from 1935 to 1936. While the Bay Area ranged between cool and warm, with noticeable humidity, the range in the south was from warm to hot, with low humidity. Surrounded by genuine mountains with winter snow, the Pomona Valley was then floored with citrus groves and avenues of tall palms and other exotic trees. The air was always clear. Using this valley as a base, one could explore by car the whole range of southern Californian landscape from the Santa Monica beach to the Palm Springs desert. The south was larger, brighter, more powerful and impressive than the quiet, genteel north, for one of my age and background.

My garden design derived from then-current California vocabularies. These were eastern formal/informal design patterns, modified to suit the special climates, topography, and plant materials of the West Coast. The plans would not have startled *House Beautiful* or *House and Garden,* but the planting was more exotic than that of the Bay Area, which in turn was more a landscape of broad-leaved evergreens than anywhere east of the Sierras and north of the Mason-Dixon line.

Although I had enjoyed puttering in the garden in Alameda, I encountered in the south, for the first time, the urge to outdoor living that the balmy weather of pre-smog southern California produced in people. It was the beginning of what later became the way of life of the southern West Coast. This was, of course, true also in the Bay Area and further north, but there it was limited by wind and season. Southern California became the great example of carefree outdoor living in the eyes of the nation.

Garden culture throughout most of North America was and still is the culture of gardening or living with nature. Vegetation remains primary. The English tradition was, and still is, dominant. But across the southern borders of the United States the Latin American tradition of patio living, in which the garden became an extension of the house's living space, exerted a strong influence from Florida to California. Here, in the garden, was a reflection of the European experience, in which Continental and Mediterranean traditions interacted, filtered

19-2

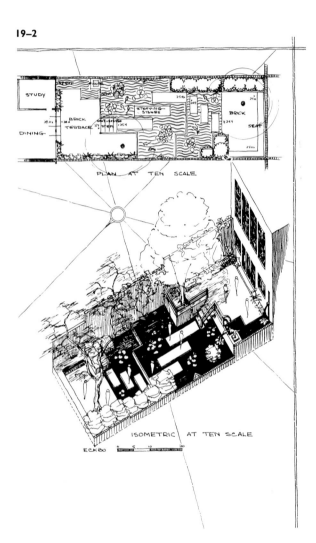

PLAN AT TEN SCALE

ISOMETRIC AT TEN SCALE

ECKBO

through the mountains that separated them. The two traditions came to America by different routes, one from England and continental Europe to the American east and midwest, the other from the Iberian peninsula through Latin America to the American southwest.

In September 1936 I arrived at Robinson Hall in Harvard's ivy- and elm-covered Yard. There I soon encountered Jim Rose and Dan Kiley. We quickly became friends and partners, each in his own way, in rebellion against the status quo.

The University of California at Berkeley's landscape department was a sound and practical school, devoid of doctrinaire assumptions. It dealt largely with the ways and means to adapt traditional theory form the East to the special climatic conditions of California. At Harvard I encountered the central distribution point for the given landscape wisdom as derived from Le Nôtre, Brown, Repton, and Olmsted. These were great and excellent sources, but their inspirations had become routines for lesser minds. While architecture in Robinson Hall fiercely debated the relative merits of, and proper responses to, the new European masters, the landscape faculty was telling us carefully that, since trees were not made in factories, we need not worry about a modern landscape architecture. Instead, the careful balance of formal/informal design theory could handle all architectural innovations.

Rose, Kiley, and I were unconvinced, and continued to explore in our individual ways the works and theories of modern art and architecture and their possible implications for landscape architecture. This contrasted with the respectable but inflexible given wisdom in our Bible, *An Introduction to the Study of Landscape Design*, by Hubbard and Kimball. This, an offshoot of the Beaux-Arts teachings that had institutionalized and regularized art and architecture in Europe since the eighteenth century, was basic to the attitudes of the northeastern American landscape brahmins, who still felt that everywhere west of the Berkshires was Indian territory. Our efforts comprised another skirmish, or perhaps battle, in the cultural wars between tradition and innovation that have marked history ever since people began to settle down on the land. This was, perhaps, a bigger battle, because it derived from the culture-shaking Industrial Revolution.

In September 1938 I published "Small Gardens in the City" in *Pencil Points* magazine, a study of design alternatives for a hypothetical block of city lots. By then I was probably becoming conscious of Thomas Church's garden design innovations in the Bay Area. The project came from my own familiarity with 25-foot row house living in San Francisco, the only West Coast example of that degree of urban density. The study made a neat exemplary laboratory in which I could focus on the variety of conceptual opportunities such small spaces could provide. By conceptual opportunities I mean varieties of physical forms and arrangements. This was a study of design possibilities—a study of physical

19–3

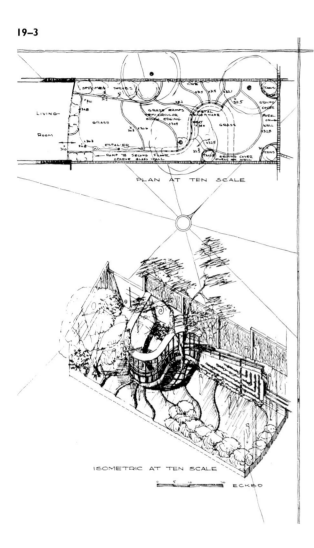

PLAN AT TEN SCALE

ISOMETRIC AT TEN SCALE

0   5   10   20   ECKBO

19–2   Plans and Axonometrics, "Small
19–3   Gardens in the City"
        Garrett Eckbo.
        [*Pencil Points,* September 1937.]

form, based on the idea that the content would develop from use over time. To quote from the text:

"Gardens are places in which people live out of doors." That was the California view. Such a concept of the garden increased the audience, and the potential clientele if you wish. In our climate, people using outdoor space must outnumber gardeners by several times.

"Gardens must be the homes of delight, of gayety, of fantasy, of illusion, of imagination, of adventure." These are not physical qualities. The assumption was that bold or free arrangements of space and material would generate such feelings and responses. Today postmodernism seems to want to begin with desired responses and find guaranteed traditional sources for them. The problem with this traditional approach is: how did they do it first?

"Design shall be three-dimensional. People live in volumes, not planes." This seems so obvious that one wonders why it is so often ignored.

"Design shall be areal, not axial." This is where we parted company from European tradition going back to Egypt—or at least Greece. By the eighteenth century the Beaux-Arts tradition was frozen in axial systems, yet the real world is only occasionally axial, and then by accident. Spatial experience is much more than a line.

"Design shall be dynamic, not static." This follows naturally from the previous statement. Axial design tends to be static, its obvious purpose being to express and freeze the status quo. We do not want to live in a static world.

This study addressed a block of 18 small gardens, all sited on a cross slope to increase the interest. Shown in detail were eleven garden designs. Primarily variations of paving, steps, and ramps, they also included water, trees and shrubs, enclosing walls, arbors and pergolas—all traditional and available materials. In plan (perhaps the innovative part), they were rectangular, diagonal, angular, curvilinear, checkerboard, formed with hexagonal paving/step blocks, primarily water with islands, and without linear form (informal? oriental?). None of these were new or original ideas, although perhaps they were developed and used in original ways. Preeminent was their use in ensembles carefully coordinated to generate unified spatial experience within each design. That is no more than serious formal/informal designers have always done.

Perhaps the best example of this approach to a garden space was one of the same size done in San Francisco by Robert Royston some years later. Designed to be seen from above as well as used, it comprised elegant free painterly patterns in colored concrete. It went beyond both Church and Eckbo.

My study for the block was completed in the spring of 1937. For my master of landscape architecture thesis, later, in the spring of 1938, I did a comparable study of suburban-scale half-acre-plus lots.

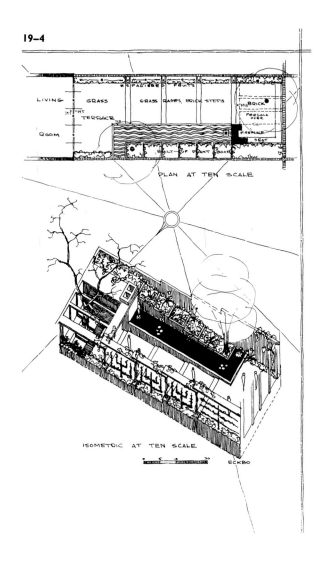

19-4

LIVING ROOM | GRASS TERRACE | ESPALIERED FRUITS | GRASS RAMPS, BRICK STEPS | BRICK

PLAN AT TEN SCALE

ISOMETRIC AT TEN SCALE

ECKBO

19–4 Plan and axonometric, "Small
Gardens in the City"
Garrett Eckbo.
[*Pencil Points,* September 1937]

19–5 Albert Wohlstetter garden
Los Angeles, California, 1950s.
Garrett Eckbo.
[Evans Slater, courtesy Garrett
Eckbo]

19–6 Higgins garden
Palm Springs, California, 1950s?
Garrett Eckbo.

In October 1938 Jim Rose published "Freedom in the Garden," a more comprehensive theory, covering landscape design in general. At about the same time Thomas Church, in active practice in San Francisco with William Wilson Wurster and other modern architects, was developing comparable theories and forms in actual gardens in the field.

Church was ten years older than I, an exemplary practitioner and human being. He did some 2,000 gardens, of a consistency in style, finesse, and comfort that has rarely been equaled. Coming from Beaux-Arts experience and training, he made in midcareer a skillful and convincing adjustment to modern design concepts of tremendous vitality. Thereafter he suited design concept to client and site situation with consummate skill, and without doctrinaire debate. He was the ultimate professional, generating refined solutions for problems of great variety.

Since 1937 I have designed close to 1,000 gardens. One can trace the original thinking of my small and medium garden studies through 30 years of experience, until I began to focus on larger-scale projects. My approach has been consistently flexible and irregular, adjusting constantly to clients and local conditions. The goals of flexibility, richness, and practicality have remained constant, as my books *The Art of Home Landscaping* and *Landscape for Living* spelled out in detail.

Christopher Tunnard arrived at Harvard soon after I left in 1938, after exceptional practice in England. He had begun to bridge European and American design practice, but he soon expanded his energies to address larger problems of urban, regional, and environmental planning. By then modern landscape architecture was off to the races.

But what was it? It was first a rejection of the idea that environmental design began with any preconceived systems of form and arrangement, such as the Beaux-Arts had dictated. We did not begin with history, tradition, and a preconceived vocabulary derived from them. We began with site and problem, client and program, materials, technology, and regional characteristics. We knew history and tradition, and respected them too much to repeat their forms and arrangements in our times and other places. We felt that environmental forms and arrangements should grow out of, or be inspired by, specific times and places. History and tradition should provide inspiration, and an implicit challenge to equal their quality in contemporary terms. They should not be treated as warehouses of concepts, details, forms, and arrangements, free to be lifted, scrambled, or used as total stage sets. That Great Planner in the Sky certainly did not intend that those first on the land—Egyptians, Greeks, et al.—should develop precedents that all subsequent societies must follow ad infinitum through endless centuries of history.

In 1950 I published my first book, *Landscape for Living,* in which I tried to develop these concepts as a complete theory of twentieth-century environmental design. They were not specific form-

19–5

19–6

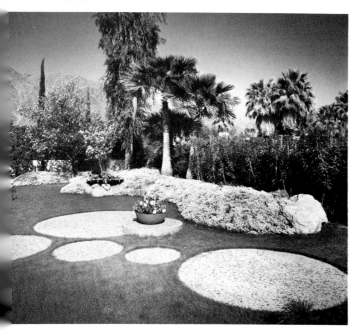

and-arrangement concepts; there was no system of form, although most of the illustrations were drawn from my own interpretations and work. I spoke of three-dimensional *space* formation as the ultimate overall goal of the arrangement of natural and structural materials on the land; of the use of *materials* in shaping space on the basis of their own innate properties and characteristics, rather than by manipulation into preconceived forms that were unnatural to them; of the importance of *people,* not only as clients and users of developed landscape spaces, but as the basic source of the cultural resources from and with which we worked; and of *specific conditions* of climate, land, water, vegetation, regionalism, and urbanism as the true source of specific character.

I gave no particular rules about form and arrangement, about degrees of formality or informality, urbanism or naturalism. All of this I felt should come from the specific site, locality, and region, both micro and macro. I was by then in the midst of an active and growing design practice in southern California. My theory may have been fathered in academia, but it was born in the field.

This was not a theory of a conscious new style, although it was intended to offset the baggage of the conscious old styles that surrounded us. It was a theory of a way of working that harked back to classical times before style consciousness developed. It was a theory of good design that solved problems but did not seek to establish binding precedents for others. It did, however, seek to challenge precedents as the means to produce better solutions to comparable problems. Not the monumentalism of the style gallery, but the living landscapes of ongoing social/natural culture.

My practice in southern California concerned projects that ranged from hundreds of gardens of one to five acres or more, through larger projects such as:

The University of New Mexico at Albuquerque: 25 years' work on a 200-acre campus that began in the urban gridiron. We gradually closed streets, moved cars to peripheral parking, and created a pedestrian campus of considerable richness and comfort, working with Van Dorn Hooker, campus architect, Guy R. Johns, campus landscape architect, and many local architects. The territorial character of the architecture led naturally to campus spatial sequences of great interest and variety.

Union Bank Square in Los Angeles: a three-acre paved plaza three floors above the street on the roof of a parking structure, at the foot of the 40-story Union Bank Tower in downtown Los Angeles. An esplanade of coral, rubber, and jacaranda trees surrounding a central sculptured island of grass and water. The architects were Harrison and Abramowitz, New York, and A. C. Martin, Los Angeles.

The Fresno Downtown Mall: we transformed ten blocks of downtown streets into pedestrian space in association with Victor Gruen Associates, Architects, and their central business district plan

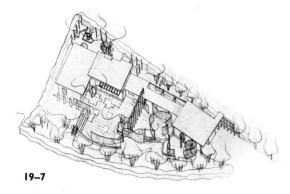

19–7

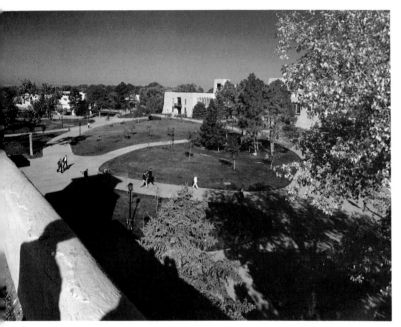

19–8

for the city. This was one of the first in a nation-wide movement to make downtown business districts competitive with suburban shopping malls. It required replanning and rerouting all traffic, parking, and service circulation within a twelve-block area, as well as providing emergency vehicle access. The mall was designed as, and has become, a social space, a focus of community interest and events, a promenade and rendezvous for friends, a play area for children and meeting place for teenagers. It stimulated the acquisition and placement of a $200,000 art collection by private citizen action. Commercial response has generally been good, though tending to vary with the times.

Ambassador College, Pasadena (also Texas and England): small private colleges with residential-scale campuses developed from existing large old residences and gardens, which gave great interest and variety, using greenery and water.

These were all built projects. The design concepts had to come as much from the institution and the locality as from my own background and design experience, and our approach was always flexible, dynamic, and yet coherent. There were also projects and proposals that were planned and designed but never built, and there were area policy planning studies that were done to establish bases for future design and development projects. Here we crossed the broad and imprecise zone between design and planning, and I became a member of the American Institute of Planners. We did planning/design policy proposals and studies for Mission Bay and Pensaquitos in San Diego; American Falls at Niagara; urban design in the city of Hayward, California; Puerto Azul Recreation Community in the Philippines; freeway alignments in Duluth, Minnesota, and Dubuque, Iowa; a large experimental date palm garden in Kuwait; and Shonan Research Village near Yokohama in Japan.

There were also many other built projects. Concern for site, microclimate, and people, all of which are specific and local, can lead to convincing, impressive, and/or enjoyable form if respect for such complex goals is built into the design process. These must be married or blended in order to produce a coherent solution. It is the modern approach that came out of the '20s and '30s, as I have described. It is a result of the Industrial Revolution and the subsequent revolts and reevaluations in all of the cultural, scientific, and technical fields. If this process, repeated many times, produces an "Eckbo style" that is identifiable no matter where the site may be, that will only be another ripple (or even wave) on the broad stream of design as it flows to the future.

The channel is never totally smooth, nor should it be. Name designs merge in the general outfall of history. More important than any single name is the production of forms and arrangements that are vital and active additions rather than dull and boring repetitions. In environmental design/landscape architecture there have been a substantial number of distinguished practitioners following

19–7 Cole garden
Oakland, California, 1941. John Dinwiddie, architect; Garrett Eckbo, landscape architect.

19–8 Central lawn, University of New Mexico
Albuquerque, 1963–1980. Garrett Eckbo.

19–9 Union Bank Square
Los Angeles, California, 1968. Harrison and Abramowitz, A. C. Martin, architects; Garrett Eckbo, landscape architect.
[Kent Oppenheimer, courtesy Garrett Eckbo]

19–9

19–10

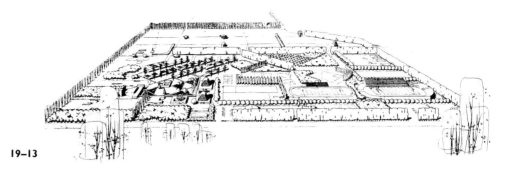

19–13

19–12

19–11

19–10 Union Bank Square
Los Angeles, California, 1968.
Harrison and Abramowitz, A. C.
Martin, architects; Garrett Eckbo,
landscape architect.
[Kent Oppenheimer, courtesy
Garrett Eckbo]

19–11 Downtown Mall
Fresno, California, early 1960s.
Victor Gruen Associates,
architect; Garrett Eckbo,
landscape architect.
[Tidyman Studios, courtesy
Garrett Eckbo]

19–12 Garden of the President's
Residence, Ambassador College
England, 1960. Garrett Eckbo.

19–13 Aerial perspective, Orange Coast
College
Southern California, 1950s. Neutra
and Alexander, architects; Garrett
Eckbo, landscape architect.

these inspirations: Thomas Church, Roberto Burle Marx, Isamu Noguchi, Luis Barragan, Lawrence Halprin, Robert Royston, Hideo Sasaki, Paul Friedberg, Rich Haag, Peter Walker, George Hargreaves, and others. We all agree that no pre-conceptions of style or fixed traditional demands should exist, only the conditions of site and society and their real traditions of quality and expectation. These are often frustrated and dishonored by traditional rulebook design processes that reproduce familiar picturebook designs at greater benefit and profit to designer than to client.

The history of design in China and Japan equals that of the West but is infinitely more subtle and flexible in form and space, less rigid in its interaction with nature, and richer in its content of people/nature relations. Yet it, too, became set in its ways and is currently going through a struggle with the influx of Western concepts and ideas. Romantic design in eighteenth-century England balanced the ideological books of Western attitudes toward nature, but was unable to bridge the gap between itself and the formal tradition. *Jardin anglais* and *jardin français* continue to exist side by side, with little pathways between.

Eclecticism, combining anything and everything from anywhere and everywhere, may not be design, but it has confused and blocked meaningful design in many parts of the world. Under the banner of postmodernism it is making a strong comeback, a sort of devil's agent trying to block serious design thought while returning to old-fashioned stylistic jamborees with little intrinsic form, principle, or regional meaning.

Modern design is what hundreds of other designers and I have said it is: another effort at good, imaginative, socially and naturally responsible design. After fifty years of production at a reasonably high level of quality and responsibility it seems to be drowning in mindless postmodernism.

There is an almost deliberate confusion, which exists all around us, between visual and verbal meaning. Structural and natural forms, which may once in simpler times have conveyed clear messages, are today garbled and confused. We are a society whose entire life, and most of its culture, are so verbalized that visual meanings tend to be lost. The world is being taken over by Disneyland, and this will lead to utter simplistic meaninglessness. The physical environment conveys specific messages, but they are not what the media and information industry would like us to get from them. The result is confusion and indigestion.

Modern design was also a theory that recognized people not only as cultural individuals and groups, but as members of local, national, and world societies. It was a socially conscious theory that soon learned that there was—and still is—a severe imbalance in relations between problems and resources in human society. Projects providing most opportunity for theoretical aesthetic development are not necessarily derived from the most pressing problems of human environment. This I

19–14

19–14 Forecast (Alcoa) Garden
Los Angeles, California, late
1950s. Garrett Eckbo.
[Julius Shulman, courtesy
Garrett Eckbo]

19–15 Forecast (Alcoa) Garden
Los Angeles, California, late
1950s. Garrett Eckbo.
[Julius Shulman, courtesy
Garrett Eckbo]

19–15

learned early on from four years' work with the Farm Security Administration of the U.S. government, 1939–1942, developing 50 combined camp/housing communities, 225 to 350 families each, for migrant agricultural workers, the lowest then and now on our very tall social ladder.[2]

The FSA program was socially and environmentally responsible; its maximum capacity was roughly 12,000 transient families and 2,000 settled families housed in 50 projects. The facilities were minimal, but they were safe and sanitary and provided opportunities for community social life. The abundance of cheap land made possible ample open space for socializing, recreation, relaxation, and private subsistence gardening. Innovative site planning, engineering, and design made the most of these opportunities by creating memorable spatial experiences. The high value of shade in these hot interior areas guaranteed maintenance and irrigation for the trees. Responsible management guaranteed safety, security, and social relaxation within the projects.

From the point of view of the bright young landscape architects and architects, fresh from our best design schools, this was an opportunity to design and build exemplary modern community social/spatial structures for the lowest economic levels. They were not corrupted by the pressures for social distinction and profitability that tended to destroy the larger environment.

If, graduated from the landscape design department at Berkeley in 1935, I became a true pilgrim on the path toward righteous or meaningful design in and of the landscape, some steps along the way should have meaning:

In the years from 1935 to 1965 I was focused primarily on private gardens, even though other kinds of work—housing, parks and community facilities, schools and colleges—assumed growing importance. The quantities were about as follows:

    Gardens, north and south: 600–800
    Housing developments: 175
    Community facilities: 76
    Education, elementary to university: 81
    Commercial: 62
    Planning: 9

In the mid '50s I listed 107 "Gardens Worth Remembering" and 65 "Public Works Worth Remembering." A few years later I listed 65 large-scale work projects to date.

This may suggest the transition in opportunity and focus from domestic garden design (the grass roots of landscape architecture—almost the only direct relationship between owner/client and user) to public/private ownership facilities open to the public, subject to general community use and to complex attention and demands from not-always-predictable sources. That is, designs extending from the specific landscape with specific boundaries to the general landscape with more relaxed boundaries. All of this within a society that believes that all land should be privately owned, controlled, and used, and that public lands, of which the United

States has vast areas, should be attentive to private demands.

In 1965 we returned to Northern California to live in Berkeley, where I joined the faculty of the University and became Chair of Landscape Architecture for four years. I was on the campus, teaching, for thirteen years, averaging about half time. The other half was devoted to professional practice through our San Francisco office. In 1978 I retired from the faculty (being at the mandatory age) and began to devote full time to professional practice. In 1983 I moved from my San Francisco office to my home studio in Berkeley, and have conducted a shrinking practice since then. Now, in 1991, I am focused more and more on stream-of-consciousness memoirs about design and environment on a continental and world scale.

Something should be said about the importance of projects, large or small, built or unbuilt. Importance may be based on size, location, content, cost, utility or benefit to local or larger populations, conceptual, spatial, or social design, contribution to cultural development, ecological content, or social content. In my work I have endeavored to focus on solving problems as presented by clients and locations, in forms and arrangements best suited to these conditions and to the development of qualitative potentials beyond the basic functions.

I still hold these truths to be self-evident: Design is the creation of environments for life, not styles for magazines and coffee table books. Design is solving problems for land, water, vegetation, animal life, and people, rather than for the last alone. If God did give humans dominion over nature it may have been a test rather than a gift. If that is true then we have failed the test. Perhaps the deluge is next.

Certainly converting landscape architecture into separate camps of designers, ecologists, and social activists is not going to solve the problem. We have all got to get into the same tub of dirty water. Design is not a superficial concern with form after social and ecological decisions are made. It is overall concern with the forms these decisions generate together in the real world of natural/human culture.

Perhaps Buddhism comes closer to the ultimate truth. It does seem as though the world in which we live is a seamless web. Whenever one of us moves—you or I or Exxon or the seals and otters—everyone else feels it.

What's next? It is very clear that the world of the twenty-first century will be very different from that of the twentieth. We began this century as a world of greedy, contentious, and self-centered nations. After two world wars and any number of smaller wars and revolutions, we may finally be learning that war just does not pay. This is as true after Iraq/Kuwait, Panama, and Grenada as it was before. Perhaps the twenty-first century can begin to reconstruct landscapes rather than destroy them.

We are still greedy, contentious, and self-centered, but now our faults are set within the larger framework of United Nations, multinational corporations, trilateral commissions, and many other international and regional organizations. Overriding all of these, though not yet much in their consciousness, is the ecological geography of the world. Increasingly it becomes clear that we must give ecological considerations at least equal play with economic, political, and social factors in world planning. The alternative may be uncomfortably close to the desert world described by Frank Marshall in the *Dune* series.

So what should landscape architects prepare to do in the next century? Of prime importance is to expand and coordinate and unify planning/design processes to the scale of the problems. We need ecological/economic planning/design processes that are truly at global, hemispheric, continental, regional, and local scale as the problems define themselves. Political demands and fears will gradually have to subordinate themselves and join the club for a decent future life. A new international regionalism, based on a marriage of human sociopolitical organization with ecological systems and areas, will produce a different and better world.[3]

The professions too will need to reorganize. The planning arts, the spatial design arts (architecture, engineering, landscape architecture, interior design), the object/furniture/utilities arts, the communication/performing arts will all need consolidation, reorganization, and reinvigoration.

Architecture/engineering has dominated world environmental development throughout history, and particularly in the twentieth century. By expanding its purview to merge with landscape/ecological concepts it can become complete environmental design, interlocked and integrated with the world, and saving it from the death by superconstruction that is implied and impending.

Notes

1 Dorothée Imbert, *The Modernist Garden in France* (New Haven: Yale University Press, 1993).

2 See John Steinbeck, *The Grapes of Wrath* (New York: Viking, 1939).

3 See Joel Garreau, *Nine Nations of North America* (Boston: Houghton Mifflin Co., 1981).

20

20–1

↑

20–1

20–I   Miller garden, plan
       Columbus, Indiana, 1957.
       Dan Kiley.

 1. House
 2. Entry drive
 3. Service drive
 4. Swimming pool
    (as originally proposed)
 5. Arborvitae hedge
 6. Staggered arborvitae hedge
 7. Honey locust allée
 8. Redbud bosque
 9. Lawn
10. Orchard
11. Sculpture (proposed)
12. Meadow
13. Weeping willows
14. Flood plain
15. Flatrock River
16. Romantic garden

Gregg Bleam is Assistant Professor of
Landscape Architecture at the University
of Virginia and a practicing landscape
architect. His research interests focus on
the relationship between landscape
architecture and architecture in the
twentieth century.

Daniel Urban Kiley's 1955 design for the Miller garden played a pivotal role in his career, effectively dividing his work into two distinct periods: those projects completed between 1936 and 1954, based primarily on form as a pure art; and those created from 1955 to the present, which were derived from ideas of modern architecture. The Miller garden was Kiley's 396th project and represented a dramatic change from his previous designs. As Kiley's "first essentially modern landscape design,"[1] it expressed spatial ideas specifically adapted from Ludwig Mies van der Rohe's German Pavilion built for the 1929 World Exposition in Barcelona, Spain.

The Miller house and garden were designed between 1953 and 1957 for Mr. and Mrs. J. Irwin Miller and family, on a plot of land between Washington Street and the Flatrock River in Columbus, Indiana (figure 20–1). The house, designed by Eero Saarinen and Kevin Roche, sits on an ivy-covered marble plinth placed on a flat, square earthen terrace approximately 15 feet above the flood plain (figure 20–2). Kiley's design divided the site into three parts: garden, meadow, and wood (figure 20–3). Highly ordered geometric gardens on the upper terrace surround the house and unfold as one moves through its spaces. A staggered pattern of clipped arborvitae hedges defines the boundary on three sides of this area. An allée of honey locusts planted parallel to the west face of the house provides shade from the sun and acts as a link between a sculpture by Henry Moore to the north and a terrace and stair leading to the meadow. The meadow, originally designed to be bounded on the south by a triple row of sycamore trees, is now a mown lawn edged by a single row of red maples. Small groups of weeping willows accentuate the space. A wood adjacent to the river, consisting of flood plain trees, forms the third part of Kiley's plan. From this lower vantage point, due to the foreshortened view, the house appears to sit above a large square lawn. Garden, meadow, and wood create a dynamic composition reminiscent of a classical tripartite order. The spaces immediately surrounding the house, however, are not classically structured; they are based upon a much different—and modern—spatial sensibility.

A comparison of the Miller garden with Kiley's previous designs raises questions concerning the reasons for the radical shift in his design vocabulary in the mid-1950s. To answer these questions, it is necessary first to establish the figures and events that were shaping his career.

Background: Kiley's Early Work

Kiley was born in Boston, Massachusetts, in 1912 and worked in the office of landscape architect Warren Manning from 1932 to 1938. In February 1936 he enrolled as a special student in the landscape architecture program at Harvard University, against the advice of Manning. There he encountered Garrett Eckbo and James Rose, who joined him in rejecting the prevalent Beaux-Arts education in order to explore themes related to modern art and architecture. In particular, the three students were influenced by the work of Walter Gropius, who was teaching at Harvard at that time. One year later, Kiley left Harvard without a diploma and moved to Washington, D.C. He began working for the United States Housing Authority as the Associate Town Planning Architect, a job previously held by Eckbo. Elbert Peets, the well-known landscape architect and town planner, was his supervisor. While working at the agency he met Louis Kahn, who offered him the opportunity to work on several Defense War Housing projects. Kiley quickly accepted, and Kahn became the first of many architects with whom he would collaborate throughout his prolific career. Kahn also introduced Kiley to a young architect named Eero Saarinen, perhaps one of his most important introductions.[2]

Kiley left the Housing Authority in 1940 and opened the Office of Dan Kiley in Washington, D.C., and Middleburg, Virginia. His first commission was a garden for the 40-acre Collier residence in Falls Church, Virginia, in Kiley's words "a 'modernistic' house, but not modern" (figures 20–4, 5).[3] The forms he used in the garden's plan were curvilinear and featured an undulating copse, juxtaposed with clipped hedges arranged in a chevron pattern; a secret garden; a vegetable garden; a children's play area; and a curving line of flowering yoshino cherries surrounding a central lawn, divided by an existing row of eastern red cedars. For four months during the garden's realization, the landscape architect lived with the Colliers, personally completing the site grading and supervising the extensive plantings.

In 1940, Kiley also designed numerous small residential projects, including the Kenneth Kassler garden in Princeton, New Jersey, and the A. A. S.

20–2

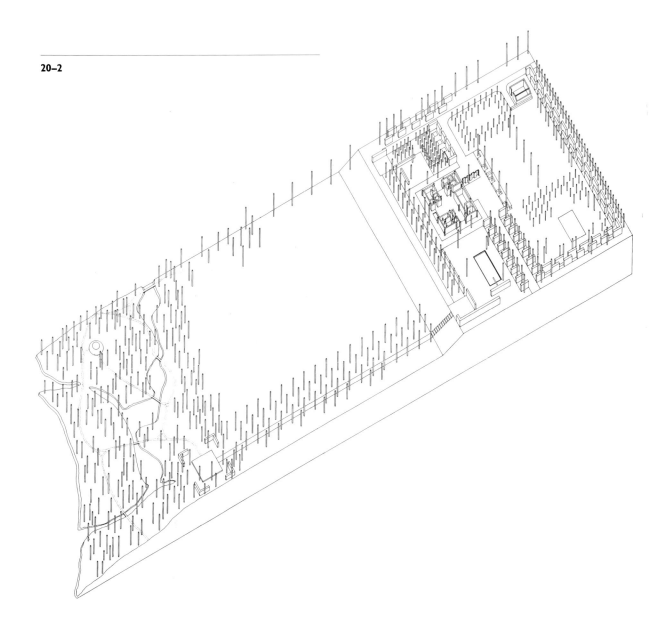

20–3

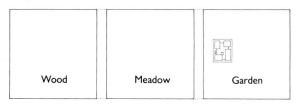

Wood	Meadow	Garden

20–2 Miller garden, axonometric diagram.

20–3 Miller garden, zoning diagram

Davy garden in Middleburg, Virginia. The Kassler and Davy designs were published in 1941 by Garrett Eckbo in *The Magazine of Art,* as examples of "fresh use of indigenous traditional material." In this article Eckbo aptly described the themes that he and Kiley were exploring at this time, which stemmed from ideas about the rural landscape:

> And there we do find innumerable definite three-dimensional space forms produced with both structural and natural material: rectangular or polygonal fields cut from solid natural wildwoods: trees in rows or belts forming planes: the regularity of orchards: straight lines of untrimmed hedges and mixed hedgerows, and of fences and old stone walls, grown up with natural plants: free-standing clumps of trees forming natural pavilions: intersecting planes of these lines of trees and hedges and walls forming a fragmentary organization of space.[4]

In a similar vein, Kiley completed a garden for the planner Edmund Bacon in 1941 and collaborated on several large housing projects with Louis Kahn, including the Lily Pond Housing Project in Washington, D.C., of 1942. Many of these designs strongly recalled the biomorphic forms associated with the work of Eckbo and Rose; there was not yet evidence of the geometric purity and classical references now typically associated with Kiley's designs.

During the war years—between 1942 and 1945—Kiley and Eero Saarinen served together in the Army Corps of Engineers in the Office of Strategic Services, in Fort Belvoir, Virginia. In 1944 Kiley collaborated on his first project with Saarinen, moonlighting on a design competition for a new Parliament building in Quito, Ecuador. In 1945 Saarinen returned to Michigan to assist his father Eliel on the design of the General Motors Technical Center in Warren, Michigan. Eero invited Kiley to collaborate on this project, but Kiley, still in active service, could not accept the invitation. Instead, he recommended three colleagues: Thomas Church, Garrett Eckbo, and James Rose.[5] Saarinen selected Church for the project that would become Saarinen's most complete architectural expression of modernism embracing a neoclassical landscape.[6]

Upon Saarinen's departure from the Office of Strategic Services, Kiley assumed his position as Chief of the Design Presentation Branch and was named as the architect for the Nuremberg Trials Courtroom in Germany.[7] This assignment afforded him the opportunity to visit Europe for the first time. While overseas, he saw the great gardens of Versailles and Parc du Sceaux, classic seventeenth-century designs by André Le Nôtre. This exposure to Le Nôtre's work—its simplicity, clarity of geometric order, and restraint—proved important in Kiley's development and would become the basis for his synthesis of a classical vocabulary with ideas of modern space in the landscape.

Following the war, Kiley moved his office to Franconia, New Hampshire, mainly because, in his words, it offered "good skiing." Practicing primarily as an architect, in 1946 he completed several small

20–4

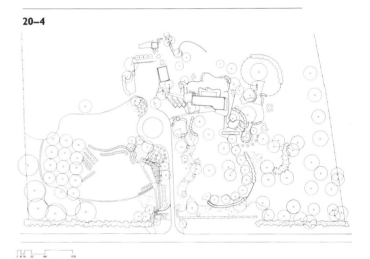

20–5

20–4 Collier residence, plan
Falls Church, Virginia, 1940.
Dan Kiley.

20–5 Collier residence, figure-ground

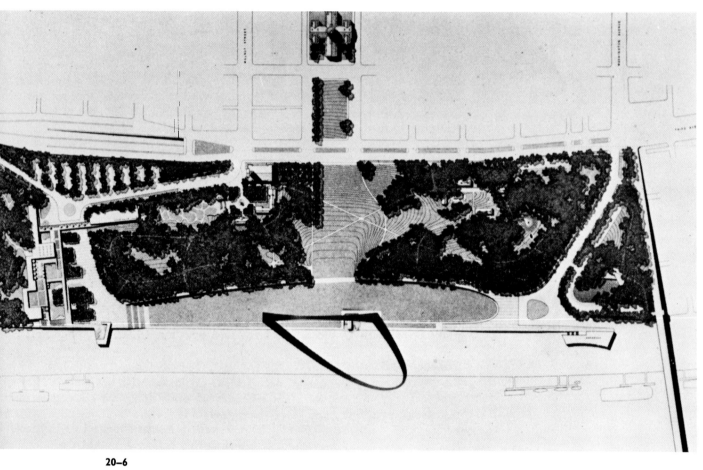

20–6

houses, including a "modernized New England farmhouse" for B. M. Kimball in New Hampshire and a flat-roofed modern house for John Atherton in Arlington, Vermont.[8] Both projects transformed the materials found in vernacular houses of the rural northeast into a modernist vocabulary.

In 1947, he collaborated again with Eero Saarinen on an entry for the Jefferson Expansion Memorial Competition in St. Louis, Missouri, which they won (figure 20–6). Both architect and landscape architect benefited by the widespread attention focused on their collaborative effort, even though completion of the project was stalled until the early 1960s.[9] Kiley completed other projects on his own at this time, including a landscape plan for the David Hamilton garden in Princeton, New Jersey, in 1949—which featured an entrance court planting of thyme in a grid pattern.[10] In 1951 he moved his residence and office to a site on Lake Champlain, facing the Adirondack Mountains, in Charlotte, Vermont. That same year he designed a series of gardens for Minoru Yamasaki's Louis Baker house in Greenwich, Connecticut, that spiraled from the center of the house outward into the wooded site (figure 20–7).[11] Prior to the completion of the Miller garden, in 1954, Saarinen recommended Kiley as landscape architect for the Robert Osborn residence, in Salisbury, Connecticut. Edward Larrabee Barnes was the architect of this Mies-inspired, bilaterally symmetrical house, published in Barnes's 1956 article "Platform Houses."[12] Here Kiley proposed his most geometric planting design to date, consisting of an entrance drive allée of elms and a bosk of red maples planted on a grid (figure 20–8). A gravel parking court, surrounded by hedges planted parallel and perpendicular to the house, sequenced the arrival. To the south of the house lay an herb garden planted in a checkerboard pattern, similar to that proposed for the David Hamilton garden. In the Osborn plan, there is a clear movement away from the fragmented forms of Kiley's earlier designs in favor of a new, geometric order (compare the figure-ground diagrams of figures 20–5 and 20–9).

In 1955, Kiley began work with Eero Saarinen on the Miller garden. Working with the established order of Saarinen's house afforded Kiley the opportunity to explore more completely the potentials of Neoplatonic geometric forms. The architect allowed Kiley the freedom to integrate the house with the surrounding garden using a shared geometric order. A comparison of Saarinen's landscape ideas with those of Mies van der Rohe will illuminate the differences in the two architects' approaches and further articulate the formal concepts that Saarinen brought to the Miller design.

20–6 Jefferson National Expansion
Memorial, plan
St. Louis, Missouri, 1947.
Eero Saarinen and Dan Kiley.
[Jefferson National Expansion
Memorial/National Park Service]

20–7

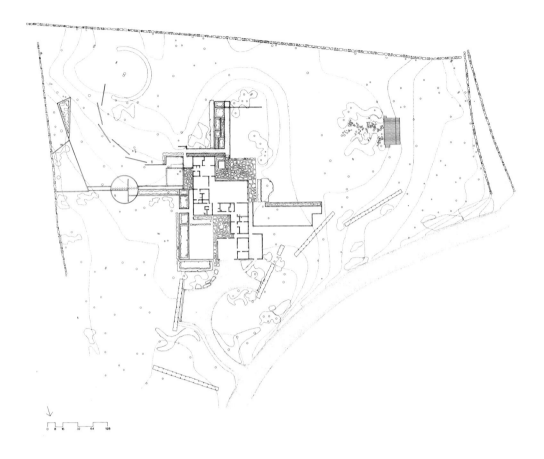

20–8

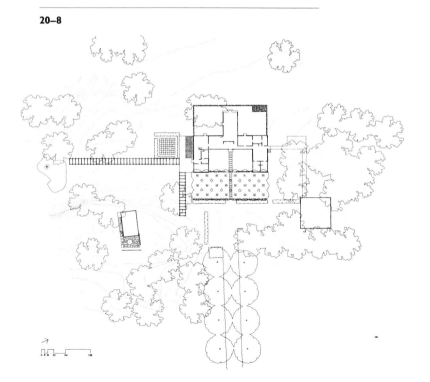

20–7 Baker house plan
Greenwich, Connecticut. Minoru
Yamasaki, architect; Dan Kiley,
landscape architect.

20–8 Robert Osborn residence, plan
Salisbury, Connecticut, 1954.
Edward Larrabee Barnes,
architect; Dan Kiley, landscape
architect.

20–9 Robert Osborn residence, figure-
ground plan

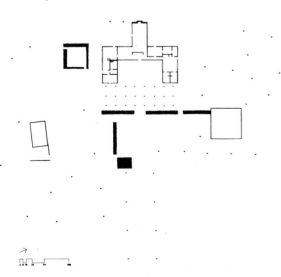

20–9

Eero Saarinen and Mies van der Rohe

Unlike many architects of his time, Saarinen placed a high value on the integration of architecture with outdoor space. In a lecture at Dickinson College in 1959, he expressed this commitment:

> I see architecture not as building alone, but the building in relation to its surroundings, whether nature or man-made surroundings. I believe that the single building must be carefully related to the whole in the outdoor space it creates. In its mass and scale and material it must become an enhancing element in the total environment. Now this does not mean that the building has to succumb to the total. Any architecture must hold its head high. But a way must be found for uniting the whole, because the total environment is more important than the single building. [13]

This position was not generally held by many architects practicing during the 1940s and '50s, who typically used plants only as a foil for their buildings rather than as structural elements to connect interior and exterior space. Saarinen, trained in the Beaux-Arts method at Yale University, carried forth both his father Eliel Saarinen's philosophy and the Scandinavian tradition of creating an architecture that benefited from a reciprocal relationship with the landscape. [14]

Throughout the years that constitute Eero Saarinen's early career, the architecture of Mies van der Rohe transformed the practice of architecture. Numerous young architects, including Saarinen himself, followed Mies's lead in adopting a strain of functionalism that utilized neoclassical design principles. "The preference for simple geometrical forms . . . and the assembly of a number of disparate volumes" was tempered initially by asymmetry—which eventually became almost complete symmetry. [15] Saarinen's General Motors Technical Center is a clear example of this formal transformation, whose prototype was provided by Mies's master plan (begun 1939) for the Illinois Institute of Technology in Chicago (figures 20–10, 11, 12, 13). Concurrent with the GM Technical Center project, Saarinen was engaged in numerous campus master plans across the country, such as those for Antioch College in Yellow Springs, Ohio, and Drake University in Des Moines, Iowa. His was perhaps the best-known campus design firm in the country; his knowledge of campus master planning allowed for a logical point of departure for the design of the GM headquarters. [16] Without the need to incorporate existing buildings into the plan, Saarinen and Church could establish the character of landscape and buildings throughout.

A comparison of Saarinen's GM Technical Center with Mies's master plan for the Illinois Institute of Technology reveals two very different attitudes about a building's relationship to the landscape. At IIT a "picturesque" landscape designed by the Prairie School landscape architect Alfred Caldwell (a disciple of Jens Jensen) surrounds Mies's classically proportioned buildings, like a nat-

20–10

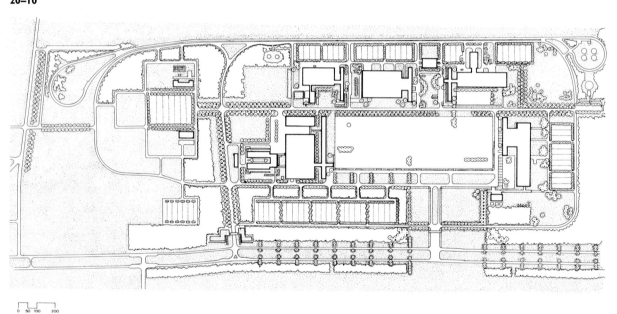

0 50 100   200

20–11

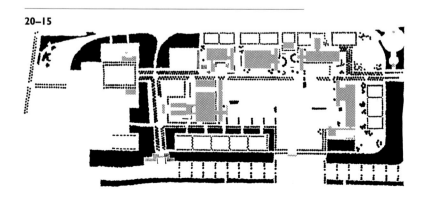

20–15

20–10 General Motors Technical Center,
site plan
Warren, Michigan, 1953. Eero
Saarinen and Thomas Church.
[after *Architect's Year Book 5*]

20–11 General Motors Technical Center,
figure-ground plan
Eero Saarinen and Thomas
Church.
[after *Architect's Year Book 5*]

20–12

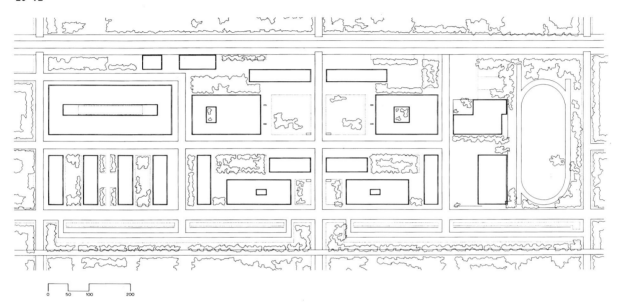

20–12 Illinois Institute of Technology, site
plan
Chicago, Illinois, 1939–1940.
Ludwig Mies van der Rohe.
[source courtesy of Illinois
Institute of Technology]

20–13 Illinois Institute of Technology,
figure-ground plan
Ludwig Mies van der Rohe and
Alfred Caldwell.
[source courtesy of Illinois
Institute of Technology]

20–14 Illinois Institute of Technology,
figure planting diagram
Ludwig Mies van der Rohe and
Alfred Caldwell.
[source courtesy of Illinois
Institute of Technology]

20–15 General Motors Technical Center,
figure planting diagram
Eero Saarinen and Thomas
Church.
[after *Architect's Year Book 5*]

20–13

20–14

20–16

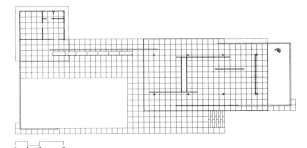

20–17

ural site around a Greek temple. Caldwell's IIT planting plan denied any orthogonal relationship with the buildings that might have extended the organization of the buildings into the surrounding outdoor spaces (figure 20–14). Conversely, the Saarinen and Church plan at GM created a highly ordered, classical landscape that effectively extended the geometry of the buildings directly into the landscape (figure 20–15). In 1956, *Architectural Forum* titled the campus project "GM's Industrial Versailles," clearly alluding to the design's vast scale and the underlying classical order of the plan.[17] Trees were planted in straight lines derived from the buildings' geometry, and hedges were clipped to define surrounding outdoor spaces. This commitment to a highly ordered landscape continued throughout Saarinen's career.

Saarinen's projects immediately following the General Motors campus remained within the Miesian idiom with respect to the architecture. Most notable is the Irwin Miller Bank of 1952 to 1955 in Columbus, Indiana, where he used a nine-square grid of columns to create a classically inspired bank. Unlike Mies, however, Saarinen was steadfast in his belief in a highly ordered, geometric landscape. Collaborating with Dan Kiley on most of his major commissions was a natural outcome of this belief; the importance that Saarinen assigned to the landscape, furthermore, was crucial in creating the Miller garden.

The Barcelona Pavilion and the Miller House

"The Barcelona Pavilion said it all, the way the walls went . . . We were fascinated with that and the spatial idea."[18]

Mies's Barcelona Pavilion is now considered one of the key structures of modern architecture (figure 20–16). Although the pavilion stood but six months (until its recent reconstruction), it was included in both *The International Style* of 1932, by Henry-Russell Hitchcock and Philip Johnson—which accompanied an exhibition at the Museum of Modern Art—and *Gardens in the Modern Landscape,* Christopher Tunnard's polemic of 1938. Kiley first studied the pavilion in architectural periodicals as a student at Harvard University. Through these publications, Kiley, Garrett Eckbo, and scores of other designers became familiar with this seminal work.[19]

The structural system of the pavilion consisted of a grid of eight cruciform columns set upon a podium; its spaces were modulated by freestanding walls that appeared to slide through space. This juxtaposition of vertical column with horizontal plane allows the pavilion to be spatially ambiguous, with a single center always denied and space flowing continuously. "It represents two important developments in Mies' work: the 'free plan' and the concept of a spatial continuum," writes David Spaeth:

In the free plan, walls are liberated from their load bearing function, becoming light screens or

planes in space. . . . The other idea that Mies
articulated in the Barcelona Pavilion is that space
exists as a continuum. It has the characteristic of
a Möbius strip in that as one moved through the
pavilion, what was once perceived as inside was
in actuality outside. Floor, roof, and wall planes
do not contain the space but define it, clarifying
and articulating its existence. As a result, the pavilion exhibits profound structural clarity; simultaneously, it is spatially ambiguous.[20]

This spatial idea, previously explored by Mies
in his brick country house design of 1924 (figure 3–
9), unified Frank Lloyd Wright's concepts of free-
flowing space and De Stijl painter Theo van Doesburg's use of overlapping geometric planes.

De Stijl spatial concepts also affected Garrett
Eckbo, who was fascinated with the Barcelona Pavilion as a Harvard graduate student and a fledgling
practitioner. In his thesis project for a "Hypothetical Superblock Park," he boldly featured the Barcelona Pavilion as a community center.[21] Eckbo's
exploration of these Miesian ideas culminated in his
1940 design for a garden in Menlo Park, California,
in which an existing orchard of pear trees was
transformed by a series of hedges arranged in a
pinwheel configuration (figure 20–17). The influence of Mies on the Menlo Park design was acknowledged by Eckbo in his book *Landscape for
Living:* "Living and dining spaces relate easily and
naturally to a large rear garden, organized with
straight rough hedges and structural extensions
from the house into a kind of free rectangularity,
reminiscent of De Stijl–van der Rohe planning."[22]

While Eckbo had explored Miesian space at
the beginning of his career, Dan Kiley did not show
similar interests until almost 15 years later in his
design for the Miller garden. By this time Kiley was
43 years old and a seasoned practitioner. Several
fortuitous circumstances—the Miller garden client,
the relatively flat open site of approximately 10
acres, and the precedent of Saarinen's Miesian
house—created the ideal climate for Kiley to translate Mies van der Rohe's spatial concepts into the
garden.

Architects Eero Saarinen and Kevin Roche
and interior architect Alexander Girard had de
signed the Miller house during a period in the early
1950s when other architects (including Louis Kahn,
John Johansen, Philip Johnson, and Mies van der
Rohe) were moving away from the asymmetrical
forms of modern architecture to more symmetrical buildings. These buildings were termed "neo-
Palladian" by the architectural critic Colin Rowe:
"Most generally the contemporary neo-'Palladian'
building presents itself as a small house equipped
with Miesian elevation and details. Conceptually a
pavilion and usually a single volume, it aspires to a
rigorous symmetry of exterior and (where possible)
interior."[23]

Architectural Forum published the Miller
house in 1958 and referred to it as "a contemporary
Palladian villa," comparing the Miller plan with a
diagram of Andrea Palladio's Villa Rotonda.[24] This

20–18

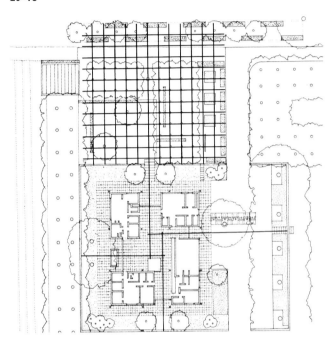

20–16 Barcelona Pavilion, grid plan
Barcelona, Spain, 1929. Ludwig
Mies van der Rohe.
[source courtesy of Museum of
Modern Art, New York, and Public
Foundation for the Mies van der
Rohe German Pavilion in
Barcelona]

20–17 Figure-ground for a garden in
Menlo Park, California
1940. Garrett Eckbo.
[after Eckbo, *Landscape
for Living*]

20–18 Miller house, floor plan/axes
diagram
Columbus, Indiana, 1953–1957.
Eero Saarinen.

20-19

20-20

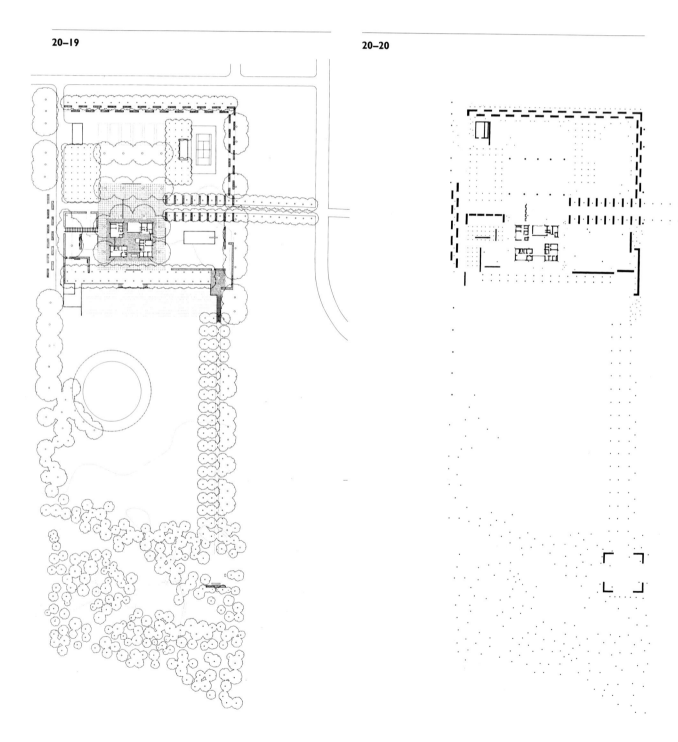

comparison requires some imagination. Contrasted to the Villa Rotonda's strongly centered plan, the theoretical center of the Miller house (the "conversation pit") is shifted off center and is not clearly defined due to the pinwheel configuration of rooms and doors (figure 20–18).

The Miller house is supported by 16 white cruciform columns arranged to form a nine-square grid. These structural columns support the steel frame, articulating the distinction between column, wall, and horizontal roof, a characteristic of Mies's mature architecture. Organized on a grid module of 2′ 6″, the free interior plan allows the four individual "houses" (or rooms) to accommodate the different programmatic needs of parents, children, guests, and service. Spatially, each of these rooms pinwheels around the ambiguous center of the house, providing Kiley with a model with which to design the surrounding garden.

The Miller Garden as Modernist Form

Kiley's study of 1955 differs programmatically (but not diagrammatically) from the most frequently published garden plan of 1957 (figure 20–19). In an early drawing of an unbuilt design, a horse paddock was proposed in the meadow and a stable under the sloping grass bank northwest of the house. Vegetable gardens and a tennis court also appear in this early scheme, but both were eliminated when the Millers decided to move them to an adjacent lot.[25] The zoning of the garden, relating to the interior functions of the house, is apparent in this early plan. Kiley placed the parents' room next to the adult garden, private garden, and dining panel. Service functions were located adjacent to the kitchen garden, laundry yard, greenhouse, vegetable gardens, and orchards. Guests were housed near tennis, swimming, and the arrival lawn. Children also had a defined lawn area for play, as well as access to the recreational areas of the garden. These program elements were organized as a series of overlapping spaces that, due to the placement of the driveway and honey locust allée, suggested a centrifugal movement similar to the plan of the house.[26] Except for those changes mentioned above, the essence of this diagram did not change in the published design of 1957 (figure 20–20).

Additional sources for Kiley's design at the Miller garden were numerous. One must acknowledge the more intuitive aspects of design formed by Kiley's relationship to the client and by the project's site conditions. Kiley's admiration for the classical geometries of Le Nôtre's gardens is also evident in his design vocabulary for the Miller garden. In the plan of 1955, for example, vegetable gardens are organized along the lines of a French potager; and a dense allée of horse chestnut trees—a common Le Nôtre device—leads to the entrance court of the house. Bosks, clipped hedges, tapis vert, and crushed-stone walks also recall the gardens of Le Nôtre. Kiley dismisses complicated explanations: "The house was designed in functional blocks, such

20–21

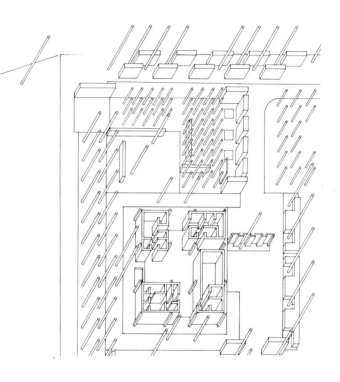

20–19 Miller garden, study plan
1955. Dan Kiley.

20–20 Miller garden, figure-ground
1957. Dan Kiley.

20–21 Miller garden, axonometric of adult
garden
1957. Dan Kiley.

as the kitchen, the dining room, the master bedroom, and the living room. So I took this same geometry and made rooms outside using trees in groves and allées."[27]

Nevertheless, the influence of the Barcelona Pavilion as a model of modern spatial ideas can readily be seen in the Miller garden. Indeed, a more comprehensive comparison of the two schemes reveals that the Barcelona Pavilion and, specifically, the adult section of the Miller garden (figure 20–21) share five design characteristics: neoclassicism, the grid, asymmetry, horizontality, and De Stijl space.

Neoclassicism

Philip Johnson wrote in 1947 that Mies's pavilion contained "in the elevation of the structure on a podium, a touch of Schinkel," alluding to German architect Karl Friedrich Schinkel, whose neoclassical designs were influential on Mies.[28] Kenneth Frampton has also noted the pavilion's indebtedness to the classical language: "The eight columns regularly spaced on a square grid and symmetrical with regard to the flat slab they support may be read as a metaphor for a classical belvedere."[29] This podium alludes to Schinkel's highly romantic design for Hofgärtnerei in the park in Potsdam; as an element of classical architecture the podium also contrasts with the modern spatial configuration Mies created through the use of walls as freestanding planes.

Elsewhere, architects of the 1950s were being reintroduced to the neoclassical roots of modern architecture. Rudolf Wittkower's *Architectural Principles in the Age of Humanism* promoted a return to plans based upon Neoplatonic and neoclassical ideals.[30] This attitude was similarly described by Reyner Banham in his *Theory and Design in the First Machine Age* of 1960, which presented functionalism as a reinterpretation of neoclassical principles (in which the forerunners of modernism had been trained). Banham elaborated his position in the entry for "Neoclassicism" in the *Encyclopedia of Modern Architecture,* and noted the ambiguity in calling a project "classical" and at the same time "modern."[31] Perhaps more than any other architect of his time, Mies represented a synthesis of what would seem to be the conflicting conceptions of neoclassicism and modernism.[32]

Dan Kiley's Miller garden also represented a synthesis of modern spatial ideas and classical structure. Speaking of this fusion Kiley has said: "I find direct and simple expressions of function and site to be the most potent. In many cases, though not all, this has led me to design using classic geometries to order spaces that are related in a continuous spatial system that indicates connections beyond itself, ultimately with the universe."[33] The Miller garden's classical garden elements of allée, bosk, clipped hedge, and tapis vert are juxtaposed with modern spatial concepts. Bosks of redbud trees planted on a grid form an L-shaped space that defines two sides of the tapis vert. The ingenious

20–22

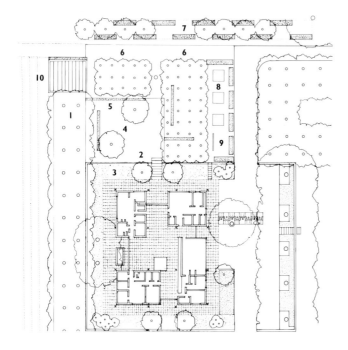

1. Honey locust allée
2. Saucer magnolia
3. Ivy
4. Yellowwood
5. Holly hedges
6. Redbud bosque
7. Arborvitae hedges
8. Kitchen garden
9. Laundry
10. Sculpture (proposed)

placement of the honey locust allée leading to the Henry Moore sculpture (added in the 1960s) runs counter to the tripartite movement of garden to meadow to wood; as a transparent wall on the western edge of the garden, it creates what Kiley has referred to as a "balustrade" in front of the platform of the house.[34] Kiley's synthesis might be seen as a response to Joseph Hudnut's admonition of 1948:

> We must continue our search for some basis of formalization if we are to create a garden for the modern house. Perhaps we can discover this basis within the house: some principle of order which, extended beyond its wall, is destined to overcome the order, or disorder, of its surroundings. One such principle at least has been suggested: that very provocative principle which is called functionalism.[35]

Functionalism provided Kiley, and other Miesian-influenced architects practicing at the time, with the opportunity to begin with a classical parti and then transform it by using asymmetrically placed walls and spaces, all ultimately controlled by the pure geometry of the square.

The Grid

The grid is certainly not an idea unique to our times, for it dates as far back as the Egyptian garden where date palms were planted in regular patterns. Early in the twentieth century, however, the grid became a symbol of all that was modern in art and architecture. Rosalind Krauss has written: "By 'discovering' the grid, cubism, De Stijl, Mondrian, Malevich . . . landed in a place that was out of reach of everything that went before, which is to say they landed in the present and everything else was declared to be the past."[36] Architecture's focus on developing forms that decentralized space and emphasized the periphery also took advantage of the continuous order the grid allowed. The grid was ideal for extending the boundaries of the building in all directions; through its repetition, it abolished the center and moved the viewer's eyes to the periphery, implying a continuous, nonhierarchical order. Le Corbusier's Maison Domino of 1914 illustrates the importance of the column grid as a support for the concrete floors above, making the free plan possible. There are also numerous instances of the adaptation of the grid in the formation of the twentieth-century garden. Walter Gropius's own house of 1938 in Lincoln, Massachusetts, was placed in the midst of a skewed grid of an existing apple orchard; Garrett Eckbo utilized the grid of an existing pear orchard, as mentioned previously, to organize his garden at Menlo Park.

In the Miller project, both Saarinen's house and Kiley's garden relied on the grid as a basic organizational device. Besides its modernist credentials, the grid had a regional appropriateness as well; for no form is more emblematic of the American Midwest as the module for farm, town, and city on the plains. Saarinen regulated the placement of

20–23

20–22 Miller garden, adult garden planting
diagram
1957. Dan Kiley.

20–23 Miller garden, photograph of adult
garden hedges
c. 1957.
[Office of Dan Kiley]

walls and columns with a 2′ 6″-square grid module that extends from the interior to the exterior podium of the house. Kiley also used a 10-foot grid to regulate the location of trees and hedges, although the podium grid of the house and the regulating grid of the garden are not aligned in plan. Other grids were used throughout the garden, in many instances inconsistent with one another, emphasizing the independence of rooms within the garden. In plan, these grids create a pattern that reinforces the centrifugal movement of space around the house. By defining a structure (the column of trees) that could be countered with walls (hedges), Kiley approximated the architectural concept of the free plan.

Asymmetry

Asymmetry, another characteristic of the Miller design, was also a hallmark of modernism. Walter Gropius, who taught in the architecture program at Harvard University during Kiley's enrollment, wrote in 1923 of the "new" principle of asymmetrical composition: "At the same time the symmetrical relationship of parts of a building and their orientation towards a central axis is being replaced by a new conception of equilibrium which transmutes this dead symmetry of similar parts into an asymmetrical but rhythmical balance."[37] This denial of the axis and preference for asymmetrical composition was fully expressed in Mies's pavilion at Barcelona. The asymmetrical organization of the plan counters the classical form of the podium and supports the free-plan organization of walls. The nonaxial entry to the pavilion and the nonalignment of the main pool with the pavilion proper also serve to heighten the contrast between classical and modern traditions (figure 20–16).

The Miller garden also presents a series of asymmetrical overlapping forms. This composition draws not only on modernism but also on Japanese design. Christopher Tunnard's *Gardens in the Modern Landscape* identified asymmetry as a hallmark of the modern garden and cited the example of the Japanese house. Similarly Kiley stated: "It is the Japanese house which excites me and influences my design with its ordering of continuous, interpenetrating spaces into a serviceable and unified whole."[38] Asymmetries abound in the adult portion of the Miller garden, beginning with the nonalignment of the lawn panels (figure 20–22). Upon this "square" of lawn, two specimen yellowwood trees are asymmetrically placed. One enters this portion of the garden from the house alongside a rectangular bosk of redbud trees, which leads to a small fountain on axis with the house door but off center with the space. These trees bound the northern and eastern sides of the garden room, while the honey locust allée borders the western edge of the space.

20–24

20–24 Miller garden, the apple grove and lawn
[Marc Treib]

Horizontality

At the Bauhaus, Gropius had promoted the "new aesthetic of the horizontal" that stemmed from the publication of Frank Lloyd Wright's work in the Wasmuth portfolio of 1910 and 1911. The Wrightian emphasis on the horizontal exerted a great influence on the work of Mies van der Rohe; it is evident in the disposition of the Barcelona Pavilion's cantilevered horizontal roof planes and their extension beyond the walls. Through these devices, the relationship of building to landscape is reinforced as the planar roof appears to hover over the ground plane.

Horizontality also dominates the Miller house and garden. Saarinen's house, a one-story rectangle in plan, has a roof that cantilevers over the surrounding podium, helping to define a transitional space between house and garden. Kiley reinforces this horizontality by evergreen plantings of arborvitae hedges clipped to a uniform height of 12 feet that function as long walls, in turn defining the edges of the garden. Geometric grid plantings of trees of the same species and height, such as the redbud bosks and honey locust allée, reinforce the horizontal dimension of the adult garden. Set against the flat floor of lawn and crushed stone, these horizontally branching plants reinforce the planar quality of the garden. The emphasis on the horizontal is especially clear when the house is viewed from the floodplain woods below. From this position, house and garden merge; the white house is set like a jewel in a green box, screened by the long horizontal line of the allée. The sharp incline creates a plinth for the house and garden and highlights the ever-present horizon line, so clearly expressed by Mies and Wright.

De Stijl Space

The Barcelona Pavilion's design creates a horizontal, centrifugal space through the arrangement of freestanding planes and cruciform columns. While undeniably Wrightian in origin (one need only compare the plans of Wright's Gerts House of 1906 and Mies's brick country house of 1924), it is a transformation of Wright's theories into the spatial concepts of De Stijl.[39] Although Mies denied the influence of De Stijl on his work, there is a strong visual connection in his buildings prior to 1930 with the paintings of Theo van Doesburg, founder of the De Stijl movement. This connection has most often been made through a comparison of van Doesburg's painting *Rhythms of a Russian Dance* of 1917 with Mies's plan for the brick country house (see figures 3–8, 9). James Rose illustrated this comparison in his 1938 article "Freedom in the Garden," calling it an example of the "recognizable continuity of the contemporary style, from pattern to architecture to landscape."[40]

The abstract paintings of Piet Mondrian, which presented portions of an ordered system that was hypothetically infinite, are perhaps the clearest expression of the De Stijl aesthetic. These paintings were based upon a theosophic, cosmic vision of space derived from the philosopher Schoenmaekers and ultimately based on platonic ideas.[41] So, too, Kiley (although certainly not a theosophist) speaks of the spiritual and of a "cosmic awareness" whereby he attempts "to express this connectedness with the universe" in his design approach.[42]

This notion of De Stijl space can be seen in the Miller garden in the form created by the small Japanese holly hedges originally planted in the adult garden (figure 20–23). Kiley's hedges were placed between the square grid of redbud tree trunks in a manner similar (at least in plan) to the walls and columns of the Barcelona Pavilion. This arrangement parallels Eckbo's use of hedges around the lawn at Menlo Park, but Kiley chose to use the same evergreen plant for all of the hedges, whereas Eckbo used a different plant for each hedge (in some instances flowering), thereby weakening the purity of the space. Unfortunately, with the removal of Kiley's "pinwheel" hedges from the adult garden, the ideas of spatial continuum and free-plan space were lost in this portion of the garden. Kiley has stated that "the major thing that changed was on the west side looking across toward the sculpture and the redbud grove. I had Mies van der Rohe–like hedges there before they were removed. This did a lot to spatially define the lawn and define the space."[43]

After the Miller Garden

For Kiley, the use of the grid, asymmetry, and horizontality represented a radical change in his approach to landscape design. After designing the Miller garden, he abandoned the type of free-form, nonorthogonal compositions that he had pursued for nearly 19 years and embarked on a series of geometric explorations as connections between landscape and architecture. The Air Force Academy of 1956–1968, Dulles Airport of 1958, and a garden for Clarence Hamilton of 1965 clearly illustrate the new ordering principles behind his work. Many architects who shared the vision of a geometrically ordered landscape intimately connected to architecture would select Kiley as collaborator. This commitment to a rigorous, more classical spatial approach is not found in the later designs of Kiley's Harvard contemporaries Garrett Eckbo and James Rose. Their compositions continued to be more open and experimental—referring to contemporary art—and seldom embraced the classical tradition that appealed to Kiley's sensibility. Certainly a great part of Kiley's success has been that he did not deny the classical language in his work but used its structure to extend modernism's free plan into the landscape.

Notes

I would like to thank the many people who contributed to this essay: Dan Kiley, who allowed me to interview him and graciously provided copies of drawings from his archives; Mr. and Mrs. J. Irwin Miller for permission to publish photographs of their garden; Marc Treib, Reuben Rainey, and Richard Wilson for their comments and suggestions on early drafts; Geoffrey and Sarah Middeleer for their assistance with editing; and my colleagues at the University of Virginia.

The drawings included in this essay would not have been possible without the support of the University of Virginia Dean's Forum Faculty Research Grant. Except where otherwise noted in the captions, they are drawn after sources used courtesy of the Office of Dan Kiley. Liza Mueller (figures 20–3, 4, 5, 7, 9, 17, 19, 20), Mary Williams (figures 20–1, 8, 10, 11, 15, 18, 22), and Helen Wilson (figures 20–2, 21), graduate students in landscape architecture at the University of Virginia, and Bradford Bellows (figures 20–12, 13, 14, 16) undergraduate in architecture at the University of Virginia, completed the drawings under my supervision.

1 Dan Kiley, "Miller Garden," *Process Architecture No. 33, Landscape Design of Dan Kiley* (October 1982), 21.

2 Dan Kiley, interview with the author, 1 June 1990.

3 Ibid.

4 Garrett Eckbo, "Outdoors and In: Gardens as Living Space," *Magazine of Art* 34 (October 1941), 426, 425.

5 Dan Kiley, interview with author, 1 June 1990.

6 The nature of Church's contribution to the design of the project is not completely known.

7 For an interview with Dan Kiley discussing his design for the Nuremberg Trials Courtroom, see Mark Pendergrast, "Trial and Error," *North by Northeast* 3, no. 3 (Winooski, Vermont: Vermont Public Radio, July 1988), 6–9, 24.

8 "The Bones of a New Hampshire Farmhouse Are Retained in This Warm Country Home," *Architectural Forum* 88 (March 1948), 81-85.

9 For a complete description of this controversy see Ruth Layton, "St. Louis Riverfront Revisited 1933–1964," *Landscape Architecture Magazine* (April 1964), 182–186.

10 This project should not be confused with Kiley's garden for Clarence Hamilton in Columbus, Indiana, completed in 1963.

11 "A House Hidden in the Woods," *Architectural Forum* 95 (December 1951), 101–107.

12 Edward L. Barnes, "Platform Houses," *Architectural Record* (October 1956), 205–212.

13 Eero Saarinen, *Eero Saarinen on His Work* (New Haven and London: Yale University Press, 1962), 6.

14 Peter Papademetriou, "Coming of Age: Eero Saarinen and Modern American Architecture," *Perspecta: 21, Yale Architectural Journal,* 120.

15 Reyner Banham, "Neoclassicism," in *Encyclopedia of Modern Architecture* (New York: Harry N. Abrams, 1964), 202.

16 Papademetriou, "Coming of Age," 128–131.

17 "GM's Industrial Versailles," *Architectural Forum* 104 (May 1956), 122–128.

18 Dan Kiley, interview with author, 1 June 1990. In this quote "We" refers to Kiley and Garrett Eckbo.

19 Juan Pablo Bonta, *An Anatomy of Architectural Interpretation: A Semiotic Review of the Criticism of Mies van der Rohe's Barcelona Pavilion* (Barcelona: Editorial Gustavo Gili, 1975), 57–58.

20 David Spaeth, "Ludwig Mies van der Rohe: A Biographical Essay," *Mies Reconsidered: His Career, Legacy, and Disciples* (New York: The Art Institute of Chicago and Rizzoli International Publications, 1986), 17–18.

21 Garrett Eckbo, *Landscape for Living* (New York: Architectural Record with Duell, Sloan, and Pearce, 1950), 178.

22 Ibid., 136.

23 Colin Rowe, "Neo-'Classicism' and Modern Architecture I," written 1956–1957, first published in *Oppositions* 1 (1973), also in *The Mathematics of the Ideal Villa and Other Essays* (Cambridge: MIT Press, 1976), 120.

24 "A Contemporary Palladian Villa," *Architectural Forum* 109, no. 3 (September 1958), 126–131.

25 Dan Kiley, interview with author, 2 June 1990.

26 Dan Kiley wrote of this centrifugal movement in "Miller House," *Process Architecture No. 33,* 21.

27 Dan Kiley, in Warren T. Byrd and Reuben Rainey, eds., *The Works of Dan Kiley: A Dialogue on Design Theory,* Proceedings of the 1st Annual Symposium on Landscape Architecture, University of Virginia, 6 February 1982, 14.

28 Philip C. Johnson, *Mies van der Rohe* (New York: The Museum of Modern Art, 1947), 58.

29 Kenneth Frampton, "Modernism and Tradition in the Work of Mies van der Rohe, 1920–1968," in *Mies Reconsidered,* 41.

30 For a description of the importance of Wittkower's book, see Henry A. Millon, "Rudolf Wittkower, *Architectural Principles in the Age of Humanism:* Its Influence on the Development and Interpretation of Modern Architecture," *Journal of the Society of Architectural Historians* 31 (1972), 83–91.

31 Reyner Banham, "Neoclassicism," 204–205.

32 Kenneth Frampton, "Notes on Classical and Modern Themes in the Architecture of Mies van der Rohe and Auguste Perret," in *Classical Tradition and the Modern Movement* (Helsinki: Finnish Association of Architects, Museum of Finnish Architecture, Alvar Aalto Museum, 1985), 22.

33 Dan Kiley, "My Design Process," *Process Architecture No. 33,* 15.

34 See Byrd and Rainey, eds., *The Works of Dan Kiley,* 30.

35 Joseph Hudnut, "Space in the Modern Garden," in *Architecture and the Spirit of Man* (Cambridge: Harvard University Press, 1949), 137, quoted by Garrett Eckbo in *Landscape for Living,* 61, and printed in Christopher Tunnard's *Gardens in the Modern Landscape,* 2d ed. (1948), 176. This short essay provides perhaps the clearest description of the "modern" garden as envisioned by Kiley, Eckbo, and Rose.

36 Rosalind E. Krauss, "Grids," in *The Originality of the Avant-Garde and Other Modernist Myths* (Cambridge: MIT Press, 1985), 10.

37 Walter Gropius, "The Theory and Organization of the Bauhaus," in Herbert Bayer, Walter Gropius, and Ise Gropius, eds., *Bauhaus 1919–1928* (New York: The Museum of Modern Art, 1938), 30.

38 Kiley, "My Design Process," 17.

39 Kenneth Frampton, *Modern Architecture: A Critical History* (London: Thames and Hudson, 1980), 164.

40 James Rose, "Freedom in the Garden," *Pencil Points* (October 1938), 640 (reprinted in this volume).

41 For a complete discussion of De Stijl theory and principles see H. L. C. Jaffé, *De Stijl 1917–1931* (Cambridge: Belknap Press of Harvard University Press, 1986).

42 Kiley, "Miller Garden," 15.

43 Dan Kiley, interview with author, 2 June 1990.

20–25

20–26

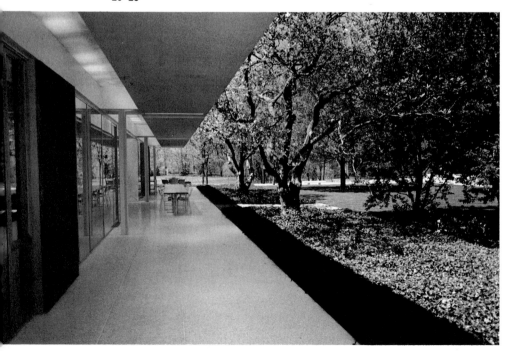

"The geometrically ordered landscape spaces extend outwards from the house in layered rhythm, providing a rich succession of spatial and visual experiences.

"The overall arrangement of planting uses simple lines and spaces to organize the property into squares and rectangles very much like the house plan does in the interior. The result is a continuing unfolding of spaces into the other."

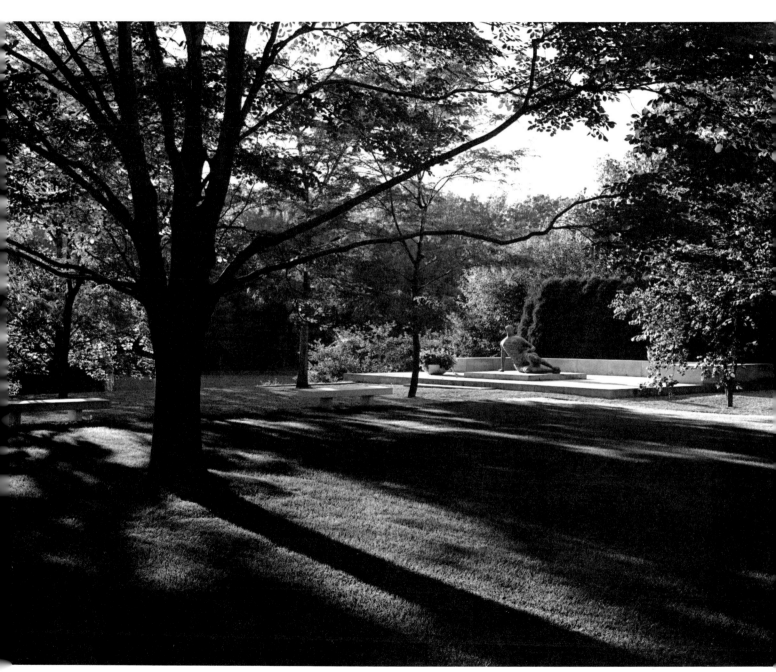

20–27

20–28 United States Air Force Academy Colorado Springs, Colorado. 1956–1968. Skidmore, Owings & Merrill, architects; Dan Kiley, landscape architect.
[courtesy Office of Dan Kiley]

20–29 United States Air Force Academy
[courtesy Office of Dan Kiley]

20–28

20–29

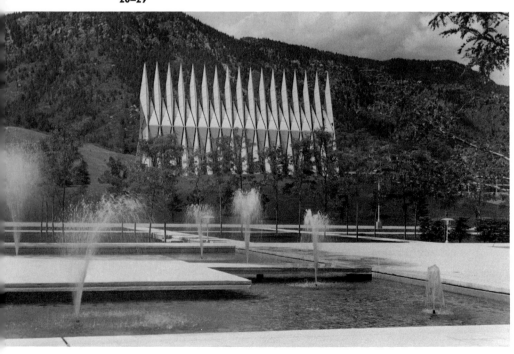

"In the academic area, which was composed of the chapel, dining hall, academic buildings and dormitories, our major feature was a 700' long 'Taj Mahal' fountain and pool system. The paving throughout this area was arranged in large modules 81' wide to accommodate a marching phalanx of cadets. Therefore, when they were off duty and on weekends, we designed the pool so they would have to walk in a broken line. The planting design outside of the academic and community areas was to integrate with the local arid Colorado conditions."

20–30 Hamilton Garden
Columbus, Indiana, 1965.
Dan Kiley.
[Marc Treib]

20–30

"An allée of moraine locust trees runs parallel to the back of the house between two pavilions. The tall slender trunks and delicate foliage of the trees screen the building from the rest of the yard.

"Interlocking arbors with diagonal structural members create interesting patterns of shade, and link various garden rooms and areas. . . . Within the hedge is the second pavilion, an open gazebo housing a small fountain."

20–31 Aerial view, Oakland Museum
Oakland, California, 1969. Roche,
Dinkeloo and Associates.
[Joe Samberg, courtesy
Oakland Museum]

20–32 Entry court, Oakland Museum
[courtesy Office of Dan Kiley]

20–31

20–32

"The building, largely underground, rises in regular tiers, and the roof of each becomes the garden terrace of the one above. Broad exterior stairways ascend the terraces, but are asymmetrically placed to encourage meandering and discovery. The lowest level, which houses children's classrooms, surrounds a sunken pool filled with fish, waterlilies from three continents, and other aquatic plants. In general the planting in each planter or group of planters is irregular in form, with formal arrangements principally at major level changes."

20–33 Chicago Filtration Plant
Chicago, Illinois. 1957. C. F.
Murphy, architect; Dan Kiley,
landscape architect.
[Balthazar Korab, Ltd, courtesy
Office of Dan Kiley]

20–34 Chicago Filtration Plant
[Balthazar Korab, Ltd, courtesy
Office of Dan Kiley]

20–33

20–34

*"Five circular pools 100 and 200 feet
in diameter, symbolizing the five Great
Lakes, are focal points of the ten acre
park at the western edge of the peninsula. Fountains which propel single
jets of water 30 to 100 feet from the
center of each pool dramatize the complex's purpose. Each pool is shaped like
a gently tapered moon crater, and the
surrounding earth slopes up to the outside rim where broad circular steps de-
scend to water level. A network of
straight walkways links the pools."*

20–35

20–36

"It seems fitting that the design for the Third Block should take its inspiration from the early plan for Philadelphia laid out by William Penn's surveyor, Thomas Holme.

"A spatial dynamism is created by 700 honey locusts set on a 12′ 6″ by 18′ 0″ grid."

20–37 Water channel, Dallas Museum of
Art
Dallas, Texas, 1985. Edward
Larrabee Barnes, architect;
Dan Kiley, landscape architect;
Christopher Dunn, associate.
[courtesy Office of Dan Kiley]

20–37

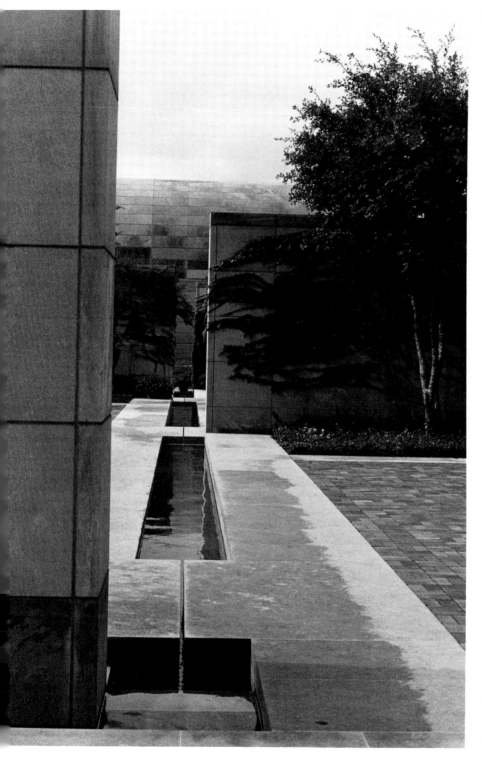

"The [sculpture] court is divided into
open-ended outdoor rooms by four freestanding limestone walls, in staggered
arrangement parallel to the building.
Traceries of Boston and English ivy on
the walls' interior surfaces provide delicate counterpoint to their austere
simplicity.

"The vertical system created by the
walls is echoed on the ground plane by
a series of narrow water channels set
perpendicularly to the walls. These
channels receive water from four sheer
waterfalls which wash down one surface of the walls, one for each garden
room."

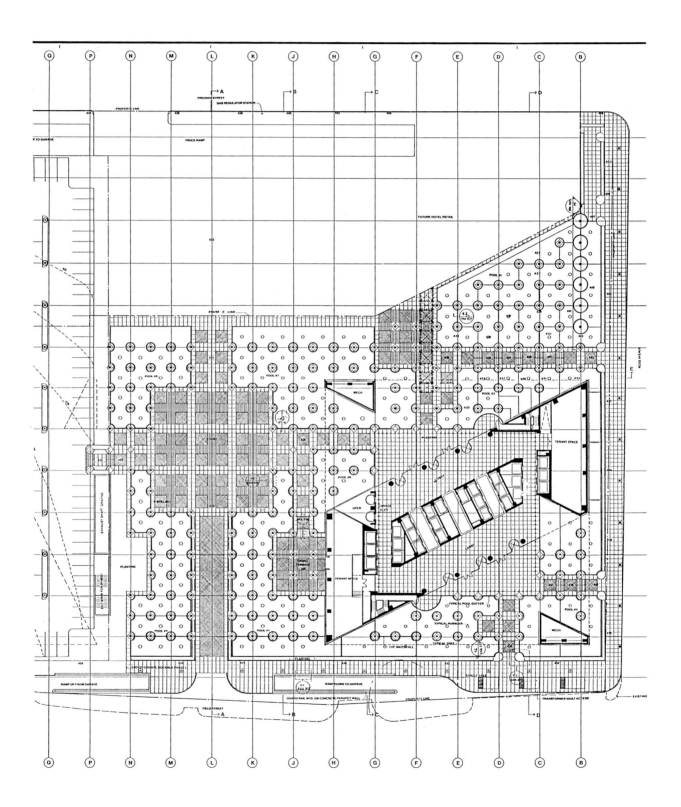

20-38 Plaza plan, Fountain Place, Allied
Bank Tower
Dallas, Texas, 1987. I. M. Pei,
Harry Cobb, Harry Weese,
architects; Kiley-Walker,
landscape architects. Dan Kiley,
landscape architect; Peter Ker
Walker, partner-in-charge.

20-39 Fountain Place, Allied Bank Tower
Dallas, Texas. 1987.
[courtesy Office of Dan Kiley]

*"In staggered rows between the [bald
cypress] trees are 263 bubbler fountains. Every fountain jet, bubbler, and
tree is individually lighted, contributing
to a nighttime display as spectacular as
the daytime one."*

20-39

20-40

20-40 Terrace/garden, North Carolina
National Bank
Tampa, Florida, 1988. Harry Wolf,
architect; Dan Kiley, landscape
architect.
[courtesy Office of Dan Kiley]

*"The plaza is a geometric plaid of grass
and pre-cast concrete shapes, interlaced
with an elaborate system of canals and
pools. The landscape design . . . uti-
lizes repetitions of architectural components and modules, inspired by the
Golden Mean and the Fibonacci series
of logarithmic patterns, to achieve an
unusual unity, spatial clarity, and elegance of forms.*

*"Nine water channels issue forth from
the canal, flow across a grid of grass
squares and pre-cast concrete walkways
on the upper level of the plaza, and end
in specially designed fountains inter-
spersed among the groves and open
spaces."*

21-1

Peter Walker is Adjunct Professor of Landscape Architecture at Harvard University, principal of Peter Walker and Partners in San Francisco, and a Fellow of the American Institute of Landscape Architects. As both a teacher and a practitioner, he has helped to rekindle an appreciation of landscape architecture as an art form.

In 1955, when I graduated from Berkeley, we were told, primarily by our architectural professors, that the past was not only dead but useless in our quest for modernist beauty. The great works of the fifteenth, the sixteenth, and particularly the seventeenth centuries were bad, as they represented decadence, waste, and authoritarian societies. Japan, not then clearly understood, was interesting, maybe even acceptable. The eighteenth-century English or Olmstedian naturalistic tradition was acceptable as context, we were told—but it should only be background for the clean, asymmetric, uncomplicated, democratic, and socially expressive new work that was certainly to follow.

We now hear again that the recent past is irrelevant to the present. Some recent critics have even dubbed the postwar designers "invisible." Due to postmodern historicist pressure, interest in Renaissance and baroque European gardens is reviving. Ironically, postmodernism has revived visual interest while at the same time discouraging interest in modernism.

Looking back, I believe architects and particularly landscape architects trained in the 1950s, '60s, and '70s were hurt by their lack of historical perspective. I feel that the new wave of disinterest in postwar experience will likewise be narrowing. The struggles of a profession are always pertinent to current activity. Even failings, if carefully analyzed, can yield insight and information, especially where research on physical design plays only a small role in the development of the art form.

The modern movement in landscape architecture of the United States began very tentatively in the late 1930s, on shaky ground. Unlike the situation in architecture, there were few European precedents, manifestos, and masterworks to direct the initial designs. In that decade, a few landscape designers—notably Fletcher Steele, Thomas Church, Christopher Tunnard, Garrett Eckbo, James Rose, and Dan Kiley—wrote articles about the need to adapt design to the conditions of modern life; but the profession of landscape architecture was slow to respond. In spite of Eckbo's passionate democratic visions, Tunnard's pragmatism, and Church's appealing good sense, for instance, there was no perceived widespread *need*—no technological revolution in the landscape industry, no revolution in political or social terms—to direct the immediate prewar and postwar work in landscape design. Rather, more subtle though pervasive changes in

American society encouraged a degree of experimentation, which became evident first in the private sphere of the home. In effect, what brought modernism to landscape design in the United States was not revolution but evolution: the gradual, profound changes in American middle-class life.

Despite significant regional differences, these changes in lifestyle were brought about by at least three important influences recognizable throughout the United States by the years immediately after World War II—increasing affluence among the middle classes; the emergence of the nuclear family as the "average" family unit; and greater informality. Some underlying conditions, including mobility of people during the depression of the 1930s and World War II and the loosening of traditional family and community ties, were perhaps equally influential. As a result of these and other changes, an unprecedented number of Americans were migrating from small towns and rural areas to metropolitan cities and suburbs; and, as they settled in newly developed subdivisions and exurban fringes of farms, forests, and canyons, new forms of social life naturally evolved.

In the eastern and midwestern United States, the natural rhythm of the four seasons, the relative proximity of extended family, and the established institutions of older cities tended to temper, if not retard, the modernist spirit. On the West Coast, however, the relative newness of urban settlements, the distance from old family ties, and a climate favoring year-round outdoor living all tended to invite more experimentation with the forms and materials of a dwelling place. In the suburbs of Los Angeles and San Francisco, then, the suburban garden and neighborhood park became the primary focus of the revived postwar profession of landscape architecture. Ambitious young designers from all over the United States flocked to the Bay Area in particular, to see the gardens publicized in *Sunset* and *House Beautiful* magazines, to work with Church or his followers, or to attend the University of California, Berkeley, then the Bay Area style's school of choice.

When I first began to work in the office of Lawrence Halprin, then almost an exact copy of Church's small atelier, or studio practice, there was only one nonresidential job in the office. Tito Patri, my classmate at Berkeley, worked around the corner at Eckbo, Royston and Williams in a similar setting with what I now consider a small stylistic

21–2

21–1   Connecticut General Life Insurance Headquarters, terrace Bloomfield, Connecticut, 1957. Skidmore, Owings and Merrill, architects; Isamu Noguchi, sculptor and landscape consultant. [Marc Treib]

21–2   Auditorium Forecourt Plaza Portland, Oregon, 1968. Lawrence Halprin. [Marc Treib]

difference, though at the time we made great distinctions between our mentors. Half of Halprin's office was comprised of Berkeley graduates; the exceptions were Halprin himself (from Cornell University, the University of Wisconsin, and Harvard), Richard Haag (from the University of Illinois and Harvard), and Mai Arbegast (from Cornell University as well as Berkeley). Over the next few years, among Halprin's young associates, Richard Vignola, Michael Painter, and I would also follow Halprin and Haag to Harvard.

Eckbo had already written about broader social and aesthetic goals; but a year later, in 1956 when I left to study with Stanley White in Illinois, Halprin's Old Orchard Shopping Center was the only exception to his work on suburban gardens.

Halprin once observed that Church's lack of social distinctions, "treating each client equally," was his tie to modern liberal thought. I agree with the sentiment, but we should remember that the underlying motives of the clients were essentially bourgeois, suburban family ideals, understandably self-indulgent after more than ten years of depression and war. What, then, was the basis of any real claim to modernism? I believe it was the particular kinds of form and their connection to the international change in formal awareness represented by surrealism, constructivism, suprematism, and later expressionism, which tied the West Coast work to the modernism of the European-informed East Coast. This formal language, generally recognized by the media of the intelligentsia, was the focus for critical discourse.

Then in the late 1950s, things changed. Opportunities for design and the subsequent demands on the office structures expanded and broadened drastically and quickly. Urban renewal as federal policy commanded the attention of large developers and all design professions. The federal highway program and financing by the Federal Housing Authority and the Veterans' Administration helped to make more suburban land available for housing and its related commercial and recreational uses. This suburban expansion affected landscape architects even more than architects.

The explosion of suburban land uses even led to a rebirth of the American new town movement, which had been dormant since before the war. U.S. corporations were assuming worldwide stature as well as expanding both production and institutional facilities across the country. No matter what motive or motives drove a designer in this generation, whether social or aesthetic, quantitative or qualitative, there was greater opportunity than had been seen in more than four decades. A new kind of office emerged. The atelier of the immediate postwar years gave way to the corporate structure we know today.

Built on a model partially remembered from Olmsted, partially imitative of the project manager/project designer teams of Skidmore, Owings and Merrill (SOM), and partly inspired by Gropius's Bauhaus ideal of collaborative practice, the office of

21-3

21-3   Constitution Square
Hartford, Connecticut, c. 1960.
Sasaki, Dawson, DeMay &
Associates.
[Marc Treib]

21-4   Water reservoir cover
Piedmont, California, 1960.
Royston, Hanamoto & Mayes.
[courtesy Robert Royston]

21-5   Foothill College
Los Altos, California, 1960.
Ernest J. Kump & Associates,
architects; Sasaki, Walker and
Associates, landscape architects.
[Gerry Campbell, The SWA
Group]

21-4

21-5

Sasaki, Walker and Associates was formed and thrived. It had a broad and hopeful vision of what design could do and the structural advantage of almost unlimited growth, as it could combine expertise in landscape, planning, architecture, and engineering as well as in many technical specialties. It could also finance, manage, and market itself, using modern corporate techniques that, as at SOM, were recognizable management tools. Sasaki, Walker and Associates thus appealed to both private and public corporate clients.

Not surprisingly, this model of corporate landscape architectural practice evolved in the northeast, where political, economic, social, and cultural institutions were already well established. Hideo Sasaki, a California native, had studied at the University of California (at both the Los Angeles and Berkeley campuses), the University of Illinois, and Harvard. He had also worked for SOM in New York and architects Perkins and Will in Chicago before setting up his own practice in Watertown, Massachusetts, near Harvard, where he taught landscape architecture. The clients of Sasaki, Walker and Associates included the corporate architectural firms as well as business corporations and government agencies. Although a few gardens were designed by his firm, Sasaki's own professional interests lay in fairly large-scale public, institutional, and corporate work. Aware of Olmsted's great legacy, Sasaki was consciously reviving the scale and the public purposes of the profession's founder. A brilliant organizer, manager, and design critic, Sasaki thrived in the context of a design team, where he profoundly influenced, rather than overtly controlled, the tangible product of the team.

EDAW, JJR, SWA, HOK, POD, and even Halprin eventually followed variations on the Sasaki format. The differences among these firms were (and are) significant. EDAW, for example, is the corporate outgrowth of a small partnership that began in San Francisco, just about the time of America's entry into World War II. Originally composed of Garrett Eckbo and Edward Williams, the partnership expanded in 1945 to include returning war veteran Robert Royston. In 1946, Eckbo moved to southern California to open a second office of the firm; but the partnership remained intact until 1957–1958 when Royston opened his own office.

Begun with a strong focus on private residential design, Eckbo's office had, by the early 1960s, begun to assume larger-scale work, including the grounds of schools, campuses, malls and shopping centers, and some regional planning studies. In the early years the office was sustained by collegial relationships with architects and planners. Gradually, however, the office began to serve more corporate and public clients. Among their more comprehensive planning projects was an open space study for the state of California, directed by Williams (in northern California) and Eckbo (in southern California).

After 1968, when Eckbo and his partners incorporated their firm, a hierarchical office manage-

21-6

21-6 Site plan, Deere & Company
Headquarters
Moline, Illinois, 1963. Eero
Saarinen, architect; Sasaki, Walker
and Associates, landscape
architects.
[courtesy Sasaki & Associates]

21-7 Site plan, Upjohn Corporation
General Office Building
Kalamazoo, Michigan, 1961.
Skidmore, Owings and Merrill,
architects; Sasaki, Walker and
Associates, landscape architects.

ment began to emerge. A younger generation of
senior staff, keenly interested in the dynamics of
running an office in a rapidly changing business climate, became managers. Meanwhile, from 1965
through 1969, Eckbo served as chairman of the department of landscape architecture at the University of California, Berkeley, while continuing to
practice. In 1972–1973 he left to form his own
smaller firm. Thereafter, EDAW, Inc. (formerly
Eckbo, Dean, Austin and Williams) moved further
beyond physical project–scale work, into larger-
scale planning for government agencies, the Navy,
and large-scale developers.

For the other acronyms—including JJR, SWA,
HOK, POD, and CHNMB (formerly Halprin's
firm)—the evolution from atelier or partnership to
corporation occurred along similar lines, each with
its own intricacies, too complex for discussion here.
Generally, the dynamics of any business thriving
within a capitalist system also operated within these
landscape firms. Initial successes brought in more
jobs that required more personnel; and growth in
sheer numbers of people led to greater hierarchy in
the organization, more complexity of fiscal management, and more financial incentive to develop a corporate entity—which would entail little or no
financial risk to individuals. In turn, particular individuals became less critical to continuing financial
success than the smooth running of the whole
operation.

Among these generalities, a few distinctions
should perhaps be made. The landscape architecture division of HOK, while completing many projects of large-scale site planning and some urban
renewal and urban design, basically worked at project level. As they were working for their own architects, they were most effective at providing the
extension and refinement of a group of buildings,
whether academic, civic, or commercial. Thus, as
extensions of, and settings for, buildings, their landscapes tended to be unobtrusive and vernacular in
expression.

POD and SWA were both involved in the new
residential expansion both at planning and at project
level. They became familiar with all parts of the
puzzle by completing individual projects—shopping
centers, commercial centers, housing, schools, and
parks. They also learned to fit these elements into
neighborhood and town plans, which included all of
the pieces. Their planning was, then, an additive
process, derived from specific experience in landscape projects.

SWA, and to some extent Sasaki's office, also
performed what I would call more traditional landscape architectural work, which is working primarily as a subcontractor to architects on large
corporate, institutional, and commercial projects,
such as university plans, downtown renewal plans,
and major commercial and housing complexes.

So here we were with these tremendous chal-
lenges and opportunities and these wonderful new
corporate tools. But what happened to the earlier
formal explorations?

There were, of course, extensions of the earlier residential-scale work, such as the work of Robert Zion and the later work of Halprin and Kiley. But the larger project areas put more emphasis on rational and practical analysis. Roads, parking, and the relationship of larger and greater numbers of buildings took the place of the simpler functional and aesthetic concerns of livable back yards. "Site planner" became the title of choice over "landscape architect." Planning, civil engineering, and managerial skills rather than visual and drawing skills gradually became the primary "products" of the larger offices. "Problem solving," "quality of services," and "process" became the buzz words heard at interviews and management meetings; and there were a lot of management meetings. Still, a large element of physical design was achieved. Many of these designs and plans were exemplars of the social and aesthetic goals of the period. Most of the strongest and most ambitious young designers joined these collaborative and idealistic enterprises.

At Sasaki's successive offices (Sasaki, Walker and Associates, SDDA, SA) and at SWA, one could still find an emphasis on landscape architecture as an *artistic* enterprise. There people still believed that the quality of the architecture and the landscape architecture were absolutely critical to success. Not surprisingly, individuals within these firms developed collegial relationships with particular architects and their firms. Eero Saarinen, SOM, Edward L. Barnes, and I. M. Pei, for instance, frequently worked with Sasaki's office, with SWA, and with Kiley. Halprin, on the other hand, worked closely with the leaders of the Bay Area style—William Wurster, Joseph Esherick, Don Emmons, Gardner Dailey—and was clearly influenced by them. Whatever the specific influence, however, these landscape firms, particularly through the 1960s and early 1970s, tended to be less process-oriented, more experimental. Striving to produce the exceptional, the iconic, was part of the firms' ethos.

The recession in the housing and building industry, from 1972 through 1975, was a turning point. The boom in housing and new-town planning abruptly ended and projects were canceled, leaving little to nourish the idealism and imagination of designers. In order to survive, SWA, HOK, POD, and other firms took on more planning jobs. And, as competition increased, these firms developed stronger orientations toward service to the client.

From these years we have many fine examples of urban spaces, housing, schools, shopping centers, and corporate work spaces. Why then do we now feel that this has been a bland or invisible period?

One reason, I believe, is the huge quantity of mediocre development work whose sheer size has become a symbol of the mindless market-oriented expansion of the suburban environment. We do not often make a distinction between high- and low-quality work of this period. For many years, even

21–7

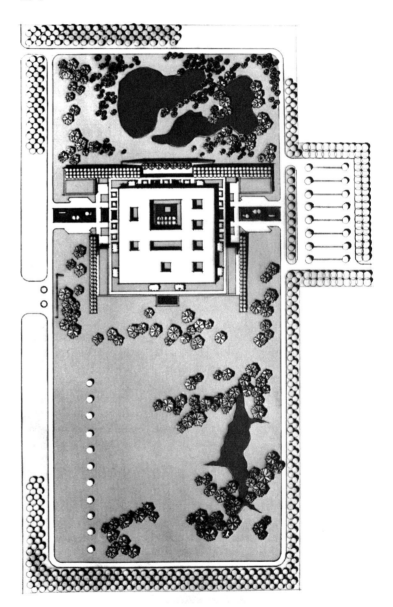

21–8

21–9

the ASLA award winners were mentioned only in the back pages of *Landscape Architecture.* More important, there was a lack of formal and expressive development. The great demand for habitat too often produced a shallow appropriation of every fashionable style, both extranational and historical. Undigested and ill-fitting combinations of formalism and naturalism were produced. Only household appliances, clothing, and perhaps American automobiles have had a more drastic devaluation in formal quality. Perhaps most important, the worlds of fine art and landscape design separated. This formal divergence eliminated the aesthetic media's important functions of wide dissemination of formal ideas and achievements. Most damaging, it eliminated critical review. The self-purifying tools of aesthetic debate virtually ceased to exist for landscape architecture. Promotion and corporate image became an aesthetic veneer on the service orientation. Comparison of products and critical discussion, even within the individual organizations, was sparse.

In the late 1960s, the environmental movement rendered its great general criticism of endless mediocre environmental activity. Ensuing debate had contradictory effects. It energized the field and broadened the landscape architect; at the same time, it furthered the tendencies toward quantitative criticism. The environmental movement further emphasized the process aspects of landscape and architectural design. As much as a third of the design fees were redirected to obtain public approval. Soon "processing" itself became a new and lucrative "service." Over the next decade the corporate design offices directed between 60 and 95 percent of their gross budgets to site planning, environmental assessments, and processing. The transformation from small physical design ateliers doing back yards to large, well-managed service organizations was almost complete—and this was well before the introduction of computers!

In a way, it is remarkable that any artifacts remain from this incredibly dynamic, and yet tragic, period. It is also encouraging and heartening that a renewed interest in physical design with recognizable visual characteristics has begun to bring balance to a field so overgrown and overambitious, and with such small real information and critical resources. I am much heartened by the beginnings of a balancing of the aesthetic, social, and ecological interests of the field. But I also recognize a clear need for greater understanding of the design products of the last twenty-five years.

I believe we should examine the exemplars of this period, separated from its excesses, and try to build on its large body of experience.

21–10

21–11

21–8 Quarry Theater, University of
California, Santa Cruz
1967. Royston, Hanamoto, Beck
and Abey.
[courtesy Robert Royston]

21–9 Syntex Research Center
Palo Alto, California, c. 1970.
MBT Associates; Clark,
Stromquist, Potter and Ehrlich,
architects; Sasaki, Walker and
Associates, landscape architects.
[Gerry Campbell, The SWA
Group]

21–10 Model, Copley Square
Boston, Massachusetts, 1966.
SDDA.
[Hutchins Photography, courtesy
Sasaki & Associates]

21–11 Concord Performing Arts Center
Concord, California, 1975. Frank
O. Gehry, architect; Sasaki,
Walker and Associates, landscape
architects.
[Dixi Carrillo, The SWA Group]

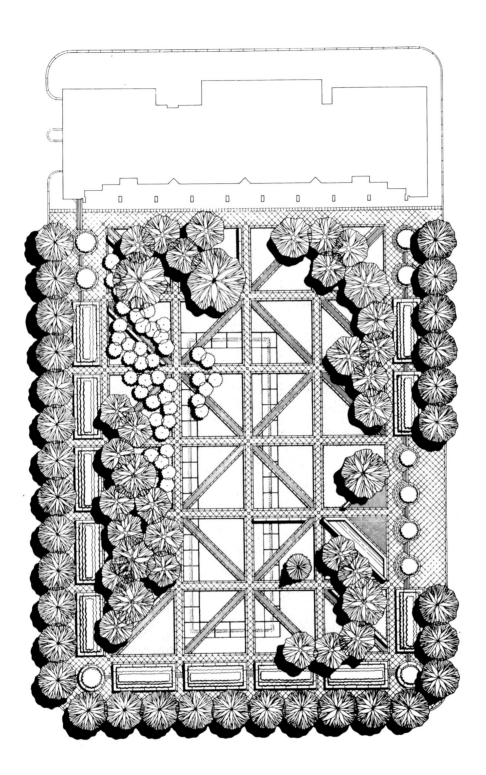

21–12

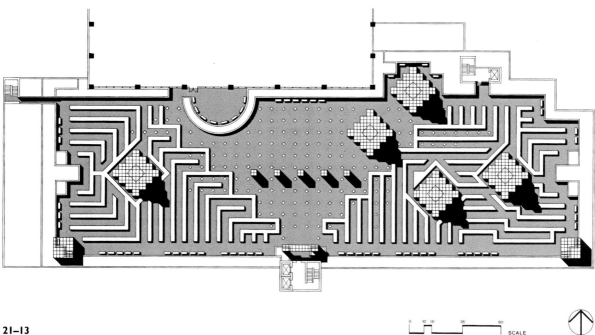

21–13

SCALE

21–14

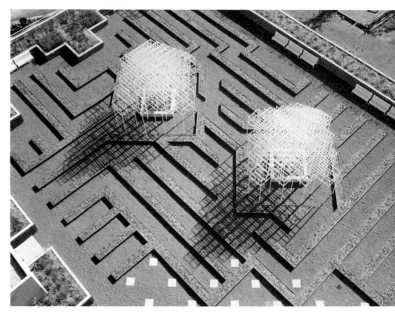

21–12 Site plan, Burnett Park
Fort Worth, Texas, 1983. Peter
Walker with The SWA Group.

21–13 Site plan, Cambridge Center roof
garden
Cambridge, Massachusetts, 1979.
Peter Walker with The SWA
Group.

21–14 Cambridge Center roof garden
Cambridge, Massachusetts, 1979.
Peter Walker with The SWA
Group.

22

22–1

Martha Schwartz is Adjunct Professor of
Landscape Architecture at Harvard
University. Trained in fine arts before
entering landscape architecture, she
believes that the landscape itself can
possess imagery, symbolism, and
intellectual content.

In this century, landscape architecture has produced a small but well-known cadre of designers
such as Roberto Burle Marx, Garrett Eckbo,
Thomas Church, Lawrence Halprin, and Dan Kiley
who, aligning themselves with modernist theory,
broke from classical and Beaux-Arts traditions.
These designers believed that landscape architecture was an art form related to the other visual
arts, and that landscape could also serve as a cultural artifact, expressive of contemporary culture
and made from modern materials. Although all
these practitioners could be lumped together as
modernists—believing that landscape could and
should reflect the needs and values of a modern society—their individual design vocabularies ranged
from surrealism to constructivism.

A more recent generation of landscape architects, including Peter Walker, Rich Haag, George
Hargreaves, and myself, practice within the same
modernist tradition—but we are also being influenced by (as well as exerting influence upon) the
art world. Today the boundary between art and
landscape design has been at least partially effaced,
and the landscape is also inhabited by artists who
practice in the landscape. Among this group are
Richard Fleischner, Andrew Leicester, Andrea
Blum, Elyn Zimmerman, Gary Reivschal, and Mary
Miss. This coalition of artists and designers presents an opportunity by which landscape is at last
seen again as an aesthetic enterprise and a legitimate art form capable of being judged on formal and
intellectual grounds.

Many aspects of modernism still hold promise
for today's world (intentions such as social egalitari-
anism, honesty in the use of materials, optimism
about the future, and the belief in human rationality), but how have these ideas exhibited themselves
in the landscapes of the recent past?

While it was based to some degree on environmental improvement, architectural modernism
has not been kind to the landscape. A great distinction divides the modernist architect's attitude toward architecture and the modernist architect's
attitude toward landscape. Architectural modernism
has been remarkably disinterested in issues of collective space, for example, focusing instead on the
space within buildings. Nor has it developed a formal attitude toward the built landscape. Instead this
was left as a moral arena, unmanipulated although
socially utilized. Curiously, even those architects
who see buildings as being able to manifest ideas

are often antagonistic toward landscapes that display visual or intellectual power. Visible landscapes, those landscapes with obvious form, are perceived as competing with buildings and too active formally. To allow the building to "read" more clearly, the content of the landscape must be drained. Although every other aspect of the designed environment—from buildings to soup spoons—has been seen as fair game by architects, modernism never envisioned the landscape as manufactured space or allowed landscape to address issues of form and composition. Well-designed, affordable manufactured products were a goal of the Bauhaus, but the landscape was to remain the pure, interstitial fabric upon which buildings were placed. It was clearly not a field in which cultural attitudes and ideas could be explored. Exterior space was, and has remained, a moral battleground and until recently has rarely been viewed aesthetically, an attitude that has resulted in a remarkable lack of design talent in the field of landscape architecture during the last three decades. Those interested in design seek their expressions in more fertile fields, such as the visual arts. This, among other factors, has contributed to our degraded visual environment.

The lack of a modernist vision for our manufactured landscapes has had a devastating effect on our urban and suburban environments. Architecture's myopic and self-serving attitude toward the landscape, as the passive, untouched setting for heroic objects, has been disastrous visually and ecologically. Ironically, it has positioned modernist architects comfortably next to those whom they perceived as their antagonists: the neoclassicist and historicist landscape architects. Modernist landscape architects have been left out on a limb, isolated by the strangely convergent attitude of the lay person and the modernist architect: the landscape should function environmentally and socially, but not intellectually or aesthetically. The fact that landscape architecture has been in existence as a profession in this country for over a century, and that only a small body of notable physical work of any intellectual rigor exists after those hundred years, attests to the unfertile ground for the proliferation of landscape design ideas.

Many ideas central to modernism are still attractive to me, and thus I distinguish my work from projects by historicist and neoclassicist designers. Of modernism's social agenda the basic optimism toward the future—where "good" design can be

22–2

22–1   "Splice" Garden, Whitehead Institute for Biomedical Research Cambridge, Massachusetts, 1986. Martha Schwartz with The Office of Peter Walker Martha Schwartz. [Alan Ward]

22–2   King County Jail Plaza Seattle, Washington, 1987. Martha Schwartz with the Office of Peter Walker Martha Schwartz. [ART on FILE, courtesy The Office of Peter Walker Martha Schwartz]

22–3

22–3   International Swimming Hall of
Fame (project), model
Fort Lauderdale, Florida, 1987.
Arquitectonica International,
architect; Martha Schwartz with
The Office of Peter Walker and
Martha Schwartz, landscape
architect.
[David Walker]

22–4   Rio Shopping Center
Atlanta, Georgia, 1988.
Arquitectonica International,
architect; The Office of Peter
Walker Martha Schwartz,
landscape architect; Martha
Schwartz, principal-in-charge.
[Ron Rizzo/Creative Services]

available to all classes—holds the most power. I view the manufacturing process not as a limitation but as an opportunity, and I see rationality in a positive light. Great landscapes can no longer be made in the tradition of carved stone and the fountains of Renaissance Europe. Instead they must be made today from concrete, asphalt, and plastic, the stuff with which we build our environment on a daily basis. Nonprecious materials and off-the-shelf items can be used artfully, and with this attitude we can build beautiful landscapes; not only for the rich, who today will no longer pay for fancy materials, but also for the middle class, who can't afford them. That we must embrace technology to find the opportunities inherent in mass production appears as valid today as it was to the early modernists. While these modernist sentiments are certainly not new attitudes in architecture, landscape architecture has been reticent to deal with the aesthetics of technology, and has evolved a profession based on the romanticization of the past.

For example, "cheap" and ubiquitous landscape materials such as asphalt and concrete are often regarded as lowly and are shunned by developers trying to sell an image of "quality." Developers often commit to budgets that can afford only lowly materials; the true (low) value of the project must be hidden from a prospective buyer by attempting to make the product look expensive. The decision to veneer or stamp concrete into stone patterns, for example, ultimately fools no one and simultaneously expresses the lack of value and discomfort with this ruse. It is possible, however, to appreciate asphalt and concrete for what they are— simple, cheap, and malleable—and for their potential to be beautiful materials if used and maintained properly. This, I believe, is a more realistic and hopeful attitude than the reliance on "fine" materials applied only superficially.

Having trained as an artist for ten years before entering graduate school in landscape architecture, I was well acquainted with the artists and art movements that had evolved from modernist painting and sculpture. Perhaps these suggest other sources more germane to my thinking than architectural modernism. My initial interest in the landscape came from sculpture made by artists such as Robert Smithson, Michael Heizer, Richard Long, Walter De Maria, and Mary Miss, artists who broke from the traditions of the studio and the commercial New York gallery scene by venturing out into the wilderness to do their work. There they created monumental landscape-inspired sculpture that could not be contained in a gallery or sold for profit. Producing early examples of both conceptual and environmental art, these artists were the bellwethers of a new wave of environmental awareness. They had gone beyond "modern" art by redefining art as something that was neither a painting to be hung on the wall nor conventional studio sculpture. Art was now reinstated as a part of our environment, not an isolated event accessible only to the effete gallery world.

From making discrete landscape objects to shaping the landscape as an integrated artwork and space seemed to me a completely logical sequence. The next step was to move from the pristine natural environment and apply the same ideas of interaction and intervention to the complexity of the city. I am both energized and challenged by this gritty arena, as the early earthwork artists took inspiration from the untouched landscapes of the American southwest.

My interest as an artist has always been in the mystical quality of geometric forms and their relationships to each other. In order to apply these ideas outdoors, the landscape must be depicted as architectural space so that it is recognizable and describable. As in architecture, people should derive a sense of orientation in space that produces a subliminal sense of comfort and security. Simple geometric forms, such as circles and squares, are familiar and memorable images. To understand the relationship of one space to another, one must first establish a sense of orientation in order to recognize new juxtapositions or changes. Simple geometries are thus best used in the landscape as mental maps. Given the nature of our built environment, the use of geometry in the landscape is more humane than the disorientation caused by the incessant lumps, bumps, and squiggles of a stylized naturalism. Geometry allows us to recognize and place ourselves in space and is more formally sympathetic to architecture. Lastly, it deals with our manufactured environments more honestly; geometry itself is a rational construct and thereby avoids the issue of trying to mask our man-made environments with a thin veneer of naturalism.

During my training in landscape architecture, I began to study the works of minimalist artists such as Robert Irwin, Carl Andre, Robert Long, and Dan Flavin, artists who deal with the description and manipulation of space. As landscape encompasses a much greater field than either painting or most sculpture, the effect must be accomplished with an economy of means. In its ability to command large areas of space with very few moves and materials the work of the minimalist artists is germane to landscape architecture. Michael Heizer joined a huge valley using only a simple bulldozed line, collapsing the vast space by connecting the viewer with the far side of the mesa. Carl Andre described a column of space above a perfectly flat plane with plates of industrially discarded metal. In a serial piece by Andre, the repetition of objects set on a floor mystically elevates the objects while focusing our attention on the visual potential of the flat plane.

Artists such as Ron Davis, Robert Mangold, Mel Bochner, Frank Stella, John Newman, and Al Held are of particular interest to me in their use of geometry. They explore a range of emotions produced by different relationships and delve into the mysticism and symbolism inherent to geometry. Mangold surprises us through his warpings and stretching of perfect form, as Le Nôtre's plans did;

22–4

22-5

though first perceived as rational, they reveal arbitrary and unpredictable relationships.

The Pop artists—Andy Warhol, Jasper Johns, and Robert Rauschenberg—interest me for their concern with banal, everyday objects and common materials. Insightful, poignant, and sympathetic to our common culture, they feed upon its energy and rawness. I respond positively to the hard-edged humor with which they illuminate the stuff of our everyday lives.

If one wishes to work on the cutting edge in either fine art or design, one must be informed of developments in the world of painting and sculpture. Ideas surface more quickly in painting and sculpture than in architecture or landscape architecture, due to many factors including the immediacy of the media and the relative low investment of money required to explore an idea.

Ideas must be challenged in order to prove their viability in a culture. Much art—such as that produced by Jeff Koons, Gordon Matta-Clark, Cindy Sherman, or Vito Acconci—may be important only in that it creates discussion and in the end critical self-reflection. Not every work of art or landscape need be a timeless masterpiece. More importantly, provocative art and design foster an atmosphere of growth by questioning and by challenging the established standards.

In conclusion, the modernist architect's break from the Beaux-Arts and classicism was an important event for landscape architecture. As the architects had to shed the old in order to develop an aesthetic and philosophical stance to deal with the social needs of post–World War I Europe, we must now shed our romance with our wilderness heritage and the English landscape in order to deal effectively with our expanding urban- and suburbanization. The nostalgia for the (imagined) English countryside (so idealized in English landscape and Hudson River School painting) has prevented us from seeing our landscape as it truly is and inhibited the evolution of an appropriate landscape approach to urbanization. We shake our heads in collective disgust at the ugliness of our man-made environments, and yet do little to fully consider the scope of the problem or its possible solution. To improve the visual blight, we place diminutive mounds in our median strips and at the bases of our buildings. Unthinkingly, we dredge up the rolling English countryside like a universal balm, without questioning its appropriateness or viability in today's environ-

22-5   Center for Innovative Technology
Fairfax, Virginia, 1988.
Arquitectonica, architect; The
Office of Peter Walker Martha
Schwartz, landscape architect;
Martha Schwartz, principal-in-
charge.
[David Walker]

22-6   The Grand Allée. The Citadel
Los Angeles, California, 1991.
Martha Schwartz / Ken Smith /
David Meyer, Inc., landscape
architects.
[Jay Venezia]

Note

The design teams for The International Swimming Hall of Fame project, the Rio Shopping Center, and the Center for Innovative Technology included Doug Findlay, David Meyer, Martin Poirier, Ken Smith, and David Walker.

ments. Our profession's narrow and moralistic view of what constitutes a "correct" landscape has disallowed the questioning of this particular aesthetic and has hampered the exploration of other ideas and solutions that might address the problems of increased urbanization. While our culture professes to be repelled by what and how we build, we still have been unable to conjure other formal vocabularies than those established by economic values, or to break from an ingrained romantic attitude toward our landscape.

Landscape architecture, as a field, has barely touched upon the questions raised by modernism. To many practitioners, modernism and its attendant aspects of growth and embrace of technology are viewed as the cause of the degradation of our natural environment. A small but continuous stream of landscape designers, however, still works within, and perhaps beyond, the modernist tradition; designers who search for meaningful relationships between our natural and built environments, without romantic sentiment but with eyes opened to the world around them.

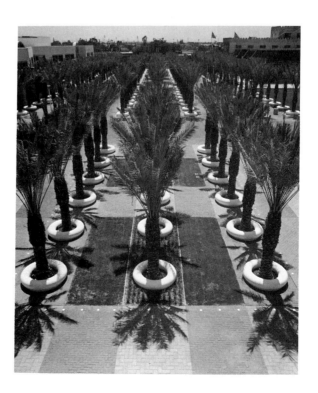

23

From the mid-1960s, the concern for ecological process and for protecting the natural environment came to dominate the consciousness of the landscape architecture profession in the United States. With this attitude firmly entrenched, landscape architects tended to neglect the specific formal characteristics of places, simplistically dismissing them as a matter of "style." In the last decade, however, designers have shown a renewed interest in the properties of form and space and have looked to the arts—particularly to land sculpture—to reinvigorate the landscape vocabulary. Artists such as Robert Smithson, Michael Heizer, and Robert Irwin have provided sources, as well as inspiration, for the making of exterior places. While some designers may merely borrow and adapt specific sculptural forms, others have shown that by better understanding the full range of factors that govern the making of art, much can be learned to enrich landscape architecture both as a profession and as a discipline. Here the work of Robert Irwin is exemplary.

Review

During the 1960s an attention to perception, rather than to the object perceived, came to occupy a more significant position in the production of art. The rise of abstract expressionism brought the channel of automism proposed by surrealism to a tentative culmination and offered painting a potential vocabulary. Art could be viewed as the tangible record of its making; marks on canvas traced the unimpeded path from the artist's subconscious to the painted panel. Cognition as a conscious activity played little part in the process; one tried to remove any mediation between the artist and the canvas. Making recognizable representations of our world had no part. As championed by the critic Clement Greenberg, painting approached its "culmination" as the directed expression of its inherent definition: it was to be characterized by physical and perceived flatness; representation and references to another ("real") world were extraneous.[1]

An extension of this path of reasoning suggested that the artwork was nothing more than its physical characteristics. The painter Frank Stella said in effect that "what you see is what it is." But if the possibility for painting or sculpture to suggest situations beyond their own forms was denied, the importance of their relationship to the wall or space

Marc Treib is Professor of Architecture at the University of California at Berkeley, a practicing designer, and a frequent contributor to architecture and design journals. He is the coauthor of *A Guide to the Gardens of Kyoto* (1980) and author of *Sanctuaries of Spanish New Mexico* (1993).

upon which or in which they were exhibited increased. One could, in fact, trace a spiral of relationships: as the mark was to the canvas, the figure to the ground, by extension so was the painting as a mark upon its support wall or the sculpture in its space. The new genre of the installation appeared, in which the objects and markings within the space as a whole were taken to be an artwork. It was then only a short step for the space itself, which had traditionally been the support, to be read as the figure rather than as the ground.[2]

In many respects Robert Irwin's personal development parallels the general course of art during the late 1950s and 1960s. Although he began his career as an abstract expressionist painter in the late 1950s, one can find in retrospect an almost purposeful evolution away from the object and toward the basic act of perception. In Irwin's words, abstract expressionism was essentially "a direct language of feeling that placed the senses before the abstractions of pictorial painting"; propelled by a growing disenchantment with the issues it addressed, he became more and more focused on the effect of painting in its particular situation. Abstract expressionism, in opposition to the traditional perspective view, questioned the notion of the frame as the limit to the work. The overall composition of the modern canvas, which found its extreme statement in the drip paintings of Jackson Pollock, suggested an extension in all directions as an infinite plane. Irwin's concern then became the quest to dissolve the edge that separated the painting from its support wall, trying effectively to merge figure and ground.

Irwin has claimed that we learn not from the solution but from formulating the particular question.[3] And it is at just that point—as we address the particular situation and formulate the question—that we find the closest parallels between the act of making art and the act of design. Irwin believes that these assumed similarities can be deceptive, however. In many ways, his attitude and working methods appear to coincide with those that propel architecture and landscape architecture. The sculptor trying to approach the site and the nature of each work with no a priori assumptions parallels the stance of the designer analyzing and formulating the statement of a design problem. Irwin is quick to point out, however, that fundamental differences of intentionality distinguish the provinces of art and design. Underlying each discipline are questions about its role in society, the ethical systems involved, and the subjects of its work. Architecture

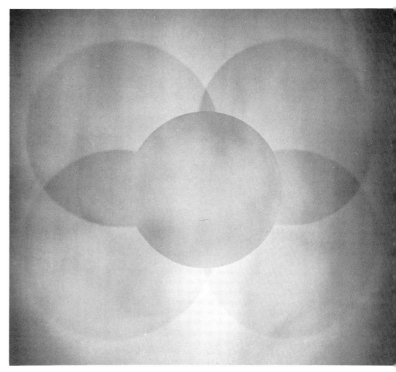

23–1

23–1 *No Title*
1966–1967. Acrylic on aluminum.
Robert Irwin.
[Whitney Museum of
American Art]

begins with a concern for places that are habitable and things that are used. Landscape architecture involves design in the natural realm, and considers environmental conditions such as climate and precipitation, structure and comfort. Habitation is the intention of both.

Pure art, on the other hand, is less directly tied to social function. "Art deals with the human potential to perceive the world around us, extending our understanding of the world. Like theoretical physics, it gives up immediate practical applications to gain a more fundamental perspective—in this sense it's like philosophy which has no actual practice. Today, much of art has been captured by different ambitions. But to me, art is a 'non-thing.' Its purpose is to help us see continually anew."[4] Art asks that quality remain central to life, Irwin believes, despite the host of factors that attempt to quantify it. Because quality is not directly measurable—although Irwin believes that it is perceptible—the artist is not directly responsible to the social entity; that is, not on a daily, project-by-project basis. For Irwin, art begins with the particularities of situation—here taken in its broadest terms. It concerns and engages the individual and the group, the physical setting, the environment, with the means at one's disposal. One does not start with a personal vocabulary or manner to be adapted to each situation. Thus, given the differences in intentionality between art and design, the artist and the designer will "plow different furrows seemingly in the same field."

An underlying characteristic of modernity, Irwin believes, is that the individual is thrown back upon his or her own resources. There is no longer a single truth, no single interpretation, no single directive for life, no single reason or way for making and lending significance to art. When one withdraws the support of doctrine, the rudder is removed and the boat of interpretation and experience is set adrift. "This creates a problem," Irwin explains. "If we are to redirect our process of knowing, we must provide a new frame of reference for doing so."[5] Everything in the making of art becomes relative, or as Irwin has phrased it, everything lies between being and circumstance.[6] Irwin feels strongly about the necessity to create works that allow, indeed coerce, the individual to feel and think for him or herself. Thus, his mature projects focus on how we perceive rather than on any particular object of our view. To him, the subject of the artistic enterprise is ultimately human consciousness and how we come to terms with our consciousness in the world.

Evolution

This approach developed slowly, through literally years of deliberation, study, and execution. A series of paintings executed from 1962 to 1964 explored the relationship of two thin, parallel lines inscribed upon a modeled monochrome field. At first, the color of the lines played against the chroma of the ground, causing a particular vibration. "These early line paintings still had a sense of composition (between the lines) and a bit of pictorial space: some lines came forward, others seemed to recede," Irwin notes. Paintings followed in which the lines were basically of the same hue and value as the ground; the lines began to merge into the field. As a result, "the eye was literally suspended between the lines and the ground."[7]

While the demands upon the artist's formal sensibility are obvious—he had to paint and judge the effect of each linear proposition—the lines were only a means to an end, not an aesthetic subject in themselves. The true goal was the perception of the field as a whole: "They're about the basic relationships of the three or four primary aspects of existence in the world: being-in-time, for example, space, presence. When you stop giving them a literate or articulate read (the kind you'd give a Renaissance painting) and instead look at them perceptually, you find that your eye ends up suspended in midair, midspace, or midstride: time and space seem to blend in the continuum of your presence."[8]

The next logical question, at least as seen in hindsight, was to make an artwork with no mark at all—"an artwork of pure phenomena." The dot paintings that followed evoked a soft radiance, a modulation of tone that attempted to create "a physical visual field occupied not by a sign, but by visual energy."[9] While appearing to have been airbrushed, they were in fact all painted with a careful hand, as visible signs of facture were essential to the artist. Irwin found that if the dots were produced according to a mechanical stencil or template, as in the work of Roy Lichtenstein for example, the surface of the painting would appear without life. If the dots were irregularly painted, on the other hand, the eye would inadvertently interpret the variations in spacing as minute clusters, thus disturbing the painted field. The solution to the problem was found in a combination of the two: that is, by using an equal, metrically determined spacing, but painting each of the dots by hand. A floating reality was achieved in which light and its perception, rather than the painted marks, became the content of the paintings. In these painted and shaped works, the compound curvature of the canvas "gave the space a charged quality," further undermining the viewer's first reaction to what was before the eyes.

Irwin allowed no photographic reproductions of his work from this period. Since the photograph can only record the marks rather than the phenomena to be experienced, it was a medium that ran completely counter to the artist's intentions: "Photography is a product of a unique perspective of the world."[10] To agree with him—to agree that percept rather than the concept constitutes the real content of painting—required a radical break with traditional notions of the artwork. The gently contoured canvas was intended not as a sculptured form; the shaping was a device to further dissolve the edge:

"Which in turn allows me to reiterate that I was not pursuing an intellectual issue here but rather a perceptual one."[11] An important discovery followed: "When the field of the painting became so reduced, my eye—for the first time—recognized the rectangle of the canvas."[12]

The progression toward the complete erasure of the perceived boundary—toward "an artwork that did not begin and end at the edge," as Irwin referred to it—was further developed in a series of disk pieces produced from 1967 to 1969. The disks became signature pieces, and they remain the most easily described of his painted works. On slightly convex metal disks, a painted color field bolstered the sense of convexity, although the net effect was still extremely subtle. The paintings were mounted a foot from the wall upon a tube hidden from view: the disk thus appeared to float, hovering in space apart from its support surface. The softly graduated color reduced the apparent contrast between painting and wall, thereby adding to the ethereal quality of the work. Four spotlights—two mounted on the floor below, two above in the ceiling—cast four overlapping shadows, conjuring an ambiguous ghost figure between the actual object and the wall. Irwin's intention was to produce a sensation that blurred the distinction between object and ground, but, quite unintentionally, the piece also acquired a reading as a figure.[13] Sensing that his involvement with painting was rapidly approaching a cul-de-sac, Irwin withdrew from the studio, as he put it, because the studio could no longer weigh the questions that he pondered: "After the disks . . . there was no reason for me to go on being a painter."[14]

When the historical connection between architecture and sculpture was severed, it permitted a rethinking of the definition of the artwork. Sculpture no longer depended upon its architectural support. In origin, in form, and in display, it secured an aesthetic independence impossible during those historical periods when art derived from its physical and social setting. But independence also provoked a consequent loss of resonance between the artwork and its situation. Modern architecture denied the importance of ornamentation, for example, and viewed painting and sculpture as discrete artifacts; works were conceptually divorced from the spaces in which they were mounted. Traditionally, the frame that enclosed the perspective view also firmly established the edge of the painting. Irwin's project, in time, aimed at eroding the distance between the object and its support, joining both in a simultaneous perception catalyzed by the artwork.

The Art and Technology project of the late 1960s provided him with the opportunity to further clarify his ideas, while distilling his means. This program was first proposed in 1967 by Maurice Tuchman, curator of modern art at the Los Angeles County Museum of Art. His idea was to bring artists and scientists together for mutual learning, and to create works that would utilize the possibilities offered by contemporary science. Irwin was invited to participate in the project and was subsequently introduced to a number of scientists to explore the potential of a dialogue. When he met psychologist Edward Wortz, he was "immediately taken with his openness and the breadth of his intelligence."[15] Early on, they agreed that such interdisciplinary discussions might benefit from the presence of a third member; as a result Irwin invited artist James Turrell to join them. Turrell later withdrew from the project, but Irwin and Wortz collaborated for over three years, a process that would have a significant impact upon Irwin's understanding of mental process and his conception of art. The collaboration produced no tangible product, but the continued discussions eventually led to an analysis of perception and philosophy and the philosophy of perception. Extracts from Irwin's notebooks published in the Art and Technology exhibition catalogue suggest that his definition of art had been substantially refined during the project:

> The works of previous artists have come from their own experience or insights but haven't given the experience itself. They set themselves up as a sort of interpreter for the layman.
> The experience is the 'thing', experiencing is the 'object.'
> All art is experience, yet all experience is not art. The artist chooses from experience that which he defines out as art, possibly because it has not yet been experienced enough, or because it needs to be experienced more.[16]

From such statements we might conclude that the scientific inquiry that characterizes psychology and the artistic enterprise virtually coincide. Irwin distinguished between the two, however:

> Of course, the two are related. Psychology can begin with the physiological characteristics of the mind, but more to the point, it asks the question: "How does the mechanism work?" The artist also looks at the mechanism and asks: How does the mechanism *feel*? The former is a quantitative question; the latter concerns itself with qualities; i.e., aesthetics. Let me give you an example. We could say that "warm" is a temperature or a phenomenon or a property. But "warm" is also a phenomenon possessing qualities, and it is the qualities of warm—what it feels like—that interest the artist.[17]

With his questions more carefully formulated, Irwin had staked out the scope of his work. "By 1970," writes Lawrence Wechsler, "Irwin had arrived at his lifethemes—the explication of presence, an awareness of perception—and everything since then has consisted in an ongoing charting of those waters."[18]

With a desire to integrate human response into his work, Irwin continued his investigations away from studio during the early 1970s. He spent nearly two years on the road, creating anonymous pieces in the southwestern desert, accepting virtually all speaking engagements and artist-in-residencies. He took time to think and reconfigure the

23–2

23–3

23–4

23–2 *No Title*
1975. Installation at the Museum
of Contemporary Art, Chicago.
Robert Irwin.

23–3 *Slant Light Volume*
1971. Installation at the Walker
Art Center. Robert Irwin.
[Walker Art Center, Minneapolis]

23–4 *Scrim Veil—Black Rectangle—
Natural Light*
1977. Installation at the Whitney
Museum of American Art.
Robert Irwin.
[Whitney Museum of
American Art]

nature of his ideas about art. In time, he returned
to creating artworks for others to experience, in-
tending to increase the awareness of perception
while playing down the identity of the vehicle; to focus attention on the music and not the form of the
instrument. He was not alone in his involvement
with perception. Minimalist sculpture of the 1960s
depended to a large degree on its perception in
space and the viewer's consciousness of that perception. In time, artists began to consider the room
as the artwork, and, like Irwin, sought to banish
the display from the displayed.

Line and Plane

It was these first investigations with space and light
that brought Irwin to the attention of designers. A
series of minimalist interventions, such as those for
the Mizuno Gallery in Los Angeles and the Museum of Contemporary Art in Chicago in 1975, reduced the signature of the artist to almost nothing.
But unlike the Duchampian strategy of granting the
status of art to an empty gallery through naming,
Irwin sought to alter the perception of the space
through reduced means, "granting the status of art
to a gallery, heightening the individual experience
of it."[19]

Early in this century Marcel Duchamp proposed that virtually anything could be art, if it was
so proposed by the artist. Through selection,
through recontextualization, the artist could grant
the status and role of artwork. Duchamp tested the
idea as well as the public's patience with his most
notorious example: a porcelain urinal he displayed
with the title *Fountain*. For Duchamp, then, it was
the artist's intention that creates the work of art,
whether or not it is accepted as such by the
viewer.[20] The aesthetic responsibility lies with the
maker. "If this is true," Irwin believed, "the next
step was to give the responsibility to the individual
viewer. This can be thought of as the politics of
Modern Art."[21] "Irwin plays with our notions of
value," asserts critic Roberta Smith, "with our expectations, with things that get in the way of the
actual experience of art, things that we attach to
art."[22]

In the case of the two Irwin exhibitions mentioned above, the medium was a strip of black tape
that acquired the authority of a police line. The narrow band staked out a segment of floor in such a
way that it read as a plane distinct from the walls it
abutted. By placing a single line of black tape, identical in width to the museum's baseboard, across
the open end of the gallery, the sides of the room
were perceptually closed and considerable visual
ambiguity resulted. If one saw the enclosed black-
lined figure as true, how could one explain the "normal" reading of the space? In effect, Irwin contrived a visual conundrum, an impossible figure. A
second line of tape was positioned exactly at eye
level around the perimeter of the room. Its effect
was to flatten the depth of the room while dividing
its walls into halves. The line drawn with tape, the

line that should provide us with clues to volumetric depth, became a single horizon that severed the upper from the lower sections of the walls. In sorting out possibility from impossibility, the viewer was forced to consider his or her own way of comprehending the world, acknowledging Irwin's belief that perception first comes, then reason: "If the information we receive from our first subliminal read of the space is insufficient, or in contradiction to our expectations, we are for the moment frozen . . . causing to examine our circumstances."[23]

In later installations, Irwin progressed from manipulating the line to manipulating the plane, although both served as means to a similar end. Scrim is a fabric long known to the theater world; its layering alters the sense of the stage by exaggerating depth. The material is so thin that it can appear transparent, translucent, or opaque depending on the angle of incidence and the intensity of the light upon its surface. In a series of installations that included the illuminated tilted plane of *Slant Light Volume* at the Walker Art Center in 1971, and the composite tape/scrim *Scrim Veil—Black Rectangle—Natural Light* at the Whitney Museum in 1977, Irwin again manipulated the reading of place. By using fabric planes and controlled light, he mystified and yet heightened the confines of the galleries. In these and in later installations at Rice University and the San Francisco Museum of Art in 1985, the scrim veiled the space and encouraged the viewer to look more closely: some parts were seen as if through a fog while other parts were lost in the space. Experiencing the spaces for the first time, one is intrigued by the muted sensation of space. To those familiar with the spaces involved, on the other hand, the effect is more disorienting; something is different, but just what is difficult to ascertain. In all instances, however, the scrim is used to counteract the effect of perspective by which we usually gauge distance and scale. The scrim installations illustrate distilled spatial manipulation, while exemplifying a simplicity of means effectively used to modify both the perception of the space and the unfolding awareness of viewing and sensing the room. Characteristically for Irwin, the scrim itself possesses a delicacy and an elegance that avoids calling attention to itself as the subject of the work.

Being and Circumstance

While these pieces utilized a medium consistent throughout any series—in this case, scrim—all ultimately derive their position and configuration from their particular site. This theory of a "site-conditioned art" Irwin verbally articulated in 1985 in his *Being and Circumstance*. In the introductory essay he outlined four types of approaches to sculpture.[24] In the first, the work is created independently of any setting and is sited only after completion. This is analogous to the easel painting; purchased and set upon a wall, the particular wall having little or no bearing on the form of the work. He terms this group *site dominant:* the setting is always incidental to the nature of the artwork. The second category, *site adjusted,* comprises those works that are created for an intended setting. Knowing the final situation, the artist considers scale, materials, and the appropriateness of the idiom—but the work still bears a distinctive signature, and is immediately identifiable as one of a family of works. With *site specific* sculpture the particularities of the site are considered to a greater degree, although the artist still uses a recognizable vocabulary. The medium may remain relatively constant, while the configuration varies to address the vagaries of the situation.

Defining the final category of *site conditioned/determined,* Irwin notes that "here the sculptural response draws all of its clues (reasons for being) from its surroundings. This requires the process *to begin* with an intimate, hands-on reading of the site."[25] One arrives without preconceptions, without any "bag of tricks." In response to "sitting, watching, and walking through the site and surrounding areas," the artist distills the reactions to determine "all the facets of the 'sculptural response': aesthetic sensibility, levels and kinds of physicality, gesture, dimensions, materials, kind and level of finish, details, etc.; whether the response should be monumental or ephemeral, aggressive or gentle, useful or useless, sculptural, architectural, or simply the planting of a tree, or maybe even doing nothing at all." Or, perhaps, doing what at first may be perceived as nothing at all. Through the seventies and into the eighties, Irwin worked toward a distillation of means and a consequent reduction of the apparent vehicle. The idea was to play down the form of the work and to play up its presence, to redirect attention from the object to the perception of the complete situation—although there was always the danger of confusion expressed in the Zen dictum: "When I point my finger at the moon, don't mistake my finger for the moon."[26]

From the gallery space, it was only a short walk to the outdoors.

Interventions

In working the landscape, Irwin uses subtle signs to alter its reading. There is no single way in which the site can be marked, no single material, no particular formal vocabulary. His method might be compared to medical practice in which a stain is applied to organic tissue to detect the presence of a foreign substance or decay. Irwin underlines an environmental situation, indoor or outdoor, to clarify or reinforce those relationships inherent or constructed in the place.

Filigreed Line (1979) was executed in the broadleaf New England landscape of the Wellesley College campus outside Boston. On his first visit, Irwin was "struck by the grace of the nature on the campus. How beautiful it all was, and without an intrusion by me." And yet there was the call to create the artwork: "The challenge to interact, work

23–5

23–5 *Filigreed Line*
1979. Wellesley College,
Wellesley, Massachusetts.
Robert Irwin.
[David Stansbury]

23–6

23–7

with nature, has always been a latent question in art, a question brought into focus in 'modern art' by the implication inherent in the edict to effect a 'marriage of figure and ground.' If one avoided the representation of natural phenomena according to convention, how could one work with nature without dominating or displacing it?"[27] How would that marriage of figure and ground take place in the world, in real space and time?

Filigreed Line is a simple profile of 3/8″ stainless steel that extends across a low ridge fronting a lake. In places, the metal sheet stands only a few inches above the ground; in other places it rises to no more than two feet above the earth's surface—far below the eye level normal for viewing sculpture.

While the steel line effectively establishes a horizon, it is not *the* horizon, and the assertiveness of its upper edge is diminished by an irregular pattern of leaves and branches, excised from the steel using plasma cutting. The impression of the work within its setting is that of a positive counteracted by two negatives; that is, the pure thrust of the simple profile is contradicted by the shadows of the real trees upon the face of the steel and by the leaf pattern that has been cut from its surface. A tension is experienced between the sharp linear plane and the irregular pattern, between the created and the natural, between certainty and hesitancy. "That Wellesley site was so lovely and pastoral," wrote Irwin in retrospect. "It really didn't require anything additional from me. All I was trying to do with my gesture, in the most subliminal fashion I could manage—and thanks to the reflectivity of the steel and the shimmer of the pond beyond it, the screen often did seem to just disappear—was to in a sense underline the beauty and perceptual vitality of the site as it already existed."[28]

An unrealized project for Ohio State University in Columbus (1979) planned to add a third dimension to what were essentially two-dimensional relationships. The Oval, the central open space of the campus, is crisscrossed by a series of walks that connect the major building destinations. The resulting network of diagonal intersections provides an active visual counterpoint to the formal layout of the buildings surrounding the lawn. If one construed these pathways as the boundaries of a series of planes, one could extrude the groundscape vertically to form a field of subtly articulated panels. This selective modeling of the mostly triangular planes constituted Irwin's proposal *Tilted Planes*.[29] The work intended to demarcate further the relationships already existing in the Oval, while creating discrete spaces that might encourage social use. For example, the raised edges could be used as a bench to provide seating along the various routes without additional street furniture. Thin walls of corten steel, the color of the earth, were to retain the soil and configure the panels. "So what I tried to do with the alteration I proposed was simply to heighten the involvement to the point where there was some recognition of one's participation, but not to heighten it to the point where you looked at the gesture as art."[30] The project was ultimately rejected by the university administration on the grounds that it was not sufficiently recognizable as artwork. Irwin writes: "The Dean's question, 'Where's the sculpture?' proves my point." In works such as these, relationships are made tangible without being obvious, apparent without being inescapable. "The piece was gentle enough not to make any issues about its existence. And it was as close as I've been able to get to simple presence."[31] Irwin wanted to reveal what existed, to "turn up by only 10 percent what was already going on there." While the proposal remains unexecuted, he regards it as "one of my best pieces; as close to the bone as you can get."[32]

Although derived from the pattern of walkways within an academic quad, the *Tilted Planes* project implicitly called into question the relationship between the landscape of living vegetation and the inert built complex. The 1981 work *Portal Park Slice,* in turn, examined the intersection of the straight and the organic, and that of the realm organized by the sculptural gesture and that instituted, de facto, by civil engineering. The site lies at the edge of the Dallas downtown, a site described by Irwin as "a dusty, abandoned jigsaw puzzle, divided everywhere by busy streets accessing the northern approach to downtown Dallas."[33] *Portal Park Slice* comprises two aligned planes of corten steel that slide through the grassed mounds graded for the new park. At the extremities of the central opening, two pedestrian-scaled rectangles were cut to reinforce the sense of opening across the street. The planes of the sculpture contrast the spaghetti-like forms of the adjacent freeway and the bulbous shapes of the park terrain, creating a datum line against which the other elements of the landscape may be judged.

In both its material and its form the sculpture also evokes the work of Richard Serra, most specifically his 1971 *Shift* in King City, Ontario. With *Shift,* Serra gauges the slope of the terrain; the form and disposition of the work are determined by the gradient and fall of the land. *Portal Park Slice,* on the other hand, establishes the primary order and remains the primary actor, inversely defined by the disorder around it. The Japanese architect Takefumi Aida once wrote that one of the greatest gifts the architect can provide in today's noisy world is a moment of silence. In an analogous manner, Irwin has created a moment of order within a formally chaotic setting, using a single yet powerful gesture defined by everything contrasting against it.

In these three projects, the approach of the sculptor to the specific formal conditions of the setting is clear. The content of the work derives from the situation and is taken as synonymous with its physical conditions. In *9 Spaces, 9 Trees* (1983), the social dimension underlies or overlays each of the formal gestures. The site is the plaza fronting the Public Safety Building in Portland, Oregon, which includes among other facilities the county jail. Ir-

23–8

23–6 Model for *Tilted Planes*
1975 (unrealized). Ohio State
University, Columbus, Ohio.
Robert Irwin.
[courtesy Robert Irwin]

23–7 *Portal Park Slice*
1981. Dallas, Texas. Robert Irwin.
[Marc Treib]

23–8 *9 Spaces, 9 Trees*
1983. Seattle, Washington.
Robert Irwin.
[Marc Treib]

23–9

23–9   *Two Running Violet V Forms*
1982. Stuart Collection, University
of California, San Diego.
Robert Irwin.
[courtesy the Stuart Collection]

win's notes from his first visit in 1979 recorded the conditions: "This is a very forlorn, isolated, even hostile plaza surrounded by gray architecture. . . . The site has three disparate vantage points: (1) that of the people passing through, (2) a strong 'graphic' read-down from the surrounding office buildings, and (3) a limited visibility from the street. Ideally all three need to be developed. Most importantly, the plaza needs greening."[34]

The first proposal, for a maze, proved to be impractical due to the limited bearing capacity of the plaza, confined by the structural grid of the parking garage below. The final configuration utilized vinyl-coated chainlink fencing to create a series of nine rooms, defined but visually open, each with a flowering plum tree and seating at its center. The nine-square grid is a common, almost trite form of organization with a long history of architectural applications. (It has been suggested, for example, that the nine-square grid was one of the pillars of the architecture of Andrea Palladio, most notably in the design of the Villa Rotonda in Vicenza.)[35] The simplest geometric division based on the square begins with a single space, then subdivides it into a 2 × 2 ordering of four squares. This configuration pivots around a single point and thus offers no spatial center. The 3 × 3 configuration, in contrast, provides a central space that anchors the composition and assures that the resulting views from room to room will be enriched. The reading of *9 Spaces, 9 Trees* is far more complex than its simple order might suggest. Due to the transparency of the fencing material, views continually develop both perpendicularly and obliquely, "an arresting kinetic interplay between the layers of blue screening and the red-violet leaves of the trees."[36] Movement through the spaces also causes a series of continually shifting moiré patterns that distort the sense of depth and distance.

A work of similar medium—but differing in effect— is *Two Running Violet V Forms,* created for the Stuart Foundation Sculpture Collection on the San Diego campus of the University of California in 1982. The name of the work is also a literal description: two V-panels of blue/violet chainlink fencing elevated some 15 to 30 feet in the air within a eucalyptus grove. The first reading, that of the geometric entity within the irregular pattern of trees, is slightly misleading. Irwin notes that this is not a natural grove—eucalyptus is not native to California—but one that was planted for an intended yield. Beneath the first level of shaggy leaf textures resides a nearly geometric ordering of trees. The fencing panels are inserted within the grove, bridging several of the paths that connect the arts complex with the library and other destinations on campus. Like the Seattle piece, the readings are more developed than the simple description would suggest. Lighting plays a major role: with front lighting, the color can be dazzling; yet when the sun is high, or when the shadows of the trees fall directly upon it, the fencing visually disappears. More often, the surface is mottled, partly effaced, partly

assertive. Irwin noted during his first site visit that "this is a rare opportunity for an interface with a beautiful natural place," and one senses little confrontation. Instead, the colored planes and the white bark coexist in a soft symbiosis. Why blue/violet? "I wanted color; it just *had* to be blue/violet"; only that color felt right.[37] Magenta-flowering plantings run linearly beneath the planes; these disappear for much of the year, but return in patches during the spring.

In its linear form and ultimate simplicity, the San Diego piece can be seen as an offspring of the *Filigreed Line.* In spite of their formal similarities, however, the works differ to a considerable degree. The Wellesley sculpture, as a shape, still could be taken as an object sensitively conceived and positioned in the landscape. The *V Forms,* however, engage the landscape more actively, and insist— albeit softly—that we regard the setting as well as the sculpture. "The natural confrontation is that rare occasion with the unsuspecting potential for letting us 'see again.' Not art per se, or ritual, but perceptual interaction with 'phenomena' unattended or overly habituated—an art that calls us to attend to the pure potential in our circumstances as a whole piece."[38]

Approach

To understand the situation in which the artistic work is created, one needs to understand the site conditions from many points of view, physical, social, and philosophical. To work in a natural landscape is a fundamentally different activity than to work in an urban context, even if the value system and the artistic intentions of the artist are the same for both. If, as Irwin believes, "you can't top nature," it is best to approach the circumstances of the site by trying to integrate the work with the natural conditions. In sum, nature is regarded as a given. In the city, on the other hand, one is dealing with "the hand of man in spades," and one must consider to a greater degree the history of the place as well as its physical configuration, the uses of the surrounding buildings, site, human factors, and most of all, scale.

In an interview held in December 1990, Robert Irwin provided the following outline of a method he *might* employ if asked to work on a hypothetical urban plaza. He might first begin with an extended visit to the site, acquiring as many impressions as possible: "without ambition; without conclusions; without any particular focus." More critical than a fixed method for making the work is trying to develop a sense of the site, in some ways recalling the *genius loci* of the English landscape garden. Next, attention is turned to the physical configuration and context, with impressions and information acquired by walking around the site in a rough circle. "I repeatedly approach the site along the lines of principal access; these initial interfaces and impressions are critical."[39] The width and attitude of the surrounding streets need to be considered,

23–10

23–10 *Wave Hill Green*
1986–1987. Wave Hill, Bronx,
New York. Robert Irwin.
[Sarah Wells]

and one must come to terms with the prevalent scale. Aspects of local buildings, their materials, details, and sense of craft, also influence the nature of the work. Driving in increasingly larger circles around the site, he surveys the characteristics of the neighborhood, aspects such as the plants used in local yards, colors in which buildings are painted. From these observations an implicit register is derived, fixing what established ideas about design, materials, color, etc. are normal for the place, and what specific properties could be used in order to surprise. He tries to avoid focusing on the wrong thing; for example, letting craft or material establish itself as the subject of the work instead of its vehicle.

The final—and very critical—step is to leave the site and let the idea crystallize. When he has formed a rudimentary response, Irwin returns to test it in place: How does it feel? Can he imagine it on site? Next follows an incubation stage, a stage of doubt, a "hypnogogic state," a questioning. It is a haptic as much as a mental construct. Once he is comfortable with the idea, the mechanics of the work can be considered. How can it be made, for example? Irwin rarely uses drawings to conceive and develop the work. But the presentation of the idea is based on the composition of the sponsoring group, and on the ability to visualize—certainly the need exists to establish the validity of the idea. The presentation drawings also provide a sense of the "thing," and they establish the proposed work as art.

The project for the Wave Hill estate in the Bronx, *Wave Hill Green; Door Light Window; Wave Hill Wood* (1986–1987), offers an opportunity to observe the hypothetical working process and witness its product. When Robert Irwin first came to Wave Hill, he was struck by the design of the total estate, the gardens, the view out to the Hudson River, and Glyndor House, now used for exhibitions. Extended visits to the site, of the type described above, only reinforced his first reactions. Irwin realized that, in spite of the original wording of the commission, there would be relatively few areas in which any intervention would be acceptable. The design of the estate seemed fixed; the trees were mature and would remain intact, as would Glyndor House. The flower beds and other plantings were carefully tended, suggesting to Irwin that this was in fact a "gardener's garden." He spent time with Wave Hill's director of horticulture, Marco Polo Stufano, and Wave Hill director Peter Sauer. Through these discussions, the zone in which he would work was circumscribed, reduced to two areas: the lawn and the woods. Above all, Irwin approached Wave Hill as a single entity; there would be no "sculpture" exhibited on the grounds. Instead, the entire situation would serve to articulate the work and vice versa. He thus operated in his fourth category of enterprise, the *site conditioned/determined* work.

When Irwin considered the lawn area, he felt that something was unsettled, that some indistinct condition between the parking area and the pergola on the far side of the lawn was not quite right.[40] While a definite Italianate air pervades the estate, the upper-level gardens lack a clearly stated axial arrangement. Rather than creating a literal axis, Irwin chose to reinforce the moment of arrival and link the parking area with the pergola on the far side of the lawn. It would serve as might an axis, although no precise path would be marked.

The means for accomplishing this linkage were disarmingly simple. First, earth was removed from a square 55 by 55 feet. Edged with corten steel, rust brown and almost the color of the soil, the depression of 18 inches was accessible by granite stairs at two ends of the recess. Because the material used to retain the depression was so thin, little discontinuity disturbed the connection between the upper and lower levels, both of which were planted with grass. Characteristically for Irwin, visitors had to wonder just where the sculpture was. Nor was the depressed panel intended to have an evident identity as a sculpture. The clarified relationship between the two sides of the site evoked a perception that one could consider aesthetic. In addition, the work "was intended to reinforce the slightly undersized pergola and the view it attends."[41] As critic Jean Feinberg described the experience: "Previously, this was a flat expanse that one looked over rather than at; now from a distance it is an active space that engages the eye. And, because your gaze is brought down into it, into a space deeper than its surroundings, the lower sod plane serves as a reflector, bouncing your eye upwards towards the Palisades that you view with renewed interest."[42]

A second area of intervention was the Nature Trail that extended along the estate's western edge. Irwin thought that the potential of this facility—the "rough" nature set against the polished lawn and flower bedding, like the *bosco* of the Italian Renaissance garden—was not fully exploited. The problem was the path's lack of announcement. Almost in the Japanese manner of implying space rather than physically enclosing it, Irwin judiciously placed three granite stones inscribed with texts. One stone abuts the curbing, extending from the realm of the polite garden. The second is positioned in the lawn, about halfway between the curb and the entry to the natural area proper. The third stone of the set suggests the path to the trail, although the manner by which the space is to be traversed is not fixed. The effect of these markers is subtle, and under some conditions almost subliminal. The stones nudge one's consciousness of the trail, without forceful markings or references. Like so much of Irwin's work, presence rests on the edge of an indistinction graced by perceptual ambiguity.

The installation at Wave Hill comprised three parts: the first, which engaged the lawn, was titled *Wave Hill Green;* the second, which marked the existence of the nature trail, was named *Wave Hill Wood;* and the third, inside Glyndor House, was

Door Light Window. Each of these titles, like the work itself, unpretentiously describes the act or condition that it names. And although each title is comprised of nouns, the effect of the works is that of a verb. Inside the building, Irwin tinted the reading of the space and the architectural elements. Sensing the axiality inherent in the plan of the house, but denied by the opaque surfaces of the doors, he replaced each of them with a glass panel. As a result, upon entry the view continues through the building, coming to active rest on the gardens beyond. Using scrim and color film tints, the circulation through the space and the quality of light have been softly modulated, the architectonic relations distilled. Etched on the glass panel of what had been the middle doorway is the title of this segment of the work: *Door Light Window.*

The Wave Hill installation raises certain questions about Irwin's more recent direction, in particular his use of language and typographic forms. Upon first reading, the work of the Scots poet/sculptor Ian Hamilton Finlay comes to mind, an association difficult to dispel given the presence of Irwin's poetry on the third stone of Wave Hill Wood: "Ever Present Never Twice the Same"—which in many ways encapsulates his quest for making present the act of perception. The use of words and the acceptance of the social coding endemic to language seems antithetical to Irwin's project, which has attempted to skirt social convention in order to throw the cognitive responsibility back upon the individual. Words address the relation between individuals. The minimal environmental disturbances of Irwin's scrim works, for example, suggested just the opposite: that is, one should engage the human being at a level preceding linguistic (social) consciousness.

Irwin argues against reading too literally, however. He sees, for example, the white canvases of Malevich not as the terminal point of painting, not as a bumper, but as a membrane through which the activity of painting could pass so as to reveal further opportunities. "Old ideas don't die," he argues, "but one can bracket out aspects of the issue to formulate new questions. I had to get rid of the painting, to reduce the condition to zero. But zero is ultimately not an answer, it is a place to begin."[43] Having himself condensed his vocabulary to the ascetic materials of scrim, light, and the single line, he now feels free to use any ideas, media, and configurations suggested by the situation and its circumstances—including natural language. "On occasion, a cannon on the front lawn can be the correct response."[44]

He admits that his new work will have its critics. "The kinds of things I'm doing now are things which, on the basis of their gross physicality, a lot of people will see as sculpture again. And they're not that different. But in my mind, I've learned to deal with the presence without the reductiveness. I'm getting more and more of all that stuff in there, but still keying it on presence. I mean, it might even get baroque at some point, just loaded with

23–11

23–12

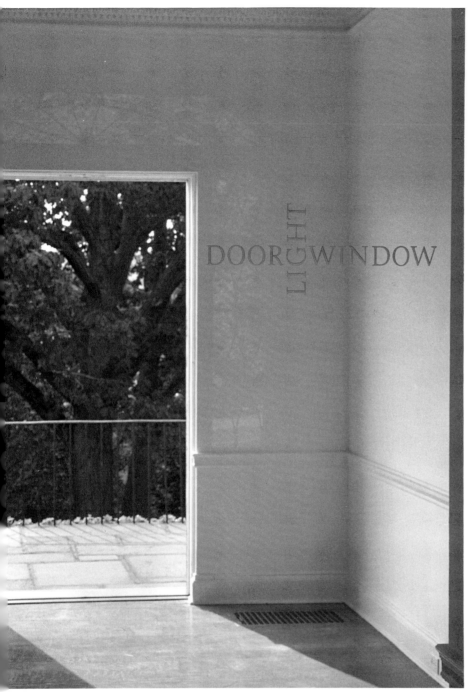

23–13

23–11 *Wave Hill Wood*
1986–1987. Wave Hill, Bronx,
New York. Robert Irwin.
[Sarah Wells]

23–12 *Elegiac Inscription*
1975. Stonypath, Dunsyre,
Lanarkshire, Scotland. Ian
Hamilton Finlay with John Andrew.
[Marc Treib]

23–13 *Door Light Window*
1986–1987. Wave Hill, Bronx,
New York. Robert Irwin.
[Sarah Wells]

richness of detail and tactility. It can become tremendously rich, as rich as the world. Restriction can be a discipline to break habits, but it need not be a final state, and it's no state of grace."[45] He supports his current activities by noting that there is no value system attached to his four categories of sculpture; each serves its own purpose: "The beauty is that you can use any of the four models; you can use any tool or medium; everything is possible."[46] The selection is based on "being and circumstance." The return to the object, and even to figuration, adds a formal complexity that could cloud the perception, however. When the means are minimal, there is nothing to literally look at; the mind is more easily focused.[47] As the formal richness increases, it may become too easy to mistake the finger for the moon.

This new direction explains the inclusion of more figurative sculptures or identifiable objects in recent projects, such as the small Sentinel Plaza adjacent to the 1990 police station in Pasadena, California (realized in collaboration with landscape architects Campbell and Campbell). The configuration of the site is a simple rectangle between two buildings, with a single watercourse marking the middle of the space. Irwin's principal device is a series of steps that suggested spatial enclosure; the plaza's foremost objects, on the other hand, are a 40-foot sycamore tree and a column comprised of a stock precast concrete post and four cast aluminum eagles forming its capital, surmounted by the blue light bulb of the police call box. Although the figuration is overt and almost too obvious, less apparent is the vestigial axis created by the plaza's column and the lightposts on the sidewalks on both sides of the street that link the small plaza to the land beyond. On the most general plane, Irwin engages the conditions of the greater situation, while still acknowledging those internal to the site.

Ultimately, we must ask about the relevance of Irwin's pilgrimage and work in relation to landscape architecture, which is ostensibly the subject of this book. If Irwin, as he does, separates the enterprise of the artist from that of the designer, one can quite rightly question the importance of his thought and work to design at any level beyond that of basic aesthetic appreciation. Of course, the forms and materials that appear in his work could easily be appropriated for landscape architecture. Or one could begin to look behind the apparent surface of the material, to find the condition that generated its selection. At this level, a scrim installation such as the Walker Art Center's is not that far from the frosted glass walls of Dan Kiley's Miller garden of 1955 or the gardens of the prewar era presented in Tunnard's *Gardens in the Modern Landscape.* In each case, the obscure-but-not-opaque surface modulated the space without effectively severing it into discrete sections.

At a deeper level, however, Robert Irwin's "questions" are of greater potential value than his answers. His basic premise that the artist looks to the qualitative aspects of existence might also be shared by the design professions. Similarly, and perhaps more profoundly, his concern with the individual, with the act of perception—and with the act of perceiving perception—might suggest to designers a multitude of routes for creating conditions beneficial to our lives and our ability to comprehend the conditions of modernity. As one critic described his project: "Irwin's work can bring about a nonverbal, purely sensational consciousness of vision that is exhilarating—even exultant—or an experience that is little more than a very interesting experience in using your eyes. His current [in 1976] work's purpose is not to be seen in itself but to expand the way we see everything, including other art and the world at large."[48]

Of course, the artist is granted certain freedoms that are proscribed the designer. Since function per se is rarely a primary consideration in the production of art, the artist may choose to acknowledge only a limited number of parameters: for example, those of form or perception alone. Landscape architecture, on the other hand, must address in its settings the characteristics of climate, the habits of the users and their culture, the forms and processes of horticulture. Human perception, the realm of Robert Irwin's investigations, is but one of a host of factors that configure landscape design; but it is the one consideration without which all the others are deprived of their reason for existence.

23–14

23–14 Sentinel Plaza
1990. Pasadena, California. Robert
Irwin with Campbell and Campbell,
landscape architects.
[Marc Treib]

23–15 Sentinel Plaza
1990. Pasadena, California. Robert
Irwin with Campbell and Campbell,
landscape architects.
[Marc Treib]

23–15

Notes

Following the original symposium, I spent most of December 12 and 13, 1990, in an extensive interview with Robert Irwin. Many of the quotations derive from that dialogue, although some were modified, clarified, and extended after his review of an advanced draft of this essay. I would like to thank Robert Irwin both for his participation in the symposium and for the time and help he has given since.

1 See Clement Greenberg, *Art and Culture: Critical Essays* (Boston: Beacon Press, 1961), in particular "Avant-Garde and Kitsch," 3–21.

2 In "Inside the White Cube," Brian O'Dougherty traces the relationship of the art object to its display space. The series of three articles originally appeared in *Artforum;* see Part II, April 1976.

3 Robert Irwin, interview with the author, December 1990. This idea, that the result of an inquiry is rooted in the form of its question, shares certain parallels with ideas advanced by Louis Sullivan, who believed that the solution to any (architectural) problem could be found in its formulation. See his *Autobiography of an Idea* (1924; New York: Dover Publishing, 1965). If one accepts this reading, analysis must be regarded as part of the synthesis.

4 Irwin, interview with the author, December 1990.

5 Robert Irwin, letter to the author, August 1991.

6 This phrase served as title for the most comprehensive presentation of Irwin's works to date (discussed below): Robert Irwin, *Being and Circumstance: Notes toward a Conditional Art* (Larkspur Landing, California: Lapis Press, 1985).

7 Irwin, letter to the author, August 1991.

8 Robert Irwin, in Lawrence Wechsler, *Seeing Is Forgetting the Name of the Thing One Sees: A Life of Contemporary Artist Robert Irwin* (Berkeley: University of California Press, 1982), 76.

9 Irwin, letter to the author, August 1991.

10 Ibid.

11 Irwin, in Wechsler, *Seeing Is Forgetting,* 90.

12 Irwin, letter to the author, August 1991.

13 Curiously, the subtle pattern of four interlocking shadows that surrounded the central disk was read by some as a mandala, in spite of the artist's declared intention to dissolve any figurative associations. Irwin has recently stated that the ideal conditions for the work may, in fact, be under strong, natural light from above, rather than directed artificial light from above and below.

14 Irwin in Wechsler, *Seeing Is Forgetting,* 107.

15 Irwin, letter to the author, August 1991.

16 Robert Irwin, in Maurice Tuchman, *A Report on the Art and Technology Program of the Los Angeles County Museum of Art, 1967–71* (Los Angeles: Los Angeles County Museum of Art, 1971), 132.

17 Irwin, interview with the author, December 1990.

18 Wechsler, *Seeing Is Forgetting,* 169.

19 Irwin, letter to the author, August 1991.

20 In an article believed to have been written by Marcel Duchamp and referring to his *Fountain,* the author wrote in closing: "Whether Mr. Mutt [the pseudonymous creator of *Fountain*] with his own hands made the fountain or not has no importance. He CHOSE it. He took an ordinary article of life, placed it so that its useful significance disappeared under a new title and point of view—created a new thought for that object." Quoted in Richard Hamilton, *Not Seen and/or Less Seen of/by Marcel Duchamp/Rrose Selavy, 1904–64* (Houston: Museum of Fine Arts, 1965).

21 Ibid.

22 Roberta Smith, "Robert Irwin: The Subject Is Sight," *Art in America* (March/April 1976), 69.

23 Irwin, letter to the author, August 1991.

24 Irwin, *Being and Circumstance,* 26–27.

25 Ibid., 27.

26 Irwin in Wechsler, *Seeing Is Forgetting,* 175.

27 Irwin, *Being and Circumstance,* 37.

28 Irwin in Wechsler, *Seeing Is Forgetting,* 192.

29 The landscape architecture by Laurie Olin of Hanna/Olin that accompanies the design of the Wexner Center for the Visual Arts by Peter Eisenman (1989) was based on a similar notion of earth uplift. Unlike the Irwin proposal, however, Olin's "fractured" planes of earth, retained in heavy walls of stone-faced concrete, were based on a logic internal to the building and its immediate site, rather than one derived from a preexisting pattern.

30 Irwin in Wechsler, *Seeing Is Forgetting,* 199.

31 Ibid.

32 Irwin, interview with the author, December 1990.

33 Irwin, *Being and Circumstance,* 95.

34 Ibid., 67.

35 This analysis is central to the thesis developed by Colin Rowe in "The Mathematics of the Ideal Villa" (1947), published in *The Mathematics of the Ideal Villa and Other Essays* (Cambridge: MIT Press, 1976), 1–28.

36 Irwin, *Being and Circumstance,* 71.

37 Irwin, interview with the author, December 1990.

38 Irwin, *Being and Circumstance,* 23.

39 Irwin, letter to the author, August 1991.

40 Irwin, interview with the author, December 1990.

41 Irwin, letter to the author, August 1991.

42 Jean E. Feinberg, in *Perceiving the Garden: Robert Irwin at Wave Hill* (Wave Hill, New York, 1987), 14.

43 Irwin, interview with the author, December 1990.

44 The perpendicular rotation of the middle words of *Wave Hill Green* and *Wave Hill Wood* serve visual as well as poetic functions. The turning of the words establishes a subtle but effective cross axis and spatial pointer. This idea is also found in the text upon the steps that lead down to the recessed lawn panel.

45 Irwin, in Wechsler, *Seeing Is Forgetting,* 200.

46 Irwin, interview with the author, December 1990.

47 The dry Zen gardens of Japan were intended to aid religious contemplation rather than to serve as zones of experiential delight. By reducing the physical elements within the garden's enclosure, the meditator was forced back upon his or her own faculties. There was no explanation for what one perceived.

48 Smith, "Robert Irwin: The Subject Is Sight," 73.

1

2

A short epilogue quickly brings us from the early 1960s, the nominal end point of the essays, to today. Thomas Church died in 1978, James Rose in the autumn of 1991, but Garrett Eckbo and Dan Kiley remain in active practice; indeed Kiley's project for the NCNB garden terrace, one should recall, was realized only four years ago. A second generation of modernists, among them Lawrence Halprin, Hideo Sasaki, Peter Walker, Robert Zion, Paul Friedberg, and A. E. Bye, have furthered the basic premises established by the quartet of American designers working in the first half of the century. Like their counterparts in architecture, these landscape architects have tended to work on projects of increasing scale, with offices that grew correspondingly large, at the service of corporate clients and municipal bodies. While less radical in style, the work of the second generation in the public domain has been more widespread—again, like parallel developments in architecture.

While the case for the contemporary idiom in landscape design has been well established, and there has been only a partial return to the use of historical styles in the last decade, the modernized version of the picturesque remains a mainstay of the profession. Landscape design executed for the corporation, for example, often situates the building in the midst of a naturalistic landscape, what architect Fred Koetter has termed the "corporate villa."[1] Reginald Blomfield[2] and Edouard André[3] would both probably be satisfied—at least to some degree—with the model employed: a more architectonic treatment around the building, softening to a naturalistic landscape beyond. One finds this archetypal landscape design from California to Maine.

And now there is a third generation, what some have termed postmodernists. Anxious, like Oedipus, to supersede the accomplishments of their fathers, they endeavor to create an even newer landscape to meet today's conditions. In many ways this is only reasonable; in other ways it is a fatuous effort. Our current American society has been bred not on primary experience but on the image, whether of photography, film, or video. This breeding has created a world in which novelty of image becomes paramount. A landscape design that caters to this hunger for titillation instead of substance, for ephemerality rather than permanence, and for the cute instead of the significant, will be of less consequence than one based on the psychology and physiology of human beings, critical ecological

4

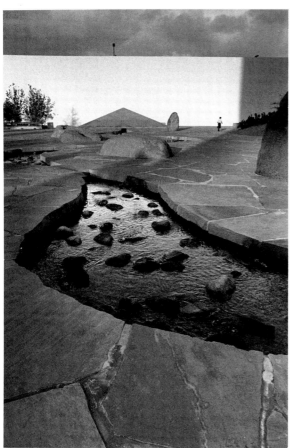

3

I	**Bornholmsgaard** Denmark, c. 1963. Carl-Theodor Sørensen. [Marc Treib]
2	**Poll garden** Holte, Denmark, c. 1971. Carl-Theodor Sørensen. [Marc Treib]
3	*California Scenario* Costa Mesa, California, 1984. Isamu Noguchi. [Marc Treib]
4	**Mustang Square** Las Colinas, Texas, 1988. The SWA Group. [Marc Treib]

factors, and current thought in the arts. Personally, I would like to see a furtherance of the questions first posed—if neither fully answered nor solved—by the modernist landscape. In a world that each day becomes more transitory, I would welcome a landscape design that can address the contemporary condition, its blessings and its horrors, while providing a place for dwelling in the world. Dwelling, to use Martin Heidegger's term, is not synonymous with living. Living is somehow getting through another day. Dwelling implies a far deeper connection with our environment, creating the means by which we may reveal and delight in its benefits as well as its mysteries.

Notes

1 See Fred Koetter, "The Corporate Villa," *Design Quarterly 135* (Minneapolis: Walker Art Center, 1987).

2 Sir Reginald Blomfield (1856–1942) argued against the naturalism and wildness of William Robinson and for a consideration of architecture in the planning of gardens. In *The Formal Garden in England* (London: Waterstone, 1892), coauthored with F. Inigo Thomas, he succinctly clarified the reasons for the formal aspect of the garden: "The formal school insists upon design; the house and the grounds should be designed together and in relation to each other; no attempt should be made to conceal the design of the garden, there being no reason for doing so" (pp. 10–11).

3 Edouard André was the principal designer of the Paris park system under the directorship of Adolphe Alphand. Like Blomfield, he proposed a composite system of orders, the *style composite,* establishing formally planned areas where appropriate to use and a contrived naturalism where necessary to suggest a more convincing image of the natural landscape. For a comprehensive study of landscape design, see his *Traité général de la composition des parcs et jardins* (1879; Marseilles: Laffitte Reprints, 1983).

5   Bamboo garden
La Villette, Paris, 1988.
Alexandre Chemetoff.
[Marc Treib]

5